Ancient Greek:
A New Approach

The MIT Press

Cambridge,
Massachusetts, and
London, England

Ancient Greek:
A New Approach

Second Edition   Carl A. P. Ruck

Sixth printing, 1993

Printed in the United States
of America

**Library of Congress Cataloging in
Publication Data**

Ruck, Carl A P
  Ancient Greek.

  1. Greek language—Grammar—
1870–I. Title.
PA258.R85 1979 488'.2'421
78–9875 ISBN 0-262-68031-9

Contents

Preface to the Second Edition

Numerous changes have been incorporated into the text of this new edition. The "horizontal" approach to syntactic forms has been retained, but the order and content of every lesson has been revised. The imperfect and aorist, for example, are introduced early to afford the student more time to become thoroughly familiar with the aorist stem and the concept of verbal aspect. Similarly, the subjunctive and optative moods occur early in the book.

The book has been redesigned both to offer more help to the self-learner and to make the text usable not only as a beginning method but also as a review book for more advanced students. To that end the inductive presentation of the grammatical patterns has been abandoned, allowing explanations to be more direct and complete.

The exercises have been reduced to a regularized format, with the type of exercise announced by the initial phrase of the directions. The MATCH exercises offer extensive practice in the horizontal manipulation of forms (that is, different forms with identical types of meaning). CHANGE exercises contrast forms that vary meaning. TRANSLATE exercises introduce examples of Greek prose (Apollodorus, Xenophon, Lysias, Andocides, Plato, Diogenes Laertius, Pausanias) or poetry. REPHRASE exercises are based on the material in the reading passages and give practice in varying the syntactic pattern. NOTE THE PATTERN exercises develop an ability to recognize a syntactic pattern and to compose additional examples of that pattern in Greek.

A distinction is made between material that must be actively learned and that which even advanced students are apt to know only passively. Thus it is not expected that the student have active recall of the six (or more) principle parts of the verb, so long as the verbal form can be analyzed into its constituent suffixes and prefixes. Exercises entitled GIVE THE LEXICAL ENTRY offer extensive practice in the recognition of future, aorist passive, and perfect stems. The thematic and athematic modes of conjugation are, moreover, taught as basic structures so that the coherence of the Greek language system can be perceived.

New vocabulary introduced in each lesson is determined by the reading passage and has been confined to a limit of approximately thirty new entries.

The Attic dialect is used as the basic tongue. An appendix introduces the student to dialectal variations.

The twenty-three lessons of the text are of approximately equal length and difficulty. The material can easily be completed in a one-semester accelerated course meeting five hours per week, or in somewhat less than two-thirds of a two-semester course of three weekly meetings.

I should like to acknowledge my gratitude to Deirdre Cosgrove for her help in testing this newly revised text with an accelerated class at Boston University, and to Danny Staples for uncovering many errors in the text.

I hope this book will be useful to those who want to learn the ancient Greek language.

A Note on Pronunciation

There are three systems of pronunciation in current use for ancient Greek. It will be easiest for the student simply to imitate the teacher and to use this note as a guide to the other pronunciations.

One system of pronunciation derives from the scholar Erasmus. Greek was actually never spoken in this manner at any period of its long history. Nevertheless, this is the pronunciation customarily learned by modern students. Its only advantage is that it poses no great difficulties and allows the student to communicate with other traditionally trained scholars.

A second system of pronunciation attempts to approximate the spoken language of ancient Greek in the classical period in Athens. Since there are no living native speakers to imitate, this pronunciation can only be an approximation based on the writings of ancient grammarians. The classical pronunciation, moreover, would have varied from city to city within the same period and probably also from social class to class. Nevertheless, the classical pronunciation is indispensable for recapturing certain onomatopoeic aspects of classical literature.

A third system pronounces ancient Greek in the same manner as modern Greek, much as Elizabethan English is usually pronounced like modern English. Although this pronunciation is not authentic for the classical period and flattens much of the varied range of vowel sounds, it nevertheless does have the advantage of uniting the ancient language with its modern continuation. This is the way ancient Greek is usually pronounced in contemporary Greece.

Whichever method the student learns, it will be useful to have an awareness of the other pronunciations. The following chart summarizes the particularities of the three systems. (Divergences from the Erasmian are indicated in columns two and three.)

Erasmian		Ancient	Modern
α A	ă *a*ha		both like ā
	ā f*a*ther	It. am*a*re	
β B	b *b*eg		v Fr. *v*ie
γ Γ	g *g*o		g Sp. ara*g*on
	n thi*n*k (before γ,		y *y*es (before
	κ, χ, ξ)		ε, ι)
δ Δ	d *d*ig	Fr. d	th *th*e
ε E	ĕ m*e*t		
ζ Z	z *z*ero	wi*sd*om	
η H	ē surv*e*y	Fr. tê*t*e	ī pol*i*ce
ϑ Θ	*th th*in	th ho*t h*ouse	
ι I	ĭ m*i*tten	Fr. v*i*te	ī pol*i*ce
	ī pol*i*ce	Fr. v*i*ve	
κ K	k *k*in	Fr. *c*ar	
λ Λ	l *l*et		
μ M	m *m*et		
ν N	n *n*et		

ξ Ξ	x la*x*		
o O	ŏ n*o*t	Ger. G*o*tt	
π Π	p *p*et	Fr. p	
ρ P	r *r*un	Scottish rolled r	
ς, σ	s *s*uch		s *s*uch
Σ		z (before β, γ, δ, μ)	z (before β, γ, δ, λ, μ, ν, ρ)
τ T	t *t*ar	Fr. t	
υ Υ	ŭ Fr. tu		
	ū Fr. sûr		ī pol*i*ce
φ Φ	ph gra*ph*ic	ph u*p* *h*ill	
χ X	ch Ger. ma*ch*en	ch ba*ckh*and	ch Ger. ma*ch*en (but like palatal ch Ger. i*ch* before ε, ι)
ψ Ψ	ps gy*ps*um		
ω Ω	ō n*o*te	s*aw*	

diphthongs:

αι	ai C*ai*ro		ĕ m*e*t
ει	ei v*ei*n	Ger. B*ee*t	ī pol*i*ce
οι	oi s*oi*l		ī pol*i*ce
αυ	ou *ou*t		av *a*void
			af *af*ter (before κ, π, τ, φ, χ, ϑ, σ, ξ, ψ)
ευ	ĕ (m*e*t) + oo (m*oo*n)		ev *e*very
			ef *ef*fort (before κ, π, τ, φ, χ, ϑ, σ, ξ, ψ)
ου	ou t*ou*r		
ηυ	ēh'-oo		
ωυ	ōh'-oo		
υι	ui q*ui*t		ī pol*i*ce
ᾳ	like ᾱ	(iota lightly pronounced)	
ῃ	like η	(iota lightly pronounced)	
ῳ	like ω	(iota lightly pronounced)	

consonant combinations:

ντ	d *d*ig (but nd when sounded in different syllables)
μπ	b *b*ut (but mb in different syllables)
τζ	dz lor*ds* (but ch if initial position)
γκ	g *g*as (but ngk in different syllables)

A Note on Lexica

The standard Greek–English lexicon was compiled by Liddell and Scott, first published in 1843, and frequently reprinted and revised at the Clarendon Press, Oxford University. It is available in various abridgments. Although this book has a glossary of all words introduced in the lesson vocabularies and in the reading selections, it is advisable that the student become acquainted with the Liddell and Scott lexicon before the completion of the elementary course because it is an invaluable tool for further study.

The student will also find useful Marinone and Guala's *Tutti i Verbi Greci/ Complete Handbook of Greek Verbs* (Casa Editrice Principato, Milano, Italia/ Schoenhof's Foreign Books, Cambridge, Massachusetts, 1961), which lists all Greek verb forms alphabetically.

Ancient Greek:
A New Approach

Introductory Material

Alphabet

Read the following quotations from Greek authors aloud with the help of the transliteration. Accented syllables are indicated by italics in the transliteration.

1. πάντων μέτρον ἄνθρωπος. —Πρωταγόρας
   pan-tōn *met*-ron *an*-thrō-pos. —Prō-ta-*go*-ras
   all measure mankind
   Mankind is the measure of everything.

2. ψυχῆς ἀγαθῆς πατρὶς ὁ ξύμπας κόσμος. —Δημόκριτος.
   psu-*khēs* a-ga-*thēs* pa-*tris* ho *ksum*-pas *kos*-mos. —Dē-*mo*-kri-tos
   soul good country the entire universe
   The entire universe is the good soul's native land.

3. νόμος ὁ πάντων βασιλεύς. —Πίνδαρος
   no-mos ho *pan*-tōn ba-si-*leus*. —*Pin*-da-ros
   law the all king
   Law is the universal ruler.

4. τῷ σοφῷ ξένον οὐδέν. —'Αντισθένης
   tōi so-*phōi* *kse*-non ou-*den*. —An-ti-*sthe*-nēs
   the wise foreign nothing
   Nothing is foreign to the wise man.

5. σκιᾶς ὄναρ ἄνθρωπος —Πίνδαρος
   ski-*as* *on*-ar *an*-thrō-pos. —*Pin*-da-ros
   shadow dream mankind
   Mankind is just a shadow's dream.

6. φωνὴ καὶ σκιὰ γέρων ἀνήρ. —Εὐριπίδης
   phō-*nē* *kai* ski-*a* ge-*rōn* a-*nēr*. —Eu-ri-*pi*-dēs
   voice and shadow old man
   An old man is just a voice and a shadow.

7. οὐδὲν ἄλγος οἷον ἡ πολλὴ ζόη. —Σοφοκλῆς
   ou-*den* *al*-gos *hoi*-on hē pol-*lē* zo-ē. —So-pho-*klēs*
   nothing pain like the much life
   There is no pain like old age.

Practice reading the quotations until you can pronounce them without the help of the transliteration.

1. πάντων μέτρον ἄνθρωπος. —Πρωταγόρας

2. ψυχῆς ἀγαθῆς πατρὶς ὁ ξύμπας κόσμος. —Δημόκριτος

3. νόμος ὁ πάντων βασιλεύς. —Πίνδαρος

4. τῷ σοφῷ ξένον οὐδέν. —'Αντισθένης

5. σκιᾶς ὄναρ ἄνθρωπος. —Πίνδαρος

6, φωνὴ καὶ σκιὰ γέρων ἀνήρ. —Εὐριπίδης

7. οὐδὲν ἄλγος οἷον ἡ πολλὴ ζόη. —Σοφοκλῆς

You will have noticed that many of the letters of the Greek alphabet resemble those of the English (Roman) alphabet. Which letters are these?

There are two forms of the Greek "s" letter. What are these two forms? Can you distinguish some principle in their use?

What Greek letter corresponds to the Roman "r"? What Roman letter does it resemble? What Greek letter represents the Roman "p"?

How does the Greek alphabet represent the double graphs "th," "ph," and "kh"? Which letters represent "ds" (or "z"), "ps," and "ks"?

How does the Greek alphabet indicate the "h" sound?

What signs indicate the accents?

Which letters indicate the vowels in the Greek alphabet?

How does the Greek alphabet distinguish between a long and short "o"? How does it distinguish between long and short "e"? Can the Greek alphabet distinguish between long and short "a," "i," or "u"?

What Greek letter represents the "n" sound?

What Greek letter represents the "m" sound? The "g"? The "l"?

Exercise

Copy the Greek quotations, using the following chart as an aid in forming the letters; note the placement and size of each letter with regard to the line of writing.

α	β	γ	δ	ε	ζ
η	ϑ	ι	κ	λ	μ
ν	ξ	ο	π	ρ	σς
τ	υ	φ	χ	ψ	ω

α A	β B	γ Γ	δ Δ	ε E	ζ Z
η H	ϑ Θ	ι I	κ K	λ Λ	μ M
ν N	ξ Ξ	ο O	π Π	ρ P	σς Σ
τ T	υ Y	φ Φ	χ X	ψ Ψ	ω Ω

Breathings

In addition to the sounds represented by the alphabet signs, the Greeks indicated the pronunciation of initial "h" by a *rough breathing* ('). The absence of this aspirate sound was shown by a *smooth breathing* ('). *Every initial vowel in Greek always is written with either a smooth or rough breathing.* In addition, υ and ρ in initial position are always written with a rough breathing:

ὄρος	(oros)	mountain
ὅρος	(horos)	boundary
ὕδωρ	(hudōr)	water
ῥήτωρ	(rhētōr)	orator

Iota Subscript

Iota as the second element in certain dipthongs (–αι, –ηι, –ωι) is customarily written beneath the preceding vowel: –ᾳ, –ῃ, –ῳ. The iota written beneath the line is called "iota subscript." It represents a writing convention: the iota of these diphthongs was early (ca. 100 B.C.) lost in pronunciation and consequently omitted in writing. Medieval Byzantine scholars academically restored the iota in the orthography, but inasmuch as it was no longer pronounced, they added the iota as a note beneath the line. Most present-day printed texts of classical authors follow this convention.

τῷ σοφῷ ξένον οὐδέν.

Punctuation

Greek uses four marks of punctuation. The *comma* and *period* have the same form as in English. The *colon* is indicated by a raised period (·) and the *question mark* is the same in form as the English semicolon (;).

Capital Letters

With the aid of the chart, copy the Greek quotations over again in capital letters. In capitals, breathing marks and accent marks are not indicated and the iota subscript is written on the line:

ΤΩΙ ΣΟΦΩΙ ΞΕΝΟΝ ΟΥΔΕΝ.

Exercise

The following chart presents the *names* (in Greek) for the letters of the Greek alphabet. Practice reading the names aloud. Write the names in both small and capital letters.

Be prepared to write the Greek quotations and the names of the Greek letters from dictation.

A	α	ἄλφα	N	ν	νῦ	
B	β	βῆτα	Ξ	ξ	ξεῖ	
Γ	γ	γάμμα	O	ο	ὂ μικρόν	
Δ	δ	δέλτα	Π	π	πεῖ	
E	ε	ἒ ψιλόν	P	ρ	ῥῶ	
Z	ζ	ζῆτα	Σ	σ, ς	σίγμα	
H	η	ἦτα	T	τ	ταῦ	
Θ	θ	θῆτα	Υ	υ	ὖ ψιλόν	
I	ι	ἰῶτα	Φ	φ	φεῖ	
K	κ	κάππα	X	χ	χεῖ	
Λ	λ	λάμβδα	Ψ	ψ	ψεῖ	
M	μ	μῦ	Ω	ω	ὦ μέγα	

Accents

There are three different marks to indicate the accent in Greek:

acute	(´)
circumflex	(˜)
grave	(`)

In the Erasmian and the modern Greek systems of pronunciation, all three marks indicate an identical stress accent. In the classical pronunciation, instead of a stress accent the language had a pitch accent, and these three marks originally indicated different pitches or tones: the acute for a rising tone (╱), the circumflex for a rising tone which glided into a falling tone (∧), and the grave for a rising tone which had been flattened into the basic tone and thereby neutralized. Even when the classical pronunciation is not employed, it is customary, as in modern Greek, to write the language with these three different accent marks.

It is admittedly difficult for the student to learn these accents—nor is it the most important task in the introductory stage of learning the language. With perseverance, however, the student can become moderately proficient in orthography. The writing of accents on Greek words is an Alexandrian convention (ca. 200 B.C.). Classical writers would not have written Greek with accents or breathing marks and they would have used nothing but capital letters, usually without indicating the division into separate words.

The following principles of accentuation will be helpful in learning the conventional orthography.

1. Accents always fall on one of the last three syllables of a Greek word and are partially determined by the rhythmic pattern of this final sequence of syllables. Long syllables are those which contain a diphthong or a long vowel. The long vowels are $\bar{α}$, $η$, $\bar{ι}$, $ω$, $\bar{υ}$, as distinct from the short vowels $α$, $ε$, $ι$, o, $υ$. It is not customary, however, to mark long syllables, and thus the letters $α$, $ι$, $υ$ can be either long or short, depending on the word or its context.

2. The accent on a diphthong is always written above the second of the two combined vowels:

βασιλεύς, καί

3. As the circumflex originally required enough time to glide from a rising to a falling tone, it can occur only on long syllables.

4. The circumflex, furthermore, occurs only upon one of the last two syllables of a word; it never falls third from the end. Moreover, it cannot occur second from the end unless the final syllable is short: οἷον, σκιᾶς.

The following chart summarizes the possible placements for the circumflex accent. (The symbol "x" is used for a syllable which is either long or short.)

. . . x ˜ ˘	ἐκεῖνος
. . . x x ˜	Σοφοκλῆς

5. The acute accent occurs on both long and short syllables and on any one of the last three syllables of a word: ἄνθρωπος, Πρωταγόρας, βασιλεύς. The acute, however, cannot fall third from the end unless the final syllable is short.

The following chart summarizes the possible placements for the acute accent.

. . . x́ x ⌣   ἄνθρωπος

. . . x x́ x   Ἀντισθένης

. . . x x x́   ἀδελφός

6. The grave accent occurs on both long and short syllables but only on the word's final syllable. It is the way a final acute is written when the word is followed by another accented word: ξένον οὐδέν, but οὐδὲν ξένον.

7. A few words in Greek do not have accents of their own but link themselves into the rhythmic pattern of the words around them. If the unaccented word links with the following word, it is called a *proclitic* ("forward-leaning"); since accentual patterns are determined by the nature of the final three syllables, a proclitic does not influence the accent in any way: ὁ ξύμπας κόσμος.

8. If the unaccented word links with the preceding word, it is called an *enclitic* ("on-leaning"). Enclitics obviously will change the accentual pattern by adding additional syllables to the rhythmic group. These changes are complex and will not be studied until later.

9. If the nature of a word's final syllable changes (either through the addition of an enclitic or a suffix), it will become necessary for the word's accent to change accordingly:

ἄνθρωπος/   (because the acute cannot fall third
   ἀνθρώπου   from the end if the final syllable is
                                       long)

οἶον/   (because the circumflex cannot fall
   οἴῳ   second from the end if the final
                                       syllable is long).

These changes too are complex and will be easier to learn as the student becomes more familiar with the language.

Exercise

The following is the beginning of the *Gospel According to John* ("In the beginning was the Word . . .").

ἐν ἀρχῇ ἦν ὁ λόγος, καὶ ὁ λόγος ἦν πρὸς τὸν Θεόν, καὶ Θεὸς ἦν ὁ λόγος. οὗτος ἦν ἐν ἀρχῇ πρὸς τὸν Θεόν. πάντα δι' αὐτοῦ ἐγένετο, καὶ χωρὶς αὐτοῦ ἐγένετο οὐδὲ ἓν ὃ γέγονεν. ἐν αὐτῷ ζωὴ ἦν, καὶ ἡ ζωὴ ἦν τὸ φῶς τῶν ἀνθρώπων. καὶ τὸ φῶς ἐν τῇ σκοτίᾳ φαίνει.
—ἐκ τοῦ εὐαγγελίου τοῦ κατὰ Ἰωάννην

Practice reading the quotation aloud. Copy it in small letters and again in capitals. Be prepared to write the passage from dictation.

1 Nominal Sentences

πάντων μέτρον ἄνθρωπος. —Πρωταγόρας

Lesson 1

Article

There are three forms of the *definite article* ("the") in Greek. Each can be used only with nouns which belong to the corresponding grammatical gender.

masculine	ὁ	ἀνήρ	the man
feminine	ἡ	γυνή	the woman
neuter	τὸ	μέτρον	the measure

Although grammatical gender sometimes corresponds to biological gender, as above, this is not always true: ὁ νόμος ("the law"), ἡ ψυχή ("the soul"), τὸ παιδίον ("the child"). You must learn the grammatical gender of each word as you encounter it.

Greek does not have an indefinite article ("a/an") and the absence of an expressed definite article corresponds to the meaning of an indefinite article: ἀνήρ ("a man" or "man").

Adjective

Adjectives (descriptive words) also have different forms for the three grammatical genders and must be expressed in the form which corresponds to (or "agrees with") the grammatical gender of the noun which it describes.

mascline	ἀγαθ-	ὸς	ἀνήρ	good man
feminine	ἀγαθ-	ή	.γυνή	good woman
neuter	ἀγαθ-	ὸν	μέτρον	good measure

Article-noun Phrase

The article obviously unites with its noun to produce a phrase (group of words which belong together): ὁ ἀνήρ "the man." Any other words which intervene between the article and its noun will belong to the same phrase.

| ὁ σοφὸς ἀνήρ | the wise man |
| ὁ πάλαι σοφὸς ἀνήρ | the wise man of long ago |

There are two other positions in which the descriptive material is bound into the article-noun phrase; in both of these positions, the descriptive material's placement is equivalent to intervening between the article and its noun.

| ὁ ἀνὴρ ὁ σοφός | the man, that is, the wise one |
| ἀνὴρ ὁ σοφός | a man, that is, the wise one |

These positions for the descriptive material are called the *attributive* position.

Nominal Sentences

Greek can express a complete idea (or sentence) simply by juxtaposing two elements, thereby implying an equation between them.

| μέτρον ἄνθρωπος. | Mankind is a measure. |
| σκιὰ ἀνήρ. | Man is a shadow. |

The two juxtaposed elements may both be nouns, as above; or one of the elements may be an adjective: σοφὸς ἀνήρ. ("A man is wise.")

Such equations are called *nominal* sentences; no verb is necessary, but if one is expressed, it must be a verb which designates the idea of "equation."

Such a verb is the enclitic (accentless) ἐστι ("is"). Before vowels or at the end of a sentence, ἐστι is written with a final –ν (ἐστιν) or, as it is called, *nu-movable*, for the sake of euphony (or ease of pronunciation). Since ἐστι is enclitic, it ordinarily does not begin a sentence, for in that position it has no preceding accented word to which it might link for its accent.

One of the two juxtaposed elements in a nominal sentence may be an article-noun phrase; the other element is called the *predicate*. The predicate can occur in any order relative to the other elements in a nominal sentence, except that it cannot be in the *attributive* position (because it would then be bound into the article-noun phrase and not be free to function as the *predicate*).

ὁ σοφὸς ἀνήρ

ὁ ἀνὴρ ὁ σοφός   the wise man

ἀνὴρ ὁ σοφός

σοφὸς ὁ ἀνήρ.

σοφός ἐστιν ὁ ἀνήρ.

σοφὸς ὁ ἀνήρ ἐστιν.

ὁ ἀνὴρ σοφός.   The man is wise.

ὁ ἀνὴρ ἐστι σοφός.

ὁ ἀνὴρ σοφός ἐστιν.

The different sequences for the elements convey differences in emphasis. The initial element is in emphatic position: σοφὸς ὁ ἀνήρ. ("*Wise* is the man.")

Vocabulary/*ONOMATA KAI PHMATA*

ὁ ἀνήρ	man
ἡ γυνή	woman
ὁ πατήρ	father
ἡ μήτηρ	mother
ὁ παῖς	boy
ἡ κόρη	girl
τὸ παιδίον	child
ὁ βασιλεύς	king
τὸ μέτρον	measure
ἡ ψυχή	soul
ἡ σκιά	shadow
ὁ νόμος	law
ὁ ἄνθρωπος	man, mankind, human
ξένος, -η, -ον	foreign
σοφός, -ή -όν	wise

καλός, -ή, -όν	beautiful, handsome
ἀγαθός, -ή, -όν	good
κακός, -ή, -όν	bad
ἐστί(ν)	is
πάλαι	long ago (adverb)
καί	and

Note: The suffix *-ιον* indicates a diminutive, hence παῖς/παιδίον.

An adjective with an article can be used as a noun: ἡ σοφή "the wise (woman)."

Exercise/*ΑΣΚΗΣΙΣ*

I. EXAMINE the seven quotations in the introductory material (p. 1); they are all examples of nominal sentences.

II. TRANSLATE.

1. μήτηρ ἡ γυνὴ ἡ καλή.

2. καλὴ ἡ γυνὴ καὶ καλὸς ὁ ἀνήρ.

3. νόμος τὸ μέτρον.

4. κακὸς ὁ ξένος βασιλεὺς καὶ καλός.

5. ὁ σοφὸς ἀγαθός.

III. LABEL each group of words as a nominal sentence or as an article-noun phrase.

1. ὁ ἀνὴρ σοφὸς

2. σοφὸς ὁ ἀνήρ

3. ὁ σοφὸς ἀνήρ

4. ἀνὴρ ὁ σοφός

5. ὁ ἀνὴρ ὁ σοφός

IV. FILL IN THE BLANKS with suitable adjectives.

1. ὁ _____ πατὴρ _____.

2. ἡ _____ γυνὴ _____.

3. _____ τὸ _____ παιδίον.

4. _____ ὁ νόμος ὁ _____.

5. _____ καὶ _____ ὁ ξένος.

V. COMPOSE ten nominal sentences using words from the vocabulary.

2　Verbal Sentences

παιδεύει ὁ ποιητής. —Πλάτων

Lesson 2
Verbal
Sentences

In addition to sentences of the nominal type which state equations, Greek sentences can be composed of a verb and express an action.

παιδεύομεν.　　　　　　　　　　We teach.

Unlike English, the verb's subject ("we") is not expressed by a separate word but instead is designated by a suffix (-μεν) which is added to the basic part of the verb or its *stem* or *theme*.

The verb does not have to occur alone but may be modified.

καλῶς παιδεύομεν.　　　　　　　We teach well.

Thematic and
Athematic
Conjugations

Different suffixes indicate different subjects for the verb.

παιδεύετε.　　　　　　　　　　You teach.

Such *personal suffixes* are added onto the verbal stem in two different ways:

either directly: δίδω - μεν

or with the intervention of a connecting vowel, which is called the *thematic vowel*: παιδεύ - ο - μεν.

These are the two systems of *conjugation* (joining of prefixes and suffixes onto the verbal stem). The system with the intervening thematic vowel is called the *thematic conjugation*; the system without the connecting vowel is called the *athematic conjugation*.

　　The chart summarizes the athematic and thematic conjugations. Note that in the athematic conjugation the final vowel of the verbal stem changes from long in the singular to short in the plural. Note also that the connecting vowel in the thematic conjugation is not always the same but varies. In order to simplify the learning of the thematic conjugation, the connecting vowel is presented together with the personal suffix, since dialectal and euphonic developments have contracted the connecting vowel with the suffix in some of the persons of the verb:

παιδεύ-ο-ασι ⟶ παιδεύ—ουσι.

Thematic

παιδεύ-	ω	1	ο–μεν
	εις	2	ε–τε
	ει	3	ουσι(ν)
	infinitive		ειν

Athematic(-μι)

δίδω- δείκνυ- τίθη- ἵστη- ἵη-	μι		δίδο- δείκνυ- τίθε- ἵστα- ἵε-	μεν	
	ς			τε	
	σι			ασι(ν)	ἱστᾶσι ἱᾶσι
				ναι	

Examples

παιδεύω.　　　　　　　　　　　I teach.

παιδεύεις.　　　　　　　　　　You (singular) teach.

παιδεύουσιν.　　　　　　　　　They teach.

παιδεύετε.　　　　　　　　　　You (plural) teach.

παιδεύειν	to teach
δίδωμι.	I give.
τίθεμεν.	We place.
τίθης.	You (singular) place.

Notes:

1. Accent on verbs is normally *recessive* (it falls as far from the end as possible) but can never fall earlier than third from the end, hence: διδόασι, τιθέασι, etc.

2. Accent on the athematic infinitive must be second from the end because the final diphthong is long: διδόναι.

3. The short vowel which corresponds to η is either α or ε. As an aid to your memory remember ἵστημι/ "stand," ἵημι/ "send."

4. Contraction occurs in the third person plural ("they") for ἵστημι and ἵημι: ἱστά-ασι → ἱστᾶσι, ἱέ-ασι → ἱᾶσι.

5. Third person plural of both conjugations may take a nu-movable before vowels or in final position in a sentence.

Subject-Verb   Although the verbal sentence is complete without a separately expressed subject, a noun may be juxtaposed (or placed in apposition) to the verb's personal suffix.

παιδεύει ὁ ποιητής.	He teaches, that is, the poet (teaches).
ὁ ποιητὴς παιδεύω.	I, the poet, teach.

This appositional subject can be added in any position before or after the verb; the order of the elements conveys emphasis.

παιδεύει ὁ ποιητής.	He *teaches*, that is, the poet (teaches).

ONOMATA KAI PHMATA

παιδεύω	teach	δίδωμι	give
διδάσκω	=παιδεύω	δείκνυμι	show
ἐθέλω	want	τίθημι	place
μανθάνω	learn	ἵστημι	stand, make stand
ἀποθνῄσκω	die	ἵημι	send, let go
ἀεί	always	ὁ ποιητής	poet
νῦν	now	οὐ	not
κακῶς	badly	οὐκ	not (before vowels)
		οὐχ	not (before aspirated vowels, such as "h")
καλῶς	well	ἀλλά	but

plurals:

οἱ ἄνδρες	men	οἱ πατέρες	fathers
αἱ γυναῖκες	women	αἱ μητέρες	mothers
οἱ παῖδες	boys	τὰ παιδία	children
αἱ κόραι	girls		

Note: Adjectives have plural forms which resemble the plural of the definite article: οἱ/αἱ/τά :: σοφοί/σοφαί/σοφά.

ΑΣΚΗΣΙΣ

I. TRANSLATE.

1. οἱ πάλαι σοφοὶ οὐκ ἀποθνῄσκουσιν ἀλλὰ παιδεύουσιν ἀεί.

2. ἐθέλομεν οἱ καλοὶ καὶ ἀγαθοὶ ἀεὶ μανθάνειν.

3. διδάσκει ὁ ποιητὴς καὶ παῖδες μανθάνετε.

4. οὐκ ἀποθνῄσκει ἡ ψυχή.

5. ἀγαθαὶ αἱ κόραι καὶ καλαί.

II. MATCH the second verb to the first by changing it into the same form.

1. παιδεύουσιν (τίθημι)	11. παιδεύετε (δίδωμι)
2. ἵστατε (ἐθέλω)	12. τιθέασιν (μανθάνω)
3. ἰᾶσιν (δίδωμι)	13. ἐθέλεις (ἵημι)
4. διδόναι (ἀποθνῄσκω)	14. δίδομεν (διδάσκω)
5. μανθάνεις (τίθημι)	15. παιδεύει (ἵστημι)
6. ἐθέλειν (ἵημι)	16. τιθέναι (ἀποθνῄσκω)
7. ἀποθνῄσκει (δείκνυμι)	17. δίδως (μανθάνω)
8. δείκνυς (ἐθέλω)	18. ἵησι (δίδωμι)
9. δεικνύασιν (διδάσκω)	19. δείκνυμεν (ἐθέλω)
10. ἱστᾶσιν (ἐθέλω)	20. ἵης (παιδεύω)

III. FILL IN THE BLANKS with suitable words.

1. _____ οἱ ξένοι.

2. οἱ πάλαι σοφοὶ _____ .

3. _____ αἱ καλαί.

4. οὐκ ἐθέλομεν_____ .

5. τὰ _____ παιδία _____ .

IV. COMPOSE five nominal sentences.

3   Accusative Case

χρόνος δίκαιον ἄνδρα δείκνυσι μόνος. —Σοφοκλῆς

Lesson 3
Accusative/Nouns
as Adverbs

As you have seen, a verb in a verbal sentence can be modified by an adverb.

καλῶς παιδεύομεν.   We teach well.

In Greek, nouns can also modify verbs. Through the addition of a suffix, a noun can carry a sign that it functions as an adverb.

φιλοσοφίαν μανθάνομεν.   We learn philosophy.

In English, such an "adverbial noun" is called a *direct object*; the noun's function as a direct object is signaled not by a suffix but by the order of words. Since in Greek the noun's adverbial function is signaled by its suffix, the order of words conveys only emphasis.

φιλοσοφίαν μανθάνομεν.   μανθάνομεν φιλοσοφίαν.

The noun with its adverbial suffix is called the *accusative case*. Although the Greek accusative is often analogous to the direct object in English, it also has meanings which the English direct object does not have. The adverbial function of the Greek accusative can be sensed from a very awkward translation of it into English by means of the suffix "-wise."

φιλοσοφίαν μανθάνομεν.   We learn philosophy-wise.

In addition to modifying verbs, the Greek accusative, like a true adverb, can modify adjectives.

οἱ ἀεὶ νέοι ἄνδρες   the always young men

οἱ φιλοσοφίαν νέοι ἄνδρες   the men who are young as far as philosophy is concerned *or* the *philosophy-wise* young men

οἱ ἄνδρες νέοι φιλοσοφίαν.   The men are young as far as philosophy is concerned.

αἱ οὐδὲν σοφαὶ γυναῖκες   the women who are intelligent with respect to nothing or the *nothing-wise* intelligent women

Declension/
Accusative Case

The system of adding suffixes to a noun is called *declension*. The noun with its suffix is said to be in a particular *case*. The accusative declensional suffix for both the masculine and feminine genders is -ν for the singular and -νς for the plural. However, since all nouns do not end with identical final letters in their stem (that is, the noun without declensional suffix), you might expect that these accusative suffixes will be changed sometimes in certain contexts for dialectal and euphonic reasons.

    The ways in which a noun's stem may end can be categorized into three types. There are, therefore, three declensions in Greek.

Type I. Nouns with a stem ending in -α or -η: ψυχή-

Type II. Nouns with a stem ending in -ο: ἄνθρωπο-

Type III. Nouns with a stem ending in a consonant.: γυναῖκ-, ἄνδρ-, παῖδ-, μητέρ-.

Accusative/ Masculine and Feminine Endings

The chart summarizes the "endings" for the three declensions. (To simplify the learning of the declensions, the ending instead of the suffix is shown: the ending is the way the case ends after the addition of the suffix and any resulting euphonic or dialectal changes.)

Type I	Type II	Type III	
-ην/-αν	*-ον*	*-α*	Singular
-ᾱς	*-ους*	*-ας*	Plural

Note that the ending for the first two noun types or declensions is composed of the final stem vowel together with the accusative suffix: $\boxed{ψυχ\text{-}ή}\text{-}ν$, $\boxed{ἄνθρωπ\text{-}ο}\text{-}ν$. In Type III nouns, the declensional suffix has undergone euphonic change: $παῖδ\text{-}ν$, which cannot be easily pronounced and therefore becomes $παῖδ\text{-}α$. Similar euphonic changes explain the plural endings: $\boxed{ψυχ\text{-}ά}\text{-}νς → ψυχάς$; $\boxed{ἀνθρώπ\text{-}ο}\text{-}νς → ἀνθρώπους$; $παῖδ\text{-}νς → παῖδ\text{-}ας$.

Note also that the -α in Type I nouns is long: *ψυχᾱ́ς* because it is the result of *ψυχά-νς*, but the -α of Type III is short: *παῖδας*, because it is the result of the shift of -ν to -α.

Attic Dialect Type I Nouns

In the Attic dialect (the language of Athens), the final -η of the noun stem changed to -α after ε, ι, and ρ:

τὴν σκιάν
τὴν χώραν

Accusative/ Neuter Endings

For all three types of noun, the neuter accusative is *always* identical with the lexical entry (that is, the word as it is listed in the vocabulary or as it is used as a subject or in a nominal sentence). In the plural, the ending for both the subject form and the accusative case is -α.

The identity of the subject and accusative cases in the neuter results in a certain ambiguity, which is usually clarified by the context:

τὸ παιδίον διδάσκει ὁ ποιητής.

τὸ παιδίον διδάσκομεν.

διδάσκει τὸ παιδίον τοὺς ἀνθρώπους.

Gender and Declension

The three genders are not equally represented in the three declensions.

Type I. Most nouns of this declension are *feminine* although a few are masculine: *τὸν ποιητήν*. There are no neuter nouns of Type I.

Type II. Most nouns of this declension are *masculine* or *neuter* although a few are feminine: *τὴν ὁδόν*.

Type III. All three genders occur fairly equally in this declension.

Examples

I	II	III
τὴν ψυχή-ν	*τὴν ὁδό-ν*	*τὴν γυναῖκ-α*
τὰς ψυχάς	*τὰς ὁδούς*	*τὰς γυναῖκας*
τὸν ποιητή-ν	*τὸν ἄνθρωπο-ν*	*τὸν ἄνδρ-α*

τοὺς ποιητάς	τοὺς ἀνθρώπους	τοὺς ἄνδρας
(no neuter)	τὸ παιδίον	τὸ σῶμα
	τὰ παιδία	τὰ σώματα

Identification of Declensional Type

You cannot determine to what declension a noun belongs from the lexical entry (subject form), for example: ἡ γυνή is Type III (τὴν γυναῖκ-α, but ἡ ψυχή is Type I (τὴν ψυχή-ν). Similarly, τὸ σῶμα is Type III. The fact that the stem does indeed end in a consonant is not apparent except from the plural (τὰ σώματ-α). The reason for this difficulty is that the subject form has often lost the final letters for euphonic reasons. The declensional type, however, is easily recognizable from any form other than the subject form. You must, therefore, learn each noun's stem and gender as well as its subject form.

Declension/Accusatives of Adjectives

Adjectives, like nouns, also belong to different declensions on the basis of the final letter of their stem. The adjectives which you have learned thus far all have stems which end in -η/α and -o. For such adjectives, the Type I endings are used for the feminine nouns and the Type II endings are used for the masculine. The Type II neuter endings are used for the neuter nouns.

τὴν ἀγαθὴν ψυχήν	τὸν ἀγαθὸν ποιητήν	
τὴν ἀγαθὴν ὁδόν	τὸν ἀγαθὸν ἄνθρωπον	τὸ ἀγαθὸν παιδίον
τὴν ἀναθὴν γυναῖκα	τὸν ἀγαθὸν ἄνδρα	τὸ ἀγαθὸν σῶμα
τὰς ἀγαθὰς ψυχάς	τοὺς ἀγαθοὺς ποιητάς	
τὰς ἀγαθὰς ὁδούς	τοὺς ἀγαθοὺς ἀνθρώπους	τὰ ἀγαθὰ παιδία
τὰς ἀγαθὰς γυναῖκας	τοὺς ἀγαθοὺς ἄνδρας	τὰ ἀγαθὰ σώματα

Obviously, adjectives do not always belong to the same declension as the nouns they modify. Adjectives must "agree" with their nouns in gender and number (but not in declensional type, or ending).

ONOMATA KAI PHMATA

I

ἡ κόρη, τὴν κόρην
ἡ ψυχή, τὴν ψυχήν
ἡ σκιά, τὴν σκιάν
ὁ ποιητής, τὸν ποιητήν

II

ὁ ἄνθρωπος, τὸν ἄνθρωπον
ὁ νόμος, τὸν νόμον
τὸ παιδίον, *pl.* τὰ παιδία
τὸ μέτρον, *pl.* τὰ μέτρα

III

ὁ ἀνήρ, τόν ἄνδρα
ἡ γυνή, τὴν γυναῖκα
ὁ πατήρ, τὸν πατέρα
ἡ μήτηρ, τὴν μητέρα
ὁ παῖς, τὸν παῖδα

νέος, -α, -ον	young
ἡ χώρα, τὴν χώραν (I)	country
ὁ νεανίας, τὸν νεανίαν (I)	young man
ἡ φιλοσοφία, τὴν φιλοσοφίαν (I)	philosophy
ἡ ὁδός, τὴν ὁδόν (II)	road, way
τὸ σῶμα, pl. τὰ σώματα (III)	body
ὁ χρόνος, τὸν χρόνον (II)	time
οὐδείς, οὐδέν	no one, nothing
μόνος, -η, -ον	alone, only
δίκαιος, -α, -ον	just

Note that ἡ κόρη (I) was not affected by the dialectal change of -η to -α in Attic.

ΑΣΚΗΣΙΣ

I. IDENTIFY the noun type (or declension) for each of the following.

1. τὴν ὁδόν   6. τὴν γυναῖκα

2. τὴν ψυχήν   7. τὴν κόρην

3. τὸ μέτρον   8. τὴν μητέρα

4. τὸν παῖδα   9. τὴν χώραν

5. τὸν πατέρα   10. τὸν νεανίαν

II. GIVE THE PLURAL for each of the above phrases.

III. ADD AN ADJECTIVE to each of the above phrases (both singular and plural).

IV. TRANSLATE.

1. σοφὸς ὁ βασιλεὺς τὸν νόμον.

2. ὁ φιλοσοφίαν σοφὸς νεανίας ἀγαθός.

3. οἱ οὐδὲν ἀγαθοὶ ἄνδρες κακῶς μανθάνουσι τὴν φιλοσοφίαν.

4. οὐδεὶς ἄνθρωπος σοφὸς φιλοσοφίαν.

5. δεικνύασι τὰ καλὰ καὶ ἀγαθὰ ἀεὶ αἱ φιλοσοφίαν σοφαὶ γυναῖκες καὶ τὰς κόρας διδάσκουσιν.

6. μέτρα ἱστᾶσιν ἄνθρωποι.

7. οἱ πάλαι σοφοὶ ἀεὶ ἀνθρώπους παιδεύουσιν.

8. ὁ παῖς οὐδὲν σοφὸς καὶ κακῶς τὴν φιλοσοφίαν μανθάνει.

9. ἐθέλω νόμους τιθέναι καὶ διδάσκειν τὰ καλά.

10. οἱ νέοι τὴν φιλοσοφίαν μανθάνουσι κακῶς.

V. MATCH the second verb to the first by changing it into the same form.

1. διδόναι (παιδεύω)

2. ἰᾶσιν (ἐθέλω)

3. δίδομεν (δείκνυμι)

4. ἵετε (δίδωμι)

5. μανθάνετε (τίθημι)

6. διδάσκεις (δίδωμι)

7. ἀποθνῄσκομεν (ἵστημι)

8. ἱστᾶσιν (διδάσκω)

9. ἱστάναι (μανθάνω)

10. παιδεύεις (ἵστημι)

VI. COMPOSE two nominal sentences and two verbal sentences, using the accusative case.

VII. REPLACE adverbs with suitable accusatives.

1. αἱ ἀεὶ σοφαὶ γυναῖκες νῦν μανθάνουσιν.

2. οἱ πάλαι σοφοὶ ἀνθρώπους διδάσκουσιν.

4   Nominative Case

τί δὴ οἱ ἄνθρωποι; θεοὶ θνητοί. τί δὲ δὴ οἱ θεοί; ἄνθρωποι ἀθάνατοι.
—Ἡράκλειτος

Lesson 4
Nominative

Up to now we have referred to the *nominative case* as the "lexical entry." It is the form listed in vocabularies and lexica. As you have seen, however, the noun's declensional type cannot be determined from the nominative without some further information, such as the accusative form.

The nominative case is the form which is used in nominal sentences (as both subject and predicate) and also the form which is used as the apposition to the subject suffix in verbal sentences.

Declension/
Nominative Case

Since you have learned the nominative singular form as the lexical entry, it is only the plural form that you must now study. The chart summarizes the nominative endings for the three types of nouns.

	Type I			Type II		Type III	
	Masc.	Fem.	Neut.	Masc.-Fem.	Neut.	Masc.-Fem.	Neut.
Singular	-ας -ης	-α -η	*	-ος	-ον	-ς	*
Plural	-αι			-οι	-α	-ες	-α

*stem with no suffix

Note that the endings in Types I and II nouns are actually composed of the declensional suffix and the final vowel of the noun stem: αἱ $\boxed{ψυχ\text{-}α}$-ι, οἱ $\boxed{ἄνθρωπ\text{-}ο}$-ι.

Note also that the diphthongs -αι and -οι as nominative endings are short; hence the accent does not have to shift from third position: ὁ ἄνθρωπος, οἱ ἄνθρωποι, but τοὺς ἀνθρώπους. Similarly, a circumflex is admissable on long vowels in second position: ἡ χώρᾱ, τὴν χώρᾱν, but αἱ χῶραι.

Examples

I		II	III
ὁ	ποιητ-ή-ς	ἄνθρωπ-ο-ς	παῖ-ς
τὸν	ποιητ-ή-ν	ἄνθρωπ-ο-ν	παῖδ-α
οἱ	ποιητ-α-ί	ἄνθρωπ-ο-ι	παῖδ-ες
τοὺς	ποιητ-άς	ἀνθρώπ-ους	παῖδ-ας
ἡ	ψυχ-ή	ὁδ-ό-ς	γυνή
τὴν	ψυχ-ή-ν	ὁδ-ό-ν	γυναῖκ-α
αἱ	ψυχ-α-ί	ὁδ-ο-ί	γυναῖκ-ες
τάς	ψυχ-άς	ὁδ-ούς	γυναῖκ-ας
τὸ		παιδί-ο-ν	σῶμα
τὸ		παιδί-ο-ν	σῶμα
τὰ	(no neuters)	παιδί-α	σώματ-α
τὰ		παιδί-α	σώματ-α

Note that for Type III neuters, the nominative is composed of the stem with no suffix. For euphonic reasons, the final consonant of the stem often is lost: τὸ σῶματ (which must be the stem, as you can see from the plural τὰ σώματ-α) simplifies to τὸ σῶμα. Similarly, the -ς suffix of the nominative singular may be lost (together with the final consonant of the stem) for euphonic reasons: ἡ γυναῖκ-ς (cf. τὴν γυναῖκ-α) becomes ἡ γυνή. Or, again for euphonic reasons, the final stem consonant may be lost: ὁ παῖδ-ς → ὁ παῖ-ς. Sometimes the final consonant of the stem must be written as a double consonant (ψ, ξ) when the -ς suffix is added: ὁ φύλακ-ς → ὁ φύλαξ.

Remember that in the Attic dialect -η has changed to -α after ε, ι or ρ; hence, ὁ νεανί-α-ς, τὸν νεανί-α-ν; ἡ χώρ-ᾱ, τὴν χώρ-ᾱ-ν.

Particles

The Greek language has a number of short words which reflect nuances of meaning that in English can be conveyed only by the intonation of the spoken voice or hand gestures or marks of punctuation. These words are called *particles*. Since they convey the nuance rather than the meaning, they usually are not placed in the first position in a sentence but are "postpositive" or ordinarily placed as the second element or after the word to which they add the nuance.

Furthermore, Greek ordinarily does not continue from one sentence to the next without at least one of these particles to indicate the manner of connection between the sequential ideas.

ΔE.

This is the weakest or least obtrusive manner of connection. The particle δέ is always placed in a postpositive position. Its meaning is a nonemphatic "and" or "but."

οἱ θεοὶ ἀθάνατοι. οἱ δ' ἄνθρωποι θνητοί.
The gods are immortal. And/but men are mortal.

Notice that the final vowel of the particle can be lost (or "elided") before a word which begins with a vowel.

MEN... ΔE...

The particle δέ is often combined with a preceding particle μέν. In this context the adversative ("but") meaning of the particle δέ is intensified. The combination of these two particles produces a meaning similar to that of the adversative coordinating conjunction ἀλλά except that the combined μέν... δέ... allows a more specific emphasis upon exactly what two items are being contrasted.

οἱ θεοὶ ἀθάνατοι ἀλλ' οἱ ἄνθρωποι θνητοί.
The gods are immortal, but men are mortal.

οἱ μὲν θεοὶ ἀθάνατοι, οἱ δ' ἄνθρωποι θνητοί.
The gods (on the one hand) are immortal, whereas men (on the other hand) are mortal. *Or*, It is the gods who are immortal, whereas it is men who are mortal.

ἀθάνατοι μὲν οἱ θεοί, θνητοὶ δ᾽ οἱ ἄνθρωποι.
Immortal are the gods, whereas *mortal* are men.

The article alone with the contrasted μέν... δέ... can indicate two opposed persons or things.

οἱ μὲν ἀθάνατοι, οἱ δὲ θνητοί.
Some men are immortal, others are mortal.

ἡ μὲν ἀγαθή, ἡ δὲ κακή.
One woman is good, the other bad.

Whatever is placed before the particles is the emphatically contrasted item.

μανθάνουσι μὲν οἱ ἄνδρες, διδάσκει δ᾽ ὁ ποιητής.
It's learning that the men do, teaching that the poet does.

τοὺς μὲν διδάσκει, τοὺς δὲ οὔ.
Some men he teaches, others not.

ΔΗ/ΓΕ.

The particle δή places emphasis upon the word that precedes it. Its meaning is similar to that of the phrase "of course" or "indeed" or to that of an exclamation mark (!).

τί δὴ οἱ θεοί; What (!) are gods?

The particle γε (which is enclitic, or accentless) has similar meaning.

θεοί γε ἀθάνατοι. Gods (!) at least are immortal.

ΟΥΝ.

The particle οὖν indicates an inference, a meaning similar to the word "therefore."

θεοὶ οὖν ἀθάνατοι. Gods, therefore, are immortal.

ΑΡΑ.

The particle ἄρα is similar in meaning to οὖν.

τί ἄρα θεοί; What then are gods, as you would infer?

ΤΕ.

The particle τε (enclitic) is a connective ("and") and is similar to καί except that it is postpositive.

θεοὶ καὶ ἄνθρωποι ἀθάνατοι = θεοὶ ἄνθρωποί τε ἀθάνατοι.

The particle τε can be combined with a second τε or with καί to mean "both... and."

θεοί τε καὶ ἄνθρωποι ἀθάνατοι. ⎫
θεοί τε ἄνθρωποί τε ἀθάνατοι. ⎬ Both gods and men are immortal.
καὶ θεοὶ καὶ ἄνθρωποι ἀθάνατοι. ⎭

The conjunction καί, in addition to meaning "and," can mean "even" or "also" in contexts where a connective meaning would be inappropriate.

ἀθάνατοι καὶ οἱ θεοί.   Immortal also are the gods.

Interrogative Pronouns

You can ask a question in Greek with the words τίς ("who?") and τί ("what?"). The accent never changes from acute to grave. The interrogative τίς is a Type III word with the stem τίν-.

τίς;	τί
τίν-α	τί
τίν-ες	τίν-α
τίν-ας	τίν-α

ΟΝΟΜΑΤΑ ΚΑΙ ΡΗΜΑΤΑ

ὁ/ἡ θεός, τὸν/τὴν θεόν	god/goddess
ὁ φιλόσοφος, τὸν φιλόσοφον	philosopher
ὁ διδάσκαλος, τὸν διδάσκαλον	teacher
ὁ φύλαξ, τὸν φύλακα	guard
ὁ θάνατος, τὸν θάνατον	death
ἡ ζωή, τὴν ζωήν	life
πάντα	everything (neuter *pl.*)
θεῖος, -α, -ον	divine
ἀθάνατος, -ον	immortal
ἄσοφος, -ον	= οὐ σοφός
θνητός, -ή, -όν	= οὐκ ἀθάνατος
αἰσχρός, -ή, -όν	= οὐ καλός
δέ/μέν... δέ.../δή/γε/οὖν/ἄρα/τε/τε καί	
τίς; τί;	who? what?

Note that the prefix α- negates: ἀθάνατος/ὁ θάνατος, ἄσοφος/σοφός. Such compound adjectives (composed of more than one stem or of a stem with a prefix) often do not have a separate declensional form for the feminine: ἡ ἀθάνατος γυνή.

The article with an adverb or an infinitive is the equivalent of a noun phrase: οἱ πάλαι "the men of long ago"; αἱ νῦν "the women of today"; τὸ διδάσκειν "the act of teaching."

ΑΣΚΗΣΙΣ

I. TRANSLATE.

1. θνητοὶ μὲν οἱ ἄνθρωποι, ἀθάνατοι δ' οἱ θεοί.

2. ἀποθνήσκουσι καὶ οἱ φιλόσοφοι, νέοι δὲ τὰς ψυχὰς ἀεί.

3. οἱ θεοὶ πάντα σοφοί. θεῖον δ' οὖν τὸ ἀεὶ καλῶς διδάσκειν.

4. οὐδεὶς οὖν θνητὸς πάντα σοφὸς ἀλλὰ τὰ μὲν σοφός, τὰ δὲ οὔ.

5. διδάσκει μὲν ὁ θεός, μανθάνομεν δ' οἱ ἀγαθοί.

6. τιθέασι νόμους οἱ φιλόσοφοι καὶ τοὺς ἀνθρώπους διδάσκουσιν ἀεὶ τὰ καλὰ καὶ ἀγαθά.

7. τοὺς μὲν παῖδας διδάσκει ὁ πατήρ, τὰς δὲ κόρας ἡ μήτηρ.

8. τί δὴ ἡ ζωή; οὔκ-ουν τὸ ἀεί γε μανθάνειν;

9. θνητοὶ δὴ οἱ ἄνθρωποι τὰ σώματα ἀλλ᾽ οὐκ ἀποθνήσκουσιν οἱ σοφοὶ οἱ πάλαι τὰς ψυχάς.

10. τὸ μὲν δείκνυμι, τὸ δὲ οὔ.

II. MATCH the second noun to the first by changing it into the same form.

1. τὸν ποιητήν (ὁ νεανίας)

2. οἱ ἄνδρες (ὁ φιλόσοφος)

3. αἱ γυναῖκες (τὸ παιδίον)

4. τὸν θάνατον (ὁ φύλαξ)

5. τὴν ζωήν (τὸ μέτρον)

6. αἱ σκιαί (ὁ ποιητής)

7. τὰς μητέρας (ὁ θεός)

8. τὰ σώματα (ἡ κόρη)

9. τὴν φιλοσοφίαν (ἡ κόρη)

10. τοὺς φύλακας (ὁ πατήρ)

III. MATCH the second verb to the first by changing it into the same form.

1. διδόναι (ἐθέλω)

2. ἰᾶσιν (παιδεύω)

3. τίθετε (ἀποθνήσκω)

4. ἐθέλεις (ἵημι)

5. δείκνυμεν (τίθημι)

6. διδάσκουσιν (δίδωμι)

7. ἵστατε (ἐθέλω)

8. ἐστίν (δίδωμι)

9. μανθάνειν (ἵημι)

10. τιθέασιν (ἵστημι)

IV. CHANGE the subject to the opposite number (singular to plural or vice versa) and make other necessary changes.

1. ἀποθνήσκουσιν οἱ ποιηταί.

2. ὁ μὲν παιδεύει, ὁ δὲ μανθάνει.

3. τοὺς μὲν οἱ θεοὶ ἐθέλουσι διδάσκειν, τοὺς δὲ οὔ.

4. ἡ μὲν γυνὴ σοφή τε καὶ καλή, ὁ δ᾽ ἀνὴρ ἄσοφός τε καὶ αἰσχρός.

5. οἱ μὲν πάλαι σοφοί τε καὶ ἀγαθοί, οἱ δὲ νῦν οὔ.

V. COMPLETE the following sentences with any suitable antithesis.

1. τὰς μέν....

2. ἡ μὲν ψυχή....

3. τὰς μὲν γυναῖκας....

4. ὁ μὲν διδάσκαλος ὁ νῦν....

5. ἐθέλομεν οὖν διδάσκειν μέν....

VI. ANSWER the questions (in Greek) with any appropriate meaning.

1. τί δὴ οἱ θεοί;

2. τίνας παιδεύει ὁ διδάσκαλος;

3. τίς τίνας παιδεύει;

4. τίνες οἱ ἄνδρες καὶ τίνες αἱ γυναῖκες;

5. τί δ' οὖν ἡ ψυχή;

5 Pronouns

ὁδὸς ἄνω κάτω μία καὶ ἡ αὐτή. —Ἡράκλειτος

Lesson 5

Personal Pronouns Pronouns are words that can be substituted for a noun when the noun (or "antecedent") is already known from the context. The *personal pronouns* are pronouns like "I," "you," "he," etc.

The list presents the Greek personal pronouns. There were no personal pronouns in common usage in Attic prose for the third person except for the form shown.

ἐγώ	I	σύ	you	_____	he, she, it
ἐμέ/με	me	σέ/σε	him, her, it	_____	him, her, it
ἡμεῖς	we	ὑμεῖς		_____	they
ἡμᾶς	us	ὑμᾶς		σφᾶς	them

Note that the forms *με* and *σε* are enclitic and are less emphatic than the accented forms.

The nominative case of the personal pronouns is used only for emphasis inasmuch as the personal suffix of the verb already designates the subject.

μανθάνομεν.	We learn.
ἡμεῖς μανθάνομεν.	*We* learn.
μανθάνομεν ἡμεῖς γε.	We (!) learn.
μανθάνομεν ἐγώ τε καὶ σύ.	We learn, I and you.
ἐγὼ μὲν μανθάνω, ὑμεῖς δὲ οὔ.	*I* learn, not you.

ΑΥΤΟΣ /
Pronoun and
Adjective

The word *αὐτός* can be used as both an adjective and a pronoun. It is declined as an adjective like *ἀγαθός, -ή, -όν*, except that, like all pronouns, it resembles the article *τό* in the neuter singular.

αὐτός	αὐτή	αὐτό
αὐτόν	αὐτήν	αὐτό
αὐτοί	αὐταί	αὐτά
αὐτούς	αὐτάς	αὐτά

When placed in the predicate position (*not* between the article and its noun), it adds emphasis and is called an *intensive pronoun*.

αὐτοὶ μανθάνομεν.	We, ourselves, learn.
αὐταὶ αἱ γυναῖκες μανθάνουσιν. ⎫	
αἱ γυναῖκες μανθάνουσιν αὐταί. ⎭	The women, themselves, learn.

When placed in the attributive position (between article and noun), it means "the same."

| αἱ αὐταὶ γυναῖκες μανθάνουσιν. | The same women learn. |
| διδάσκω τοὺς αὐτοὺς ἄνδρας. | I teach the same men. |

In cases other than the nominative, it has a meaning like that of the lacking third person of the personal pronouns.

αὐτὴν διδάσκω.	I teach her.
αὐτοὺς διδάσκω. σφᾶς διδάσκω. }	I teach them.

Demonstrative Pronouns and Adjectives

Demonstrative pronouns and adjectives indicate or describe persons or things by pointing to them.

ΟΥΤΟΣ/ΟΔΕ.

These demonstratives point to a person or thing nearby: "this."

οὗτος	αὕτη	τοῦτο	ὅδε	ἥδε	τόδε
τοῦτον	ταύτην	τοῦτο	τόνδε	τήνδε	τόδε
οὗτοι	αὗται	ταῦτα	οἵδε	αἵδε	τάδε
τούτους	ταύτας	ταῦτα	τούσδε	τάσδε	τάδε

Note that οὗτος has a stem which changes to τουτ-/ταυτ-.

Note also the similarity of ὅδε to the article ὁ, ἡ, τό. (The article is itself a weak demonstrative.)

ΕΚΕΙΝΟΣ.

This demonstrative points to a person or thing which is not nearby: "that."

ἐκεῖνος	ἐκείνη	ἐκεῖνο
ἐκεῖνον	ἐκείνην	ἐκεῖνο
ἐκεῖνοι	ἐκεῖναι	ἐκεῖνα
ἐκείνους	ἐκείνας	ἐκεῖνα

Note that the neuter singular of ἐκεῖνος is also, like all pronouns, similar to the article. Otherwise ἐκεῖνος is declined like ἀγαθός, -ή, -όν.

All demonstratives are always placed in predicate position.

ἐκεῖνος ὁ ἀνήρ.	That is the man.
ἐκείνη ἡ γυνὴ φιλόσοφος.	That woman is a philosopher.
ταύτην τὴν γυναῖκα διδάσκω.	I teach this woman.

Οὗτος and ὅδε sometimes differ in meaning. Οὗτος refers to what is nearby by being before, whereas ὅδε refers to what is nearby by being after.

τοῦτο μὲν σοφὸς ὁ ἀνήρ, τόδε δὲ οὔ. With respect to this (which I have just mentioned), the man is wise, but with respect to this (which I'm about to mention), he isn't.

These three demonstratives were used to supply the nominative function of the missing third person of the personal pronouns.

παιδεύουσιν οὗτός τε καὶ αὕτη.	He and she teach.

Reflexive Pronouns

When a pronoun is *not* in the nominative case but, nevertheless, has the subject of the sentence as its antecedent, it is called *reflexive* (that is, it "turns back" upon the subject).

ἐμαυτὸν παιδεύω.	I teach myself.
ἑαυτὸν παιδεύει.	He teaches himself.
ἑαυτὸν μὲν παιδεύει, αὐτὸν δὲ οὔ.	He teaches himself, but not him.

Note that the reflexive in Greek is not identical with the intensive pronoun.

ἐμαυτὸν αὐτὸς παιδεύω ἔγωγε.	I (!), myself, teach myself.

The list presents the Greek reflexive pronouns.

masc.	fem.	neut.	
ἐμαυτόν	ἐμαυτήν		myself
ἡμᾶς αὐτούς	ἡμᾶς αὐτάς		ourselves
σεαυτόν/σαυτόν	σεαυτήν/σαυτήν		yourself
ὑμᾶς αὐτούς	ὑμᾶς αὐτάς		yourselves
ἑαυτόν/αὐτόν	ἑαυτήν/αὐτήν	ἑαυτό/αὐτό	him/ her/ itself
ἑαυτούς/αὐτούς	ἑαυτάς/αὐτάς	ἑαυτά/αὐτά	themselves

Conjugation of *EIMI*

The verb εἰμί is athematic. Its stem is ἐσ- as can be seen from the form ἐσμέν. Sigma, however, is unstable in certain positions in Greek and is easily lost for dialectal and euphonic reasons. The verb εἰμί is, therefore, *irregular* (that is, its forms cannot be predicted simply on the athematic pattern) and must be memorized. The verb is enclitic except for the second person singular and the infinitive.

εἰ-μί	ἐσ-μέν	I am, etc.
εἶ	ἐσ-τέ	
ἐσ-τί(ν)	εἰ-σί(ν)	
	εἶ-ναι	

(The verb forms shown with the final accent are enclitic: it is conventional to accent them thus when they occur alone out of context.) You will learn accent patterns for enclitics later. Enclitics retain their accents when they are emphasized. The form ἐστί is accented ἔστι when it begins a sentence and when it signifies "exists" instead of "is."

ONOMATA KAI PHMATA

ἐγώ/ἐμέ/ἡμεῖς/ἡμᾶς	ὅδε, ἥδε, τόδε
σύ/σέ/ὑμεῖς/ὑμᾶς	ἐκεῖνος, -η, -ο
σφᾶς	ἐμαυτόν, -ήν
αὐτός, -ή, -ό	σεαυτόν, -ήν

οὗτος, αὕτη, τοῦτο	ἑαυτόν, -ήν, -ό
εἰμί	
οὐδέ	= καὶ οὐ/οὐ δέ
εἷς, μία, ἕν	one
οὐδείς, οὐδεμία, οὐδέν	= οὐδὲ εἷς, οὐδὲ μία, οὐδὲ ἕν
πᾶς, πᾶσα, πᾶν	every, all
ὁ Ἕλλην, τὸν Ἕλληνα	Greek (person)
ἡ Ἑλλάς, τὴν Ἑλλάδα	Greece
ὁ γέρων, τὸν γέροντα	= opposite of νεανίας
γεραιός, -ά, -όν	= opposite of νέος
γάρ	(*particle postpositive*) for, because
ἄνω	upward
κάτω	downward
τὸ δῶρον, pl. τὰ δῶρα	gift

Note that οὐδείς is composed of οὐδὲ εἷς. The declension of εἷς and οὐδείς is Type III for the masculine and neuter, with the stem ἑν-: ἕνα, οὐδένα, but Type I for the feminine: μίαν, οὐδεμίαν.

Note that πᾶς, πᾶσα, πᾶν is like εἷς in being declined as Type III for the masculine and neuter, with the stem πάντ-, but as Type I for the feminine: πάντα ἄνθρωπον, πᾶσαν γυναῖκα, πᾶν παιδίον. The position of this adjective is usually predicate but it can be used in both predicate and attributive positions: πάντες οἱ ἄνθρωποι/οἱ πάντες ἄνθρωποι.

Note that the particle γάρ indicates an explanation and is *postpositive*, (never in first position): ἀποθνῄσκουσι πάντες οἱ ἄνθρωποι. θνητοὶ γάρ εἰσιν.

ΑΣΚΗΣΙΣ

I. TRANSLATE.

1. Ἕλληνες ἀεὶ παῖδές ἐστε, γέρων δὲ Ἕλλην οὐκ ἔστιν. νέοι γάρ ἐστε τὰς ψυχὰς πάντες. —Πλάτων

2. τὴν Ἑλλάδα παιδεύει ὁ ποιητής. —Πλάτων

3. εἷς ἀνὴρ οὐδεὶς ἀνήρ. —Greek proverb

4. αὗται αἱ ὁδοὶ οὐκ εἰσὶν αἱ αὐταί. ἡ μὲν γὰρ ἄνω ἐστίν, ἡ δὲ κάτω.

5. πάντες δ' οὖν μανθάνομεν ἀεὶ οὐδὲ σοφὸς οὐδείς ἔστι θνητὸς ἀλλ' ἄσοφοι ἡμεῖς πάντες τε καὶ πᾶσαι.

6. ἡ ἄνω ὁδὸς καὶ ἡ κάτω μία ἐστὶ καὶ ἡ αὐτή.

7. οἱ πάντες ἄνθρωποι ἕν τε καὶ τὸ αὐτό.

8. ὁ δὲ Σωκράτης γέρων οὐκ ἔστιν. τὸ μὲν γὰρ σῶμά γε γεραιός, τὴν δὲ ψυχήν ἐστι νεανίας.

9. ζωήν τε καὶ θάνατον οἱ θεοὶ διδόασιν. ψυχὴ γὰρ ἀθάνατος καὶ ἐσμεν σῶμα θνητοὶ πάντες οἱ ἄνθρωποι.

10. τὸ μὲν ἑαυτὸν πάντα διδάσκειν καλόν ἐστι καὶ ἀγαθόν, τὸ δ' οὐδὲν ἐθέλειν μανθάνειν ἀεὶ αἰσχρόν. οἱ γὰρ σοφοί γε τὰς ψυχὰς ἐσμεν νεανίαι.

II. MATCH the second noun to the first by changing it into the same form.

1. οἱ Ἕλληνες (ὁ ποιητής)
2. αἱ γυναῖκες (ἡ ὁδός)
3. τὸν φύλακα (ὁ πατήρ)
4. τοὺς θεούς (ὁ νεανίας)
5. τοὺς διδασκάλους (ἡ κόρη)
6. τὰς σκιάς (τὸ δῶρον)
7. τὴν ψυχήν (ἡ ὁδός)
8. τὴν γυναῖκα ὁ (παῖς)
9. αἱ χῶραι (τὸ μέτρον)
10. οἱ νόμοι (τὸ σῶμα)

III. MATCH the second verb to the first by changing it into the same form.

1. ἐθέλειν (ἵημι)
2. τιθέασιν (διδάσκω)
3. παιδεύεις (τίθημι)
4. ἐσμέν (δίδωμι)
5. ἴης (εἰμί)
6. εἶναι (δείκνυμι)
7. εἶ (ἵστημι)
8. τιθέναι (ἀποθνῄσκω)
9. ἱᾶσιν (παιδεύω)
10. εἰσίν (ἵστημι)

IV. COMPLETE the following sentences with any suitable antithesis.

1. ἡμεῖς μὲν οἱ ἄνδρες ἐσμὲν φιλόσοφοι....

2. ὁ μὲν διδάσκαλος ἑαυτὸν διδάσκει....

3. πᾶσαι μὲν αἱ κόραι ἐθέλουσι μανθάνειν....

4. τὰς μὲν ψυχάς ἐστε πάντες οἱ ἄνθρωποι ἀθάνατοι....

5. σὺ μέν γε εἶ σοφή....

V. ANSWER the questions (in Greek) with any appropriate response.

1. τίνες οὗτοι οἱ γέροντες;

2. τίνες αὗται;

3. τίς παιδεύει ἐκείνους τοὺς παῖδας;

4. τί μανθάνουσιν ἐκεῖνοι οἱ φιλόσοφοι;

5. τίς τίθησι τούτους τοὺς νόμους;

VI. FILL IN THE BLANKS with suitable pronouns.

1. _____ μὲν σοφοί, ὑμεῖς δὲ ἄσοφοι.

2. ἀποθνῄσκομεν _____ τε καὶ _____.

3. ὑμᾶς μὲν αὐτοὺς διδάσκετε, _____ δ' ἐγώ.

4. σεαυτὸν μὲν σύ, ἐμαυτὸν δ' _____ διδάσκομεν.

5. _____ μὲν καλή, _____ δὲ αἰσχρή.

6

Thematic Conjugation of Imperfect and Aorist

ἡ γλῶσσα πολλοὺς εἰς ὄλεθρον ἤγαγεν. —Μένανδρος.

Lesson 6:

Verbal Aspect

The verbal conjugations which you have learned thus far describe action that occurs in the present time or "tense." The present tense cannot distinguish whether the action is described as something that is going on continually (that is, "progressive") or something that occurs in a punctual manner. That is to say, the verb *μανθάνομεν* means either "we learn" or "we are learning." In the past tense, however, the Greek language can make such a distinction between the progressive and punctual ideas. This distinction is called the verb's *aspect*.

Imperfect and Aorist

The past tense which expresses the action as a continuing or progressive idea is called the *imperfect* ("not finished"), whereas the past tense which views the action as a punctual occurrence is called the *aorist* ("indeterminate").

ἐ-μανθάν-ο-μεν.	We were learning. (imperfect)
ἐ-μάθ-ο-μεν.	We learned. (aorist)

Past Tense

The past tense of a Greek verb is indicated by a combination of two signs, a prefix and a special system of past tense (or *secondary*) personal suffixes, which differ in some persons from the present (or *primary*) personal suffixes. This is true of all verbs that indicate action which occurred at some past time.

Thematic Past Tense Conjugations

As always, there are two ways of adding the personal suffixes to a verb's stem: either with the intervention of a connecting vowel (the thematic conjugation) or without the connecting vowel (the athematic conjugation). In this lesson you will learn the thematic conjugations for the imperfect and aorist aspects of a verbal action in past time.

Augment

The prefix which indicates past tense is called the verbal *augment*. There are two varieties of augment. If the verb's stem begins with a consonant, the augment consists of the addition of *ἐ-* in front of the stem.

ἐ-	*μανθάν-ο-μεν.*		*ἐ-*	*μάθ-ο-μεν.*

If the verb's stem begins with a vowel, the augment consists of the lengthening of that initial vowel.

ἠ-	*θέλ-ο-μεν.*	(*see* present *ἐθέλ-ο-μεν*)

ἦ-	*γ-ο-μεν.*	(*see* present *ἄγ-ο-μεν*)

Secondary Verbal Suffixes

The past tense (or secondary) suffixes are identical to the present (or primary) personal suffixes in the plural first and second persons: *-μεν, -τε*. The other persons are different.

-ν	1	-μεν
-ς*	2	-τε
-	3	-ν*

*variants: -ς/-σθα, -ν/-σαν

It is important to remember that these suffixes indicate the subject of the verb but only together with the augment do they indicate past time.

Imperfect and Aorist Stems

Past tense is indicated by the augment and the secondary personal suffixes. The difference between the progressive (imperfect) and punctual (aorist) aspects is signaled by a modification of the verb's stem.

The imperfect adds the augment prefix and the personal suffixes to the stem which you already have learned as the present tense or the lexical entry.

μανθάν-ο-μεν/ἐ-μανθάν-ο-μεν.

The aorist stem is different from the lexical entry and must be memorized as part of the necessary information about any verb (its so-called principle parts), like the alternation in English between "lead" and "led."

ἐ-μάθ-ο-μεν.   (μανθαν-/μαθ-)

Imperfect and Aorist Conjugations

The chart summarizes the imperfect and aorist thematic conjugations.

Imperfect		Aorist		Present (for comparison)	
ἐ-	μάνθαν- o-ν	ἔ-	μαθ- -o-ν	μανθάν-	ω
	ε-ς		ε-ς		εις
	ε-*		ε-*		ει
	o-μεν		o-μεν		o-μεν
	ε-τε		ε-τε		ε-τε
	o-ν		o-ν		ουσι*

*Nu-movable: ἐμάνθανεν/ἔμαθεν/μανθάνουσιν.

The accent on verbs is normally recessive: ἐμανθάνομεν/ἔμαθον.

EIMI/ Imperfect

The variant secondary personal suffixes appear in the conjugation of the imperfect of εἰμί. This verb has no aorist.

Imperfect			Present (for comparison)
ἦ-	ν	/ἦ	εἰμί
ἦ-	σθα		εἶ
ἦ-	ν		ἐστί (ν)
ἦ-	μεν		ἐσμέν
ἦ-	τε	/ἦσ-τε	ἐστέ
ἦ-	σαν		εἰσί (ν)

Separable Prefixes

Greek verbs often are compounded with adverbial prefixes which intensify or clarify particular meanings.

ἀπο-θνῄσκω   die *away*   προσ-άγω   lead *toward*

κατα-θνῄσκω	die *down*	ἀνα-φέρω	carry *up*
κατ-άγω	lead *down*	προσ-ανα-τρέχω	run *up towards*
κατα-πίνω	drink *down*	ἐκ-φέρω	carry *out*

The particular nuance of meaning which these prefixes add is often idiomatic and not so simple as in the examples given.

Since the augment always is prefixed onto the verb stem, it will occur after such adverbial prefixes.

ἀπ-ε-θνῄσκ-ο-μεν	προσ-αν-ε-τρέχ-ο-μεν
προσ-ήγ-ο-μεν	ἐξ-ε-φέρ-ο-μεν

The augment may cause the final vowel of the adverbial prefix to be elided (eliminated for euphonic reasons). It should also be noted that although the accent on verbs is normally recessive (that is, it falls as far back as possible), it cannot fall further back than the augment: κατ-ῆγ-ο-ν.

These adverbial prefixes are called *separable prefixes* because they sometimes separate completely from the verb and act just like a separate adverb.

Prepositions

The separable prefixes often clarify the abverbial modification of other words in the sentence and are felt to have a very close relationship with such words, often being placed in some special proximity to them. When this occurs, the prefixes are called *prepositions* (that is "placed in front"). The preposition together with the word it is clarifying is called a prepositional phrase.

ἡμᾶς πρὸς θάνατον ἦγεν.   He was leading us toward death

ONOMATA KAI PHMATA

θνῄσκω, ἔθανον	die
μανθάνω, ἔμαθον	learn
ἄγω, ἤγαγον	lead
πάσχω, ἔπαθον	experience, suffer
λείπω, ἔλιπον	leave, depart
τρέχω, ἔδραμον	run
τίκτω, ἔτεκον	give birth, beget
φεύγω, ἔφυγον	flee
ἔχω, ἔσχον (imperfect εἶχον)	have (καλῶς ἔχω/κακῶς ἔχω be well off, etc.)
λέγω, εἶπον	speak, say
λαμβάνω, ἔλαβον	take, grasp
εὑρίσκω, ηὗρον	find (*also augments to* εὑ-)
πίνω, ἔπιον	drink
πίπτω, ἔπεσον	fall

φέρω, ἤνεγκον	carry, bring
τυγχάνω, ἔτυχον	happen by chance
πρός	toward, to
εἰς	toward, into
κατά	down toward, according to
ἀνά	up toward
ἡ γλῶσσα, τὴν γλῶσσαν	tongue, language (γλῶσσαν ἵημι speak a language)
ὁ ὄλεθρος, τὸν ὄλεθρον	= θάνατος
ὁ φίλος, τὸν φίλον	friend
πολλοί, -αί, -ά	many
δεινός, -ή, -όν	terrible
ἐμός, -ή, -όν	my
σός, -ή, -όν	your
ἅπαξ	once
συνεχῶς	continually
εὖ	= καλῶς
κακῶς	= οὐ καλῶς

Note that the aorist stem cannot be predicted from the present. There are similarities or patterns, however, in some instances. Present stems that end in -αν-ο/ε-(λαμβ-άν-ω, μανθάνω, τυγχάνω) always lose that ending in the aorist. This is because -αν-ο/ε- is actually a *present verbal suffix* and cannot therefore occur in the aorist: λαμβάνω/ἔλαβον, τυγχάνω/ἔτυχον, μανθάνω/ἔμαθον. So also is the ending -ν-ο/ε-; hence, πίνω/ἔπιον. The ending -(ι)σκ-ο/ε- is similarly a present suffix; hence, θνῄσκω/ἔθανον, πάσχω/ἔπαθον, εὑρίσκω/ηὗρον. The same is true of the suffix -τ-ο/ε-; hence, πίπτω/ἔπεσον, τίκτω/ἔτεκον.

Note also that there are often similarities between the aorist stem and nouns with related meanings: ἔτυχον/ἡ τύχη ("chance"), ἔθανον/ ὁ θάνατος (death), ἔλαβον/ἡ λαβή (handle), εἶπον/τὸ ἔπος (word), ἔμαθον/τὸ μάθημα (lesson), ἔδραμον/τὸ δρᾶμα (action), ἔπαθον/τὸ πάθος (suffering).

ΑΣΚΗΣΙΣ

I. CHANGE each verb to the present.

1. ἀπέθανεν
2. ἠγάγετε
3. ἐφεύγομεν
4. ἔσχες
5. ἔτρεχον
6. ἔδραμον

7. εἶπεν

8. ἔλεγεν

9. ἐλαμβάνετε

10. ἐλείπομεν

11. ἤνεγκες

12. κατέφερεν

13. κατέπιες

14. ηὗρεν

15. προσηγάγετε

16. ἐθάνομεν

17. προσανεδράμομεν

18. ἀνήνεγκες

19. ἐπέσετε

20. κατέθανον

II. CHANGE present to imperfect and then to aorist.

1. τίκτουσιν

2. ἀπολείπομεν

3. ἔχεις

4. εὑρίσκει

5. λέγουσιν

6. τυγχάνομεν

7. πίνετε

8. ἄγουσιν

9. τίκτετε

10. φεύγεις

11. ἀναφέρει

12. προσανατρέχουσιν

13. κατάγεις

14. πάσχομεν

15. μανθάνω

16. ἀποθνήσκει

17. πίπτουσιν

18. λείπεις

19. ἔχομεν

20. καταμανθάνουσιν

III. NOTE THE PATTERN in each of the quotations and compose a translation of the English sentences using the same pattern.

1. δεινὸν τὸ τίκτειν. —Σοφοκλῆς

Learning is good.

It is ugly to suffer.

To give is divine.

2. νέοι ἐστὲ τὰς ψυχὰς πάντες. —Πλάτων

They were in no way divine.

The woman was wise as far as speaking was concerned.

No one himself is wise at everything.

3. ἡ γλῶσσα πολλοὺς εἰς ὄλεθρον ἤγαγεν. —Μένανδρος

The gods brought him to philosophy.

The god was leading you to the way.

The women carried the gifts to Greece.

IV. CHANGE verbs from aorist to imperfect. (Substitute συνεχῶς for ἅπαξ to emphasize the change in aspect.)

1. τοὺς δὲ θεοὺς ηὗρον ἔγωγε κακοὺς ἅπαξ.

2. κακῶς δ' ἔπαθον ἅπαξ πάντες καὶ πολλά.

3. ἔτεκον δ' Ἑκάβη καὶ Πρίαμος παῖδας ἅπαξ.

4. οἱ δὲ νεανίαι ἔμαθον ἅπαξ τὸ καλὸν καὶ ἀγαθόν.

5. ἅπαξ ἔδραμον πρὸς τοὺς ἀδελφοὺς τοὺς ἐμούς.

6. δῶρα δ' ἤνεγκες πρὸς τὴν σὴν μητέρα ἅπαξ.

7. ἐπίομεν ἡμεῖς ἅπαξ.

8. ἐλάβετε δὲ δῶρα καλὰ ἅπαξ.

9. ἅπαξ δ' ἔφυγεν τὴν Ἑλλάδα.

10. φιλοὺς δὲ πολλοὺς ἔσχομεν ἅπαξ.

V. FILL IN THE BLANKS with the appropriate aspect of the past tense of the verb in parentheses.

1. αὕτη ἡ μήτηρ ἡ ἐμή. ἐμὲ γὰρ _____ . (τίκτω)

2. αὐτὸν δ' ἔλιπεν ἡ ψυχὴ καὶ _____ . (ἀποθνήσκω)

3. οἱ μὲν καλῶς _____ ἀεί, οἱ δὲ κακῶς. (ἔχω)

4. γλῶσσαν ἱέναι παῖδες _____ . (μανθάνω)

5. κατὰ δὲ τὸν νόμον οἱ μὲν ἀγαθοὶ ἀεὶ εὖ _____ , οἱ δὲ κακοὶ ἀεὶ κακῶς. (πάσχω)

7

Athematic Conjugation of Imperfect and Aorist

μία ἡμέρα τὸν μὲν καθεῖλεν ὑψόθεν, τὸν δ᾽ ἦρ᾽ ἄνω. —Εὐριπίδης

Lesson 7
Athematic Past Tense Conjugations

In the athematic past tense conjugations, the verbal stem is augmented in the usual manner and the past (or secondary) personal suffixes are added directly onto the verbal stem without the intervention of a connecting vowel.

Imperfect

Just as in the present tense, the final vowel of the verbal stem for the imperfect athematic conjugation changes from long in the singular to short in the plural.

τίθη-μι/τίθε-μεν

ἐ-τίθη-ν/ἐ-τίθε-μεν

The chart summarizes the athematic conjugation of the imperfect tense.

Imperfect

ἐ-τίθη-	ν	1*
ἵστη-	ς	2*
ἵη-	—	3*
ἐ-δείκνῡ-		

Present (for comparison)

δίδω-	μι	1
τίθη-	ς	2
ἵστη-	σι	3
ἵη-		
δείκνῡ-		

ἐ-τίθε-	μεν	1
ἵστα-	τε	2
ἵε-	σαν	3
ἐ-δείκνυ-		
ἐ-δίδο-		

δίδο-	μεν	1
τίθε-	τε	2
ἵστα-	ασι	3*
ἵε-		
δείκνυ-		

*Exceptions:

ἐ-δίδ-ουν, -ους, -ου   ἱστᾶσι

ἐ-τίθ-ην, -εις, -ει   ἱᾶσι

ἵ-ην, -εις, -ει

Note that there are exceptions to the regular pattern in the singular of the imperfect of δίδωμι, τίθημι, and ἵημι. These verbs have shifted to the thematic conjugation in some forms: ἐ-τίθη-ν is athematic, but ἐτίθεις is actually thematic, resulting from the contraction of ἐ-τίθε-ε-ς. (The contraction of ε-ε to ει is something you will see occurring in other thematic verbs which you will learn later.)

Aorist ("First")/ -ΣΑ- Suffix

As in the thematic conjugation, the aorist is signaled by a change in the verbal stem itself. Although this change cannot be predicted and must be learned as a "principle part" of the verb, one very common type of change involves the addition of the suffix -σα- onto the verbal stem of the present. This is the so-called sigmatic aorist or first aorist. The past (secondary) personal suffixes are added directly onto the aorist stem without the intervention of a connecting vowel.

ἐ-παιδεύ-σα-μεν

Aorist ("Second")/ Without Suffix   The other type of athematic aorist does not use this -σα- suffix but, nevertheless, is similarly conjugated in the athematic manner. (It therefore resembles the imperfect athematic conjugation, except for the difference between present and aorist verbal stems.) Aorists which do not have the -σα- suffix, including the thematic aorist which you learned in the previous lesson, are sometimes called *second aorists*.

Sigmatic aorist

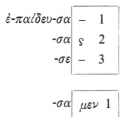

Aorist without suffix

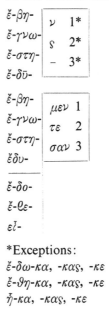

*Exceptions:
ἔ-δω-κα, -κας, -κε
ἔ-θη-κα, -κας, -κε
ἦ-κα, -κας, -κε

Note that some aorist stems do *not* show the regular shift to the short stem vowel in the plural: ἔβη-ν/ἔβη-μεν.

Note that verbs may shift from one type of conjugation to the other: βαίν-ο-μεν/ἔ-βη-μεν. Such shifts cannot be predicted and must be learned from the principle parts of the verb: βαίνω/ἔβην.

Note that ἔδωκα, ἔθηκα, and ἦκα are exceptions to the regular pattern. In the singular they are actually sigmatic aorists with a -κα- suffix (which is a variant of the -σα- suffix). Notice that these three verbs are the only ones that have the short stem vowel in the plural. You will remember that these same three verbs were also the ones that shifted to the thematic conjugation in some persons of the imperfect.

Note that most words ending in -σι, and all verbs of the third person which end in -ε, can take a nu-movable: ἐπαίδευσεν.

Special Meanings of the Aorist and Imperfect   Although the basic meaning of the imperfect and aorist contrasts verbal aspect (progressive vs. punctual or indeterminate) in past time, there are special meanings of the imperfect and aorist which evolve from particular contexts or from certain cultural presuppositions.

Gnomic Aorist

The aorist is used to express homilitic truths or proverbs. Whereas in English one would say, "A stitch in time saves nine," the Greek language would express such homilies in the aorist. The quotations which are in the headings for Lessons 6 and 7 are examples of this so-called gnomic aorist. The reason that a past tense is used for general truths probably has something to do with the Greek oral tradition of myth and history which presupposed that truth was a timeless paradigm from the past.

Imperfect for Attempted Action in the Past

Since the aspect of the imperfect is progressive, in certain contexts the "incomplete" (or imperfect) nature of the action may suggest the idea that the action was attempted and therefore not yet completed.

ἔπειθεν ὑμᾶς. "He was persuading you." In certain contexts, this could mean, "He was trying to persuade you."

Imperfect for Customary Action in the Past.

The progressive aspect of the imperfect in certain contexts may express repeated or customary action in the past.

Σωκράτης ὥσπερ ἐγίγνωσκεν οὕτως ἔλεγε. —Ξενοφῶν
Socrates used to speak just as he thought.

Speaker's Attitude Instead of Reality

It is important to notice that the choice between imperfect and aorist is not determined by the real nature of the action described but by the speaker's attitude or perception of the reality. Thus Socrates' death occurred in reality as it actually occurred, but a speaker can describe it in either its progressive or punctual aspect.

γενναίως ἀπέθανεν ὁ Σωκράτης. Socrates died nobly.
γενναίως ἀπέθνησκεν ὁ Σωκράτης. The whole procedure of what Socrates was doing in dying was done nobly.

ONOMATA KAI PHMATA

παιδεύω, ἐπαίδευσα	
διδάσκω, ἐδίδαξα	
ἐθέλω, ἠθέλησα	
πείθω, ἔπεισα	persuade
γράφω, ἔγραψα	write (see τὸ γράμμα, pl. τὰ γράμματα letter)
πέμπω, ἔπεμψα	send
πράττω, ἔπραξα	do
δείκνυμι, ἔδειξα	
μένω, ἔμεινα	stay, remain

ἀγγέλλω, ἤγγειλα	announce (*see ὁ ἄγγελος, τὸν ἄγγελον* messenger)
φθείρω, ἔφθειρα	destroy, corrupt
κρίνω, ἔκρινα	judge, decide (a contest or dispute); (*see ὁ κριτής, τὸν κριτήν* judge)
τίθημι ἔθηκα	
δίδωμι, ἔδωκα	
ἵημι, ἧκα	
βαίνω, ἔβην	walk
γιγνώσκω, ἔγνων	know, recognize
φέρω, ἤνεγκα/ἤνεγκον	
αἴρω, ἦρα	raise
_____, εἷλον	take (*see καθ-εῖλον*)
ἵστημι, ἔστησα/ἔστην	
δύω, -έδυσα/ἔδυν	go down, enter, cause to enter
ἡ ἡμέρα, τὴν ἡμέραν	day
ὀρθός, -ή, -όν	upright
ὑψόθεν	from on high (*adv.*)
ὥς...οὕτως	just as . . . so/thus
-περ	(intensive particle, enclitic; like *γε*)
γενναῖος, -α, -ον	noble (*see γενναίως*)

Note that the -σα- suffix will combine with certain final consonants of the verbal stem to be written as the double letter ψ or ξ (π/β/φ + σ → ψ; κ/γ/χ + σ → ξ): ἔγραψα, ἔπεμψα).

Note that when the -σα- suffix is added onto a verbal stem that ends in a "liquid" consonant (λ, ρ) or a "nasal" consonant (μ, ν), the σ is lost and the vowel of the preceding syllable is lengthened to compensate for the loss: κρίνω/ἔκρῑνα, μένω/ἔμεινα.

Note that a few verbs have two aorists, both a "first" aorist (aorist with the athematic -σα- suffix) and a "second" aorist (aorist without the -σα- suffix, conjugated either thematically like ἔμαθον or athematically like ἔβην). In such verbs, a distinction can often be made between transitive (with accusative) and intransitive (without accusative) meanings: ἔστησα αὐτὸν ὀρθόν. "I stood him upright." Or γυναῖκα ἔστησα κριτήν. "I appointed a woman as judge." But ἔστην αὐτὸς ὀρθός "I, myself, stood upright." In the present tense this distinction cannot be made except from context, and the same verb form, therefore, is used for both meanings: ἵστημι αὐτὸς ὀρθός/γυναῖκα ἵστημι κριτήν.

Note that δύω has both a first and second aorist but that the first aorist never seems to have been used without a separable prefix: κατ-έδυσεν εἰς θάνατον τὴν ψυχήν. "He made the soul go down into death." κατέδυ εἰς θάνατον. "He went down into death."

Note that the suffix -της denotes the *doer* of an action and that all nouns with this suffix belong to the Type I declension: ὁ κριτής ("judge"), ὁ μαθητής ("student"), ὁ ποιητής ("creator").

ΑΣΚΗΣΙΣ

I. IDENTIFY each of the verbs in the vocabulary with respect to its type of aorist.

II. CHANGE each verb to the present.

1. ἀνέβη ἡ ψυχὴ εἰς τοὺς θεούς.

2. ἠθέλησαν οἱ μαθηταὶ μανθάνειν.

3. νόμους ἔθηκεν ὁ φιλόσοφος καὶ ἔγραψεν.

4. τοὺς δικαίους γέροντας ἔστησαν κριτάς.

5. ὁ Σωκράτης τοὺς νεανίας ἔφθειρεν.

6. πολλοὺς ἀνθρώπους ἐδίδαξεν ὁ Εὐριπίδης.

7. ἡμᾶς ἔγνωτε πάντας.

8. δεινὰ εἶπέ τε καὶ ἔγραψεν ὁ βασιλεύς.

9. δῶρα ἔδομεν.

10. ἀγγέλους ἔπεμψας πρὸς τοὺς ἄνδρας.

11. ἔκρινε καλῶς ὁ θεός.

12. αὐτὰς ἐπείσαμεν.

13. πολλὰς γυναῖκας ἡ γλῶσσα ἤγαγεν εἰς ὄλεθρον.

14. δῶρον ὁ ποιητὴς ἔπεμψε πρὸς τοὺς κριτάς.

15. ἐστήσατε τοὺς ἄνδρας ὀρθούς.

16. ὀρθαὶ ἔστητε.

17. μία ἡμέρα μόνον κατέπεμψε τὸν ἄδικον ὑψόθεν.

18. ἐκεῖνον τὸν ἀγαθὸν ᾖρε μία ἡμέρα ἄνω.

19. ἀνέδραμες πρὸς τοὺς θεούς.

20. τὴν αὐτὴν γλῶσσαν εἶμεν πάντες οἱ Ἕλληνες.

III. CHANGE each of the above verbs to the imperfect.

IV. MATCH the second verb to the first by changing it into the same form.

1. ἔμαθεν (ἵστημι)

2. ἀπεθάνετε (βαίνω)

3. ἔθηκα (φεύγω)

4. εἶχεν (δύω)

5. ἔδωκα (φθείρω)

6. ἔπεμπες (κρίνω)

7. ἔγνωσαν (κρίνω)

8. ἐδίδαξαν (τρέχω)

9. ἐτίκτομεν (ἐθέλω)

10. ἔπραξας (μένω)

11. ἠγγέλλετε (ἵστημι)

12. ἠγγείλατε (ἵστημι)

13. ἧκεν (πείθω)

14. ἐδείκνυτε (γιγνώσκω)

15. ἤνεγκαν (λείπω)

16. ἔδυτε (φέρω)

17. ἐτίθην (προσβαίνω)

18. ἔδοσαν (ἵημι)

19. ἔπραττον (ἵστημι)

20. ἔσχετε (λέγω)

V. NOTE THE PATTERN in each of the quotations and compose a translation of the English sentences using the same pattern.

1. ἔγνως ὡς θεός εἰμι. —Ὅμηρος (ὡς/ὅτι "that")

You realized that the student was teacher.
You decided that the poet was good.
He said that Socrates was a philosopher.
You wrote that Socrates corrupted young men.
The guard announced that Socrates was dead.

2. μία ἡμέρα τὸν μὲν καθεῖλεν ὑψόθεν, τὸν δ' ἦρ' ἄνω. —Εὐριπίδης

Everyone judged one man good, the other bad.
The gods sent some souls upward and others down.
The student learned some things well and others badly.

3. Σωκράτης ὥσπερ ἐγίγνωσκεν οὕτως ἔλεγε. —Ξενοφῶν

The noble teacher used to do just as he taught.
Poets don't always speak just as they write.

8

Genitive Case

ψυχῆς ἀγαθῆς πατρίς ὁ ξύμπας κόσμος. —Δημόκριτος

As you have seen, an adjective can modify a noun: it is *adnominal*.

ἡ ἀγαθὴ πατρίς   the good country

In Greek, nouns can also be adnominal. Through the addition of a declensional suffix, a noun can carry a sign that it is functioning as an adjective.

ἡ ψυχῆς πατρίς   the soul's country

Note these other examples:

ἡ 'Αθηναία πολιτεία   the Athenian constitution
ἡ τῶν 'Αθηναίων πολιτεία   the Athenians' constitution
τὸ παίδειον μάθημα   the childish lesson
τὸ τοῦ παιδὸς μάθημα   the child's lesson
ὁ ἀνθρώπινος νόμος   human law
ὁ τῶν ἀνθρώπων νόμος   humans' law, the law of man

The genitive case in its adnominal function obviously supplies the same kind of information as an adjective and commonly expresses the idea of *possession*.

ἡ ἐμὴ μήτηρ/ἡ μήτηρ μου

The adnominal function of the genitive, however, (unlike the "possessive case" in English) is not limited to the idea of possession. In contexts of evaluation, for example, the genitive often expresses the *price* or *value*.

δῶρον ἄξιον ἔδωκεν.   He gave a worthy gift.
δῶρον μιᾶς δραχμῆς ἔδωκεν.   He gave a one drachma gift.

The genitive case conforms to the same pattern as the adjective with respect to the distinction between attributive and predicative positions.

ὁ τῶν ἀνθρώπων νόμος ἀγαθός.   Mankind's law is good.
ὁ νόμος τῶν ἀνθρώπων ἐστίν.   The law is mankind's.

ἀνδρός σοφοῦ ἐστι τὸ διδάσκειν.   It is a wise man's task to teach.
τὸ δῶρόν ἐστι μιᾶς δραχμῆς.   The gift is worth a drachma.

The genitive case, like the accusative case, can also allow a noun to function adverbially. The genitive adverbial function, however, has a different meaning from that of the accusative. The genitive always expresses a less complete involvement than the accusative.

ἐσθίω ἄρτον.   I eat bread (customarily or completely).

ἐσθίω ἄρτου.   I eat some bread.

τὸν οἶνον πίνω.   I drink wine.

τοῦ οἴνου πίνω.   I drink some wine.

τὸν ἄνδρα ἀκούω.   I hear the man (as he moves through the bushes).

τοῦ ἀνδρὸς ἀκούω.   I listen to the man.

τὸν παῖδα παίω.   I hit the boy.

τοῦ παιδὸς ψαύω.   I touch the boy.

Some verbs, by the very nature of their meaning, can allow only the genitive adverbial modification: ψαύω ("touch"), μετέχω (share). Such verbs are said to "pattern with the genitive" or to "take the genitive."

Genitive/ With Verbal Nouns

Some nouns have the same root or basic part as related verbs and are called *verbal nouns*. Obviously, with such nouns, the adnominal and adverbial functions of the genitive will coincide. For example, the noun βασιλεύς is formed from the same root as the verb βασιλεύω. Therefore, the phrase βασιλεὺς ἀνδρῶν could mean either "men's king" (the possessive idea) or "king of men" (the adverbial idea that occurs in the sentence βασιλεύω ἀνδρῶν/ "I rule men as their king").

Many *idiomatic* (or special) meanings of the genitive derive from this usage with nouns (or adjectives) that are based upon verbal roots.

τοῦ ὕδατος ἐπιθυμία   desire for water (*see* ἐπιθυμέω/ ἐπίθυμος, -ον)

ὁδῶν ἔμπειρος   experienced about the roads (*see* ἡ ἐμπειρία/ἐμπειρέω)

ὕδατος πλησμονή   fullness with water (*see* πληρόω)

These idiomatic meanings are usually obvious from the context and you will become more familiar with them as you read more Greek.

Genitive/Ablatival Function

In addition to the meanings of the genitive which derive from its adnominal and adverbial functions, the genitive can also express the idea of separation. This meaning was originally expressed by a separate case (the *ablative*) in the more ancient language from which the Greek language developed. A few remnants of this lost ablative case can be seen in words that end in -θεν, which was originally the ablative suffix: ὑψόθεν "from on high"/ 'Αθήνηθεν "from Athens"/πόθεν "from where?" When the ablative case was lost the functions of the ablative case devolved upon the genitive.

The reason that the genitive could assume the ablatival function is apparently because the genitive in some of its functions already approximated the idea of "separation." For example, in certain contexts, the adverbial use of the genitive suggests the idea of separation: πόνων μετέχω "I have a share of troubles" (*see* μετά "with" + ἔχω), "Along with others, I have a part separated away from the totality of troubles." Or πόνων λήγουσιν "They cease from troubles," that is, "They move away from troubles." Or ἄρτου ἐσθίω "I eat something separated from the totality of all bread." In such contexts, it is impossible to know whether the genitives are true genitives in an adverbial function or genitives that have assumed the function of the lost ablative case.

Partitive

In the ablatival function, the genitive often indicates the totality from which a part is separated. This meaning is the so-called partitive genitive.

οὐδεὶς ἀνθρώπων	no one (out of the totality) of men
πολλαὶ γυναικῶν	many (out of the totality) of women

The partitive genitive is usually placed in predicate position.

αἱ σοφαὶ τῶν γυναικῶν	the wise ones (out of the totality) of women, that is, the wise amongst women
Σωκράτης τῶν φιλοσόφων ἦν.	Socrates was (one out of the totality) of philosophers.

With Prepositions

The ablatival function of the genitive is often clarified by the use of specific prepositions (or separable prefixes) that designate separation.

ἀπὸ τῶν ἀνθρώπων ἔδραμεν.	He ran away from the men.
ἐκ τοῦ οἴκου τρέχει.	He runs out of the house.
μετὰ φίλων μανθάνεις.	You are learning with (that is, as one out of a group of) friends.
παρὰ μητρὸς φεύγει.	He flees from (the side of) his mother.
Ὀλύμπου κατέβην.	I walked down from Olympus. (In this example, the separable prefix is still attached to the verb in the more ancient manner. This is more common in poetic usage.)

These prepositions merely clarify the meaning of the ablatival function of the genitive case. You have already seen, however, that the accusative case can also be used with prepositions that clarify the nature of the adverbial modification. The use of different cases with prepositions is idiomatic and will become more familiar as you read more Greek, but there are general principles to be noted. The prepositions make up for the loss of various cases that no longer exist in the Greek language. In addition to the ablative (-θεν) suffix there is also a suffix -δε (or -σε) which occurs with a few words to indicate *destination*: ᾿Αθήναζε (that is, ᾿Αθήνας-δε) "toward Athens," οἴκαδε "toward home," ὑφόσε "toward on high." Apart from these words, however, Greek expresses the idea of destination by the accusative with certain prepositions.

παρὰ μητέρα φεύγει.	He flees to (the side of) his mother. *See* παρὰ μητρὸς φεύγει. He flees from (the side of) his mother.

Declension/ Genitive Case

The chart summarizes the genitive endings for the three types of nouns.

	Type I			Type II			Type III		
	Masc.	Fem.	Neut.	Masc.	Fem.	Neut.	Masc.	Fem.	Neut.
Singular	-ου	-ᾱς / -ης		-ου			-ος		
Plural	-ῶν			-ων			-ων		

Note that the accent for Type I plural genitive is *always* a circumflex on the ending, which represents a contraction for -άων → -ῶν.

Note that otherwise if the accent normally falls on the final syllable, it will be a circumflex (except for Type III singular, which is not a long vowel): ἡ ψυχή/τὴν ψυχήν/τῆς ψυχῆς.

Note that masculine nouns of Type I have the same genitive singular ending as masculine nouns of Type II.

Examples

I		II	III
ὁ	ποιητ-ή-ς	ἄνθρωπ-ο-ς	παῖ-ς
τὸν	ποιητ-ή-ν	ἄνθρωπ-ο-ν	παῖδ-α
τοῦ	ποιητ-οῦ	ἀνθρώπ-ου	παιδ-ός
οἱ	ποιητ-α-ί	ἄνθρωπ-ο-ι	παῖδ-ες
τοὺς	ποιητ-ᾱς	ἀνθρώπ-ους	παῖδ-ας
τῶν	ποιητ-ῶν	ἀνθρώπ-ων	παῖδ-ων
ἡ	ψυχ-ή	ὁδ-ό-ς	γυνή
τὴν	ψυχ-ή-ν	ὁδ-ό-ν	γυναῖκ-α
τῆς	ψυχ-ῆς	ὁδ-οῦ	γυναικ-ός
αἱ	ψυχ-α-ί	ὁδ-ο-ί	γυναῖκ-ες
τὰς	ψυχ-ᾱς	ὁδ-ούς	γυναῖκ-ας
τῶν	ψυχ-ῶν	ὁδ-ῶν	γυναικ-ῶν
τὸ		παιδί-ο-ν	σῶμα
τὸ		παιδί-ο-ν	σῶμα
τοῦ		παιδί-ου	σώματ-ος
τὰ (no neuters)		παιδί-α	σώματ-α
τὰ		παιδί-α	σώματ-α
τῶν		παιδί-ων	σωμάτ-ων

Syncopated Nouns

The suffix -ηρ/-ερ (like -της) indicates the *doer* of an action. You have seen this suffix on Type III nouns such as ὁ πατήρ ("begett-er," "fath-er," etc.), ἡ μήτηρ, ἡ θυγάτηρ, ὁ ἀνήρ. The vowel in this suffix varies from -ηρ to -ερ in different declensional forms; the vowel may also be absent, the so-called zero-grade, that is, -ρ. This is the reason, for example, that the accusative of ὁ πατήρ is τὸν πατέρα. The zero-grade occurs in the genitive τοῦ πατρός. (This variation is called *syncopation*).

ὁ	πατ-ήρ	ἀν-ήρ	ἡ	μήτ-ηρ	θυγάτ-ηρ daughter
τὸν	πατ-έρ-α	ἀν-δρ-α	τὴν μητ-έρ-α		θυγατ-έρ-α
τοῦ	πατ--ρ-ός	ἀν-δρ-ός	τῆς μητ--ρ-ός		θυγατ--ρός
οἱ	πατ-έρ-ες	ἄν-δρ-ες	αἱ μητ-έρ-ες		θυγατ-έρ-ες
τοὺς	πατ-έρ-ας	ἄν-δρ-ας	τὰς μητ-έρ-ας		θυγατ-έρ-ας
τῶν	πατ-έρ-ων	ἀν-δρ-ῶν	τῶν μητ-έρ-ων		θυγατ-έρ-ων

Note that in all these syncopated nouns, the accent shifts so that it always falls on the -έρ- suffix and always falls on the end with the zero-grade -ρ-.

Note that ὁ ἀνήρ has -δρ- instead of -ερ- for euphonic reasons.

Type III Monosyllabic Nouns
In Type III nouns which are composed of a single syllable, the accent always shifts to the end in the genitive (both singular and plural): ἡ νύξ, τὴν νύκτα, τῆς νυκτός/τῶν νυκτῶν. The noun ἡ γυνή, although not monosyllabic, conforms to this pattern of accent shift: ἡ γυνή, τὴν γυναῖκα, τῆς γυναικός/ τῶν γυναικῶν.

The noun ὁ παῖς and adjective πᾶς are exceptions in that they conform to this pattern of accent shift only in the singular: τοῦ παιδός, τῶν παίδων/ παντός, πάντων.

ONOMATA KAI PHMATA

ἡ δραχμή, τῆς δραχμῆς	drachma (unit of money equal to six obols: a working man earned one or two obols per day)
ἡ πολιτεία, τῆς πολιτείας	constitution
ἡ ἐπιθυμία, τῆς ἐπιθυμίας	desire
ἡ πατρίς, τῆς πατρίδος	(father) land, country (*see* ἡ χώρα)
ὁ κόσμος, τοῦ κόσμου	universe, ornament
ὁ ἄρτος, τοῦ ἄρτου	bread
ὁ οἶνος, τοῦ οἴνου	wine
ὁ πόνος, τοῦ πόνου	pain, work
ἡ θυγάτηρ, τῆς θυγατρός	daughter
τὸ ὕδωρ, τοῦ ὕδατος	water
τὸ μάθημα, τοῦ μαθήματος	lesson (*see* μανθάνω)
ἔμπειρος, -ον	experienced, acquainted with
ξύμπας, ξύμπασα, ξύμπαν	= a more emphatic πᾶς, πᾶσα, πᾶν

ἄξιος, -α, -ον	worth, worthy
ἀνθρώπινος, -η, -ον	human
ἡ νύξ, τῆς νυκτός	night (opposite of ἡ ἡμέρα)
ἐσθίω, ἔφαγον	eat
ἀκούω, ἤκουσα	hear, listen
παίω, ἔπαισα	hit
ψαύω, ἔψαυσα	touch
μετέχω, μετέσχον	share
βασιλεύω, ἐβασίλευσα	rule as βασιλεύς
μετά	with (+ partitive genitive)
ἐκ	out of (+ ablative genitive)
ἀπό	away from (+ ablative genitive)
παρά	away from the side of (+ abl. gen.)
κατά	down from (+ abl. gen.); toward, in accordance with (+ acc.)
πίμπλημι, ἔπλησα	fill
λήγω, (ἔλληξα)	cease from
ἐγώ, ἐμέ/με, ἐμοῦ/μου, ἡμεις, ἡμᾶς, ἡμῶν	
σύ, σέ/σε, σοῦ/σου, ὑμεῖς, ὑμᾶς, ὑμῶν	
ὁ οἶκος, τοῦ οἴκου	house

Note that in this vocabulary list the nouns' declensional types are indicated by the genitive form rather than the accusative. This is the convention of the lexica you will be using.

ΑΣΚΗΣΙΣ

I. IDENTIFY each of the nouns in the vocabulary with respect to its declensional type.

II. IDENTIFY each of the verbs in the vocabulary with respect to its type of aorist conjugation.

III. CHANGE each phrase from whatever case it is to the genitive.

1. τὰ ἀνθρώπινα μαθήματα

2. αἱ καλαὶ νύκτες

3. τὸ καλὸν ὕδωρ

4. οἱ ἔμπειροι ἄνδρες

5. τὸν ἀγαθὸν οἶνον

6. πάντας τοὺς ἄρτους

7. τὸν ξύμπαντα κόσμον

8. πᾶσαν πολιτείαν

9. ἐκείνην τὴν πατρίδα

10. πολλαὶ δραχμαί

11. οὗτος ὁ σοφὸς ἄνθρωπος

12. ὑμεῖς οἱ πατέρες

13. θυγατέρας σοφάς

14. τοὺς ἀσόφους παῖδας

15. αἱ αὐταὶ ὁδοί

16. νεανίαν τὸν αἰσχρόν

17. τοὺς ἀθανάτους θεούς

18. οἱ σοφοὶ ποιηταί

19. αἰσχροὺς θανάτους

20. τὴν ἀγαθὴν χώραν

IV. MATCH the second noun to the first by changing it into the same form.

1. τῆς πολιτείας (ἡ πατρίς)

2. αἱ μητέρες (ὁ ἄρτος)

3. τὴν νύκτα (ἡ ἡμέρα)

4. τῆς χώρας (ὁ ποιητής)

5. τοῦ οἴκου (τὸ ὕδωρ)

6. τῆς κόρης (ἡ ἐπιθυμία)

7. τῆς Ἑλλάδος (ὁ νεανίας)

8. τοὺς παῖδας (ἡ θυγάτηρ)

9. τῶν θεῶν (ὁ Ἕλλην)

10. τῶν γερόντων (ἡ ψυχή)

11. τοῦ παιδίου (τὸ σῶμα)

12. τῆς φιλοσοφίας (τὸ μέτρον)

13. τοὺς διδασκάλους (ἡ γυνή)

14. τῶν σκιῶν (ὁ νόμος)

15. τοῦ ἀνθρώπου (ἡ ὁδός)

16. μητρός (ὄλεθρος)

17. κριτής (ἄνθρωπος)

18. μέτρα (μάθημα)

19. παιδός (οἶνος)

20. ἡμέρας (νύξ)

V. TRANSLATE.

1. ἐμοῦ μὲν ἔψαυσεν, σὲ δὲ ἔπαισεν.

2. τὰ δὲ φίλων μαθήματα ἄξια ἦσαν πολλοῦ καὶ πάντες μ' ἐδίδαξαν πολλά.

3. οἱ μὲν πολλοὶ μαθητῶν οὐκ ἔμαθον τὸ μάθημα, ἡμεῖς δὲ συνεχῶς ἠκούομεν τοῦ φιλοσόφου καὶ πάντες ἀγαθοὶ μαθηταὶ ἦμεν.

4. ἡμᾶς δ' ἔπλησαν οἱ θεοὶ πόνων, τούς τε κακοὺς καὶ τοὺς ἀγαθούς. κακῶς δ' οὖν εἴχομεν συνεχῶς.

5. οὗτος ὁ φύλαξ ἔμπειρος ἦν τῆς χώρας καὶ ἡμᾶς ἤγαγεν ἐκ τῶν Ἀθηνῶν (Ἀθήνηθεν) πρὸς τὸν φιλόσοφον.

6. ἐπιθυμίαν τοῦ ἀγαθοῦ ἐδίδασκεν ἀεὶ ὁ Σωκράτης ἀλλ' οὐκ ἤθελον οἱ μαθηταὶ αὐτοῦ συνεχῶς τὰ ἀγαθὰ πράττειν.

7. οὐδεμίαν τῶν γυναικῶν ἔγνωμεν. ξένοι γὰρ ἦμεν καὶ ἄπειροι (ἀ- + ἔμπειροι) ταύτης τῆς χώρας.

8. μεθ' ὑμῶν ἠθέλομεν συνεχῶς οἴνου τε πίνειν καὶ ἄρτου ἐσθίειν.

9. παντὸς ἀνθρώπου οὐκ ἔστι τὸ φιλοσοφίαν μανθάνειν. οὐ γὰρ ἐθέλουσιν οἱ πολλοὶ ἀνδρῶν μαθηταὶ εἶναι.

10. πάντες ἄνθρωποι τοῦ αὐτοῦ ἄξιοι, οἵ τε νεανίαι καὶ οἱ γέροντες. πάντες γὰρ θνητοὶ καὶ ἀποθνήσκουσιν.

VI. NOTE THE PATTERN in each of the quotations and compose a translation of the English sentences using the same pattern.

1. Ἔρως τῶν θεῶν βασιλεύει. —Πλάτων (ὁ Ἔρως, τοῦ Ἔρωτος. θεὸς καὶ παῖς Ἀφροδίτης.)

Plato ruled over all philosophers as their king.

No one is king of the Greeks.

The soul is the body's king.

The gods rule men as kings.

2. νόμος ὁ πάντων βασιλεύς, θνητῶν τε καὶ ἀθανάτων. —Πίνδαρος

Man is the measure of everything, both of what is good and of what is bad.

Philosophy is the teacher of everybody, both of all men and of all women.

3. ψυχῆς ἀγαθῆς πατρὶς ὁ ξύμπας κόσμος. —Δημόκριτος

Every country's soul is its constitution and its laws.

The entire body is our soul's house.

4. οἱ ἄνθρωποι ἀθανασίας μετέχουσιν. —Πλάτων (ἡ ἀθανασία, τῆς ἀθανασίας from ἀ- + θάνατος "immortality")

The body has a share of life.

The good cease from troubles.

I drank some wine.

The young men were listening to the old teacher.

9 Middle and Passive Voices of the Verb

γῆ πάντα τίκτει καὶ πάλιν κομίζεται. —Μένανδρος

Lesson 9

Active Voice

The *voice* of a verb indicates the manner of relationship that exists between the subject (or personal suffix) and the verbal root. The verbs you have learned thus far have all been in the *active voice*. In the active voice, the subject designates the doer of the action.

διδάσκομεν. | We teach. (It is the subject "we" that does the teaching.)

Passive Voice

In the *passive voice*, the subject is the recipient of the verbal action. In Greek, the passive voice is indicated by a different set of personal suffixes.

διδασκόμεθα. | We are taught. (It is the subject "we" that receives the teaching.)

Middle Voice

In addition to the active and passive voices, the Greek verb also has a *middle voice*, in which the subject is still the doer of the action, as in the active voice, but the subject also receives some kind of playback from the action, almost as though it were in some way the recipient as in the passive voice. The personal suffixes for the middle voice are identical with those for the passive in most tenses of the verb, and the distinction between middle and passive meaning in such tenses, therefore, can only be designated by the context. The aorist and the future tenses, however, have separate forms for the passive. You will learn these later.

Since English does not have a middle voice for the verb, you will find that it will take some experience in reading Greek before you begin to get a natural feeling for this idea of playback. The following three types of playback will serve as a guide to the possibilities of meaning for the middle voice.

1. The middle voice may indicate that the subject is *acting on its own behalf.*

ὁ δῆμος νόμους τίθεται. | "The populace legislates laws (for itself)." Whereas in the active voice, the lawgiver establishes laws for others: ὁ νομοθέτης νόμους τίθησιν.

μεταπεμπόμεθα τὸν παῖδα. | We send for the boy (to come to us).

ἀποπεμπόμεθα τὸν παῖδα. | We send the boy away (from ourselves).

γευόμεθα οἴνου. | "We taste the wine." Whereas in the active voice, we give him a taste of wine: αὐτὸν γεύομεν οἴνου.

2. The middle voice may indicate that the subject is *acting on something that belongs to itself.*

διδασκόμεθα τοὺς παῖδας. | We teach *our* sons.

3. The middle voice may indicate that the subject is *acting on itself.* This meaning is similar to that of the reflexive pronoun as the verbal object.

φαινόμεϑα.

"We appear." Whereas in the active voice, we show: φαίνομεν. See φαίνομεν ἡμᾶς αὐτούς, we show ourselves.

λούει σύ.

"You bathe." Whereas in the active voice, you wash the body: λούεις τὸ σῶμα. See λούεις σεαυτόν, you wash yourself.

Some verbs have meanings which so much imply the middle voice that they actually occur only in that voice. Such verbs are called *deponent* verbs and are listed in the vocabulary in the middle voice.

δυνάμεϑα.

We are able.

βουλόμεϑα.

We want.

Middle-Passive Voice/Personal Suffixes

The chart lists the personal suffixes for the middle-passive voice. Just as with the active voice, these suffixes are added to the verbal root either thematically or athematically. The "primary" personal suffixes are used for the present tense; the "secondary" personal suffixes are used for the imperfect and aorist tenses. The suffix for the infinitive is -σϑαι.

Primary Personal Suffixes				Secondary Personal Suffixes			
-μαι	1	-μεϑα		-μην	1	-μεϑα	
-σαι	2	-σϑε		-σο	2	-σϑε	
-ται	3	-νται		-το	3	-ντο	

Middle-Passive/ Thematic Conjugation

The chart shows the thematic mode of conjugation (that is, with the variable vowel).

Present Middle-Passive	Imperfect Middle-Passive	Aorist Middle (only)
παιδεύ-ο-μαι	ἐ-παιδευ-ό-μην	ἐ-λαβ-ό-μην
-ει*	-ου*	-ου*
-ε-ται	-ε-το	-ε-το
-ό-μεϑα	-ό-μεϑα	-ό-μεϑα
-ε-σϑε	-ε-σϑε	-ε-σϑε
-ο-νται	-ο-ντο	-ο-ντο

Note (*) that in the second person singular, the sigma of the personal suffix is lost when it occurs between vowels and the variable vowel contracts with the ending: παιδεύ-ε-σαι⟶παιδεύ-ει/ ἐ-παιδεύ-ε-σο⟶ἐ-παιδεύ-ου/ ἐ-λάβ-ε-σο⟶ἐ-λάβ-ου

Note that the accent is recessive (that is, it falls as far back as possible). The diphthong -αι is short.

**Middle-Passive/
Athematic
Conjugation**

The chart shows the athematic mode of conjugation.

Present Middle-Passive		Imperfect Middle-Passive		Aorist Middle (only) sigma-alpha suffix	"second"	
δίδο-	μαι	ἐ-διδό-	μην	ἐ-παιδευ-σά-μην	ἐ-στή-	μην
τίθε-		ἐ-τιθέ-			ἐ-θέ-	
ἵστα-	σαι	ἱστά-	σο	-σω*	ἐ-δό-	σο*
ἵε-	ται	ἱέ-	το	-σα-το	εἷ-	το
δείκνυ-	μεθα	ἐ-δεικνύ-	μεθα	-μεθα		μεθα
	σθε		σθε	-σθε		σθε
	νται		ντο	-ντο		ντο

Note (*) that in the second person singular of the aorist, the sigma of the personal suffix is lost with subsequent contraction in some verbs: ἐ-παιδεύ-σα-σο⟶ἐ-παιδεύ-σω/ ἔ-θε-σο⟶ἔ-θου/ ἔ-δο-σο⟶ἔ-δου. This contraction always occurs in the sigmatic aorist. The other "second" aorists are not contracted: εἷ-σο, ἔ-στη-σο.

Note that the verbal stem in the present and the imperfect occurs with the short final vowel, as in the plural (only) of the present and imperfect active: δίδω-μι, but δίδο-μαι, ἐ-διδό-μην. In the "second" aorist, some verbs maintain the long final stem vowel and others have the short final stem vowel, as in the chart for aorist active on page 35.

**Agent for the
Passive Voice**

As you have seen, the subject in the passive voice is the recipient of the action instead of its agent or doer. The agent, however, can be expressed in a sentence with a passive verb by using a prepositional phrase which identifies the doer as the *source from whom* the action came into being. Since this kind of meaning is an ablatival idea, the genitive case is used with the preposition. The most common preposition for this usage in prose is ὑπό, but other prepositions also occur (ἐκ, ἀπό, παρά).

οἱ παῖδες διδάσκονται ὑφ' ἡμῶν.   The boys are taught by us.

**Middle-Passive/
Ambiguity**

Since in some tenses the middle and the passive voices have identical forms, the context is the only indication of whether the voice is middle or passive.

διδασκόμεθα τοὺς παῖδας.   We teach our sons.
διδασκόμεθα ὑπὸ τοῦ διδασκάλου.   We are taught by the teacher.

ONOMATA KAI PHMATA

ἡ γῆ, -ῆς   earth

ὁ ποταμός, -οῦ   river

ὁ ὕπνος, -ου   sleep

τὸ πῦρ, -ρός   fire

ὁ δῆμος, -ου   populace

ὁ νομοθέτης, -ου	lawgiver (*see* νόμος/τίθημι)
ὁ ὄνειρος, -ου	dream (= τὸ ὄναρ)
ὁ οἶκος, -ου	house
ὁ θήρ, -ρός	beast, animal
πρῶτος, -η, -ον	first
δεύτερος, -α, -ον	second
ἕτερος, -α, -ον	other, different
ἄλλος, -η, -ον	other, another
γίγνομαι, ἐγενόμην	be, come to be, become, be born
κομίζω, ἐκόμισα	convey, escort
σῴζω/σώζω, ἔσωσα	save
ὀνομάζω, ὠνόμασα	name (*see* τὸ ὄνομα, -ατα name)
λούω, ἔλουσα	wash
δύναμαι, _____	be able
βούλομαι, _____	want
γεύω, ἔγευσα	give a taste of
φαίνω, ἔφηνα	show (*in mid. voice,* appear)
ἀπ-όλλυμι, ἀπ-ώλεσα, middle ἀπ-ωλόμην	destroy (*in mid. voice,* perish. *See* ὁ ὄλεθρος.)
ὑπο-κρίνομαι, ὑπ-εκρινάμην (ἀπο-κρίνομαι, ἀπ-εκρινάμην)	answer, reply
μέλλω, ἐμέλησα	be about to, intend
_____, ἔγημα	marry (*in mid. voice,* a woman marries)
_____, ἔδοξα	seem, think
τρέφω, ἔθρεψα	nourish
ἤ	or
πάλιν	back, backwards, again
ὡς	as
ὅτι	that (conjunction)
ὅτε	when (conjunction)
ἐπεί/ἐπειδή	when, since (conjunction)

Remember that the suffix -της denotes the doer of an action and that all nouns with this suffix belong to the Type I declension: ὁ κριτής, ὁ μαθητής, ὁ ποιητής, ὁ νομοθέτης, ὁ οἰκέτης, (household slave), ὁ ὀνειροκρίτης (dream interpreter).

Note that the suffix -ι/αζω is used to form many verbs, which are all similar in the aorist: σῴζω, κομίζω, ὀνομάζω.

ΑΣΚΗΣΙΣ

I. TRANSLATE: The Birth of Paris.

Πρίαμος ὁ τῶν Τρώων βασιλεὺς ὠνομάζετο καὶ Ποδάρκης. οὗτος δὲ γυναῖκα
ἔγημε πρώτην Ἀρίσβην τὴν Μέροπος καὶ ἐξ αὐτῆς παῖς ἐγένετο Αἴσακος.
Πρίαμος δέ ταύτην ἐξέδωκε τὴν Ἀρίσβην καὶ δευτέραν ἔγημεν Ἑκάβην
τὴν Δύμαντος ἢ ὡς ἕτεροι λέγουσι, Σαγγαρίου ποταμοῦ καὶ Μερώπης.
5 ἔτεκε δ' αὕτη πρῶτον μὲν Ἕκτορα, δεύτερον δ' ὅτε τίκτειν ἔμελλε παιδίον,
ἔδοξε καθ' ὕπνους πῦρ γίγνεσθαι ἀντὶ παιδὸς ἐξ αὐτῆς. τοῦτο δὲ τὸ πῦρ,
ὡς ἔδοξε, πᾶσαν ἐπενέμετο τὴν χώραν καὶ πάντα ἔκαιεν. ἐπειδὴ δ' ἔμαθε
Πρίαμος παρ' Ἑκάβης τὸν ὄνειρον, Αἴσακον τὸν πρῶτον παῖδα μετεπέμψατο. ἦν γὰρ ὀνειροκρίτης ὁ Αἴσακος. οὗτος δ' ὑπεκρίνατο καὶ εἶπεν ὅτι
10 τὸ δεύτερον παιδίον ἔμελλε τῆς πατρίδος εἶναι τὸν ὄλεθρον. ὁ δ' οὖν
Πρίαμος, ὅτ' ἐγένετο τὸ παιδίον, ἐξέθηκεν εἰς Ἴδην. ἀλλ' οὐ μὲν
ἀπέθανεν τό παιδίον οὐδ' ἀπώλετο, ἐτρέφετο δ' ὑπὸ θηρὸς καὶ ἐσῴζετο.
Ἀγέλαος δ' ὁ Πριάμου οἰκέτης τὸ παιδίον ηὗρέ τε καὶ ἐκομίσατο εἰς οἶκον.
ὡς δ' ἑαυτοῦ τὸν παῖδα ἔτρεφεν ὠνόμασέ τε Πάριν. ὁ δ' ἐπεὶ ἐγένετο
15 νεανίας, τῶν ἄλλων διέφερε παίδων καὶ ἐφαίνετο βασίλειος εἶναι.
οὕτως δ' αὐτὸν ἔγνωσαν Πρίαμός τε καὶ Ἑκάβη. —Adapted from
Ἀπολλόδωρος

Reading Notes:

(2) τὴν Μέροπος, a patronymic (the genitive of the father's name was used as a last name) =τὴν Μέροπος θυγατέρα. *See* Ἑκάβη ἡ Δύμαντος.

(3) ἐξέδωκε/ἐκ + δίδωμι

(6) ἀντί intead of

(7) ἐπενέμετο/ἐπι-νέμομαι encroach upon, spread over (νέμομαι graze like cattle)

(7) ἔκαιεν/καίω burn

(11) ἐξέθηκεν/ἐκ + τίθημι expose (a child to die)

(11) εἰς Ἴδην on Mount Ida

(15) διέφερε/δια-φέρω differ (+ ablatival genitive)

(15) βασίλειος, kingly, royal. *See* βασιλεύς.

II. CHANGE each of the following verbs to the present.

1. ἐπράττοντο

2. μετεπεμψάμην

3. ἠθέλησαν

4. ἔθου

5. ἀπέθανεν

6. ἐδράμετε

7. ἐγράφου	14. εἴχετε
8. ἔδωκα	15. ἐγιγνώσκεσθε
9. ἐδόμην	16. ἐγένεσθε
10. ἵεσο	17. ἔγνων
11. ἔβημεν	18. εἶντο
12. ἐκρίνω	19. ἐφάγομεν
13. ἔστητε	20. ἀπώλλυτο

III. MATCH the second verb to the first by changing it to the same form.

1. ἐβουλόμεθα (δύναμαι)	11. εἱλόμεθα (μετέχω)
2. μετείχετε (ψαύω)	12. ἔμειναν (γιγνώσκω)
3. ἐγράφου (λαμβάνω)	13. ἐκρίνετο (φθείρω)
4. ἔδοντο (παιδεύω)	14. πείθεσθε (δίδωμι)
5. ἠθέλησαν (δείκνυμι)	15. ἔβης (τίθημι)
6. ἔθηκα (λούω)	16. ἦκε (τρέχω)
7. ἐθέμην (ἀγγέλλω)	17. ἐπραξάμην (φέρω)
8. ἐγένου (διδάσκω)	18. ἔδυν (αἴρω)
9. ἐκομίζετο (ἀπόλλυμι)	19. ἐλάβου (μετέχω)
10. ἐδύναντο (τίθημι)	20. ἀπωλέσατε (ἀποπέμπω)

IV. REPHRASE each of the following sentences so that they express the same idea in the passive voice, using a prepositional phrase to indicate the agent.

1. ὁ Πρίαμος ἐξετίθει τὸν παῖδα εἰς Ἴδην.

2. ἐξ ὀλέθρου θὴρ ἔσῳζε τὸ παιδίον.

3. τὸν ὄνειρον ἔκρινεν ὁ ὀνειροκρίτης.

4. τὸ πῦρ πάντα ἔκαιεν.

5. ἐξεδίδου ὁ Πρίαμος τὴν πρώτην γυναῖκα.

6. θῆρες ἔτρεφον τὸ παιδίον.

7. ὁ οἰκέτης τὸ παιδίον ηὕρισκεν.

8. ὁ οἰκέτης ὠνόμαζε τὸν παῖδα Πάριν.

9. ἐκόμιζεν ὁ οἰκέτης τὸ παιδίον εἰς οἶκον.

10. ὁ πατὴρ ἐγίγνωσκε τὸν παῖδα.

V. NOTE THE PATTERN in each of the quotations and compose a translation of the English sentences using the same pattern.

1. γῆ πάντα τίκτει καὶ πάλιν κομίζεται. —Μένανδρος

God gives the soul and then takes it back (to himself).

The lawgiver establishes the constitution and the populace legislates its own laws.

2. ἀνδρὸς δικαίου καρπὸς οὐκ ἀπόλλυται. —ὁ αὐτός
   (ὁ καρπὸς, -οῦ fruit, harvest)

A bad teacher's lesson is not learned.

The wise poet's lesson was not heard.

3. ἐμπείρως ἔχω τοῦ λέγειν. —Δημοσθένης
   (ἐμπείρως, adverb related to ἔμπειρος, -ον; ἔχω with an adverb is
   idiomatic for "to be," for example: καλῶς ἔχω, "I am well.")

Students are experienced in listening.

The poet was experienced in writing.

10

Dative Case

τῷ σοφῷ ξένον οὐδέν. —'Αντισθένης

Lesson 10
Dative/
Attributive

The dative case conveys the idea of *attribution* (or giving). It can occur in both nominal and verbal sentences.

τὸ ὄνομα τῷ ἀνδρὶ Πλάτων.
The man's name is Plato (that is, the name given to the man is Plato).

ἔθετο ἡ μήτηρ ὄνομα τῷ παιδὶ Πλάτων.
The mother named her son Plato (that is, the mother established Plato as the name given to her son).

The dative case often corresponds to the meaning of the *indirect object* in English.

πάντα ἀγαθὰ ὁ θεὸς ἀνθρώποις ἔδωκεν.
God gave everything good to mankind.

In this same function as indirect object, the dative case indicates the person or thing indirectly involved in the verbal idea, usually either by receiving some *benefit* from it or by being put at some *disadvantage* by it.

ὁ νομοθέτης 'Αθηναίοις νόμους ἔθηκεν.
The lawgiver established laws for the Athenians.

ἀπέθανεν ὁ πατήρ μοι.
My father died on me (that is, his death was my misfortune).

Thus, certain verbs which express the idea of benefit or disadvantage commonly take the dative case as their complement instead of the accusative case.

ἐβοήθησαν οἱ 'Αθηναῖοι τοῖς ξένοις.
The Athenians helped the foreigners.

The dative is also used idiomatically with certain other verbs and with certain adjectives and adverbs. In general, the English words "to" or "for" translate the function of the dative in these structures.

θνητὰ θνητοῖς πρέπει. —Πίνδαρος
Mortals are appropriate for mortals.
τοῖς θεοῖς εὔχομαι.
I pray to the gods.
φίλος αὐτῷ εἰμι.
I am a friend to him.

Dative/Locative

In addition to its true dative function, the dative case also had certain functions that it had assumed from cases that no longer existed in the Greek language. You have already seen an example of such assimilation with regard to the ablatival function of the genitive case.

The language from which Greek evolved had a separate case to indicate *place*, the so-called locative case. The dative assumed this function in Greek and, therefore, can indicate the *place in which* something is, either spacially or temporally. The spacial *locative* meaning of the dative is usually clarified by the use of a preposition (or of a separable prefix on the verb).

ἐν τῷ ποταμῷ ἀπέθανεν ὁ θήρ.
The beast died in the river.

πάρειμι τῷ φίλῳ.
I am at the side of the friend.
(παρὰ τῷ φίλῳ εἰμί.)

τῇ αὐτῇ ἡμέρᾳ ἀπέθανεν.
He died on the same day.

Contrast this locative meaning with the accusative, which indicates *place throughout which* (instead of in which) something is, either temporally or spacially.

παρὰ τὸν ποταμὸν ἔδραμεν ὁ θὴρ καὶ παρὰ τῷ ἀνδρὶ ἀπέθανεν.	The beast ran along the side of the river and died beside the man.
πᾶσαν τὴν πρώτην ἡμέραν ἔμεινεν ὁ ξένος ἀλλὰ τῇ δευτέρᾳ ἀπέθανεν.	All the first day, the foreigner stayed, but on the second day, he died.

Dative/ Instrumental- Comitative

The language from which Greek evolved also had a separate case to indicate the *instrument with which* or the *person in the company with whom* something was done. The function of this lost "instrumental" case was also assumed by the dative.

τῇ γλώσσῃ λέγομεν.	We speak with the instrument of our tongue.
τῷ φιλοσόφῳ διαλεγόμεθα.	We converse with the philosopher.
μετέχομεν ὑμῖν τοῦ οἴνου.	We have a share of the wine with you.

The comitative idea (or the person in the company with whom something is done) is sometimes clarified by a preposition or by a separable prefix on the verb.

σὺν ὑμῖν εἰμι πάσας τὰς ἡμέρας. —Ματθαῖος	I am with you throughout all the days.
συνεπίομεν αὐτῷ.	We drank with him (*Note* that the idea of accompaniment or "with" can be expressed also as an ablatival idea: συνεπίομεν μετ' αὐτοῦ. We drank with him as one out of the group.)

Contrast the instrumental idea (which is expressed by the dative) with the ablatival idea of the agent (which is expressed by the genitive).

λόγοις διδασκόμεθα ὑπὸ τοῦ διδασκάλου.	We are taught by (the agency of) the teacher by (the instrument of) his words.

Declension/ Dative Case

The declensional suffix for the dative case is -ι for the singular and -ις/-σι for the plural.

The chart summarizes the endings for the three types of nouns.

	Type I	Type II	Type III
	Masc., Fem.	Masc., Fem., Neut.	Masc., Fem., Neut.
Singular	$-\eta/\alpha$	$-\omega$	$-\iota$
Plural	$-\alpha\iota\varsigma$	$-o\iota\varsigma$	$-\sigma\iota(\nu)$

Note that the singular of Type II has lengthened the stem vowel.

Note also that in the singular of Types I and II, the $-\iota$ suffix is written as the iota subscript (*see* page 3).

Note that the plural of Type III can take the nu-movable.

Examples

I		II	III
ὁ	ποιητ-ή-ς	ἄνθρωπ-ο-ς	παῖ-ς
τὸν	ποιητ-ή-ν	ἄνθρωπ-ο-ν	παῖδ-α
τοῦ	ποιητ-οῦ	ἀνθρώπ-ου	παιδ-ός
τῷ	ποιητ-ῇ	ἀνθρώπ-ῳ	παιδ-ί
οἱ	ποιητ-ά-ί	ἄνθρωπ-ο-ι	παῖδ-ες
τοὺς	ποιητ-άς	ἀνθρώπ-ους	παῖδ-ας
τῶν	ποιητ-ῶν	ἀνθρώπ-ων	παίδ-ων
τοῖς	ποιητ-α-ῖς	ἀνθρώπ-ο-ις	παι-σί(ν)
ἡ	ψυχ-ή	ὁδ-ό-ς	γυνή
τὴν	ψυχ-ή-ν	ὁδ-ό-ν	γυναῖκ-α
τῆς	ψυχ-ῆς	ὁδ-οῦ	γυναικ-ός
τῇ	ψυχ-ῇ	ὁδ-ῷ	γυναικ-ί
αἱ	ψυχ-α-ί	ὁδ-ο-ί	γυναῖκ-ες
τάς	ψυχ-άς	ὁδ-ούς	γυναῖκ-ας
τῶν	ψυχ-ῶν	ὁδ-ῶν	γυναικ-ῶν
ταῖς	ψυχ-α-ῖς	ὁδ-ο-ῖς	γυναιξί(ν)
τὸ		παιδί-ο-ν	σῶμα
τὸ		παιδί-ο-ν	σῶμα
τοῦ		παιδί-ου	σώματ-ος
τῷ		παιδί-ῳ	σώματ-ι
	(no neuters)		
τὰ		παιδί-α	σώματ-α
τὰ		παιδί-α	σώματ-α
τῶν		παιδί-ων	σωμάτ-ων
τοῖς		παιδί-ο-ις	σώμα-σι(ν)

Note that the -σι suffix for Type III nouns may cause the final consonant of the noun stem to be eliminated for euphonic reasons (παιδ-σί → παι-σί, *see* the nominative παιδ-ς → παῖ-ς), or it may combine with the final consonant and be written as a double consonant (γυναικ-σί → γυναιξί).

Note that syncopated nouns (*see* page 43) have the zero-grade, -ρ-, in the dative: πατρί/πατράσι (in the plural, an alpha is inserted after the rho for euphonic reasons), μητρί/μητράσι, θυγατρί/θυγατράσι. The accent for these nouns shifts so that it always falls on the epsilon-grade suffix, -ερ-, or on the alpha which is inserted for euphony; otherwise, in the zero-grade the accent shifts to the final syllable.

Remember the accent pattern for Type III monosyllabic nouns (*see* page 44). The dative shows the same accent shift to the end as occurs in the genitive: ἡ νύξ, τὴν νύκτα, τῆς νυκτός, τῇ νυκτί, αἱ νύκτες, τὰς νύκτας, τῶν νυκτῶν, ταῖς νυξί. The declension of γυνή shows the same accent pattern. The dative plural of παῖς (but not the genitive plural) also shows this shift in accent to the end; πᾶς shows the shift only in the singular.

ONOMATA KAI PHMATA

τὸ ὄνομα, -ατος	name
ἡ ἀρχή, -ῆς	beginning
ἡ πενία, -ας	poverty (*see* ὁ πόνος, -ου work, pain)
τὸ χρῆμα, -ατος	thing, a thing that one uses, *pl.* money
ὁ ὄμβρος, -ου	rain
ὁ λίθος, -ου	stone
ὁ/ἡ ἀδελφός, -οῦ/-ῆς	brother/sister
ἡ κεφαλή, -ῆς	head
ἡ δόξα, -ης	opinion, public opinion
ἡ θάλασσα, -ης	sea
ἐχθρός, -ά, -όν	hated, hateful, hostile, inimical (opposite of φίλος)
ἴσος, -η, -ον	equal, like
δειλός, -ή, -όν	cowardly
βροτός, -ή, -όν	= θνητός
ἐπιτήδειος, -α, -ον	suitable, useful, necessary (οἱ ἐπιτήδειοι = οἱ φίλοι)
πλάττω, ἔπλασα	form, mould
βάλλω, ἔβαλον	throw
δια-λέγομαι, διελεξάμην	converse, have a dialogue

παύω, ἔπαυσα	stop
τεύχω, ἔτευξα	produce (by work of art), make
εὔχομαι, ηὐξάμην	pray
_____, ἐβοήθησα	help, aid
_____, ἠγανάκτησα	be vexed, be angry
_____, ἐποίησα	make
πρέπω, ἔπρεψα	be conspicuous. resemble (πρέπει it is fitting)
σύν	with (+ dative)
ἄνευ	without (+ genitive)

ἐγώ, ἐμέ/με, ἐμοῦ/μου, ἐμοί/μοι, ἡμεῖς, ἡμᾶς, ἡμῶν, ἡμῖν

σύ, σέ/σε, σοῦ/σου, σοί/σοι, ὑμεῖς, ὑμᾶς, ὑμῶν, ὑμῖν

τίς, τίνα, τίνος, τίνι, τίνες, τίνας, τίνων, τίσι

Note that nouns which have a stem ending in σ, λλ, or a double consonant have η instead of α in the genitive and dative singular: ἡ δόξα, τὴν δόξαν, τῆς δόξης, τῇ δόξῃ/ἡ θάλασσα, τὴν θάλασσαν, τῆς θαλάσσης, τῇ θαλάσσῃ. So also, the feminine of the adjective πᾶς: πᾶσα, πᾶσαν, πάσης, πάσῃ.

ΑΣΚΗΣΙΣ

I. TRANSLATE: The Creation of Man and the Great Flood.

Προμηθεὺς δ' ἐξ ὕδατος καὶ γῆς ἀνθρώπους ἔπλασεν. ἔδωκεν δ' αὐτοῖς καὶ πῦρ. φίλος γὰρ ἀνθρώποις ἦν καὶ οὕτως ἐβοήθησεν αὐτοῖς. ἀλλ' ὁ Ζεὺς, ὅτ' ἔμαθεν, σφόδρα ἠγανάκτησεν αὐτῷ. τὸ γὰρ πῦρ ἑαυτοῦ ἦν οὐδ' ἐβούλετο τοῦτ' ἀνθρώποις διδόναι. ἐχθρὸς γὰρ αὐτοῖς ἦν ὁ θεὸς ἐξ
5 ἀρχῆς καὶ ἔμελλε πάντας ἀπολλύναι. ἀλλὰ πυρὶ ἐσῴζοντο οἱ βροτοὶ οὐδ' ἀπέθανον. πυρὶ γὰρ ἐγένοντο οἱ θνητοὶ ἴσοι θεοῖς. διόπερ οὖν ὁ Ζεὺς τὴν πρώτην ἔπλασε γυναῖκα. ταύτῃ δ' ἔθετο ὄνομα Πανδώρα ἐπεὶ αὐτῇ οἱ θεοὶ πάντες καὶ πᾶσαι δῶρα ἔδοσαν. αὐτὴν δὲ ὁ Ζεὺς ἐξέδωκε γυναῖκα τῷ Προμηθέως ἀδελφῷ. οὗτος δ' ὠνομάζετο Ἐπιμηθεύς. ὁ μὲν γὰρ
10 Προμηθεὺς σφόδρα ἦν σοφός, ὁ δ' Ἐπιμηθεὺς ἄσοφος καὶ οὕτως ἔγημε τὴν Πανδώραν. οὐ γὰρ ἔγνω ὅτι ἐχθρὸς ἦν ὁ Ζεὺς ἑαυτῷ οὐδ' ὅτι ἡ Πανδώρα ἔμελλεν ἀρχὴ εἶναι πολλῶν κακῶν ἀνθρώποις.
    Προμηθέως δὲ παῖς Δευκαλίων ἐγένετο. οὗτος μὲν ἐβασίλευε τῶν περὶ τὴν Φθίαν τόπων, ἔγημε δὲ Πύρραν τὴν Ἐπιμηθέως καὶ Πανδώρας. ὁ
15 δὲ Ζεὺς πάλιν ἠθέλησεν ἀνθρώπους ἀπολλύναι, ἀλλ' ὁ Προμηθεὺς τῷ ἀδελφῷ ὑπέθετο λάρνακα τεύχειν. διόπερ τοῦτο Δευκαλίων ἐποίησεν καὶ πάντα τὰ ἐπιτήδεια ἐνέθετο καὶ εἰς ταύτην μετὰ Πύρρας εἰσέβη. ὁ δὲ Ζεὺς ὄμβρους πολλοὺς ἔτευχε καὶ πᾶσαν τὴν Ἑλλάδα κατέκλυσεν. πολλοὶ μὲν ἀνθρώπων διεφθείροντο καὶ ἀπώλοντο, ὁ δὲ Δευκαλίων
20 μετὰ τῆς γυναικὸς ἐν λάρνακι διὰ τῆς θαλάσσης ἐφέρετο ἡμέρας ἐννέα καὶ νύκτας τὰς ἴσας. τῷ δὲ Παρνασῷ προσέσχε καὶ ἐκεῖ, ὅτ' ἐπαύσαντο οἱ ὄμβροι, ἐξέβη καὶ Διὶ ηὔχετο. Ζεὺς δ' ἔπεμψεν Ἑρμῆν πρὸς

αὐτόν. οὗτος δ᾽ εἶπεν ὅτι ὁ Ζεὺς νῦν φίλος ἦν αὐτῷ καὶ ἐβούλετο δῶρα
αὐτῷ διδόναι. ὡς δὲ δῶρον ἑαυτῷ ἠθέλησεν ὁ Δευκαλίων ἀνθρώπους
25 πάλιν εἶναι. ἦν γὰρ μόνος μετὰ τῆς γυναικὸς καὶ ἄνευ φίλων οὐδὲ
διελέγετο οὐδενὶ ἀνθρώπων. οὕτως δὲ, ὡς αὐτῷ ὁ Ἑρμῆς ὑπέθετο, λίθους
ἦραν ἀπὸ τῆς γῆς καὶ ὑφόθεν κατέβαλον ὑπὸ τῆς κεφαλῆς. ἐκ μὲν τῶν
λίθων τῶν τοῦ Δευκαλίωνος ἄνδρες ἐγένοντο ἐκ τῆς γῆς, ἐκ δὲ τῶν τῆς
Πύρρας γυναῖκες. οὕτως δὲ μήτηρ πάντων τε καὶ πασῶν ἡ γῆ ἐγένετο.
—Adapted from Ἀπολλόδωρος

Reading Notes:

(3) σφόδρα exceedingly

(6) διόπερ wherefore

(9) Προμηθέως genitive of Προμηθεύς. See Ἐπιμηθέως.

(13) περί around (+accusative), that is, throughout the region around

(14) τόπων/ὁ τόπος, -ου place, region

(16) ὑπέθετο/ὑπό+τίθημι enjoin, instruct, place under concern

(16) λάρνακα/ἡ λάρναξ, -ακος box, chest

(17) ἐνέθετο/ἐν "on"+τίθημι

(18) κατέκλυσεν/κατά+κλύζω wash, flood

(20) ἐν on, in (+dative)

(20) διά through (+genitive)

(21) ἐννέα nine

(21) Παρνασῷ Parnasos (the mountain at Delphi)

(21) προσέσχε (πρός+ἔχω) put a boat in toward land

(21) ἐκεῖ there (locative). See the ablatival ἐκεῖθεν.

(22) Διί/ὁ Ζεύς, Διός (Note that Zeus has a different root for the genitive.)

(25) μόνος -η, -ον alone, only

(27) κατέβαλον/κατά+βάλλω, ἔβαλον throw down

II. CHANGE each phrase from whatever case it is to the dative.

1. πάντα τὰ ἐπιτήδεια

2. πᾶσαι αἱ θεοί

3. τὸ κακὸν χρῆμα

4. ἡ ἀγαθὴ δόξα

5. τοὺς ἐχθροὺς βροτούς

6. θυγατέρας σοφάς

7. ὅδε ὁ ἀνήρ

8. τῆς καλῆς θαλάσσης

9. τοῦτο τὸ πῦρ

10. τὸν ξύμπαντα κόσμον

11. οἱ σοφοὶ ποιηταί

12. τὰς ἴσας νύκτας

13. οὗτος ὁ σοφὸς νεανίας

14. τοὺς ἀθανάτους νόμους

15. πᾶσαν πολιτείαν

16. πολλῶν δραχμῶν

17. ταύτης τῆς ἀγαθῆς χώρας

18. ἐκείνας τὰς δειλὰς γυναῖκας

19. αἱ αὐταὶ ὁδοί

20. οἱ ἔμπειροι ἄνδρες

III. MATCH the second noun to the first by changing it into the same form.

1. τῷ ὀνόματι (ὁ κριτής)

2. τὴν γῆν (ὁ ἀνήρ)

3. ποταμοῦ (ὄνομα)

4. πενίᾳ (ἡ θάλασσα)

5. τῶν κεφαλῶν (ἡ δόξα)

6. τῇ κόρῃ (ἡ γυνή)

7. ταῖς γυναιξί (ὄμβρος)

8. τῷ δήμῳ (τὸ πῦρ)

9. ὑμῶν (ὁ ὕπνος)

10. θηρί (ὁ νομοθέτης)

11. οἴκῳ (χώρα)

12. οἴνοι (πολιτεία)

13. μητράσιν (πόνος)

14. ἄρτους (ἐπιθυμία)

15. πατρίδι (πατήρ)

16. τῇ ψυχῇ (ἡ ἡμέρα)

17. ὀλέθρῳ (ἡ γλῶσσα)

18. οὐδεμίᾳ (ὁ Ἕλλην)

19. δώροις (παῖς)

20. ζωήν (θάνατος)

IV. MATCH the second verb to the first by changing it into the same form.

1. εἶπεν (διαλέγομαι)

2. ἔγημαν (ἀποπέμπω)

3. ὑπέθετο (ἀπόλλυμι)

4. ἐβουλόμεθα (εὔχομαι)

5. ηὔξω (μεταπέμπομαι)

6. ἀπέδωκεν (ὀνομάζω)

7. εἴχετε (εὑρίσκω)

8. ἐξέβησαν (προσάγω)

9. ἐμανθάνομεν (λαμβάνω)

10. κατέπεσον (καταπίνω)

11. προσέσχες (ἀποθνήσκω)

12. μετεῖχες (ἀκούω)

13. ἀπεπέμπου (δίδωμι)

14. ἔστησαν (τυγχάνω)

15. ἔδραμες (ἵημι)

16. ἀπώλλυ (τίθημι)

17. ἐξεδίδους (πάσχω)

18. ἔτεκον (ἐκβαίνω)

19. ἔδου (γίγνομαι)

20. ὑπεκρίνω (ἀπόλλυμι)

V. NOTE THE PATTERN in each of the quotations and compose a translation of the English sentences using the same pattern.

1. χρήματα ψυχὴ δειλοῖς βροτοῖς. —Ἡσίοδος

Poverty is hateful to mortals.

The sea is the beginning for all life.

Water is death for fire.

The philosopher's name is Plato.

2. τῷ σοφῷ ξένον οὐδέν. —Ἀντισθένης
To all young men, the universe is beautiful.

Life is a dream for old men.

For many, the tongue is the beginning of disaster.

3. πᾶς ἀνὴρ αὑτῷ πονεῖ. —Σοφοκλῆς (αὑτῷ = ἑαυτῷ, see page 25. πονεῖ "he works," see ὁ πόνος, ἡ πενία.)

Every woman works for herself.

No one legislates laws for himself.

The universe came into being for mankind.

4. θνητὰ θνητοῖς πρέπει. —Πίνδαρος (Note that a neuter plural subject can be used in agreement with a singular verb.)

Immortal things are fitting for immortal beings.

Nothing is fitting for everyone.

5. οὐκ ἔστιν οὐδὲν χωρὶς ἀνθρώποις θεῶν. —Εὐριπίδης (χωρίς = ἄνευ. Double negatives in Greek intensify the expression of negation and do not equal a positive statement as in English.)

There is no money for men without work.

Without men, there are no gifts for the gods.

6. ἐλπὶς ἐν ἀνθρώποις μόνη θεὸς ἐσθλὴ ἔνεστιν. —Θέογνις (ἡ ἐλπίς, -ίδος hope; ἐν in; μόνος, -η, -ον alone, only; ἔνεστιν/ἐν + εἰμί; ἐσθλός, -ή, -όν = ἀγαθός)

Good reputation alone is a law in mortals.

Man alone in the universe was the measure.

7. δόξα χρημάτων οὐκ ὠνητή. —Ἰσοκράτης (ὠνητός, -ή, -όν to be bought. See page 40 for the structure.)

The house was worth much money.

The wine was for sale for one drachma.

(Note also: ἐλπὶς χρήμασιν ὠνητή. —Θουκυδίδης)

11

Infinitive, Participle, and Genitive Absolute

πάλιν γὰρ αὖθις παῖς ὁ γηράσκων ἀνήρ. —Σοφοκλῆς

Lesson 11
Participle/Verbal
Adjective

The participle is an adjective which is formed from a verb.

ὁ γεραιὸς ἀνήρ	the old man
ὁ γηράσκων ἀνήρ	the aging man

Since the participle is adjectival, it agrees with the word which it modifies or describes.

οἱ γηράσκοντες ἄνδρες	the aging men
ἡ γηράσκουσα γυνή	the aging woman

Like any adjective, the participle can be placed either in attributive position or in predicate position.

παῖς ὁ γηράσκων ἀνήρ.	The aging man is a child.
ὁ ἀνὴρ γηράσκων παῖς.	The man is an aging child.

Like any verbal form, however, the participle can be expressed in the active, middle, or passive voice and it can be modified by adverbs or any adverbial complement (accusative, genitive, dative).

ὁ διδασκόμενος παῖς	the boy being educated
ὁ οἴνου πίνων ἀνήρ	the man drinking wine
ὁ καλῶς ἔχων ἄνθρωπος	the man in good condition

As you have seen, the Greek language has different verbal roots to express the progressive (*τρέχ-*) and punctual (*δράμ-*) *aspects*. The participle can be formed from different verbal roots and will, therefore, express this distinction in aspect.

εἶδον τὸν παῖδα τρέχοντα.	I saw the boy running.
εἶδον τὸν παῖδα δραμόντα.	I saw the boy run.

The participle, however, never expresses tense (or time). For this reason, *the participle is not augmented.* The context of the main verb establishes the time by inference for the participle, which expresses only aspect.

ἤκουσα τοῦ φιλοσόφου διδάσκοντος.	I listened to the philosopher (while he was) teaching.
ἀκούω τοῦ φιλοσόφου διδάσκοντος.	I listen to the philosopher (while he is) teaching.
ἀκούω τοῦ φιλοσόφου διδάξαντος.	I listen to the philosopher teach.

The so-called "present participle" is, therefore, a misnomer since it is present not in tense but only because it is formed from the present verbal stem. In like manner, the "aorist participle" is formed from the aorist stem (without augment). These two participles differ only in aspect.

The punctual aspect of the aorist participle, however, may infer that the participial action is already completed prior to the time of the main verb.

πολλὰ φαγὼν ἀπέθανον.	(After) eating much, I died.
πολλὰ ἐσθίων ἀπέθανον.	(While) eating much, I died.

**Participle/
Declension**

In Greek, the participle is formed by adding a suffix, either thematically or athematically, to the verbal root and then declining the form like an adjective. For the middle-passive voice, the suffix is -μεν-ος, -η, -ον, which is declined like adjectives such as ἀγαθός, -ή, -όν. Since the aorist root which you have learned is only middle, the participle which is formed from it is also only middle; you will learn the aorist passive and its participle later. For the active voice, the suffix is -ντ-, which is declined as Type III for the masculine and neuter: -ντ-α, -ντ-ος, -ντ-ι, etc.; for the feminine, an additional suffix (-ι-) is added with a resultant euphonic change (-ντ-ι-→-σ-, which causes the preceding vowel to be lengthened as compensation for the lost consonants), and the form is declined as Type I: -σαν, -σης, -ση, etc. (For the shift from alpha to eta, *see* page 59.)

Examples

THEMATIC
Present Active

masculine	neuter	masculine	neuter
παιδεύ-ω-ν*	παιδεύ-ο-ν*	λαβ-ώ-ν*	λαβ-ό-ν*
-ο-ντ-α	-ο-ν	-ό-ντ-α	-ό-ν
-ο-ντ-ος	-ο-ντ-ος	-ό-ντ-ος	-ό-ντ-ος
-ο-ντ-ι	-ο-ντ-ι		etc.
-ο-ντ-ες	-ο-ντ-α		
-ο-ντ-ας	-ο-ντ-α		
-ό-ντ-ων	-ό-ντ-ων		
-ουσι*	-ουσι*		

(Here are shown under **Aorist Active** the masculine and neuter columns.)

Present Middle-Passive

παιδευ-ό-μεν-ος, -η,-ον

Aorist Middle (only)

λαβ-ό-μεν-ος, -η, -ον

ATHEMATIC
Present Active

masculine	neuter
τιθείς/ἱστάς/	τιθέ-ν/ἱστά-ν/
ἱείς/, διδούς/	ἱέ-ν/ διδό-ν/
δεικνύς*	δεικνύ-ν*

τιθέ-	ντ-α/	-ν
ἱστά-	ντ-ος	
ἱέ-	ντ-ι	
διδό-	ντ-ες/	-ντ-α
δεικνύ-	ντ-ας/	-ντ-α
	ντ-ων	

τιθεῖ-σι/ἱστᾱ-σι/ἱεῖ-σι/
διδοῦ-σι/δεικνῦ-σι*

Aorist Active

masculine	neuter
θείς/στάς/	θέ-ν/στά-ν/
εἵς/δούς/	ἕ-ν/ δό-ν/
βᾱς/γνούς/	βά-ν/γνό-ν/
δύς*	δύ-ν*

θέ-	ντ-α/	-ν
στά-	ντ-ος	
ἕ-	ντ-ι	
δό-	ντ-ες/	-ντ-α
βά-	ντ-ας/	-ντ-α
γνό-	ντ-ων	
δύ-		

θεῖ-σι/στᾱ-σι/εἷ-σι/
δοῦ-σι/βᾱ-σι/γνοῦ-σι/
δῦ-σι*

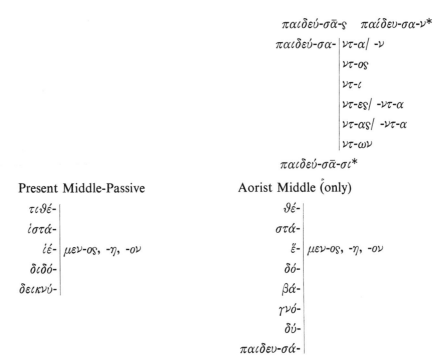

$$\pi\alpha\iota\delta\varepsilon\acute{\upsilon}\text{-}\sigma\bar{\alpha}\text{-}\varsigma \quad \pi\alpha\acute{\iota}\delta\varepsilon\upsilon\text{-}\sigma\alpha\text{-}\nu*$$

$$\pi\alpha\iota\delta\varepsilon\acute{\upsilon}\text{-}\sigma\alpha\text{-}\left|\nu\tau\text{-}\alpha\right| \text{-}\nu$$

$$\nu\tau\text{-}o\varsigma$$

$$\nu\tau\text{-}\iota$$

$$\nu\tau\text{-}\varepsilon\varsigma / \ \text{-}\nu\tau\text{-}\alpha$$

$$\nu\tau\text{-}\alpha\varsigma / \ \text{-}\nu\tau\text{-}\alpha$$

$$\nu\tau\text{-}\omega\nu$$

$$\pi\alpha\iota\delta\varepsilon\acute{\upsilon}\text{-}\sigma\bar{\alpha}\text{-}\sigma\iota*$$

Present Middle-Passive	Aorist Middle (only)
$\tau\iota\vartheta\acute{\varepsilon}\text{-}$	$\vartheta\acute{\varepsilon}\text{-}$
$\acute{\iota}\sigma\tau\acute{\alpha}\text{-}$	$\sigma\tau\acute{\alpha}\text{-}$
$\acute{\iota}\acute{\varepsilon}\text{-} \mid \mu\varepsilon\nu\text{-}o\varsigma, \text{-}\eta, \text{-}o\nu$	$\acute{\varepsilon}\text{-} \mid \mu\varepsilon\nu\text{-}o\varsigma, \text{-}\eta, \text{-}o\nu$
$\delta\iota\delta\acute{o}\text{-}$	$\delta\acute{o}\text{-}$
$\delta\varepsilon\iota\kappa\nu\acute{\upsilon}\text{-}$	$\beta\acute{\alpha}\text{-}$
	$\gamma\nu\acute{o}\text{-}$
	$\delta\acute{\upsilon}\text{-}$
	$\pi\alpha\iota\delta\varepsilon\upsilon\text{-}\sigma\acute{\alpha}\text{-}$

Note (*) that in the nominative singular and in the dative plural, euphonic changes occur: $\pi\alpha\iota\delta\varepsilon\acute{\upsilon}\text{-}o\text{-}\nu\tau\text{-}\varsigma \rightarrow \pi\alpha\iota\delta\varepsilon\acute{\upsilon}\text{-}\omega\text{-}\nu$ (that is, loss of $\text{-}\tau\text{-}\varsigma$, with compensatory lengthening of the preceding vowel); $\pi\alpha\iota\delta\varepsilon\acute{\upsilon}\text{-}o\text{-}\nu\tau\text{-}\sigma\iota \rightarrow \pi\alpha\iota\delta\varepsilon\acute{\upsilon}\text{-}o\upsilon\text{-}\sigma\iota$ (a similar loss of $\text{-}\nu\tau\text{-}$, with compensatory lengthening of the preceding vowel by conversion to a diphthong); so also in the athematic declension, $\tau\iota\vartheta\acute{\varepsilon}\text{-}\nu\tau\text{-}\varsigma \rightarrow \tau\iota\vartheta\varepsilon\acute{\iota}\varsigma / \tau\iota\vartheta\acute{\varepsilon}\text{-}\nu\tau\text{-}\sigma\iota \rightarrow \tau\iota\vartheta\varepsilon\acute{\iota}\text{-}\sigma\iota / \pi\alpha\iota\delta\varepsilon\acute{\upsilon}\text{-}\sigma\alpha\text{-}\nu\tau\text{-}\varsigma \rightarrow \pi\alpha\iota\delta\varepsilon\acute{\upsilon}\text{-}\sigma\bar{\alpha}\text{-}\varsigma$. In the nominative and accusative *neuter*, the declensional suffix for Type III is normally (*see* page 17) the absence of any additional sign; the $\text{-}\tau\text{-}$ alone is lost for euphonic reasons, and the preceding vowel is not affected: $\pi\alpha\iota\delta\varepsilon\acute{\upsilon}\text{-}o\text{-}\nu\tau \rightarrow \pi\alpha\iota\delta\varepsilon\acute{\upsilon}\text{-}o\text{-}\nu / \tau\iota\vartheta\acute{\varepsilon}\text{-}\nu\tau \rightarrow \tau\iota\vartheta\acute{\varepsilon}\text{-}\nu / \pi\alpha\acute{\iota}\delta\varepsilon\upsilon\text{-}\sigma\alpha\text{-}\nu\tau \rightarrow \pi\alpha\acute{\iota}\delta\varepsilon\upsilon\text{-}\sigma\alpha\text{-}\nu$.

Note that the accent is normally recessive (*see* page 10), but that in the aorist active (except for the aorists with the athematic $\text{-}\sigma\alpha\text{-}$ suffix), the accent always falls immediately before the participial suffix: $\lambda\alpha\beta\text{-}\acute{o}\text{-}\nu\tau\text{-}\alpha / \tau\iota\vartheta\acute{\varepsilon}\text{-}\nu\tau\text{-}\alpha / \tau\iota\vartheta\varepsilon\acute{\iota}\text{-}\varsigma / \tau\iota\vartheta\varepsilon\acute{\iota}\text{-}\sigma\iota$.

Note that the "reduced" stem vowel (short instead of long) occurs throughout the athematic forms: ($\tau\iota\vartheta\eta / \varepsilon$) $\tau\iota\vartheta\acute{\varepsilon}\text{-}\nu\tau\text{-}\alpha$, etc.

Note that the dative plural, like normal Type III forms (*see* page 57), allows the nu-movable: $\pi\alpha\iota\delta\varepsilon\acute{\upsilon}o\upsilon\sigma\iota(\nu)$.

THEMATIC Feminine

Present Active	Aorist Active
$\pi\alpha\iota\delta\varepsilon\acute{\upsilon}\text{-}o\upsilon\sigma\text{-}\alpha$	$\lambda\alpha\beta\text{-}o\bar{\upsilon}\sigma\text{-}\alpha$
$\pi\alpha\iota\delta\varepsilon\acute{\upsilon}\text{-}o\upsilon\sigma\text{-}\alpha\nu$	$\lambda\alpha\beta\text{-}o\bar{\upsilon}\sigma\text{-}\alpha\nu$
$\pi\alpha\iota\delta\varepsilon\upsilon\text{-}o\acute{\upsilon}\sigma\text{-}\eta\varsigma$	$\lambda\alpha\beta\text{-}o\acute{\upsilon}\sigma\text{-}\eta\varsigma$
$\pi\alpha\iota\delta\varepsilon\upsilon\text{-}o\acute{\upsilon}\sigma\text{-}\eta$	etc.

παιδεύ-ουσ-αι

παιδευ-ούσ-ᾱς

παιδευ-ουσ-ῶν

παιδευ-ούσ-αις

ATHEMATIC Feminine

Present Active	Aorist Active
τιθεῖσ-α/ἱστᾶσ-α/ἱεῖσ-α/	θεῖσ-α/στᾶσ-α/εῖσ-α/
διδοῦσ-α/δεικνῦσ-α	δοῦσ-α/βᾶσ-α/γνοῦσ-α/
	δῦσ-α

τιθεῖσ-αν	θεῖσ-αν
τιθείσ-ης	θείσ-ης
etc.	etc.

παιδεύ-σᾱσ-α

παιδεύ-σᾱσ-αν

παιδευ-σάσ-ης

etc.

Note the pattern of compensatory lengthening: παιδεύ-ο-ντ-ια→παιδεύ-ουσ-α/παιδεύ-σα-ντ-ια→παιδεύ-σᾱσ-α/θέ-ντ-ια→θεῖσ-α.

Note the same accent pattern for the aorists as in the masculine and neuter.

**Participle/
Declension of
*EIMI***

The chart summarizes the declension of the participle of the verb εἰμί.

masc.	fem.	neut.
ὤν	οὖσ-α	ὄν
ὄντ-α	οὖσ-αν	ὄν
ὄντ-ος	οὖσ-ης	ὄντ-ος
ὄντ-ι	οὖσ-η	ὄντ-ι
ὄντ-ες	οὖσ-αι	ὄντ-α
ὄντ-ας	οὖσ-ᾱς	ὄντ-α
ὄντ-ων	οὖσ-ῶν	ὄντ-ων
οὖ-σι	οὖσ-αις	οὖ-σι

**Participle/
Genitive Absolute**

The Greek language uses the participle more extensively than does English. The range of possible contexts is best learned from reading Greek. For example, several participial phrases often will be dependent upon the main clause.

πολλὰ φαγὼν καὶ πολλὰ πινὼν καὶ πολλὰ κακ' εἰπὼν ἀνθρώπους κεῖμαι Τιμοκρέων ᾿Ρόδιος. —Τιμοκρέων (After) eating much and drinking much and saying much evil (about) men, I lie here (dead), Timokreon, the Rhodian. (*Note* that the participle of εἶπον is irregular in retaining the augment.)

The participle, as you have seen, always agrees with its antecedent (the word it modifies or describes). Very commonly, however, the antecedent can be a word that has no direct grammatical connection to the main clause. In such instances, both the antecedent and the participle are in the genitive case; the participial phrase expresses the general circumstances for the action in the main clause (that is, an ablatival idea of source like that which is expressed by the preposition μετά). This structure is called the "unconnected" or *absolute genitive*.

τοῦ φιλοσόφου διδάσκοντος, ἐμανθάνομεν.	(With) the philosopher teaching, we learned. (Contrast this absolute structure with one which is not absolute: ὁ φιλόσοφος διδάσκων εἶπεν.) (While) teaching, the philosopher spoke.

Infinitive/Verbal Noun

The infinitive is that form of the verb which expresses the verbal idea without stating its subject (that is, "infinitely" or without limitation of person and number); it is a noun formed from the verb and retains certain verbal characteristics such as allowing adverbial (instead of adjectival) modification.

ἤθελον αὐτοῦ ἀκούειν.	They wanted to hear him.

τὸ γὰρ γνῶναι ἐπιστήμην λαβεῖν ἐστιν. —Πλάτων	To know is to acquire knowledge.

Infinitive/ Declension

In Greek, the infinitive is formed by adding a suffix, either thematically or athematically, to the verbal root. Like the participle, the *infinitive does not express tense or time*, but only aspect; for that reason, *it is never augmented*. The present infinitive expresses continual or repeated action, whereas the aorist expresses punctual action.

There is only one form of the infinitive; it is declined by declining only its article. τὸ γνῶναι, τοῦ γνῶναι, τῷ γνῶναι.

THEMATIC

Present Active
παιδεύ-ε-ιν

Aorist Active
λαβ-ε-ῖν

Present Middle-Passive
παιδεύ-ε-σθαι

Aorist Middle (only)
λαβ-έ-σθαι

ATHEMATIC

Present Active

τιθέ-
ἱστά-
ἱέ- | ναι
διδό-
δεικνύ-

Aorist Active

θεῖ-/στῆ-
εἱ-/δοῦ-
βῆ-/γνω- | ναι
δῦ-
παιδεῦ-σαι

Present Middle-Passive

τίθε-
ἵστα-
ἵε- | σθαι
δίδο-
δείκνυ-

Aorist Middle (only)

θέ-
δό-
ἕ- | σθαι
παιδεύ-σα-

Note that the accent is normally recessive, except that it always falls immediately before the -ναι suffix and always falls on the thematic vowel (or diphthong) in the aorist.

Note that the reduced stem vowel occurs in the athematic forms except for the aorist active.

Infinitive/ Indirect Discourse

Since the infinitive is modified adverbally, the accusative case can function either as the infinitive's direct object or as its subject.

τὸ αὐτὸν ἑαυτὸν γνῶναι	him to know himself

Such infinitive phrases can function as the object of the main verb.

βουλόμεθα αὐτὸν ἑαυτὸν γνῶναι.	We want him to know himself.

If the main verb is one of saying or thinking, the infinitive phrase, by context, will indicate the substance of what was said or thought, indirectly quoted. This is the structure for so-called indirect discourse.

ἔφην αὐτὸν ἑαυτὸν γνῶναι.	I said that he knew himself.

Indirectly quoted material can also be expressed by a clause introduced by the subordinating conjunctions ὅτι or ὡς ("that").

λέγει ὅτι ὁ σοφὸς ἑαυτὸν γιγνώσκει.	He says that the wise man knows himself.

In general, the infinitive structure is more common with the verb φημί and the subordinate clause is more common with the verb λέγω.

When the subject of the main verb is identical with that of the infinitive, the nominative case of the main verb's subject takes precedence and the infinitive's subject either is not separately expressed or it must also be in the nominative case, to agree with the subject of the main clause.

ἔφη ὁ φιλόσοφος ἑαυτὸν γνῶναι.	
ἔφη ὁ φιλόσοφος αὐτὸς ἑαυτὸν γνῶναι.	The philosopher said that he knew himself.

Negatives/ΜΗ and ΟΥ

There are two negative adverbs in Greek, μή and οὐ. Both also occur in compounds such as οὐδείς/μηδείς, οὐδέ/μηδέ. Generally, μή is used to negate infinitives except when the infinitive is in the structure for indirect discourse. Μή also negates hypotheses (clauses introduced by εἰ 'if'') and participles when the participle has the implication of an hypothesis.

τὸ μὴ σεαυτὸν γνῶναι κακόν ἐστιν.	Not to know yourself is a bad thing.
ἔφη οὐκ ἑαυτὸν γνῶναι.	He said he did not know himself.
εἰ μὴ ἔγνω ἑαυτὸν, οὐκ ἦν σοφός.	If he did not know himself, he was not wise.
ὁ μὴ ἑαυτὸν γνοὺς οὐκ ἔστι σοφός.	Whoever does not know himself is not wise.
οἴνου μηκέτ᾽ ὄντος οὐκ ἔστιν Κύπρις	(With) there being no longer any

οὐδ' ἄλλο τερπνὸν οὐδὲν ἀνθρώποις ἔτι. —Εὐριπίδης	wine, there is no Cyprian goddess of love nor any longer anything else pleasurable for mankind.

ΟΝΟΜΑΤΑ ΚΑΙ ΡΗΜΑΤΑ

ἡ ἐπιστήμη, -ης	knowledge (*see* epistemology; *see* ἐπίσταμαι)
ἡ αἰτία, -ας	cause (*see* aetiology)
ἡ εὐνή, -ῆς	bed
ἡ χείρ, -ρός	hand
ἡ μάχη, -ης	battle (*see* μάχομαι)
ἡ πάρθενος, -ου	virgin, maiden, κόρη
ἡ νύμφη, -ης	bride (*see* ὁ νυμφίος, -ου)
πρότερος, -α, -ον	previous, earlier
πρεσβύτερος, -α, -ον	older
ἑκάτερος, -α, -ον	each of two
τερπνός, -ή, -όν	delightful, pleasurable
ὅμοιος, -α, -ον	similar, like
ἄλλος, -η, -ο	other (*see* ἀλλά)
πολύς, πολλή, πολύ	much, many
μέγας, μεγάλη, μέγα	big
γηράσκω, ἐγήρασα	grow old (*see* ὁ γέρων, -οντος/γεραιός)
ἔρχομαι, ἦλθον	go, come
κεῖμαι	lie repose (athematic: κεῖ-μαι/ἐκεί-μην)
_____, εἶδον	see
φημί, ἔφησα, ἔφην	say (participle: φάσκων or φάς, φᾶσα, φάν)
ἐπι-στρατεύω, ἐπ-εστράτευσα	make war upon (*see* ὁ στρατός, -οῦ army)
_____, ἐνίκησα	win (*see* ἡ νίκη, -ης victory)
_____, ἡγησάμην	lead the way (δι-ηγησάμην narrate)
ἀπο-κτείνω, ἀπ-έκτεινα	kill
τότε	then, at that time
αὖθις	= πάλιν

ἐν	in, on (+locative dative)
ἐπί	on (+genitive, dative, or accusative)
παρά	beside (+gen., dat., or acc.)
πρό	before (+genitive)
περί	around, concerning (+gen., dat., or acc.)
μή	=οὐ (see μηδέ/οὐδέ, μηδείς/οὐδείς)
ἔτι	still (see μηκέτι/οὐκέτι)

Note that the verbal suffix -(ι)σκ-ο/ε- is "inceptive" in meaning (that is, "coming into the state of being"): γηράσκω "grow old." See ἀπο-θνήσκω, γιγνώσκω, εὑρίσκω. It is, moreover, a present forming suffix (*see* page 31): γηράσκω/ἐγήρασα.

Note that the athematic verb φημί is enclitic (*see* page 5) and that it has a stem vowel which alternates with alpha for its reduced form (like ἵστημι): φημί/φα μέν.

Note that the neuter of ἄλλος is ἄλλο (without a *nu*). This is the normal form for *all neuter pronouns* (*see* pp. 23–25): αὐτό, τό, τόδε, ἐκεῖνο, ἑαυτό, αὐτό, τοῦτο.

Note that the adjectives πολύς and μέγας are slightly irregular in having a different stem for the masculine and neuter nominative and accusative singular only: πολύς, πολλή, πολύ/πολύν, πολλήν, πολύ, but πολλοῦ, πολλῆς, πολλοῦ, etc.; μέγας, μεγάλη, μέγα/μέγαν, μεγάλην, μέγα, but μεγάλου, μεγάλης, μεγάλου, etc.

ΑΣΚΗΣΙΣ

I. TRANSLATE: The Birth of Heracles.

ἐκ μὲν Ἀλκαίου καὶ Ἀστυδαμείας τῆς Πέλοπος Ἀμφιτρύων ἐγένετο. γήμας δ' Ἀλκμήνην τὴν Ἠλεκτρύονος, τοῦ τότε βασιλεύοντος Μυκηνῶν, παρεγένετο σὺν αὐτῇ ἐπὶ Θήβας. παρθένον δὲ τὴν νύμφην φυλάξας καὶ ἐν Θήβαις λιπών, ἐπεστράτευσεν ἐπὶ Τηλεβόας. τούτους δὲ μάχῃ νικήσας,
5 πάλιν προσήρχετο εἰς Θήβας.
   πρὸ τοῦ δ' Ἀμφιτρύωνα παραγενέσθαι εἰς Θήβας, Ζεύς, διὰ νυκτὸς ἐλθὼν καὶ τὴν μίαν τριπλασιάσας νύκτα, ὅμοιος Ἀμφιτρύωνι γενόμενος Ἀλκμήνῃ συνηυνάζετο καὶ τὰ γενόμενα περὶ Τηλεβοῶν διηγήσατο. Ἀμφιτρύων δὲ παραγενόμενος, ὡς οὐκ εἶδεν φιλόφρονα οὖσαν πρὸς αὐτὸν
10 τὴν γυναῖκα, ἐπυνθάνετο τὴν αἰτίαν. εἰπούσης δὲ ὅτι τῇ προτέρᾳ νυκτὶ παραγενόμενος αὐτῇ συνηυνάζετο, μανθάνει παρὰ Τειρεσίου τὴν γενομένην τοῦ Διὸς συνουσίαν. Ἀλκμήνη δὲ δύο ἐγέννησε παῖδας, Διὶ μὲν Ἡρακλέα, μιᾷ νυκτὶ πρεσβύτερον, Ἀμφιτρύωνι δ' Ἰφικλέα. τοῦ δὲ παιδὸς ὄντος ὀκταμηνιαίου, δύο δράκοντας μεγάλους Ἥρα ἐπὶ τὴν εὐνὴν
15 ἔπεμψε, ἀποκτεῖναι τὰ παιδία θέλουσα. ἐπιβοησαμένης δ' Ἀλκμήνης Ἀμφιτρύωνα, Ἡρακλῆς διαναστὰς ἄγχων ἑκατέραις ταῖς χερσὶν αὐτοὺς διέφθειρε. Φερεκύδης δέ φησιν Ἀμφιτρύωνα, βουλόμενον μαθεῖν ὁπότερος

ἦν τῶν παίδων ἐκείνου, τοὺς δράκοντας εἰς τὴν εὐνὴν ἐμβαλεῖν, καὶ τοῦ
μὲν Ἰφικλέους φυγόντος, τοῦ δὲ Ἡρακλέους ὑποστάντος μαθεῖν ὡς
20 Ἰφικλῆς ἐξ αὐτοῦ ἦν. —Adapted from Ἀπολλόδωρος

Reading Notes:

(2) Μυκηνῶν/αἱ Μυκῆναι Mycenae

(3) παρεγένετο/παρα-γίγνομαι (+dat.) "be beside," but here with ἐπὶ Θήβας
the idea of motion directed toward a place (where Amphitryon will be beside
someone) predominates. *Note* that the case used with prepositions is always
determined by the basic meaning of the case which is simply clarified by the
preposition. Thus some prepositions can occur with all three cases but always
with a distinction in meaning. *See* εἰς Θήβας "into Thebes," πρὸς Θήβας
"toward Thebes," ἐπὶ Θήβας ἦλθεν "he went toward upon Thebes," ἐπὶ
Θήβαις ἔμεινεν "he stayed (locative) in Thebes," ἐπὶ γῆς ἦν "he was on
(a spot out of the entire) earth." etc.

(3) Θήβας/αἱ Θῆβαι

(3) φυλάξας/φυλάττω guard, keep (*see* ὁ φύλαξ, -ακος)

(4) Τηλεβόας/οἱ Τηλεβόαι

(5) προσήρχετο/προσ-έρχομαι

(6) πρὸ τοῦ... The entire infinitive phrase is object of the preposition.

(7) τριπλασιάσας/τριπλασιάζω, ἐτριπλασίασα triple (*see* τρίς thrice, τρεῖς
three)

(8) συνηυνάζετο/συν-ευνάζω put to bed with. Passive: sleep with (*see* ἡ
εὐνή)

(9) ὡς = ὅτε when, as

(9) φιλόφρονα/φιλόφρων, -ον (-ονος) friendly

(11) Τειρεσίου/ὁ Τειρεσίας a prophet

(12) Διός/ὁ Ζεύς, τοῦ Διός

(12) συνουσίαν/ἡ συν-ουσία, -ας (*see* οὖσα, participle of εἰμί) sexual inter-
course

(12) ἐγέννησε = ἔτεκε

(13) Ἡρακλέα accusative of Ἡρακλῆς. See Ἰφικλέα.

(13) μιᾷ νυκτί (*see* page 56). The dative (instrumental) can express the
means by which one thing differs from another; hence, "older by one
night."

(14) ὀκταμηνιαίου/ὀκταμηνιαῖος, -α, -ον eight months old (*see* ὀκτώ
eight/ ὁ μείς, μηνός month/ἡ μήνη, -ης moon)

(14) δράκοντας/ ὁ δράκων, -οντος serpent (*see* dragon)

(15) ἐπιβοησαμένης/ἐπ-εβόησα shout (*see* ἡ βοή, -ῆς shout)

(16) διαναστάς/δι-αν-ίστημι

(16) ἄγχων/ἄγχω strangle

(17) Φερεκύδης a sixth century B.C. historian

(17) ὁπότερος, -α, -ον which of two

(18) ἐμβαλεῖν/ἐμ-βάλλω, ἐν-έβαλον

(19) Ἰφικλέους genitive of Ἰφικλῆς. See Ἡρακλέους.

II. MATCH the verb to the noun by changing it into a participle in the same case.

1. αἱ πάρθενοι (εἶδον)

2. τὰς νύμφας (ἔρχομαι)

3. τοῖς πρεσβυτέροις (ἀπέκτεινα)

4. τὴν χεῖρα (ἐλουσάμην)

5. οἱ γέροντες (διηγησάμην)

6. τῷ ὀνείρῳ (ἐγενόμην)

7. τοῦ ποιητοῦ (βούλομαι)

8. οἱ νομοθέται (ἐβοήθησα)

9. τὸν δῆμον (ἀπωλόμην)

10. τὸν πατέρα (δύναμαι)

11. οἱ θῆρες (ἀπόλλυμι)

12. τοῦ φιλοσόφου (ὑπεκρινάμην)

13. τῶν παίδων (ἔπεσον)

14. τοῖς θεοῖς (ηὗρον)

15. τῶν ἀνδρῶν (ἔπιον)

16. τὰς ψυχάς (ἔτυχον)

17. οἱ ἄγγελοι (ἤγγειλα)

18. τῇ γυναικί (εἶπον)

19. τῶν σοφῶν (ἔγνων)

20. τῇ θυγατρί (δίδωμι)

III. REPHRASE each of the following sentences, substituting a participial phrase for the subordinate clause (ἐπεί, ὅτε, etc.). Some sentences will require the genitive absolute structure; in others, the participle will agree with its antecedent.

1. ὅτε δ' ἔγημεν ὁ Ἀμφιτρύων τὴν νύμφην, εἰς τὰς Θήβας ἦλθεν.

2. ὅτε δ' οἱ παῖδες ἔτι νέοι ἦσαν, δύο θῆρας μεγάλους ἡ Ἥρα ἐπὶ τὴν εὐνὴν ἔπεμψεν.

3. ἐπειδὴ δ' πρότερος μιᾷ ἡμέρᾳ ἐγένετο ὁ Ἡρακλῆς, πρεσβύτερος ἦν.

4. ἐπειδὴ δ' ἡ Ἥρα ἠθέλησε τὸν παῖδα ἀποκτεῖναι, δύο θῆρας μεγάλους ἐπὶ τὴν εὐνὴν ἔπεμψεν.

5. ὅτε δ' ἐνέβαλε τοὺς θῆρας εἰς τὴν εὐνήν, ἔμαθεν ὁ πατὴρ τὸν παῖδα ἐξ ἑαυτοῦ οὐκ εἶναι.

6. ὅτε δὲ διανέστη ὁ παῖς καὶ τοὺς θῆρας ἀπέκτεινεν, ἔγνω ὁ Ἀμφιτρύων αὐτὸν ἐξ ἑαυτοῦ οὐκ εἶναι.

7. ἐπειδὴ δ' ἔφυγεν ὁ παῖς, οὐκ ἀπέθανεν.

8. ὅτε δ' ἐπεστράτευεν ὁ Ἀμφιτρύων ἐπὶ τοὺς Τηλεβόας, ὁ Ζεὺς διὰ νυκτὸς ἦλθεν εἰς τὰς Θήβας.

9. ὅτε δ' ἐβασίλευεν ὁ Ἠλεκτρύων τῶν Μυκηνῶν, ἔγημεν ὁ Ἀμφιτρύων τὴν

Ἀλκμήνην καὶ μετ' αὐτῆς προσῆλθεν ἐπὶ τὰς Θήβας.

10. ἐβούλετο δ' ἡ Ἥρα τὸν παῖδα ἀποκτεῖναι ἐπειδὴ ἐκ τοῦ Διὸς ἐγένετο οὐδ' ἑαυτῆς ἦν.

IV. REPHRASE each of the following quotations as an infinitive phrase in the structure for "indirect discourse" (see page 68) with φημί.

1. πάντων μέτρον ἄνθρωπος. —Πρωταγόρας (answer: ὁ Πρωταγόρας φησὶ (or ἔφη) πάντων μέτρον ἄνθρωπον εἶναι.)

2. σκιὰ γέρων ἀνήρ. —Εὐριπίδης

3. ψυχῆς ἀγαθῆς πατρὶς ὁ ξύμπας κόσμος. —Δημόκριτος

4. τὴν Ἑλλάδα παιδεύει ὁ ποιητής. —Πλάτων

5. χρόνος δίκαιον ἄνδρα δείκνυσι μόνος. —Σοφοκλῆς

6. ὁδὸς ἄνω κάτω μία καὶ ἡ αὐτή. —Ἡράκλειτος

7. ἡ γλῶσσα πολλοὺς εἰς ὄλεθρον ἤγαγεν. —Μένανδρος

8. μία ἡμέρα τὸν μὲν καθεῖλεν ὑψόθεν, τὸν δ' ἦρ' ἄνω. —Εὐριπίδης

9. γῆ πάντα τίκτει καὶ πάλιν κομίζεται. —Μένανδρος

10. πάλιν γὰρ αὖθις παῖς ὁ γηράσκων ἀνήρ. —Σοφοκλῆς

11. χρήματα ψυχὴ δειλοῖς βροτοῖς. —Ἡσίοδος

12. θνητὰ θνητοῖς πρέπει. —Πίνδαρος

13. ἐμπείρως ἔχω τοῦ λέγειν. —Δημοσθένης

14. Ἔρως τῶν θεῶν βασιλεύει. —Πλάτων

15. πολλὰ φαγὼν καὶ πολλὰ πιὼν καὶ πολλὰ κακ' εἰπὼν ἀνθρώπους κεῖμαι Τιμοκρέων Ῥόδιος. —Τιμοκρέων

V. MATCH the second verb to the first by changing it into the same form.

1. ἀπεκτείναμεν (γιγνώσκω)   11. ἠγγείλατε (πίνω)

2. γνῶναι (διαλέγομαι)   12. τυχούσαις (πράττω)

3. ἔβαλλε (παύω)   13. ἐνεγκεῖν (πέμπω)

4. εἰπόντες (τίθημι)   14. ἀποθανόντας (δίδωμι)

5. θεῖναι (λαμβάνω)   15. ἴασι (πείθω)

6. γενομένοις (ἵστημι)   16. ἔλεγον (μετέχω)

7. ἔσθαι (μανθάνω)   17. ἔκρινες (τίθημι)

8. βᾶσιν (γράφω)   18. ἧκα (ἐθέλω)

9. ἔθηκες (δείκνυμι)   19. γνοῦσι (διδάσκω)

10. θείσης (παιδεύω)   20. ἔφαγες (ἀκούω)

VI. NOTE THE PATTERN in each of the following quotations and compose a translation of the English sentences using the same pattern.

1. Ἡράκλειτος τὴν ἀρχὴν εἶναί φησι ψυχήν. —Ἀριστοτέλης (ἡ ἀρχή, -ῆς beginning)

Timocreon said that he ate a lot.

The god says men do not know themselves.

Timocreon says that he died.

Antisthenes said that nothing was strange for a wise man.

2. τὸ γὰρ γνῶναι ἐπιστήμην λαβεῖν ἐστιν. —Πλάτων

To grow old is to learn many new things.

To die is to be a human being.

To see is to become experienced with the world. (*See* page 41.)

3. γηράσκω ἀεὶ πολλὰ διδασκόμενος. —Σόλων

The philosopher used to walk while constantly conversing with his students.

Hera sent the two beasts, wanting to kill the child.

The lawgiver established laws while praying to the gods.

4. οἴνου μηκέτ' ὄντος οὐκ ἔστιν...οὐδὲν τερπνὸν ἀνθρώποις. —Εὐριπίδης

While the woman was speaking, the man died.

If there are no gods, man alone is the measure of the universe.

Since no one out of the class of men is wise, the gods alone can teach. (*See* page 42 for the partitive genitive.)

5. παρὼν ἐτύγχανον. —Σοφοκλῆς

I chanced to be traveling to Thebes.

They all happened to be Athenians.

I happened to have eaten a lot.

He happened to die during the night.

6. παθὼν δέ τε νήπιος ἔγνω. —Ἡσίοδος (τε = καί intensive; *see* page 19/ νήπιος, -α, -ον childish, stupid. For the meaning of the gnomic aorist, *see* page 36.)

After drinking a lot, even a philosopher is not in good condition. (κακῶς ἔχω)
After they die, even the bad become wise.

ἕκαστος κρίνει καλῶς ἃ γιγνώσκει καὶ τούτων ἐστὶν ἀγαϑὸς κριτής.
—’Αριστοτέλης

Lesson 12

Relative Pronoun   A relative pronoun is a pronoun that refers back (or "relates") to an antecedent (or a word that means the same thing as it does). In the following
example, two independent sentences are combined into one sentence by using
a relative pronoun to replace the noun in the second sentence which is common
to the first.

τοῦ ἀνδρὸς ἀκούω. ὁ ἀνὴρ λέγει.	I listen to the man. The man is speaking.
τοῦ ἀνδρὸς ἀκούω ὃς λέγει.	I listen to the man *who* is speaking.

Just as the nouns in the above example are in the cases required for their functions, so also will the relative pronoun have the appropriate case for its function within its own clause.

λέγει ὁ φιλόσοφος. τοῦ φιλοσόφου ἀκούω.	The philosopher is speaking. I listen to the philosopher.
λέγει ὁ φιλόσοφος οὗ ἀκούω.	The philosopher is speaking *to whom* I am listening.

Since the relative pronoun refers back to its antecedent (and designates the
same person or thing), it will always have *the same gender and number as the
antecedent*.

τῆς γυναικὸς ἀκούω. ἡ γυνὴ λέγει.	I listen to the woman. The woman is speaking.
τῆς γυναικὸς ἀκούω ᾗ λέγει.	I listen to the woman *who* is speakng.
ἕκαστος κρίνει καλῶς ταῦτα ἃ γιγνώσκει.	Each man judges well these things *which* he knows.

In situations where the antecedent is easily inferred from the relative, the antecedent may be omitted.

ἕκαστος κρίνει καλῶς ἃ γιγνώσκει.	Each man judges well *what* he knows.

Note, however, that exceptions to the above principles do occur. Despite the
general rule that a relative is in the case required for its function within its
own clause, *sometimes* the relative is "assimilated" to the case of its antecedent if the antecedent is in the genitive or dative case.

ἦλθον μεϑ’ οὗ γιγνώσκεις.	I came with *whom* you know. (instead of μετὰ αὐτοῦ ὅν)
δῶρον ἔδωκα οἷς γιγνώσκεις.	I gave a gift *to whom* you know. (instead of αὐτοῖς οὕς)

Relative Pronoun/   The relative pronoun resembles the definite article except that it has a rough
Declension   breathing (’) instead of the initial τ. It is like all pronouns in having -ο (instead
of -ον) in the neuter singular nominative and accusative (pp. 23–25).

		Article				Relative	Pronoun	
M	F	N			M	F	N	
ὁ	ἡ	τό	N		ὅς	ἥ	ὅ	
τόν	τήν	τό	A		ὅν	ἥν	ὅ	
τοῦ	τῆς	τοῦ	G		οὗ	ἧς	οὗ	
τῷ	τῇ	τῷ	D		ᾧ	ᾗ	ᾧ	
οἱ	αἱ	τά	N		οἵ	αἵ	ἅ	
τούς	τάς	τά	A		οὕς	ἅς	ἅ	
τῶν	τῶν	τῶν	G		ὧν	ὧν	ὧν	
τοῖς	ταῖς	τοῖς	D		οἷς	αἷς	οἷς	

Indefinite Pronoun-Adjective   You have learned that the omission of the definite article in Greek is equivalent to the English indefinite article ("a").

| ἔδωκα τὸ δῶρον. | I gave *the* gift. |
| ἔδωκα δῶρον. | I gave *a* gift. |

The Greek language expresses an idea which is still more indefinite by the use of an indefinite pronoun or adjective.

| ἔδωκα δῶρόν τι. | I gave some gift or other. |
| ἔδωκά τι. | I gave something or other. |

Indefinite Pronoun-Adjective/ Declension   The indefinite pronoun-adjective is identical with the interrogative pronoun-adjective (*see* pp. 20 and 59) except that it is enclitic (*see* page 5).

τις	τι
τιν-α	τι
τιν-ος	τιν-ος
τιν-ι	τιν-ι
τιν-ες	τιν-α
τιν-ας	τιν-α
τιν-ων	τιν-ων
τισι	τισι

Accent Patterns With Enclitics   Review the rules for accentuation in Greek (*see* pp. 4–5).

The enclitic is an unaccented word that leans back upon the preceding word for its accent and forms one accentual group together with it. The addition of an enclitic to a word will, therefore, sometimes place the word's accent more than three from the end of the new accentual group (word + enclitic) and some change will be necessary to restore the three-syllable accent pattern.

Acute Accent
The acute accent can fall on syllables one, two, or three from the end.

1. ___ ___ ___́ + ___ (___)   σοφός τις
       word   enclitic of   σοφοί τινες
                   1 or 2 syllables

No additional accent is ever necessary because the addition of the longest enclitic (two syllables) will still leave the accent three from the end of the word
+ enclitic accentual group.

2. ___ ___ ___́ + ___ ('or~)(___)   λόγος τις   λόγων τινῶν
                              λόγοι τινές

An additional accent (either acute or circumflex, depending on the quantity of
last syllable) may be necessary to prevent the accent from falling more than
three from the end of the group. (The accent is added to the enclitic, because
the addition of another accent to the word would produce the impossible accent pattern of two successive acute accents.)

3. ___ ___́ ___́ + ___ (___)   ἄνθρωπός τις
                              ἄνθρωποί τινες

The word itself picks up an additional acute accent on the last syllable to carry
it over the enclitic.

Circumflex Accent

The circumflex accent can fall only on the last or second to last syllable.

1. ___ ___ ___̂ + ___ (___)   σοφῶν γε
                              σοφῶν τινων

No accent is ever necessary, since the addition of the longest enclitic will still
preserve the three-syllable accent pattern.

2. ___ ___̂ ___́ + ___ (___)   δῶρόν τι   παῖδές τινες

The word itself picks up an additional acute to carry it over the enclitic.

Interrogatives, Relatives, Demonstratives/ Compared

The following chart summarizes the correspondences which can be noted between pronominal adjectives and adverbs of different types. Notice, for example, that the indefinite is always enclitic, that the relative always has an
initial rough breathing, and that the interrogative has an initial π.

Interrogative quality	Indefinite	Demonstrative	Relative
ποῖος, -α, -ον what kind(of)?	ποιος, -α, -ον some kind (of)	τοιόσδε, τοιάδε, τοιόνδε (τοῖος + ὅδε)/τοιοῦτος, τοιαύτη, τοιοῦ- το (τοῖος + οὗτος) such a kind (of)	οἷος, -α, -ον/ὁποῖ- ος, -α, -ον which kind (of)

quantity

πόσος, -η, -ον how much?	ποσος, -η, -ον some amount (of)	τόσος, η, -ον/ τοσόσδε, τοσήδε, τοσόνδε (τόσος + ὅδε)/τοσοῦτος, τοσαύτη, τοσοῦτο (τόσος + οὗτος) so much	ὅσος, -η, -ον/ ὁπόσος, -η, -ον as much as

place (locative)

ποῦ where?	που somewhere	ἐνθάδε/ἐκεῖ there	οὗ/ὅπου where, in which place

place (ablatival)

πόθεν whence, from which place?	ποθεν from some place	ἐνθένδε/ἐκεῖθεν thence, from that place	ὅθεν/ὁπόθεν whence, from which place

time

πότε when?	ποτε at some time	τότε then, at that time	ὅτε/ὁπότε when, at which time

manner

πῶς how?	πως somehow	ὧδε/οὕτως thus	ὡς, ὅπως as, by which way

ONOMATA KAI PHMATA

ὁ χρησμός, -οῦ	oracular response, oracle
τὸ ὅπλον, -ου	weapon, armor, tool
ὁ ἵππος, -ου	horse
ὁ ἆθλος, -ου	contest
ὁ γάμος, -ου	wedding
τὸ ἅρμα, -ατος	chariot
ὁ ἔρως, -ωτος	love
ἡ ἀρά, -ᾶς	curse
ὁ χρόνος, -ου	time
τὸ φῶς, -ωτός	light
τὸ γράμμα, -ατος	letter, lines of a drawing
ὁ τρόπος, -ου	manner, way of life
μνηστεύω, ἐμνήστευσα	seek in marriage, court

δεῖ (ἔδει)	it is (was) necessary
διώκω, ἐδίωξα	pursue
τέμνω, ἔτεμον	cut
καλύπτω, ἐκάλυφα	cover
ἕκαστος, -η, -ον	each
ὅσος, -η, -ον	as much as
δώδεκα	twelve
μέχρι	as far as (*prep.* + genitive, partitive idea)
ποῦ	where?
πόθεν	whence?
πότε	when?
πῶς	how?
εὐθέως or εὐθύς	*adv.* straight

Note that several words in the vocabulary are related to nouns formed with the -της suffix (*see* page 38): ὁ ὁπλίτης, -ου (armed soldier), ὁ ἱππότης, -ου (cavalry soldier), ὁ ἀθλητής, -οῦ (athlete).

Note that the verb δεῖ is usually impersonal. It is structured with an infinitive phrase as its subject: δεῖ γράμματα μαθεῖν "To learn writing is necessary" or "It is necessary to learn writing." *See* ἡμᾶς δεῖ γράμματα μαθεῖν "For us to learn writing is necessary" or "We must learn writing."

ΑΣΚΗΣΙΣ

I. TRANSLATE: The Courtship of Hippodameia.

τοῦ δὲ βασιλεύοντος Πίσης Οἰνομάου θυγατέρα ἔχοντος Ἱπποδάμειαν
καί, ὥς τινες λέγουσιν, χρησμὸν ἔχοντος ἀποθανεῖν ὑπὸ τοῦ γήμαντος
αὐτήν, οὐδεὶς αὐτὴν ἐλάμβανεν εἰς γυναῖκα. οἱ γὰρ μνηστευόμενοι ἀεὶ
ἀπεκτείνοντο ὑπ᾽ αὐτοῦ μὴ θέλοντος αὐτὴν ἀνδρί τινι διδόναι. ἔχων γὰρ
5 ὅπλα τε καὶ ἵππους παρὰ θεοῦ τινος ἆθλον ἐτίθει τοῖς μνηστῆρσι τὸν
γάμον καὶ ἕκαστον τὸν μνηστευόμενον ἔδει ἀναλαβόντα τὴν Ἱπποδάμειαν
εἰς τὸ οἰκεῖον ἅρμα φεύγειν μέχρι τοῦ Κορινθίων ἰσθμοῦ, τὸν δὲ Οἰνόμαον
εὐθέως διώκειν καὶ καταλαβόντα τὸν μνηστῆρα κτείνειν. ὃν δὲ μὴ κατέλαβεν ἔχειν γυναῖκα τὴν Ἱπποδάμειαν. καὶ τοῦτον τὸν τρόπον πολλοὺς
10 μνηστευομένους ἀπέκτεινεν, ὡς δέ τινες λέγουσι, δώδεκα. τὰς δὲ κεφαλὰς
τῶν μνηστήρων ἐκτεμὼν τῇ οἰκίᾳ προσεπαττάλευε.
παραγίγνεται τοίνυν καὶ Πέλοψ ἐπὶ τὴν μνηστείαν. οὗ τὸ κάλλος ἰδοῦσα
ἡ Ἱπποδάμεια ἔρωτα ἔσχεν αὐτοῦ καὶ πείθει Μυρτίλον τὸν Ἑρμοῦ παῖδα
συλλαβέσθαι αὐτῷ. ἦν δὲ Μυρτίλος ἡνίοχος Οἰνομάου. Μυρτίλος οὖν
15 ἔρωτα ἔχων αὐτῆς καὶ βουλόμενος αὐτῇ χαρίσασθαι, διέφθειρε τὸ
Οἰνομάου ἅρμα ἐν ᾧ ἔτρεχε καὶ οὕτως ἐποίησεν αὐτὸν ἀποθανεῖν. ἐν δὲ

τῷ ἀποθνῄσκειν ἀρὰς ἔθετο κατὰ τοῦ Μυρτίλου, γνοὺς τὴν ἐπιβουλὴν καὶ θέλων αὐτὸν ἀπολέσθαι. —Adapted from Ἀπολλόδωρος

Reading Notes:

(1) Πίσης/ἡ Πῖσα, -ης a fountain at Olympia, which also gave its name to the entire country

(1) Οἰνομάου/ὁ Οἰνόμαος, -ου The structure is a genitive absolute: Οἰνομάου ...ἔχοντος, with τοῦ βασιλεύοντος Πίσης a participial phrase modifying Οἰνομάου.

(2) ἀποθανεῖν The structure is indirect quotation (see page 68) of the χρησμός.

(3) εἰς γυναῖκα "to wife," "for a wife"

(5) μνηστῆρσι/ὁ μνηστήρ, -ῆρος See the meaning of the -ηρ suffix, page 43.

(5–6) τὸν γάμον The structure is an adverbial accusative (see page 12), the socalled accusative of "respect," modifying μνηστῆρσι.

(6) ἀναλαβόντα/ἀνα-λαμβάνω

(7) οἰκεῖον/οἰκεῖος, -α, -ον one's own, personal, belonging to one's house or family (see ὁ οἶκος, -ου)

(7) ἰσθμοῦ/ὁ ἰσθμός, -ου isthmus

(8) καταλαβόντα/κατα-λαμβάνω

(8) κτείνειν/ἀπο-κτείνω

(9) ἔχειν This infinitive is also structured with ἔδει, with the relative clause as the infinitive's accusative subject: ὃν μὴ κατέλαβεν.

(9) τοῦτον τὸν τρόπον The structure is an adverbial accusative: "in this way." (= οὕτως)

(11) τῇ οἰκίᾳ/ἡ οἰκία, -ας = ὁ οἶκος, -ου.

(11) προσεπαττάλευε/προσ-πατταλεύω fasten, peg, bolt, impale. See ὁ πάτταλος, -ου peg.

(12) τοίνυν/τοι + νῦν = οὖν

(12) ὁ Πέλοψ, -οπος

(12) τὴν μνηστείαν/ἡ μνηστεία, -ας courtship. See μνηστεύω.

(12) τὸ κάλλος beauty. See καλός, -ή, -όν.

(14) συλλαβέσθαι/συν + λαμβάνω, here equivalent to βοηθῆσαι, "help."

(14) ὁ ἡνίοχος, -ου reinsman, chariot driver (ἡ ἡνία, -ας reins + ἔχω).

(15) χαρίσασθαι/χαρίζω show kindness to (+ dative).

(17) ἐπιβουλήν/ἡ ἐπιβουλή, -ῆς plot formed against someone.

II. REPHRASE each of the following sentences, replacing the participial phrase with a relative clause.

1. βασιλεύων δὲ Πίσης, ὁ Οἰνόμαος χρησμὸν ἔσχεν αὐτὸς ἀποθανεῖν ὑπὸ τοῦ Ἱπποδαμείας νυμφίου. (Answer: ὁ δ᾽ Οἰνόμαος, ὃς Πίσης ἐβασίλευε, χρησμὸν ἔσχεν αὐτὸς ἀποθανεῖν ὑπὸ τοῦ Ἱπποδαμείας νυμφίου.)

2. τὸν Ἱπποδάμειαν γήμαντα ἔδει τὸν πατέρα ἀποκτεῖναι.

3. οὐδεὶς δὲ τὴν Ἱπποδάμειαν, θυγατέρα οὖσαν τοῦ Οἰνομάου, ἔλαβεν εἰς γυναῖκα.

4. οἱ μνηστευόμενοι ἀεὶ ἀπεκτείνοντο ὑπὸ τοῦ Οἰνομάου.

5. ἕκαστος δὲ νυμφίος ἀεὶ ἀπεκτείνετο ὑπὸ τοῦ Οἰνομάου μὴ θέλοντος αὐτὴν διδόναι ὡς γυναῖκα.

6. ὅπλα τε καὶ ἵππους ἔχων παρὰ θεοῦ, ὁ Οἰνόμαος ἆθλον ἐτίθει τοῖς νυμφίοις.

7. τὸν δὲ μὴ φυγόντα ἔδει ἀποθανεῖν ὑπὸ τοῦ πατρός.

8. εἶδε δ᾽ ἡ Ἱπποδάμεια τὸν ἄνδρα καλόν τε ὄντα καὶ νέον.

9. ἀρὰς δ᾽ ἔθετο ἀποθανὼν ὁ βασιλεὺς κατὰ τοῦ Μυρτίλου.

10. ἡνίος δ᾽ ὢν τοῦ Οἰνομάου, ὁ Μυρτίλος ἐβοήθησε τῷ Πέλοπι.

III. REPHRASE each of the following pairs of sentences by combining them into a single sentence, using a relative clause.

1. παρεγένετο δ᾽ ὁ Πέλοψ. αὐτὸν δ᾽ εἶδεν ἡ γυνή. (Answer: παρεγένετο δ᾽ ὁ Πέλοψ ὃν εἶδεν ἡ γυνή or ἡ δὲ γυνὴ εἶδε τὸν Πέλοπα ὃς παρεγένετο.)

2. εἶδε δὲ ἡ Ἱπποδάμεια τὸν ἄνδρα. αὐτοῦ δ᾽ ἔρωτα εἶχεν ὄντος καλοῦ.

3. ἆθλον δ᾽ ἔθηκεν ὁ πατήρ. οὐ γὰρ ἐβούλετο τὴν θυγατέρα δοῦναι οὐδενὶ εἰς γυναῖκα.

4. ἐξέτεμε δὲ τὰς κεφαλὰς ὁ Οἰνόμαος. ἐνίκησε γὰρ δραμών.

5. ὁ μὲν νυμφίος ἔφυγε μέχρι τοῦ ἰσθμοῦ, ὁ δὲ πατὴρ ἐδίωξεν. αὐτῶν δὲ ὁ νικήσας ἔσχε τὴν Ἱπποδάμειαν ὡς νύμφην.

6. ἀπώλοντο δὲ δώδεκα μνηστευόμενοι. αὐτῶν δ᾽ ἐξέτεμε τὰς κεφαλάς.

7. ἄρας δ᾽ ἔθετο κατὰ τοῦ Μυρτίλου. οὗτος γὰρ διέφθειρε τὸ ἅρμα.

8. ἄρας δ᾽ ἔθετο κατὰ τοῦ Μυρτίλου. ἔγνω γὰρ ἀποθανὼν ὁ Οἰνόμαος τὸν Μυρτίλον κακὸν ὄντα καὶ βοηθήσαντα τῷ Πέλοπι.

9. ἔδει τὸν μὴ νικήσαντα ἀποθανεῖν. οὐ γὰρ ἔφυγε μέχρι τοῦ ἰσθμοῦ.

10. ἐβασίλευε δ᾽ ὁ Οἰνόμαος Πίσης. χρησμὸν δ᾽ ἔσχεν αὐτὸς ἀποθανεῖν ὑπὸ τοῦ γήμαντος τὴν Ἱπποδάμειαν.

IV. ADD ACCENTS where needed to the underlined words.

1. ποῖος τις ἄνθρωπος ἦν ὁ βασιλεύων Πίσης;

2. οὐδείς ποτε ἐβούλετο γῆμαι τὴν Ἱπποδάμειαν.

3. ἔχων δ᾽ ὅπλα τινα παρά τινος θεοῦ ἐνίκησεν ἀεὶ ὁ πατήρ.

4. τὰς δὲ κεφαλάς ποτε πάντων τῶν μνηστευομένων ὅσοι τινες δραμόντες

οὐκ ἐνίκησαν ἐξέτεμε ὁ Οἰνόμαος.

5. καὶ τοῦτον τὸν τρόπον ἄνδρας τινας ἀπέκτεινε τὰς κεφαλὰς ἐκτεμών.

6. ἦλθε δὲ μνηστευόμενος ἄνθρωπος τις ᾧ ὄνομα ἦν Πέλοψ.

7. ἐτίθει δ᾽ ἆθλον τινα πᾶσι τοῖς θέλουσι γῆμαι τὴν ἑαυτοῦ θυγατέρα.

8. ἔδραμε τε διώκων καὶ ὅσους φεύγοντας κατέλαβεν ἀπέκτεινε.

9. καὶ εἶδε τινα ἄνδρα καλόν τε ὄντα καὶ νέον ᾧ ἤθελε γήμασθαι.

10. ἀλλὰ χρησμόν ποθεν εἶχεν τις ἀποθανεῖν ποτε ὑπό τινος ἀνθρώπου γήμαντος τὴν νύμφην.

V. MATCH the second verb to the first by changing it into the same form.

1. ἔγνωσαν (καταλαμβάνω)

2. καλυψαμένη (τέμνω)

3. προσήλθετε (γηράσκω)

4. ἀποκτείνας (τεύχω)

5. θέντος (γίγνομαι)

6. δοῦναι (ἵημι)

7. οὔσαις (λούω)

8. ἐβασίλευσας (ἐσθίω)

9. ἤκουον (πίνω)

10. πιοῦσα (ἵστημι)

11. ἔθηκας (γιγνώσκω)

12. ἐτίθει (ἀπόλλυμι)

13. ἐδίδου (ἵημι)

14. ἐδίδαξε (λέγω)

15. ἰδοῦσα (τυγχάνω)

16. εὑρόντι (τρέχω)

17. ἔπασχες (ἔχω)

18. ἤγαγε (ἀποθνήσκω)

19. γράψαντα (εὑρίσκω)

20. ἐπίομεν (πέμπω)

VI. NOTE THE PATTERN in each of the following quotations and compose a translation of the English sentences using the same pattern.

1. ὃν οἱ θεοὶ φιλοῦσιν ἀποθνήσκει νέος. —Μένανδρος (φιλοῦσιν "they love"; this verb is like other thematic verbs except that its ending has contracted with the final vowel of the verbal stem: φιλέουσι → φιλοῦσι.)

What the lawgiver said was immortal.

What I found remained mine.

What I drank was wine.

The child whom she bore happens to be me. (*See* page 74 no. 5.)

As many as he taught were worthy men.

2. ἕκαστος κρίνει καλῶς ἃ γιγνώσκει. —᾽Αριστοτέλης

Everybody gave continually what he had.

Many people always heard what he said.

Oinomaos always killed as many as he caught.

3. ὅ τι καλὸν φίλον ἀεί. —Εὐριπίδης

Whatever is good is divine.

Whoever is bad is always ugly. (ὅς τις→ὅστις)

Whoever are women are always wise.

4. γράμματα μαθεῖν δεῖ. —Μένανδρος

It is necessary to know yourself.

You must die young. (*See* page 79, note.)

Everybody had to give some gift or other.

5. ἄνθρωπον ὄντα δεῖ φρονεῖν τἀνθρώπινα. —Μένανδρος (φρονέ-ειν→ φρονεῖν "think"; τἀνθρώπινα = τὰ ἀνθρώπινα)

Being noble, one must do noble things.

Inasmuch as they are human, women must be equal to men.

6. πάντ᾽ ἐκκαλύπτων ὁ χρόνος εἰς τὸ φῶς ἄγει. —Σοφοκλῆς (πάντ᾽ = πάντα; ἐκ-καλύπτω—take the cover *off*)

As it leaves the body, the soul goes to the gods.

While setting up laws for the Athenians, the lawgiver sent a letter to his friends. (A written message or letter is composed of many drawn lines or letters; hence, τὰ γράμματα.)

7. μέγα κακὸν τὸ μὴ δύνασθαι φέρειν κακόν. —Βίων

It is a noble thing not to want to do evil.

A terrible thing it is to bear just one child.

13   Subjunctive

πῶς οὖν μάχωμαι θνητὸς ὢν θείᾳ τύχῃ; —Σοφοκλῆς

Lesson 13
Verbal Mood

The *mood* of a verb indicates the *function* for which the verb is used. Thus far, you have learned the *indicative mood* of the Greek verb (παιδεύομεν/παιδευόμεθα), which is the mood in which the verb functions as an indication of a statement about reality or an assertion of fact. There are, however, other functions for which a verb may be used.

Subjunctive/
Volition

The *subjunctive* is another mood of the verb. Its function is the *direct and emotive expression of volition or will*.

μάχωμαι θείᾳ τύχῃ.	Let me fight with divine chance!
πῶς μάχωμαι θείᾳ τύχῃ;	How may I fight with divine chance?

Notice that the volition is directly and emotively expressed. Contrast the subjunctive with the unemotive indicative statement of the same idea. In the indicative there is simply a statement of the fact that the volition exists in reality rather than the subjunctive's emotive expression of that volition.

βούλομαι μάχεσθαι θείᾳ τύχῃ.	I want to fight with divine chance.

This use of the subjunctive to express volition is the so-called hortatory subjunctive (expressing an exhortation). It commonly occurs only in the first person and usually only in the plural.

Subjunctive/
Aspect

Like the infinitive and the participle, the subjunctive does not express tense or time but only aspect.

μαχώμεθα.	Let's (be constantly) fight(ing)! (progressive, formed from the present root)
μαχησώμεθα.	Let's fight (once and for all)! (punctual, formed from the aorist root)

Subjunctive/
Purpose (*INA*,
OΠΩΣ)

The subjunctive mood is much more common in dependent clauses than, as above, in independent clauses. The word "subjunctive" is in fact a translation of a Greek grammatical term meaning "subjoined" or dependent.

The uses of the subjunctive for particular kinds of dependent clauses originally derived from its basic meaning as an expression of volition. For example, notice that the juxtaposition of an hortatory subjunctive to another statement in certain contexts easily implies the idea of purpose.

στρατευόμεν. μαχώμεθα θείᾳ τύχῃ.	We are going to war. Let's fight with divine chance! (This implies that we are going to war *for the purpose of* fighting with chance.)

The implication of purpose is intensified by the addition of an appropriate subordinating conjunction (ἵνα or ὅπως).

στρατευόμεν ἵνα μαχώμεθα θείᾳ τύχῃ.	We are going to war in order to fight with divine chance. (Literally: We are going to war whereby let's fight with divine chance.)

In its dependent uses, the subjunctive is common in all persons of the verb. Since the subjunctive has no tense but only aspect, the time is determined by the context of the main clause.

ἐστράτευσε ἵνα μάχηται θείᾳ τύχῃ.
> He went to war to be fighting (at that time) with divine chance.

Subjunctive/Fear (MH, MH OΥ)

When juxtaposed to an expression of fear, the subjunctive indicates what it is that is feared in terms of a negative exhortation.

φοβερός εἰμι μὴ μάχωμαι θείᾳ τύχῃ.
> I am fearful lest I fight with divine chance. (Literally: I am fearful: may I not fight with divine chance.)

To express what one fears may not happen, the negative οὐ is added.

φοβερός εἰμι μὴ οὐ μάχωμαι θείᾳ τύχῃ.
> I am fearful lest I not fight with divine chance. (Literally: I am fearful: may I not fight with divine chance.)

Subjunctive/ Generalized Clauses

In addition to the idea of volition, the independent subjunctive in Homeric Greek could also express *anticipation* or eventuality. This meaning was often clarified by the addition of the particle ἄν. In Greek of the classical period, this independent usage does not occur, but the anticipatory idea is still found in a very common kind of dependent clause.

Any subordinate or dependent clause (that is, temporal ὅτε, ἐπεί, ἐπειδή; inferential (since) ἐπεί, ἐπειδή; hypothetical εἰ; relative; etc.) can be made more general in meaning by the use of a *subjunctive with the particle ἄν*. The ἄν is often combined with the subordinating conjunction, but it need not be and can be placed anywhere within the clause.

ἀεὶ καλὸς πλοῦς ἐσθ' ὅταν φεύγῃς κακά. —Σοφοκλῆς (ὅταν = ὅτε ἄν/ἐσθ' = ἐστι)
> Always good sailing is it *whenever* you are fleeing from troubles.

Contrast the expression of the same idea without the generalized clause.

ἀεὶ καλὸς πλοῦς ἐσθ' ὅτε φεύγεις κακά.
> Always good sailing is it when (on some particular occasion) you are fleeing from troubles.

Notice also these additional examples.

κακῶς ἔχει ἅπας ἰατρὸς ἐὰν μηδεὶς κακῶς ἔχῃ. —Φιλήμων
> Every doctor is in bad condition if ever no one is in bad condition. (Contrast: . . . εἰ μηδεὶς κακῶς ἔχει/ . . . if on some particular occasion no one is in bad condition.)

πατρὶς γάρ ἐστι πᾶσ' ἵν' ἄν πράττῃ τις εὖ. —Ἀριστοφάνης (πᾶσ' = πᾶσα)
> Every native country is wherever some one is well off. (*Note* that ἵνα does not introduce a purpose clause here because the particle ἄν indicates that the subjunctive must be in a generalized clause.)

Negation/*M H*

The negative for all uses of the subjunctive is always *μή* (see page 68).

Subjunctive/ Conjugation

A lengthened variable (or thematic) vowel is the sign of the subjunctive. To this vowel are added primary personal suffixes (the same as for the present indicative). Since the subjunctive does not have tense, it is never augmented.

Indicative	Subjunctive
παιδεύ-ε-τε	*παιδεύ-η-τε*
παιδεύ-ε-σθε	*παιδεύ-η-σθε*
ἐ-λάβ-ο-μεν	*λάβ-ω-μεν*

Since the subjunctive sign is the lengthened variable vowel, all verbs are conjugated in the thematic manner in the subjunctive. Those verbs which are athematic in the indicative (except for verbs like *δείκνυμι*) contract the final stem vowel with the lengthened variable vowel of the subjunctive.

τίθε-τε	*τιθέ-η-τε → τιθῆτε*
τίθε-σθε	*τιθέ-η-σθε → τιθῆσθε*
ἵστα-τε	*ἱστά-η-τε → ἱστῆτε*
ἐ-παιδεύ-σα-τε	*παιδεύ-σ(α)-η-τε → παιδεύσητε**
ἔ-βη-τε	*βά-η-τε → βῆτε*
δίδο-τε	*διδό-η-τε → διδῶτε***
ἔ-δο-τε	*δό-η-τε → δῶτε***
ἔ-γνω-τε	*γνό-η-τε → γνῶτε***

Note (*) that the athematic –*σα*– suffix does not cause a shift in accent.

Note (**) that the verb stems which end in *o* always contract to *ω* in all persons of the subjunctive.

The following chart summarizes the subjunctive conjugation.

Present

παιδεύ-ω	*παιδεύ-ω-μαι*	*τιθ*｜*-ῶ*	*τιθ*｜*-ῶ-μαι*
-ης	*-ῃ**	*ἱστ*｜*-ῇς*	*ἱστ*｜*-ῇ**
-ῃ	*-η-ται*	*ἱ*｜*-ῇ*	*ἱ*｜*-ῇ-ται*
-ω-μεν	*-ώ-μεθα*	*-ῶ-μεν*	*-ώ-μεθα*
-η-τε	*-η-σθε*	*-ῆ-τε*	*-ῆ-σθε*
-ωσι	*-ω-νται*	*-ῶσι*	*-ῶ-νται*

		διδ-ῶ	*διδ-ῶ-μαι*
		-ῷς	*-ῷ**
		-ῷ	*-ῶ-ται*
		-ῶ-μεν	*-ώ-μεθα*
		-ῶ-τε	*-ῶ-σθε*
		-ῶσι	*-ῶ-νται*

$$\delta\varepsilon\iota\kappa\nu\acute{\upsilon}\text{-}\omega$$
$$\text{-}\eta\varsigma$$
$$\text{-}\eta$$
etc.

Aorist

$\pi\alpha\iota\delta\varepsilon\acute{\upsilon}\text{-}\sigma\text{-}\omega$	$\pi\alpha\iota\delta\varepsilon\acute{\upsilon}\text{-}\sigma\text{-}\omega\text{-}\mu\alpha\iota$				
-ης	-η*	β	-ῶ	β	-ῶ-μαι
-η	-η-ται	ϑ	-ῇς	ϑ	-ῇ*
-ω-μεν	-ώ-μεθα	στ	-ῇ	στ	-ῇ-ται
-η-τε	-η-σθε	ʻ	-ῶ-μεν	ʻ	-ώ-μεθα
-ωσι	-ω-νται		-ῇ-τε		-ῇ-σθε
			-ῶσι		-ῶ-νται
$\lambda\acute{\alpha}\beta\text{-}\omega$	$\lambda\acute{\alpha}\beta\text{-}\omega\text{-}\mu\alpha\iota$	δ	-ῶ	δ	-ῶ-μαι
-ης	-η*	γν	-ῷς	γν	-ῷ*
-η	-η-ται		-ῷ		-ῶ-ται
etc.	etc.		-ῶ-μεν		-ώ-μεθα
			-ῶ-τε		-ῶ-σθε
			-ῶσι		-ῶ-νται

Note (*) that the second person singular of the middle (-passive) has lost the *sigma* of the -σαι suffix and contracted so that the resultant form is identical with the third person singular of the active.

The verb εἰμί has the following forms in the subjunctive;

ὦ	ὦ-μεν
ᾖς	ἦ-τε
ᾖ	ὦσι

ONOMATA KAI PHMATA

ἡ συμφορά, -ᾶς	event, circumstance, mishap
ἡ πέτρα, -ας	= ὁ λίθος, -ου, rock
ὁ/ἡ κύων, κυνός	dog
ὁ/ἡ ὄρνις, ὄρνιθος	bird, (bird of) omen
ἡ ἀρετή, -ῆς	excellence
ὁ ὅρκος, -ου	oath
ὁ θησαυρός, -οῦ	treasury (*see* thesaurus)
ἡ τύχη, -ης	chance, luck (*see* τυγχάνω, ἔτυχον)
ἡ ἀπαλλαγή, -ῆς	deliverance, release (*see* ἀπ-αλλάσσω)
ὁ ἰατρός, -οῦ	doctor
ὁ πλοῦς, -οῦ	sailing, voyage

ὁ νοῦς, -οῦ	mind, intellect
τὸ πρόβατον, -ου	cattle (*see* προ-βαίνω)
ὁ λύκος, -ου	wolf
φοβερός, -ά, -όν	fearful, afraid
μάχομαι, ἐμαχησάμην	fight (*see*, ἡ μάχη, -ης)
ἀπ-ερύκω, ἀπ-ήρυξα	keep off or away
ἀν-ελίσσω, ἀν-είλιξα	unroll (*see* ἐλίσσω roll), read a book roll
ἐρίζω, ἤρισα	contend, strive
λύω, ἔλυσα	untie, release
νομίζω, ἐνόμισα	think, consider
_____, ὑπ-εσχόμην	promise (*see* ἔχω, ἔσχον)
ἀναγκάζω, _____	force, compel
_____, ἔδησα	bind, tie
_____, ἔχρησα	proclaim an oracle (*mid.*, consult an oracle)
ἥδομαι, _____	enjoy, take pleasure in (+ dat.)
μηνίω, ἐμήνισα	have wrath, be wroth against (+ dat.)

εἰ/ἐάν (εἰ ἄν)/ἄν (contracted for ἐάν)/κἄν (contracted for καὶ ἐάν)

ὅτε/ὅταν (ὅτε ἄν)

Note that the nouns πλοῦς and νοῦς are Type II, but like other similar nouns they contract the adjacent *omicrons* and *omegas* in the Attic dialect: νόος → νοῦς, νοῦν, νοῦ, νῷ, νοῖ, νοῦς, νῶν, νοῖς.

ΑΣΚΗΣΙΣ

I. TRANSLATE: Socrates on the Pleasures and Benefits of Friendship.
ἐγὼ δ' οὖν καὶ αὐτός, ὥσπερ ἄλλος τις ἢ ἵππῳ ἀγαθῷ ἢ κυνὶ ἢ ὄρνιθι ἥδεται, οὕτω καὶ ἔτι μᾶλλον ἥδομαι φίλοις ἀγαθοῖς, καὶ ἐάν τι ἔχω ἀγαθόν, διδάσκω, καὶ ἄλλοις συνίστημι παρ' ὧν ἂν νομίζω βοηθῆσαί τι αὐτοῖς εἰς ἀρετήν. καὶ τοὺς θησαυροὺς τῶν πάλαι σοφῶν ἀνδρῶν, οὓς ἐκεῖνοι
5 κατέλιπον ἐν βιβλίοις γράψαντες, ἀνελίττων κοινῇ σὺν τοῖς φίλοις διέρχομαι καὶ ἄν τι ἴδωμεν ἀγαθὸν ἐκλεγόμεθα. καὶ μέγα νομίζομεν ἀγαθὸν ἐὰν ἀλλήλοις φίλοι γιγνώμεθα. —Ξενοφῶν

Perseus and Andromeda.
ὁ δὲ Περσεὺς παραγενόμενος εἰς Αἰθιοπίαν, ἧς ἐβασίλευε Κηφεύς, ηὗρε τὴν τούτου θυγατέρα παρακειμένην βορὰν θαλασσίῳ θηρί. Κασσιέπεια
10 γὰρ ἡ αὐτοῦ γυνὴ Νηρηίσιν ἤρισε περὶ κάλλους καὶ πασῶν εἶναι ἀρίστη

ηὔχησεν. ὅθεν αἱ Νηρηίδες ἐμήνισαν καὶ ηὔξαντο τῷ Ποσειδῶνι πλήμυράν τε ἐπὶ τὴν χώραν πέμψαι καὶ ϑῆρα. Ἄμμωνος χρήσαντος τὴν ἀπαλλαγὴν τῆς συμφορᾶς, ἐὰν τὴν Κασσιεπείας ϑυγατέρα προϑῶσι τῷ ϑηρὶ βοράν, τοῦτο ἀναγκαζόμενος ὁ Κηφεὺς ὑπὸ τῶν Αἰϑιόπων ἔπραξε καὶ προσέδησε
15 τὴν ϑυγατέρα πέτρᾳ. ἣν δ' ἰδὼν ὁ Περσεὺς ἀποκτεῖναι ὑπέσχετο τῷ πατρὶ τὸν ϑῆρα. ἔρωτα γὰρ ἔχων τῆς ϑυγατρὸς ἐβούλετο γῆμαι ἐὰν δῷ αὐτὴν αὐτῷ ὁ πατὴρ σώσαντι. ἐπὶ τούτοις δὲ γενομένων ὅρκων, ὑποστὰς τὸν ϑῆρα ἔκτεινε καὶ τὴν Ἀνδρομέδαν ἔλυσεν. — Adapted from Ἀπολλόδωρος

Reading Notes:

(1) ὥσπερ just as (*See* page 78 for ὡς and page 37 for -περ.)

(2) οὕτω before consonants = οὕτως (*See* page 78.)

(2) μᾶλλον adv. more

(3) συνίστημι/συν-ίστημι stand with, form a league with (+comitative dat.)

(3) αὐτοῖς redundant reference (in the dat. with βοηϑῆσαι) to the same people already mentioned in. . . . ἄλλοις · · · παρ' ὧν.

(3) τι adverbial accusative: βοηϑῆσαί τι αὐτοῖς εἰς ἀρετήν aid them *anyway* toward excellence.

(5) κατέλιπον/ κατα-λείπω leave *behind*

(5) ἀνελίττων/ἀν-ελίσσω Old Attic writers often used -ττ- where most other dialects have -σσ-.

(5) κοινῇ (that is, κοινῇ ὁδῷ instrumental comitative dat., "by a common way, together") = κοινῶς. The feminine dative of adjectives often has this adverbial meaning.

(6) διέρχομαι/δι-έρχομαι go *through*

(6) ἰδῶμεν subjunctive from εἶδον

(6) ἐκλέγομαι/ἐκ-λέγομαι select (λέγω means "pick" as well as "say.")

(9) παρακειμένην/παρα-κεῖμαι

(9) βοράν/ἡ βορά, -ᾶς food (for carnivorous animals)

(9) ϑαλασσίῳ/ϑαλάσσιος, -α, -ον (see ἡ ϑάλασσα, -ης)

(10) Νηρηίσιν/αἱ Νηρηίδες patronymic, daughters of Νηρεύς, a sea god

(10) κάλλους genitive of τὸ κάλλος (see καλός, -ή, -όν)"beauty" (This is a Type III noun about which you will learn later: it has a stem ending in a sigma, but sigma is lost between vowels and the adjacent vowels are then contracted; hence: κάλλεσ-ος → κάλλους.)

(10) ἀρίστη/ἄριστος, -η, -ον (see ἀρετή)

(11) ηὔχησεν/αὐχέω, ηὔχησα boast

(11) ὅθεν *see* page 78

(11) πλημυράν/ἡ πλημυρά, -ᾶς flood tide

(12) Ἄμμωνος/ὁ Ἄμμων, -ωνος the Libyan Zeus

(13) προθῶσι/προ-τίθημι place *forth*

(14) προσέδησε/προσ-έδησα tie *to*

(17) ὑποστάς/ὑφ-ίστημι withstand, *undertake*

II. CHANGE each verb to the subjunctive.

1. νομίζετε	11. ἔθηκα
2. ἔλυσαν	12. ἔβημεν
3. ἠρίσαμεν	13. ἔδωκας
4. ἀναγκάζεις	14. ἔγνω
5. ἐμαχησάμην	15. ἐγένου
6. μνηστεύουσι	16. ἔστησαν
7. εἶδον	17. εἵμην
8. ἦλθες	18. γηράσκω
9. ἐκάλυψα	19. ὑπεκρίνω
10. ἱστᾶσι	20. βουλόμεθα

III. MATCH the second verb to the first by changing it into the same form.

1. πέμψαι (λούω)	11. ἀπολώμεθα (γίγνομαι)
2. ἔτεμον (διέρχομαι)	12. σώσαντι (δείκνυμι)
3. παρακείμεθα (δύναμαι)	13. ἐπιστρατεύσητε (ἔρχομαι)
4. ἴδητε (γιγνώσκω)	14. ἡγήσατε (κρίνω)
5. ἀπέκτεινες (τρέχω)	15. ἤνεγκα (γράφω)
6. δοῦναι (πάσχω)	16. διδῷς (δείκνυμι)
7. ὦμεν (ἵημι)	17. ἱστῇ (δίδωμι)
8. διδούς (τίθημι)	18. λίπωσι (ἄγω)
9. ἐχρήσατε (διώκω)	19. ἔμαθες (ἀποθνήσκω)
10. στῶσι (ὀνομάζω)	20. πίῃς (γιγνώσκω)

IV. REPHRASE each dependent clause in the following sentences to make it more general, using the subjunctive. Give both the progressive (present) and the punctual (aorist) for each.

1. μέγα νομίζομεν ἀγαθὸν εἰ ἀλλήλοις φίλοι γιγνόμεθα.

2. βιβλία ἀνελίσσοντες κοινῇ μετ' ἀλλήλων ἐκλεγόμεθα ἅτινα εὑρίσκομεν ἀγαθά.

3. εἴ τι ἔχομεν ἀγαθόν, διδάσκομεν ἀεὶ ἀλλήλοις βοηθήσαντες.

4. φίλοις συνίστημι παρ᾽ ὧν νομίζω βοηθῆσαί τι αὐτοῖς εἰς ἀρετήν.

5. τοὺς θησαυροὺς τῶν πάλαι σοφῶν ἀνδρῶν, οὓς ἐκεῖνοι καταλίπουσι ἐν βιβλίοις γράψαντες, ἀνελίσσομεν κοινῇ.

6. ὅτε παραγίγνεται ὁ Περσεὺς εἰς Αἰθιοπίαν, εὑρίσκει τὴν κόρην παρα-κειμένην βορὰν θαλασσίῳ θηρί.

7. ὁ Περσεὺς βούλεται γῆμαι τὴν θυγατέρα εἰ δίδωσιν αὐτὴν αὐτῷ ὁ πατὴρ σώσαντι.

8. ὁ θεὸς ἐχρήσατο τὴν ἀπαλλαγὴν τῆς συμφορᾶς εἰ τὴν θυγατέρα προτιθέασι τῷ θηρὶ βοράν.

9. ὅτε εὔχονται αἱ Νηρηίδες τῷ θαλασσίῳ θεῷ, πέμπει θηρά τινα ἐπὶ τὴν χώραν.

10. ὅτε σῴζει τὴν κόρην, ὁ πατὴρ δίδωσιν αὐτὴν τῷ ἀνδρὶ γυναῖκα.

V. REPHRASE each of the following coupled sentences so that the second expresses the purpose for the first (both progressive and punctual).

1. ἀνελίσσομεν βιβλία κοινῇ μετ᾽ ἀλλήλων. ἀγαθὰ δέ τινα εὑρίσκομεν τῶν πάλαι σοφῶν ἀνδρῶν.

2. φίλοις συνίστημι. διερχόμεθα δὲ κοινῇ τὰ βιβλία τῶν πάλαι σοφῶν ἀνδρῶν.

3. ἀποκτείνει ὁ Περσεὺς τὸν θῆρα. σῴζει δὲ τὴν κόρην.

4. προτιθέασι τὴν κόρην τῷ θηρὶ βοράν. ἀπαλλαγὴ δὲ τῆς συμφορᾶς ἐστι.

5. γράφουσιν ἄνδρες βιβλία. θησαυροὺς δὲ καταλείπουσιν ἀνθρώποις.

VI. REPHRASE each of the following sentences, making it the substance of what you fear (φόβερός εἰμι . . .). Contrast this structure with what would be required if the idea were introduced by ἔφη. . . .

1. οὐκ ἐβοήθησε ὁ φιλόσοφος τοῖς φίλοις εἰς ἀρετήν.

2. ἤρισε ἡ Κασσιέπεια ταῖς Νηρηίσιν.

3. οὐκ ἔσχον τι ἀγαθὸν διδάσκων.

4. οὐκ ἔσωσε τὴν κόρην ὁ νυμφίος.

5. εἶδεν ὁ θὴρ τὴν κόρην παρακειμένην βοράν.

VII. NOTE THE PATTERN in each of the quotations and compose a trans-lation of the English sentences, using the same pattern.

1. ἀκούσωμεν τοῦ ἀνδρός. —Πλάτων

Let's drink some wine!

Let's see what you found in the book!

2. νέος δ᾽ ἀπόλλυθ᾽ ὅντιν᾽ ἂν φιλῇ θεός. —Στοβαῖος (ἀπόλλυθ᾽ = ἀπόλλυται; ὅντιν᾽ = ὅντινα; φιλῇ contraction for the verb φιλέῃ "love")

We select whatever we find worthy.

Whomever the gods don't kill dies an old man.

3. οὐδὲν ἡ μάθησις ἂν μὴ νοῦς παρῇ. —Μένανδρος (ἡ μάθησις = τὸ μαθεῖν; παρῇ/πάρ-ειμι)

Life is nothing unless (ἐὰν μὴ) you enjoy friends.

Giving birth is nothing unless you happen to be a woman. (*See* page 74 no. 5.)

4. ἀρετὴ δὲ κἂν θάνῃ τις οὐκ ἀπόλλυται. —Εὐριπίδης

Chance rules over mankind even if the gods ever do exist.

5. ἢν ἐγγὺς ἔλθῃ θάνατος, οὐδεὶς βούλεται θνήσκειν. —Εὐριπίδης (ἢν = ἐάν; ἐγγύς adv. near)

If ever all mankind is well off, no doctor can be well off.

6. κύνας τρέφεις ἵνα σοι τοὺς λύκους ἀπὸ τῶν προβάτων ἀπερύκωσι. —'Ηρόδοτος

We read books in order to aid our friends.

7. πατρὶς γάρ ἐστι πᾶσ' ἵν' ἂν πράττῃ τις εὖ. —'Αριστοφάνης

Home is wherever one has friends.

14   Optative

πλούσιον νομίζοιμι τὸν σοφὸν εἶναι. —Πλάτων

Lesson 14

**Optative/
Independent
Usage: 'Hope'**

The optative, like the indicative and the subjunctive, is another mood of the Greek verb. Its function is the *direct and emotive expression of a hope, wish, or prayer* (so named from the Latin *opto* 'wish').

πλούσιον νομίζοιμι τὸν σοφὸν εἶναι.   May I consider the wise man wealthy.

Contrast such an optative expression with the indicative and the subjunctive moods.

πλούσιον νομίζω τὸν σοφὸν εἶναι.   I consider the wise man wealthy. (Indicative: statement of fact.)

πλούσιον νομίζωμεν τὸν σοφὸν εἶναι.   Let's consider the wise man wealthy. (Subjunctive: direct expression of volition.)

**Optative/
Aspect**

Like the participle, infinitive, and subjunctive, the optative does not express tense or time but only verbal aspect. The indicative alone in Greek can express tense.

πλούσιον νομίζοιμι τὸν σοφὸν εἶναι.   May I (be constantly) consider(ing) the wise man wealthy. (Formed from the present verbal stem.)

πλούσιον νομίσαιμι τὸν σοφὸν εἶναι.   May I (once and for all) consider the wise man wealthy. (Formed from the aorist stem.)

**Optative/
Independent
Usage:
'Possibility'**

You have already seen that the particle *ἄν* implies *eventuality* and that it can be used with a subjunctive in subordinate clauses to give the clause a generalized meaning (*See* page 85).

The particle *ἄν* can also be used with the *optative in independent clauses to express a possibility or potential*. Although the optative cannot express tense but only aspect, this structure implies that the possibility or potential exists either now or at some future time.

*ὕδωρ δὲ πίνων οὐδὲν ἂν τέκοι σοφόν.
—Κρατῖνος*   "While drinking water, he is not likely to give birth to anything intelligent." That is, no one is apt to compose anything good if he drinks water instead of wine. Another way of translating this structure is "he may give birth," which contrasts with the structure without *ἄν*: *τέκοι* "May he give birth."

Contrast the progressive statement of the same idea.

ὕδωρ δὲ πίνων οὐδὲν ἂν τίκτοι σοφόν.   No one sober is apt to be giving birth to anything intelligent.

**Indicative with *AN*
/Past Possibility**   When this same particle *ἄν* is used with a *past tense of the indicative*, it expresses an eventuality, possibility, or potential that existed in the past.

ὕδωρ δὲ πίνων οὐδὲν ἄν ἔτικτε σοφόν.   No one sober was likely to be giving birth to anything intelligent. *Or* might be giving birth . . ..

ὕδωρ δὲ πίνων οὐδὲν ἄν ἔτεκε σοφόν.   No one sober was likely to give birth to anything intelligent.

In both the present potential (optative with ἄν) and the past potential (past indicative with ἄν), the position of the particle ἄν does not matter. It usually has some proximity to the verb that it modifies, but sometimes for particular effects or emphasis it is placed elsewhere or even stated more than once.

Optative/ Dependent Usage: Secondary Subordination

In addition to the independent uses of the optative, the verb in any dependent clause can be optative when the main clause is in a past (or secondary) tense. The optative in this usage is never obligatory: it functions as a *possible* substitute in past tense contexts for verbs in many kinds of dependent clauses, both indicative (indirect quotation, indirect question) and subjunctive (purpose, fear, generalizing). This so-called optative of secondary subordination is never accompanied by the particle ἄν, even when it is substituted for a generalized clause (subjunctive with ἄν) in past contexts.

Indirect quotation:

λέγει ὅτι ὁ σοφὸς ἑαυτὸν γιγνώσκει.   He says that the wise man knows himself.

ἔλεγε ὅτι ὁ σοφὸς ἑαυτὸν {ἐγίγνωσκε. / γιγνώσκοι.}   He said that the wise man knew himself.

Purpose:

στρατεύομεν ἵνα μαχώμεθα θείᾳ τύχῃ.   We are going to war in order to fight with divine chance.

ἐστρατεύομεν ἵνα {μαχώμεθα / μαχοίμεθα} θείᾳ τύχῃ.   We were going to war in order to fight with divine chance.

Fear:

φοβερός εἰμι μὴ μάχωμαι θείᾳ τύχῃ.   I am afraid lest I fight with divine chance.

φοβερὸς ἦ μὴ {μάχωμαι / μαχοίμην} θείᾳ τύχῃ.   I was afraid lest I fight with divine chance.

Generalized clause:

ἀεὶ καλὸς πλοῦς ἐσθ' ὅταν φεύγῃς κακά.   It is always fair sailing whenever you flee troubles.

ἀεὶ καλὸς πλοῦς ἦν {ὅταν φεύγῃς / ὅτε φεύγοις} κακά.   It was always fair sailing whenever you fled troubles.

All subordinate clauses indirectly quoted in past tense contexts:

ἔφη ἕκαστον κρίνειν καλῶς ἃ γιγνώσκοι.   He said each man judged well what he knew. *Or* . . . whatever he knew. (The distinction between particular and generalized clauses is lost.)

ἔφη εἰ ἔχοι τι διδόναι τοῖς φίλοις.　　He said that if he had anything he gave it to his friends.

In all instances, the optative structures are the more ordinary way of expressing the idea; retention of the verb in the indicative or subjunctive is more vivid or emphatic. *Note*, however, that the optative is appropriate for past contexts; present indicatives do not shift to the optative: *ἔφη ἕκαστον κρίνειν καλῶς ἃ γιγνώσκει*/ "He said each man judges (or judged) well what he knows."

Negation/ MH and OT

The adverb *οὐ* is used to negate past potentials (past tense of the indicative plus *ἄν*) and present-future potentials (optative plus *ἄν*) since these are both statements of fact, but the adverb *μή* is used to negate the independent optative expressing "hope," etc. and for the optative of secondary subordination when it is substituted into a structure that would ordinarily have required *μή* (*see* page 68).

Optative/ Conjugation

The sign of the optative is the suffix *-ι-* or *-ιη-*. This suffix is added to the verbal stem either thematically (the variable vowel is always *o* for the optative) or athematically. Secondary personal suffixes (*see* page 28) are used for the optative.

Thematic

　παιδευ-o-ί-μην

　　λαβ-o-ί-μην

Athematic

　　ἱστα-ί-μην

　　τιθε-ί-μην

　παιδευσα-ί-μην

　　βα-ί-μην

The optative is never augmented since it does not indicate tense or time. The chart on the next pages adds the optative conjugation (final column) to the verbal forms you have learned thus far and is therefore suitable for review and reference as well as for learning the new conjugation.

Note that in the athematic verbs the optative sign *-ι-/-ιη-* combines with the stem to form a diphthong in pronunciation: *τιθείην, τιθείμην*.

Note that the optative suffix *-ιη-* occurs only in the singular active of the athematic conjugation. Contrast the forms *παιδεύοιμι* and *τιθείην*.

Note that in the athematic conjugation the verbal stem always occurs in its reduced form (that is, *τιθε-* rather than *τιθη-*) in both the subjunctive (where it has contracted with the endings) and in the optative. The unreduced form occurs only in the singular of the indicative present and imperfect *active*.

Note that *δείκνυμι* is thematically conjugated in the optative and does not contract in the subjunctive: *δεικνύῃς/δεκνύοις*.

Formed from the present stem (all indicate progressive action except the indicative, which does not distinguish between progressive and punctual aspects):

Thematic

Primary		Secondary	
Present	Subjunctive	Imperfect	Optative
παιδεύ- ω	ω	$\boxed{ἐ}$ παίδευ- ον	παιδεύ- οιμι
εις	ῃς		ες	οις
ει	ῃ	ε	οι
ομεν	ωμεν	ομεν	οιμεν
ετε	ητε	ετε	οιτε
ουσι	ωσι	ον	οιεν
ομαι	ωμαι	όμην	οί μην
ει	ῃ	ου	οιο
εται	ηται	ετο	οιτο
όμεθα	ώμεθα	όμεθα	οί μεθα
εσθε	ησθε	εσθε	οισθε
ονται	ωνται	οντο	οιντο

Athematic except for the subjunctive (which is always thematic)

τίθη- δίδω- ἵστη- ἵη- δείκνῡ- } μι ς σι	τιϑ- ἱστ- ἱ- διδ- } ῶ ῆς* ῇ*	ἐτίθη- ἵστη- ἵη- ἐδείκνῡ- } ν* ς* ─*	τιθε- ἱστα- διδο- ἱε- } ίην ίης ίη
τίθε- δίδο- ἵστα- ἵε- δείκνυ- } μεν τε ασι*	ὦμεν ῆτε* ὦσι	ἐτίθε- ἵστα- ἵε- ἐδείκνυ- ἐδίδο- } μεν τε σαν	ἵμεν ἵτε ἵεν
μαι	ὦμαι	μην	ί μην
σαι	ῇ*	σο	ἵο
ται	ῆται*	το	ἵτο
μεθα	ώμεθα	μεθα	ἵμεθα
σϑε	ῆσϑε*	σϑε	ἵσϑε
νται	ὦνται	ντο	ἵντο

*ἱστᾶσι, ἱᾶσι

*δίδωμι has ω throughout διδῷς, διδῷ, διδῶτε, etc.

*ἐδίδ-ουν, -ους, -ου
ἐτίϑ-ην, -εις, -ει
ἵ-ην, -εις, -ει

Formed from the aorist stem (all indicate punctual aspect):

Thematic

Primary	Secondary	
Subjunctive	Aorist Indic.	Optative
λάβ-ω	ἔ-λαβ-ον	λάβ-οιμι
ης	ες	οις
η	ε	οι
ωμεν	ομεν	οιμεν
ητε	ετε	οιτε
ωσι	ον	οιεν
ωμαι	ό μην	οί μην
η	ου	οιο
ηται	ετο	οιτο
ώμεθα	ό μεθα	οί μεθα
ησθε	εσθε	οισθε
ωνται	οντο	οιντο

Athematic

παιδεύσ-ω	ἐ-παίδευ-σα	παιδεύσα-ιμι
ης	-σα-ς	ις
η	-σε	ι
ωμεν	-σα-μεν	ιμεν
ητε	-σα-τε	ιτε
ωσι	-σα-ν	ιεν
ωμαι	-σα μην	ι μην
η	-σω	ιο
ηται	-σα-το	ιτο
ώμεθα	-σα-μεθα	ιμεθα
ησθε	-σα-σθε	ισθε
ωνται	-σα-ντο	ιντο

β	ω̄	ἔ-βη	ν*	βα	ίην
γν		ἔ-γνω		γνο	
ϑ	η̄ς	ἔ-στη	ς*	ϑε	ίης
στ		ἔ-δῡ	—*	στα	ίη
δ	η̄			δο	
̔				έ	
	ω̄μεν	ἔ-ϑε	μεν		ίμεν
	η̄τε	ἔ-δο	τε		ίτε
	ω̄σι	ει	σαν		ίεν

β	ὦμαι	ἔ-βη	μην		βα	ἴμην
**γν	ἦ	ἔ-γνω	σο		γνο	ἴο
ϑ	ἧται	ἔ-στη	το		ϑε	ἶτο
στ	ὤμεϑα	ἔ-δῦ	μεϑα		στα	ἴμεϑα
**δ	ἦσϑε	***ἔ-ϑε	σϑε		δο	ἶσϑε
	ὦνται	***ἔ-δο	ντο		ἐ	ἶντο
		εἶ				

Note (*): ἔδωκ-α, -ας, -ε/ἔϑηκ-α, -ας, -ε/ἧκ-α, -ας, -ε.

Note (**): maintains ω throughout: γνῶ, γνῷς, γνῷ, etc. /δῶ, δῷς, δῷ, etc.

Note (***): *see* page 50 note.

Note that in the second person singular optative middle-passive *sigma* is lost: παιδεύ-ο-ι-σο → παιδεύ-ο-ι-ο, etc.

Review also infinitives and participles, pages 64–66.

Optative Conjugation of EIMI

The conjugation of the "irregular" athematic verb εἰμί is formed with its stem ἐσ- with the *sigma* lost: ἐσ-μέν/ἐ(σ)-ω-μεν → ὦ-μεν/ἤ(σ)-μεν → ἦ-μεν/ ἐ(σ)-ιη-μεν → ε-ἴη-μεν.

Pres. Indicative	Subjunctive	Imper. Indic.	Optative
εἰμί	ὦ	ἦ/ἤν	εἴην
εἶ	ἦς	ἦσϑα	εἴης
ἐστί	ἦ	ἦν	εἴη
ἐσμέν	ὦμεν	ἦμεν	εἴημεν/εἶμεν
ἐστέ	ἦτε	ἦτε	εἴητε/εἶτε
εἰσί(ν)	ὦσι(ν)	ἦσαν	εἴησαν/εἶεν

ONOMATA KAI PHMATA

ἡ φρήν, φρενός	= ὁ νοῦς, midriff (as seat of life, intellect), heart (as seat of passions)
τὸ ἔργον, -ου	work, deed
τὸ ζῷον, -ου	living creature, animal (*see* ἡ ζωή)
ἡ γνώμη, -ης	thought, mind
τὸ φάρμακον, -ου	drug
ὁ κρατήρ, -ῆρος	mixing bowl in which wine was mixed with water
ὁ φόβος, -ου	fear (*see* φοβερός, -ά, -όν)
τὸ δεῖπνον, -ου	dinner

ὁ λέων, -οντος	lion
τὸ δέρμα, -ατος	skin, hide (*see* δέρω flay, skin)
ὁ δοῦλος, -ου	slave, servant
ὁ δεσπότης, -ου	master
δῆλος, -η, -ον	manifest, visible (*see* the more intensive κατάδηλος, -ον)
ἑτοῖμος, -η, -ον	at hand, ready
θερμός, -ή, -όν	hot
λοιπός, -ή, -όν	remaining over, left (*see* λείπω)
ἀμφότερος, -α, -ον	both
εὐδαίμων, -ον (gen. -ονος)	blessed with a good spirit, fortunate (εὐ + δαίμων a divine power)
πλούσιος, -α, -ον	wealthy (*see,* ὁ πλοῦτος, -ου wealth)
κρατιστεύω, _____	be mightiest (*see* τὸ κράτος might, power/ κράτιστος, -η, -ον mightiest)
οἴχομαι, _____	be gone
ἁρπάζω, ἥρπασα	snatch away, seize
καθίζομαι (or καθέζομαι), ἐκαθισάμην	sit down
θέλγω, ἔθελξα	enchant, beguile
σπεύδω, ἔσπευσα	strive after, hasten, be eager
ἡδέως	*adv.* with pleasure, pleasurably (*see* ἥδομαι/ἀηδῶς, that is ἀ + ἡδέως)
πάνυ	altogether, very (*see* πᾶς, πᾶσα, πᾶν)
αὐτίκα	immediately
σπουδῇ	hastily (*see* σπεύδω/ἡ σπουδή, -ῆς)
ἄγαν	very much, too much

Note the agential suffix -ηρ (*see* page 43) on κρατήρ, the mix*er* (κεράννυμι mix).

Note the diminutive suffix -ιον (*see* page 81) on ζῷον.

Note the verbal suffix -ι/αζω (*see* page 52) on ἁρπάζω.

ΑΣΚΗΣΙΣ

I. TRANSLATE: On Man's Godlike Superiority over Beasts.
   οὐ γὰρ πάνυ σοι κατάδηλον ὅτι παρὰ τἆλλα ζῷα ὥσπερ θεοὶ ἄνθρωποι

βιοτεύουσι, τῷ σώματι καὶ τῇ ψυχῇ κρατιστεύοντες; οὔτε γὰρ θηρός τινος
ἂν ἔχων σῶμα, ἀνθρώπου δὲ γνώμην ἐδύνατ' ἄν τις πράττειν ἃ ἐβούλετο.
—Adapted from Ξενοφῶν

Socrates' Clever Remarks at Dinner.

῎Αλλου δὲ λέγοντος ὅτι ἀηδῶς ἐσθίοι, "᾽Ακουμενός," ἔφη ὁ Σωκράτης,
5 "τούτου φάρμακον ἀγαθὸν διδάσκει." ἐρομένου δέ, "Ποῖον;" "Παύεσθαι
ἐσθίοντα," ἔφη.

῎Αλλου δ' αὖ λέγοντος ὅτι θερμὸν εἴη παρ' ἑαυτῷ τὸ ὕδωρ ὃ πίνοι, "῞Οταν
ἄρ'," ἔφη, "βούλῃ θερμῷ λούεσθαι, ἑτοῖμον ἔσται σοι." —Ξενοφῶν

Two Prayers for Friendship.

Μή μοι ἀνὴρ εἴη γλώσσῃ φίλος, ἀλλὰ καὶ ἔργῳ,
10 χερσίν τε σπεύδοι χρήμασί τ', ἀμφότερα.
μηδὲ παρὰ κρητῆρι λόγοισιν ἐμήν φρένα θέλγοι,
ἀλλ' ἔρδων φαίνοιτ', εἴ τι δύναιτ', ἀγαθόν.

Εὐδαίμων εἴην καὶ θεοῖς φίλος ἀθανάτοισιν,
Κύρν', ἀρετῆς δ' ἄλλης οὐδεμῆς ἔραμαι. —Θέογνις

A Troezenian Legend about the Young Theseus.

15 Τῶν δὲ ἐν Τροιζῆνι λόγων, οὓς ἐς Θησέα λέγουσίν, ἐστιν ὡς Ηρακλῆς ἐς
Τροίζηνα ἐλθὼν παρὰ Πιτθέα καθέζοιτο ἐπὶ τῷ δείπνῳ, τοῦ λέοντος τὸ
δέρμα κατατιθείς, ἐσέλθοιεν δὲ παρ' αὐτὸν ἄλλοι τε Τροιζηνίων παῖδες
καὶ Θησεὺς ἔτι νέος ὤν. τοὺς μὲν δὴ λοιποὺς παῖδας, ὡς τὸ δέρμα εἶδον,
φεύγοντάς φασιν οἴχεσθαι, Θησέα δὲ ὑπεξελθόντα οὐκ ἄγαν σὺν φόβῳ
20 παρὰ τῶν διακόνων ἁρπάσαι πέλεκυν καὶ αὐτίκα μάχεσθαι σπουδῇ,
λέοντα εἶναι τὸ δέρμα νομίζοντα. —Adapted from Παυσανίας

Reading Notes:

(1) παρὰ τἆλλα ζῷα/παρὰ τὰ ἄλλα ζῷα "(put) beside," that is "in contrast
to"... (accusative with goal directed motion, see page 56).

(1) ὥσπερ/distinguish ὡς relative adverb (see page 78) from ὡς = ὅτι and
ὡς = ὅτε. It is accented here because it is followed by the enclitic particle
—περ.

(2) βιοτεύουσι/βιοτεύω "live" (see ὁ βίος, -ου "life")

(4) ᾽Ακουμενὸς ἰατρὸς ἦν.

(5) ἐρομένου/ἔρομαι "ask" (genitive absolute with the second element omitted:
ἄλλου ἐρομένου)

(5) ποῖον;/ποῖος, -α, -ον (see page 78)

(8) θερμῷ (namely ὕδατι)

(8) ἔσται/future of ἐστί

(9) γλώσσῃ ... ἔργῳ Greek authors often contrast what is said (λόγος) with
what in fact is done (ἔργον).

(10) χερσίν = χειρσί(ν)

(10) ἀμφότερα adverbial accusative

(11) λόγοισιν = λόγοις The additional ending -ι(ν) is often added to the dative plural of noun Types I and II in poetry.

(12) ἔρδων/ἔρδω "do" (see ἔργον)

(13) κρητῆρι = κρατῆρι Theognis writes in the Ionic dialect (the language as it was spoken on the Ionian islands and in certain cities on the coast of Asia Minor). In this dialect, η after ε, ι, or ρ did not change to α (see page 13); hence (14). οὐδεμιῆς = οὐδεμιᾶς.

(14) Κύρν'/Κύρνε, a man's name (ὁ Κύρνος) in the declensional case used for direct naming or calling (vocative)

(14) ἔραμαι "love" (see ὁ ἔρως, -ωτος), athematic like δύναμαι

(15) ἡ Τροιζήν, -ῆνος Troizen, a town on the northern coast of the Argolid where Theseus was born and spent his childhood

(15) ἐς = εἰς

(17) κατατιθείς/κατα-τίθημι

(17) ἐσέλθοιεν/ἐσ-έρχομαι

(19) ὑπεξελθόντα/ὑπ-εξ-έρχομαι

(20) διακόνων/ὁ διάκονος, -ου = δοῦλος (see deacon)

(20) πέλεκυν accusative of ὁ πέλεκυς, axe

II. CHANGE each verb to the optative.

1. ἁρπαζόμεθα	11. ἦλθον
2. ἔσπευσε	12. εἶδεν
3. νομίζεις	13. ἐποίησα
4. ὑπέσχου	14. οἴχει
5. ἐμαχήσω	15. δύνασαι
6. κατέθηκε	16. βούλει
7. ἤδεσθε	17. ἀπόλλυσαι
8. ἀπέδοσαν	18. ἐγένετο
9. ἧκα	19. ἦσαν
10. ἔτεμες	20. ὑπεκρίνω

III. MATCH the second verb to the first by changing it into the same form.

1. ᾠχόμην (ἀποτίθημι)	6. ὑποσχέσθαι (ἐσθίω)
2. ἤδωμαι (μάχομαι)	7. βαίης (δίδωμι)
3. ἱείη (νομίζω)	8. εἴλετε (τίκτω)
4. παιδεῦσαι (ἔχομαι)	9. ἀποθνήσκοιεν (ἀποδίδωμι)
5. ἀποκτεῖναι (ἀφίστημι)	10. εἶχε (πάσχω)

11. μάθῃς (βασιλεύω)   16. δούς (κρίνω)

12. δύναιο (γιγνώσκω)   17. ἧκας (φέρω)

13. εὕροις (γράφω)   18. στῶσι (δείκνυμι)

14. εἴην (ἵημι)   19. εἴποιμι (ἵημι)

15. γνῷ (λαμβάνω)   20. πείθοιμι (ἵστημι)

IV. REPHRASE each sentence, changing it from an expression of a past potential ("it was likely…") to a present-future potential ("it is likely…").

1. πλούσιον ἐνόμιζεν ἂν ὁ Σωκράτης τὸν σοφὸν εἶναι.

2. οὐκ ἂν ἐδύνατο πράττειν τις ἃ ἐβούλετο.

3. οὐ πάνυ σοι κατάδηλον ἂν ἦν.

4. τοῦ ἀεὶ ἀηδῶς ἐσθίειν φάρμακον ἀγαθὸν ἐδίδαξεν ἂν ὁ ἰατρός.

5. θερμῷ ἐλούεσθε ἂν ὕδατι.

6. οὗτος ἂν ἦν μοι φίλος ἀγαθὸς λόγῳ μὲν, οὐδὲ ἔργῳ.

7. εὐδαίμονες ἂν ἦμεν ἀποθανόντες.

8. τάδε εἴπετε ἄν.

9. ἔστη ἂν ἀεὶ ὁ φίλος παρὰ τῇ κρατῆρι.

10. ἔπιεν ἂν ὕδατος θερμοῦ.

V. REPHRASE each sentence, changing to a past tense context and using the optative of secondary subordination.

1. οἱ Τροιζήνιοί φασιν ὅτι ὁ Ἡρακλῆς ἦλθέ ποτε παρὰ Πιτθέα.

2. λέγουσιν ὡς ᾤχοντο φεύγοντες οἱ ἄλλοι παῖδες πάντες.

3. κατατίθησιν ὁ Ἡρακλῆς τὸ δέρμα ἵνα φάγῃ τε καί πίῃ μετὰ τῶν φίλων.

4. οὐκ ἄγαν φοβερός ἐστιν ὁ παῖς μὴ ἀποκτείνῃ αὐτὸν ὁ λέων.

5. ἀπερύκω ἀπ᾽ ἐμαυτοῦ φίλους τινὰς κακοὺς ἵνα μὴ θέλγωσιν ἐμὴν φρένα παρὰ τῇ κρατῆρι στάντες.

6. λέγει ὡς τυγχάνει ὁ Ἡρακλῆς φίλος ὢν ἑαυτῷ.

7. οὐχ ἥδομαι πίνων ὅταν ὦ μετὰ φίλων κακῶν.

8. ἀεὶ μάχεται οἷς ἂν ἴδῃ. (*See* page 75 note.)

9. ἀρετὴ κἂν θάνῃ τις οὐκ ἀπόλλυται.

10. δύνασαι ὕδατι λούεσθαι θερμῷ ὅταν βούλῃ.

VI. NOTE THE PATTERN in each of the quotations and compose a translation of the English sentences, using the same pattern.

1. δοῦλοι γὰρ ἂν καὶ δεσπόται οὐκ ἂν ποτε γένοιντο φίλοι. —Πλάτων

Word and deed are never likely to be the same thing.

Man and animal may both be beasts of some kind.

2. θεῶν διδόντων οὐκ ἂν ἐκφύγοις κακά. —Αἰσχύλος

When we die, the soul may not leave the body.

With the gods as enemies, we are not likely to be fortunate.

3. τοῦτο δὲ κἂν παῖς γνοίη. —Πλάτων

Not even an enemy would do that.

Even a doctor may be sick. (*See* page 85.)

4. τί ἂν ὑμῶν ἕκαστος ἐποίησεν? —᾿Ανδοκίδης

How many of the Greeks would have gone? (*See* page 78.)

How was he likely to have found the treasury?

5. πλούσιον νομίζοιμι τὸν σοφὸν εἶναι. —Πλάτων

May no one beguile my wits.

May the gods always be my friends.

15

Thematic Contract Verbs

τὸ γαμεῖν, ἐάν τις τὴν ἀλήθειαν σκοπῇ, κακὸν μέν ἐστιν, ἀλλ' ἀναγκαῖον κακόν. —Μένανδρος

Lesson 15
Contraction

In the Attic dialect, thematic verbs with stems ending in -ε-, -α-, and -ο- contracted the stem vowel with the following thematic (variable) vowel. (You have already seen similar contractions in the subjunctive of athematic verbs: page 86.)

ποιέ-ο-μεν ⟶ ποιοῦ-μεν
τιμά-ο-μεν ⟶ τιμῶ-μεν
δηλό-ο-μεν ⟶ δηλοῦ-μεν

These contractions are predictable (resulting from the slurring together of the two adjacent vowel sounds), but you will want to become familiar with the contracted forms since some very common verbs are of this type. In some of the other literary dialects, these contractions do not occur and you should, therefore, also be aware of the uncontracted forms.

The following rules summarize the nature of the contractions.

1. Two like vowels (that is, two *a*-sounds, two *e*-sounds, two *o*-sounds without regard to quantity) unite to form the common long ($\bar{\alpha}$, η, ω). Exceptions: $\varepsilon + \varepsilon \rightarrow \varepsilon\iota$; $o + o \rightarrow o\upsilon$.

2. An *o*-sound followed by an *a*- or an *e*-sound becomes ω. Exceptions: $o + \varepsilon$ or $\varepsilon + o \rightarrow o\upsilon$.

3. When an *a*-sound precedes or follows an *e*-sound, the first in order prevails: $\alpha + \varepsilon \rightarrow \bar{\alpha}$; $\varepsilon + \alpha \rightarrow \eta$.

4. Iota is never lost in contraction, although it may sometimes be written as the iota-subscript.

Conjugation

The chart presents the conjugations of three paradigmatic contract verbs. The -ό-ω contract verbs are less common than the others.

There are two exceptions to the paradigms. The verbs ζάω, χράω, and a few others always contract to an -η- wherever the paradigm has an -α-; and -έω verbs of two syllables (πλέω, πνέω, etc.) do not contract ε with ο or ω: hence, πνέ-ο-μεν, πνέ-ω-μεν, πλέ-ουσι.

Indicative Present

ΠΟΙΕ-
ΤΙΜΑ-
ΔΗΛΟ-

-ω ⟶	ποιῶ	τιμῶ	δηλῶ
-εις	ποιεῖς	τιμᾷς	δηλοῖς
-ει	ποιεῖ	τιμᾷ	δηλοῖ
-ο-μεν	ποιοῦμεν	τιμῶμεν	δηλοῦμεν
-ε-τε	ποιεῖτε	τιμᾶτε	δηλοῦτε
-ουσι	ποιοῦσι	τιμῶσι	δηλοῦσι
-ο-μαι	ποιοῦμαι	τιμῶμαι	δηλοῦμαι
-ει	ποιεῖ	τιμᾷ	δηλοῖ

-ε-ται	ποιεῖται	τιμᾶται	δηλοῦται
-ό-μεθα	ποιούμεθα	τιμώμεθα	δηλούμεθα
-ε-σθε	ποιεῖσθε	τιμᾶσθε	δηλοῦσθε
-ο-νται	ποιοῦνται	τιμῶνται	δηλοῦνται

Indicative Imperfect

ἐ-/ /-ο-ν⟶	ἐποίουν	ἐτίμων	ἐδήλουν
-ε-ς	ἐποίεις	ἐτίμας	ἐδήλους
-ε	ἐποίει	ἐτίμα	ἐδήλου
-ο-μεν	ἐποιοῦμεν	ἐτιμῶμεν	ἐδηλοῦμεν
-ε-τε	ἐποιεῖτε	ἐτιμᾶτε	ἐδηλοῦτε
-ο-ν	ἐποίουν	ἐτίμων	ἐδήλουν
-ό-μην	ἐποιούμην	ἐτιμώμην	ἐδηλούμην
-ου	ἐποιοῦ	ἐτιμῶ	ἐδηλοῦ
-ε-το	ἐποιεῖτο	ἐτιμᾶτο	ἐδηλοῦτο
-ό-μεθα	ἐποιούμεθα	ἐτιμώμεθα	ἐδηλούμεθα
-ε-σθε	ἐποιεῖσθε	ἐτιμᾶσθε	ἐδηλοῦσθε
-ο-ντο	ἐποιοῦντο	ἐτιμῶντο	ἐδηλοῦντο

Subjunctive

-ω⟶	ποιῶ	τιμῶ	δηλῶ
-ῃς	ποιῇς	τιμᾷς	δηλοῖς
-ῃ	ποιῇ	τιμᾷ	δηλοῖ
-ω-μεν	ποιῶμεν	τιμῶμεν	δηλῶμεν
-η-τε	ποιῆτε	τιμᾶτε	δηλῶτε
-ω-σι	ποιῶσι	τιμῶσι	δηλῶσι
-ω-μαι	ποιῶμαι	τιμῶμαι	δηλῶμαι
-ῃ	ποιῇ	τιμᾷ	δηλοῖ
-η-ται	ποιῆται	τιμᾶται	δηλῶται
-ώ-μεθα	ποιώμεθα	τιμώμεθα	δηλώμεθα
-η-σθε	ποιῆσθε	τιμᾶσθε	δηλῶσθε
-ω-νται	ποιῶνται	τιμῶνται	δηλῶνται

Optative

-ο-ι(η)-ν/-μι⟶	ποιοίην	τιμῴην	δηλοίην
	(ποιοῖμι)	(τιμῷμι)	(δηλοῖμι)
-ο-ι(η)-ς	ποιοίης	τιμῴης	δηλοίης
	(ποιοῖς)	(τιμῷς)	(δηλοῖς)
-ο-ι(η)	ποιοίη	τιμῴη	δηλοίη
	(ποιοῖ)	(τιμῷ)	(δηλοῖ)

-ο-ι(η)-μεν	ποιοῖμεν (ποιοίημεν)	τιμῷμεν (τιμῴημεν)	δηλοῖμεν (δηλοίημεν)
-ο-ι(η)-τε	ποιοῖτε (ποιοίητε)	τιμῷτε (τιμῴητε)	δηλοῖτε (δηλοίητε)
-ο-ι(η)-σαν/-εν	ποιοῖεν (ποιοίησαν)	τιμῷεν (τιμῴησαν)	δηλοῖεν (δηλοίησαν)
-ο-ι-μην	ποιοίμην	τιμῴμην	δηλοίμην
-ο-ι-ο	ποιοῖο	τιμῷο	δηλοῖο
-ο-ι-το	ποιοῖτο	τιμῷτο	δηλοῖτο
-ο-ι-μεθα	ποιοίμεθα	τιμῴμεθα	δηλοίμεθα
-ο-ι-σθε	ποιοῖσθε	τιμῷσθε	δηλοῖσθε
-ο-ι-ντο	ποιοῖντο	τιμῷντο	δηλοῖντο

Note that the accent is recessive and falls where it would have fallen in the uncontracted form: ποιέ-εις→ποιεῖς/ἐποίε-ε-ς→ἐποίεις/ἐποιέ-ε-(σ)ο→ἐποιοῦ, etc.

Note that there are alternative forms for the optative active, using either the *-ι-* or the *-ιη-* optative sign. The forms in parentheses are less frequently used than the others.

Participle

Active

ΠΟΙΕ-
ΤΙΜΑ-
ΔΗΛΟ-

masculine

*-ο-ν(τ-ς)→*ποιῶν		τιμῶν	δηλῶν
-ο-ντ-α ποιοῦντα		τιμῶντα	δηλοῦντα
-ο-ντ-ος ποιοῦντος		τιμῶντος	δηλοῦντος

etc.

(dat. *pl.*)*-ο-ντ-σι* ποιοῦσι		τιμῶσι	δηλοῦσι

neuter

-ο-ν(τ)→ ποιοῦν		τιμῶν	δηλοῦν
-ο-ν(τ) ποιοῦν		τιμῶν	δηλοῦν
-ο-ντ-ος ποιοῦντος		τιμῶντος	δηλοῦντος

feminine

-ο-ντ-ια→ ποιοῦσα		τιμῶσα	δηλοῦσα
-ο-ντ-ιαν ποιοῦσαν		τιμῶσαν	δηλοῦσαν
-ο-ντ-ιης ποιοῦσης		τιμῶσης	δηλοῦσης

Middle-Passive

*-ο-μενος,→*ποιούμενος, *-η, -ον* *-η, -ον*		τιμώμενος, *-η, -ον*	δηλούμενος, *-η, -ον*

Infinitive

Active

$-ειν \rightarrow$	$ποιεῖν$	$τιμᾶν$	$δηλοῦν$

Middle-Passive

$-ε-σθαι \rightarrow$	$ποιεῖσθαι$	$τιμᾶσθαι$	$δηλοῦσθαι$

ΟΝΟΜΑΤΑ ΚΑΙ ΡΗΜΑΤΑ

ἡ ἀλήθεια, -ας	truth
ὁ βίος, -ου	life (usually "mode of life" instead of "animal life," ἡ ζωή, -ῆς)
ὁ πένης, -ητος	= ἀνὴρ οὐ πλούσιος ὤν (see ὁ πόνος, -ου work, suffering/πονηρός, -ή, -όν = κακός)
ἡ ἑορτή, -ῆς	festival
ὁ βωμός, -οῦ	altar
ἡ φωνή, -ῆς	sound, tone, voice, any articulate sound
ὁ φθόγγος, -ου	any clear sound, voice, utterance
ἡ φήμη, -ης	utterance prompted by the gods, prophetic saying, any voice or words, common report (see φημί)
ὁ οἰωνός, -οῦ	bird (usually a large bird of prey), omen (drawn from the appearance of such a bird)
ὁ ἱερός, -οῦ/ἡ ἱέρεια, -ας	priest/priestess (see ἱερός, -ή, -όν sacred)
τὸ ἱμάτιον, -ου	article of outer wear clothing, worn over the chiton, ὁ χιτών
ἀναγκαῖος, -α, -ον	necessary (see ἡ ἀνάγκη, -ης necessity)
καινός, -ή, -όν	new, novel (see νέος, -α, -ον new, young)
μέγιστος, -η, -ον	biggest, greatest (see μέγας, μεγάλη, μέγα)
θαυμάζω, ἐθαύμασα	wonder at (see τὸ θαῦμα, -ατος marvel)
θύω, ἔθυσα	sacrifice
σημαίνω, ἐσήμηνα	show by sign, signal (see τὸ σῆμα,

	-ατος sign, a sign marking a grave, that is, a grave monument)
τεκμαίρομαι, ἐτεκμηράμην	judge from signs and omens (*see* τὸ τέκμαρ *indeclinable* boundary sign)
αἰσθάνομαι, ἠσθόμην	perceive, see, hear
ἀδικέω, ἠδίκησα	be unjust, do wrong (*see* δίκαιος, -α, -ον/ἄδικος, -ον)
ὁράω (imperf. ἑώρων), εἶδον	see
ποιέω, ἐποίησα	do, make (*see* ὁ ποιητής, -οῦ/τὸ ποίημα -ατος)
χράομαι, ἐχρησάμην	have in use, have as something or someone necessary (with dative); *see* χρή it is necessary (with an infinitive phrase: χρὴ τὸν ποιητὴν ποιήματα ποιεῖν)/χρηστός, -ή, -όν good; distinguish the different set of meanings in χράω proclaim an oracle/χράομαι consult an oracle
ἀξιόω, ἠξίωσα	esteem worthy, place a value upon, with genitive for the price or estimation of value (*see* page 40); *see* ἄξιος, -α, -ον
τιμάω, ἐτίμησα	honor, (in legal language: estimate the amount of punishment for a condemned person, with genitive for amount, *see* page 40); ἡ τιμή, -ῆς esteem, honor, price
ζάω, ἔζησα	live, be alive (*see* ἡ ζωή, -ῆς/βιόω live, pass one's life)
γαμέω, ἔγημα	marry (*see* ὁ γάμος, -ου)
σκοπέω, _____	contemplate, consider, examine
δηλόω, ἐδήλωσα	make manifest, show (*see* δῆλος, -η, -ον/distinguish δείκνυμι point out, show)
εὐτυχέω, ηὐτύχησα	be fortunate (*see* εὖ = καλῶς + ἡ τυχή, -ῆς/ contrast the antonym δυστυχέω)
πολλάκις adv.	many times (*see* πολύς, πολλή, πολύ)

Note that the aorist stem of thematic contract verbs *often* is formed by adding the -σα- suffix on to the present stem with its final vowel lengthened: τιμάω, ἐ-τίμη-σα/ποιέω, ἐ-ποίη-σα/ δηλόω, ἐ-δήλω-σα.

Note that thematic contract verbs in -άω are derived from Type I nouns

($\tau\iota\mu\acute{\alpha}$-$\omega$, $\acute{\eta}$ $\tau\iota\mu\acute{\eta}$, -$\tilde{\eta}\varsigma$) and contract verbs in -$\acute{\epsilon}\omega$ and -$\acute{o}\omega$ are den.
from Type II nouns ($\gamma\alpha\mu\acute{\epsilon}$-$\omega$, $\acute{o}$ $\gamma\acute{\alpha}\mu o\varsigma$, -$ov$/$\beta\iota\acute{o}$-$\omega$, $\acute{o}$ $\beta\acute{\iota}o\varsigma$, -$ov$).

Note that the abverbial suffix -$\alpha\kappa\iota\varsigma$ denotes repetition: $\pi o\lambda\lambda\acute{\alpha}\kappa\iota\varsigma$ "many times"/
$\dot{\epsilon}\kappa\alpha\sigma\tau\acute{\alpha}\kappa\iota\varsigma$ "each time"/$\tau\epsilon\tau\rho\acute{\alpha}\kappa\iota\varsigma$ "four times"/$\acute{o}\sigma\acute{\alpha}\kappa\iota\varsigma$ "as many times as" (*see* page 78)/$\acute{o}\lambda\iota\gamma\acute{\alpha}\kappa\iota\varsigma$ "few times."

Note that the imperfect of $\acute{o}\rho\acute{\alpha}\omega$ has an irregular augment: $\dot{\epsilon}\acute{\omega}\rho\omega\nu$.

Review the present forming suffix -$\alpha\nu$-o/ϵ- (*see* page 31) on $\alpha\dot{\iota}\sigma\vartheta$-$\acute{\alpha}\nu$-$o$-$\mu\alpha\iota$/
$\tilde{\eta}\sigma\vartheta$-$\acute{o}$-$\mu\eta\nu$.

$\mathit{A\Sigma KH\Sigma I\Sigma}$

I. TRANSLATE: The Indictment against Socrates for Impiety.

$\Pi o\lambda\lambda\acute{\alpha}\kappa\iota\varsigma$ $\dot{\epsilon}\vartheta\alpha\acute{v}\mu\alpha\sigma\alpha$ $\tau\acute{\iota}\sigma\iota$ $\pi o\tau\grave{\epsilon}$ $\lambda\acute{o}\gamma o\iota\varsigma$ $'A\vartheta\eta\nu\alpha\acute{\iota}ov\varsigma$ $\acute{\epsilon}\pi\epsilon\iota\sigma\alpha\nu$ $o\acute{\iota}$ $\gamma\rho\alpha\psi\acute{\alpha}\mu\epsilon\nu o\iota$
$\Sigma\omega\kappa\rho\acute{\alpha}\tau\eta\nu$ $\dot{\omega}\varsigma$ $\acute{\alpha}\xi\iota o\varsigma$ $\epsilon\check{\iota}\eta$ $\vartheta\alpha\nu\acute{\alpha}\tau ov$ $\tau\tilde{\eta}$ $\pi\acute{o}\lambda\epsilon\iota$. $\acute{\eta}$ $\mu\grave{\epsilon}\nu$ $\gamma\grave{\alpha}\rho$ $\gamma\rho\alpha\phi\grave{\eta}$ $\kappa\alpha\tau'$ $\alpha\dot{v}\tauo\tilde{v}$
$\tauo\iota\acute{\alpha}\delta\epsilon$ $\tau\iota\varsigma$ $\tilde{\eta}\nu$· $\acute{\alpha}\delta\iota\kappa\epsilon\tilde{\iota}$ $\Sigma\omega\kappa\rho\acute{\alpha}\tau\eta\varsigma$ $o\ddot{v}\varsigma$ $\mu\grave{\epsilon}\nu$ $\acute{\eta}$ $\pi\acute{o}\lambda\iota\varsigma$ $\nu o\mu\acute{\iota}\zeta\epsilon\iota$ $\vartheta\epsilon o\grave{v}\varsigma$ $o\dot{v}$ $\nu o\mu\acute{\iota}\zeta\omega\nu$,
$\acute{\epsilon}\tau\epsilon\rho\alpha$ $\delta\grave{\epsilon}$ $\kappa\alpha\iota\nu\grave{\alpha}$ $\delta\alpha\iota\mu\acute{o}\nu\iota\alpha$ $\epsilon\dot{\iota}\sigma\phi\acute{\epsilon}\rho\omega\nu$· $\acute{\alpha}\delta\iota\kappa\epsilon\tilde{\iota}$ $\delta\grave{\epsilon}$ $\kappa\alpha\grave{\iota}$ $\tauo\grave{v}\varsigma$ $\nu\acute{\epsilon}ov\varsigma$ $\delta\iota\alpha\phi\vartheta\epsilon\acute{\iota}\rho\omega\nu$.
5 —$\Xi\epsilon\nu o\phi\tilde{\omega}\nu$

Socrates' Reply to the Indictment for Impiety.

$'A\lambda\lambda'$ $\dot{\epsilon}\gamma\grave{\omega}$, $\tilde{\omega}$ $\acute{\alpha}\nu\delta\rho\epsilon\varsigma$, $\tauo\tilde{v}\tauo$ $\mu\grave{\epsilon}\nu$ $\pi\rho\tilde{\omega}\tauo\nu$ $\vartheta\alpha\nu\mu\acute{\alpha}\zeta\omega$ $M\epsilon\lambda\acute{\eta}\tauov$, $\acute{o}\tau\omega$ $\pi o\tau\grave{\epsilon}$ $\gamma\nuo\grave{v}\varsigma$
$\lambda\acute{\epsilon}\gamma\epsilon\iota$ $\dot{\omega}\varsigma$ $\dot{\epsilon}\gamma\grave{\omega}$ $o\ddot{v}\varsigma$ $\acute{\eta}$ $\pi\acute{o}\lambda\iota\varsigma$ $\nu o\mu\acute{\iota}\zeta\epsilon\iota$ $\vartheta\epsilon o\grave{v}\varsigma$ $o\dot{v}$ $\nu o\mu\acute{\iota}\zeta\omega$· $\dot{\epsilon}\pi\epsilon\grave{\iota}$ $\vartheta\acute{v}o\nu\tau\acute{\alpha}$ $\gamma\acute{\epsilon}$ $\mu\epsilon$ $\dot{\epsilon}\nu$
$\tau\alpha\tilde{\iota}\varsigma$ $\kappa o\iota\nu\alpha\tilde{\iota}\varsigma$ $\dot{\epsilon}o\rho\tau\alpha\tilde{\iota}\varsigma$ $\kappa\alpha\grave{\iota}$ $\dot{\epsilon}\pi\grave{\iota}$ $\tau\tilde{\omega}\nu$ $\delta\eta\mu o\sigma\acute{\iota}\omega\nu$ $\beta\omega\mu\tilde{\omega}\nu$ $\kappa\alpha\grave{\iota}$ $o\acute{\iota}$ $\acute{\alpha}\lambda\lambda o\iota$ $o\acute{\iota}$
$\pi\alpha\rho\alpha\tau\upsilon\gamma\chi\acute{\alpha}\nuo\nu\tau\epsilon\varsigma$ $\dot{\epsilon}\acute{\omega}\rho\omega\nu$ $\kappa\alpha\grave{\iota}$ $\alpha\dot{v}\tau\grave{o}\varsigma$ $M\acute{\epsilon}\lambda\eta\tauo\varsigma$, $\epsilon\dot{\iota}$ $\dot{\epsilon}\beta o\acute{v}\lambda\epsilon\tauo$. $\kappa\alpha\iota\nu\acute{\alpha}$ $\gamma\epsilon$ $\mu\grave{\eta}\nu$
10 $\delta\alpha\iota\mu\acute{o}\nu\iota\alpha$ $\pi\tilde{\omega}\varsigma$ $\grave{\alpha}\nu$ $\dot{\epsilon}\gamma\grave{\omega}$ $\epsilon\dot{\iota}\sigma\phi\acute{\epsilon}\rho o\iota\mu\iota$ $\lambda\acute{\epsilon}\gamma\omega\nu$ $\acute{o}\tau\iota$ $\vartheta\epsilon o\tilde{v}$ $\mu o\iota$ $\phi\omega\nu\grave{\eta}$ $\phi\alpha\acute{\iota}\nu\epsilon\tau\alpha\iota$
$\sigma\eta\mu\alpha\acute{\iota}\nuo\upsilon\sigma\alpha$ $\acute{o}$ $\tau\iota$ $\chi\rho\grave{\eta}$ $\pi o\iota\epsilon\tilde{\iota}\nu$; $\kappa\alpha\grave{\iota}$ $\gamma\grave{\alpha}\rho$ $o\acute{\iota}$ $\phi\vartheta\acute{o}\gamma\gamma o\iota\varsigma$ $o\dot{\iota}\omega\nu\tilde{\omega}\nu$ $\kappa\alpha\grave{\iota}$ $o\acute{\iota}$ $\phi\acute{\eta}\mu\alpha\iota\varsigma$
$\dot{\alpha}\nu\vartheta\rho\acute{\omega}\pi\omega\nu$ $\chi\rho\acute{\omega}\mu\epsilon\nuo\iota$ $\phi\omega\nu\alpha\tilde{\iota}\varsigma$ $\delta\acute{\eta}\pi ov$ $\tau\epsilon\kappa\mu\alpha\acute{\iota}\rho o\nu\tau\alpha\iota$. $\acute{\eta}$ $\delta\grave{\epsilon}$ $\Pi v\vartheta o\tilde{\iota}$ $\dot{\epsilon}\nu$ $\tau\tilde{\omega}$
$\tau\rho\acute{\iota}\pi o\delta\iota$ $\acute{\iota}\acute{\epsilon}\rho\epsilon\iota\alpha$ $o\dot{v}$ $\kappa\alpha\grave{\iota}$ $\alpha\dot{v}\tau\grave{\eta}$ $\phi\omega\nu\tilde{\eta}$ $\tau\grave{\alpha}$ $\pi\alpha\rho\grave{\alpha}$ $\tauo\tilde{v}$ $\vartheta\epsilon o\tilde{v}$ $\delta\iota\alpha\gamma\gamma\acute{\epsilon}\lambda\lambda\epsilon\iota$;
—$\Xi\epsilon\nu o\phi\tilde{\omega}\nu$

Some of Socrates' Clever Remarks.

15 $\dot{\eta}\xi\acute{\iota}ov$ $\delta\grave{\epsilon}$ $\kappa\alpha\grave{\iota}$ $\tauo\grave{v}\varsigma$ $\nu\acute{\epsilon}ov\varsigma$ $\sigma\upsilon\nu\epsilon\chi\grave{\epsilon}\varsigma$ $\kappa\alpha\tauo\pi\tau\rho\acute{\iota}\zeta\epsilon\sigma\vartheta\alpha\iota$, $\check{\iota}\nu'$ $\epsilon\dot{\iota}$ $\kappa\alpha\lambda o\grave{\iota}$ $\epsilon\check{\iota}\epsilon\nu$, $\acute{\alpha}\xi\iota o\iota$
$\gamma\acute{\iota}\gamma\nuo\iota\nu\tauo$. $\epsilon\dot{\iota}$ δ' $\alpha\dot{\iota}\sigma\chi\rho o\acute{\iota}$, $\pi\alpha\iota\delta\epsilon\acute{\iota}\alpha$ $\tau\grave{\eta}\nu$ $\delta\upsilon\sigma\epsilon\acute{\iota}\delta\epsilon\iota\alpha\nu$ $\dot{\epsilon}\pi\iota\kappa\alpha\lambda\acute{v}\pi\tauo\iota\epsilon\nu$.
$\check{E}\lambda\epsilon\gamma\acute{\epsilon}$ $\tau\epsilon$ $\tauo\grave{v}\varsigma$ $\mu\grave{\epsilon}\nu$ $\acute{\alpha}\lambda\lambda ov\varsigma$ $\dot{\alpha}\nu\vartheta\rho\acute{\omega}\pi ov\varsigma$ $\zeta\tilde{\eta}\nu$ $\check{\iota}\nu'$ $\dot{\epsilon}\sigma\vartheta\acute{\iota}o\iota\epsilon\nu$, $\alpha\dot{v}\tau\grave{o}\varsigma$ $\delta\grave{\epsilon}$ $\dot{\epsilon}\sigma\vartheta\acute{\iota}\epsilon\iota\nu$
$\check{\iota}\nu\alpha$ $\zeta\acute{\omega}\eta$.
$A\dot{\iota}\sigma\chi\acute{\iota}\nuov$ $\delta\grave{\epsilon}$ $\epsilon\dot{\iota}\pi\acute{o}\nu\tauo\varsigma$, "$\pi\acute{\epsilon}\nu\eta\varsigma$ $\epsilon\dot{\iota}\mu\grave{\iota}$ $\kappa\alpha\grave{\iota}$ $\acute{\alpha}\lambda\lambda o$ $\mu\grave{\epsilon}\nu$ $o\dot{v}\delta\grave{\epsilon}\nu$ $\acute{\epsilon}\chi\omega$, $\delta\acute{\iota}\delta\omega\mu\iota$ $\delta\acute{\epsilon}$
20 $\sigma o\iota$ $\dot{\epsilon}\mu\alpha\upsilon\tau\acute{o}\nu$," "$\acute{\alpha}\rho'$ $o\check{v}\nu$," $\epsilon\check{\iota}\pi\epsilon\nu$, "$o\dot{v}\kappa$ $\alpha\dot{\iota}\sigma\vartheta\acute{\alpha}\nu\eta$ $\tau\grave{\alpha}$ $\mu\acute{\epsilon}\gamma\iota\sigma\tau\acute{\alpha}$ $\mu o\iota$ $\delta\iota\delta o\acute{v}\varsigma$;"
$T\tilde{\eta}\varsigma$ $\delta\grave{\epsilon}$ $\gamma\upsilon\nu\alpha\iota\kappa\grave{o}\varsigma$ $\epsilon\dot{\iota}\pi o\acute{v}\sigma\eta\varsigma$, "$\dot{\alpha}\delta\acute{\iota}\kappa\omega\varsigma$ $\dot{\alpha}\pi o\vartheta\nu\acute{\eta}\sigma\kappa\epsilon\iota\varsigma$," "$\sigma\grave{v}$ $\delta\acute{\epsilon}$," $\acute{\epsilon}\phi\eta$, "$\delta\iota\kappa\alpha\acute{\iota}\omega\varsigma$
$\dot{\epsilon}\beta o\acute{v}\lambda ov$;"
$M\acute{\epsilon}\lambda\lambda o\nu\tau\acute{\iota}$ $\tau\epsilon$ $\alpha\dot{v}\tau\tilde{\omega}$ $\tau\grave{o}$ $\kappa\acute{\omega}\nu\epsilon\iota o\nu$ $\pi\acute{\iota}\epsilon\sigma\vartheta\alpha\iota$ $'A\pi o\lambda\lambda\acute{o}\delta\omega\rho o\varsigma$ $\acute{\iota}\mu\acute{\alpha}\tau\iota o\nu$ $\dot{\epsilon}\delta\acute{\iota}\delta ov$ $\kappa\alpha\lambda\grave{o}\nu$
$\check{\iota}\nu'$ $\dot{\epsilon}\nu$ $\dot{\epsilon}\kappa\epsilon\acute{\iota}\nu\omega$ $\dot{\alpha}\pi o\vartheta\acute{\alpha}\nu\eta$. $\kappa\alpha\grave{\iota}$ $\acute{o}\varsigma$, "$\tau\acute{\iota}$ $\delta\acute{\epsilon}$," $\acute{\epsilon}\phi\eta$, "$\tau\grave{o}$ $\dot{\epsilon}\mu\grave{o}\nu$ $\acute{\iota}\mu\acute{\alpha}\tau\iota o\nu$ $\dot{\epsilon}\mu\beta\iota\tilde{\omega}\nu\alpha\iota$
25 $\mu\grave{\epsilon}\nu$ $\dot{\epsilon}\pi\iota\tau\acute{\eta}\delta\epsilon\iota o\nu$, $\dot{\epsilon}\nu\alpha\pi o\vartheta\alpha\nu\epsilon\tilde{\iota}\nu$ $\delta\grave{\epsilon}$ $o\dot{v}\chi\acute{\iota}$;" —$\Delta\iota o\gamma\acute{\epsilon}\nu\eta\varsigma$ $\Lambda\alpha\acute{\epsilon}\rho\tau\iota o\varsigma$

Reading Notes:

(1) $\tau\acute{\iota}\sigma\iota$...$\lambda\acute{o}\gamma o\iota\varsigma$ interrogative instrumental dative with $\acute{\epsilon}\pi\epsilon\iota\sigma\alpha\nu$ ($\pi\epsilon\acute{\iota}\vartheta\omega$)

(1) $o\acute{\iota}$ $\gamma\rho\alpha\psi\acute{\alpha}\mu\epsilon\nuo\iota$/$\gamma\rho\acute{\alpha}\phi o\mu\alpha\iota$ in legal language "indict"; *see* $\acute{\eta}$ $\gamma\rho\alpha\phi\acute{\eta}$, -$\tilde{\eta}\varsigma$ "indictment"

(2) $\vartheta\alpha\nu\acute{\alpha}\tau ov$ *see* page 40, the genitive of value, here expressing the penalty

(2) τῇ πόλει/ἡ πόλις Type III, "city"; dative: τῇ πόλε-ι

(2) κατ' αὐτοῦ/κατά + genitive, "against"(basically an ablative idea in Greek: "down away from, detracting from")

(3) τοιάδε see page 77

(4) δαιμόνια/τὸ δαιμόνιον, -ου diminutive (see page 8) of ὁ/ἡ δαῖμων, -ονος "divine power" (that is, demon)

(4) εἰσφέρων/εἰσ-φέρω

(6) ὦ ἄνδρες vocative case (that is, the form for direct calling): "O Gentle-men!"

(6) Μελήτου/ὁ Μέλητος, -ου. Meletos was one of Socrates' accusers at the trial; he was apparently a religious fanatic and perhaps a poet. The genitive here modifies τοῦτο.

(6) ὅτῳ = ὅτινι/ὅστις, ἥτις, ὅτι. In addition to the forms you have learned for the interrogative-indefinite adjective-pronouns τίς, τί (see page 76), there are alternative forms for the genitive and dative singular: τίνος, τοῦ (τινος, του)/τίνι, τῷ (τινι, τῳ). The dative here is instrumental with γνούς.

(8) δημοσίων/δημόσιος, -α, ον "belonging to the populace," ὁ δῆμος, -ου

(9) παρατυγχάνοντες/παρα-τυγχάνω

(9) μήν emphatic particle (see page 19)

(11) οἱ φθόγγοις ... χρώμενοι is the entire participial phrase.

(12) δήπου = δή που. The emphatic particle δή (see page 19) is attenuated or softened by the indefinite locative που (see page 78): "!, perhaps."

(13) ἡ ... ἱέρεια is the entire noun phrase. Πυθοῖ is a locative (see page 42); hence also: Πυθώδε and Πυθώθεν. Pytho was the region in which lay Apollo's oracular sanctuary of Delphi. The prophetic priestess of the god was called the Pythia.

(13) διαγγέλλει/δι'-αγγέλλω

(15) συνεχές = συνεχῶς

(15) κατοπτρίζεσθαι/κατ'-οπτρίζομαι "look into a mirror," τὸ κάτοπτρον, -ου

(16) παιδείᾳ/ἡ παιδεία, -ας"education, training" (see παιδεύω)

(16) δυσείδειαν/ἡ δυσείδεια, -ας "ugliness" (see δυσ-, εἶδον)

(16) ἐπικαλύπτοιεν/ἐπι-καλύπτω

(20) ἆρ'/ἆρα a particle that introduces questions ("?"); distinguish from ἄρα (see page 19)

(23) τὸ κώνειον, -ου juice of the herb "hemlock" (Conium maculatum), a poi-son by which criminals were put to death at Athens

(24) ὅς/ὅς, ἥ usually a relative pronoun, but also a demonstrative functioning as a personal pronoun ("he, she") in certain contexts, chiefly after καί and only in the nominative, usually in conjunction with a verb for saying

(24) ἐμβιῶναι = ἐμβίουν/ἐμ-βιόω (Diogenes Laertius has used the athematic infinitive suffix -ναι with a thematic verb.)

(25) ἐναποθανεῖν/ἐν-απο-θνῄσκω

(25) οὐχί no

II. CHANGE each verb into its contracted form.

1. γαμέω
2. ποιέομεν
3. ηὐτύχεον
4. γαμεοίην
5. σκοπέητε
6. χράεσθε
7. ἐποιέοντο
8. ζάεις
9. ἀξιόεις
10. ἠξίοου

11. ἐτίμαον
12. ἐποίεε
13. ἑώραε
14. ὁράει
15. γαμέετε
16. ποιέοιμεν
17. χραοίμεθα
18. ποιέησθε
19. ποιέῃ
20. δηλόομεν

III. MATCH the second verb to the first by changing it into the same form.

1. θαυμάζοιτε (ποιέω)
2. ἐσήμαινεν (γαμέω)
3. τεκμαιρόμεθα (χράομαι)
4. ᾐσθόμην (ποιέω)
5. οἴχωνται (χράομαι)
6. ἐδίδου (γαμέω)
7. ἔθηκας (ὁράω)
8. εἶχες (ὁράω)
9. ἔθελγε (ἀξιόω)
10. ἔδραμες (γαμέω)

11. νομίζοιμι (ποιέω)
12. ἡδόμην (χράομαι)
13. λάβοιτε (ποιέω)
14. βάλλοιεν (τιμάω)
15. παύοντες (ἀξιόω)
16. εὔχοιο (χράομαι)
17. ἐτίθει (ὁράω)
18. ἔγνω (τιμάω)
19. λέγειν (εὐτυχέω)
20. ἐγένετο (γαμέω)

IV. REPHRASE each sentence, changing it from an expression of a likelihood in the past (past potential) to a likelihood in the present (present-future potential, see page 93).

1. ἠδίκει ἂν Σωκράτης καινοὺς θεοὺς εἰσφέρων.
2. ἐσκοποῦμεν ἂν πάντες τὴν ἀλήθειαν γήμαντες.

3. ἑώρων ἂν Σωκράτην θύοντα ἐν ταῖς κοιναῖς ἑορταῖς καὶ ἐπὶ βωμῶν.

4. Σωκράτης ἂν ἠξίου ἀνθρώπους ζῆν ἵνα ἐσθίοιεν.

5. ἠδικοῦμεν ἂν οὓς θεοὺς οἱ πολλοὶ νομίζουσιν οὐ νομίζοντες.

6. ἑώρας ἂν τὴν ἱέρειαν θύουσαν ἐπὶ τοῦ βωμοῦ.

7. ἠξιοῦτο Σωκράτης ἂν θανάτου τοὺς νεανίας διαφθείρων.

8. καὶ ὑμεῖς ἂν ἑωρᾶσθε οὐ ποιοῦσαι ὅ τι χρή.

9. ἀνὴρ πονηρὸς ἂν ἐδυστύχει.

10. γυναῖκα μὴ ἔχων ἔζης ἂν καλῶς.

V. REPHRASE each sentence, changing to a past tense context and using the optative of secondary subordination (*see* page 94).

1. ὁ Σωκράτης ἀεὶ ἐσθίει ἵνα ζῇ.

2. οἱ πολλοὶ ἀνθρώπων ζῶσιν ἵνα ἐσθίωσιν.

3. οὐ γαμεῖ ὁ φιλόσοφος ἵνα μὴ ἔχῃ κακά.

4. οὐκ ἀδικεῖ Σωκράτης ἵνα μὴ ἀξιῶται θανάτου.

5. λέγουσιν οἱ γραφάμενοι Σωκράτην ὡς οὐχ ἑώρων αὐτόν ποτε ἐπὶ τῶν βωμῶν θύοντα.

6. φοβερός εἰμι μὴ οὐ ποιῇ Σωκράτης τὰ ἐπιτήδεια.

7. ἀξιῶ τοὺς νεανίας παιδεύεσθαι ἵνα καλοί τε γίγνωνται καὶ ἄξιοι.

8. σκοποῦμεν τὴν ἀλήθειαν ἵνα μάθωμεν.

9. Μέλητός φησι Σωκράτην ἀδικεῖν οὐ νομίζοντα οὓς ἂν θεοὺς οἱ πολλοὶ νομίζωσιν.

10. γράφεται Μέλητος Σωκράτην θανάτου ὡς ἀδικεῖ τοὺς νέους διαφθείρων.

VI. NOTE THE PATTERN in each of the quotations and compose a translation of the English sentences, using the same pattern.

1. βίον καλὸν ζῇς ἂν γυναῖκα μὴ ἔχῃς. —Μένανδρος

We are fortunate if ever we contemplate the truth.

A bad man is always condemned to death if ever he does wrong.

2. θέλομεν καλῶς ζῆν πάντες ἀλλ' οὐ δυνάμεθα.
ζῶμεν γὰρ οὐχ ὡς θέλομεν, ἀλλ' ὡς δυνάμεθα. —Μένανδρος

You all want to do what is necessary, but you always do wrong because you act not as you want but as you can.

3. ἀνὴρ δίκαιός ἐστιν οὐχ ὁ μὴ ἀδικῶν,
ἀλλ' ὅστις ἀδικεῖν δυνάμενος μὴ βούλεται. —Μένανδρος

Just women are not the ones who do no wrong, but all those who can do wrong but don't want to.

4. ἀνὴρ πονηρὸς δυστυχεῖ κἂν εὐτυχῇ. —Μένανδρος

Good men are fortunate even if they ever be unfortunate.

A rich man is honored even if be ever he unjust.

5. ἀνάγκη ὃς ἂν γένηται, τούτῳ χρῆσθαι. —Δημόκριτος

It is necessary to put up with (that is, use) whatever daughter is born.

It is necessary to make use of whatever friends one has.

6. ἤδη του ἤκουσα τῶν σοφῶν ὡς τὸ σῶμά ἐστιν ἡμῖν σῆμα. —Πλάτων (ἤδη adverb "already;" for του, see page 110, note 6; notice the pun on σῶμα/σῆμα)

I already learned from some one of the poets that the poor man is fortunate.

16

Aorist Passive

πῶς ἐπράχθη τὸ πραχθέν; —Πολύβιος

Lesson 16
Aorist Passive Voice

In the aorist (or punctual aspect) of the Greek verb, the passive voice can be distinguished from the middle as well as from the active voices by a separate stem.

ἐπαιδεύσαμεν	Aorist active
ἐπαιδευσάμεθα	Aorist middle
ἐπαιδεύθημεν	Aorist passive: We were taught. (Contrast the imperfect middle-passive: ἐπαιδευόμεθα We were being taught. *Or*, we were teaching (for ourselves).

As always, only the augmented forms of the Greek verb express past tense. All other forms constructed upon the aorist passive stem convey only the passive voice in its punctual aspect.

παιδευθέντες	Participle: taught
παιδευθῶμεν	Subjunctive: Let's be taught!
παιδευθεῖμεν	Optative: May we be taught!
παιδευθῆναι	Infinitive: to be taught

Aorist Passive/ Conjugation

The aorist passive stem is formed by adding either the suffix -θη- or the suffix -η- to the present stem.

ἐ-παιδεύ-θη-μεν	(the so-called first aorist passive)
ἐ-γράφ-η-μεν	(the so-called second aorist passive)

The -θη- suffix may cause euphonic changes in the final consonant of the present stem.

λείπ-ο-μεν	ἐ-λείφ-θη-μεν
ἄγ-ο-μεν	ἤχ-θη-μεν
φυλάττ-ο-μεν	ἐ-φυλάχ-θη-μεν
νομίζ-ο-μεν	ἐ-νομίσ-θη-μεν
πείθ-ο-μεν	ἐ-πείσ-θη-μεν

It may also happen that there occur internal variations between the present and aorist passive stems.

βάλλ-ο-μεν	ἐ-βάλ-ο-μεν	ἐ-βλή-θη-μεν

Furthermore, for some verbs the aorist active stem and the aorist passive stem are actually completely different verbs from the present stem.

ὁρά-ο-μεν (ὁρῶμεν)	εἴδ-ο-μεν	ὤφ-θη-μεν

It is obvious, therefore, that the aorist passive stem cannot be predicted and must be listed as one of the *principle parts* of a Greek verb. Except for some of the more common verbs, however, it probably is not necessary to memorize the aorist passive stem completely so long as you can recognize the aorist passive easily and can analyze it into its probable lexical entry.

Both -θη- and -η- are athematic suffixes (*see* the -σα- suffix of the aorist active and middle stem) and, therefore, all verbs are conjugated athematically in the aorist passive, except, as always, the subjunctive, whose sign is the lengthened variable vowel. Since the indicative has past tense, it is augmented and has secondary endings.

Note that the aorist passive uses *active* rather than *middle-passive* personal suffixes.

Note that the reduced version of the -θη-/-η- suffixes occurs in the subjunctive, optative and participle. In the subjunctive, the reduced vowel of the suffix contracts with the subjunctive "endings:" παιδευ-θέ-ω-μεν → παιδευθῶμεν.

The chart summarizes the aorist passive conjugation.

Indicative		Subjunctive		Optative	
ἐ-παιδεύ-θη-	ν	παιδευ-θ-	ῶ	παιδευ-θε-	ίην
ἐ-γράφ-η-	ς	γραφ-	ῇς	γραφ-ε-	ίης
	—		ῇ		ίη
	μεν		ῶ-μεν		ῖμεν/ ίημεν
	τε		ῆ-τε		ῖτε/ ίητε
	σαν		ῶσι		ῖεν/ ίησαν

Participle (masc.)		(fem.)		(neut.)	
παιδευ-θε-	ίς	παιδευ-θε-	ῖσα	παιδευ-θέ-	ν
γραφ-ε-	ντ-α	γραφ-ε-	ῖσαν	γραφ-έ-	ν
	ντ-ος		ίσης		ντ-ος
etc.		etc.		etc.	
dat. pl.	ῖσι		ίσαις		ῖσι

Infinitive

παιδευ-θῆ-	
γραφ-ῆ-	ναι

Principle Parts/ Some Common Verbs That You Already Know

ἄγω, ἤγαγον, ἤχθην

ἀκούω, ἤκουσα, ἠκούσθην

ἀπο-δύω, ἀπ-έδυν, ἀπ-εδύθην

ἁρπάζω, ἥρπασα, ἡρπάσθην

βάλλω, ἔβαλον, ἐβλήθην

βούλομαι, _____, ἐβουλήθην

γιγνώσκω, ἔγνων, ἐγνώθην

γράφω, ἔγραψα, ἐγράφην

δείκνυμι, ἔδειξα, ἐδείχθην

δίδωμι, ἔδωκα, ἐδόθην

εὑρίσκω, ηὗρον (or εὗρον), ηὑρέθην (or εὑρέθην)
ἵημι, ἧκα, εἵθην
ἵστημι, ἔστησα (ἔστην), ἐστάθην
λαμβάνω, ἔλαβον, ἐλήφθην
λείπω, ἔλιπον, ἐλείφθην
νομίζω, ἐνόμισα, ἐνομίσθην
ὁράω, εἶδον, ὤφθην (see τά ὀπ-τικά "optics" for aor. pass. stem)
πείθω, ἔπεισα, ἐπείσθην
πέμπω, ἔπεμψα, ἐπέμφην
πίνω, ἔπιον, ἐπόθην
πράττω, ἔπραξα, ἐπράχθην
σῴζω, ἔσωσα, ἐσώθην
τίθημι, ἔθηκα, ἐτέθην
φαίνω, ἔφηνα, ἐφάνθην "be revealed" (ἐφάνην intrans. "appeared")
φέρω, ἤνεγκα (ἤνεγκον), ἠνέχθην

ΟΝΟΜΑΤΑ ΚΑΙ ΡΗΜΑΤΑ

ὁ οὐρανός, -οῦ	sky, heaven
ἡ γραῖα, -ας	old woman (see ὁ γέρων, -οντος/ γεραιός, -ά, -όν/ γηράσκω)
ὁ πυρός, -οῦ	wheat (distinguish from τὸ πῦρ, πυρός)
πτηνός, -ή, -όν	winged, flying
ἐράω, _____, ἠράσθην	love (see ὁ ἔρως, -ωτος/ ὁ ἐραστής, -οῦ "lover") + genitive
ζητέω, ἐζήτησα, _____	seek, search for
καλέω, ἐκάλεσα, ἐκλήθην	call
αἱρέω, εἷλον, ἡρέθην	take (middle choose, that is, take for oneself)
βοάω, ἐβόησα, _____	shout (see ἡ βοή, -ῆς "shout")
οἰκέω, ᾤκησα, ᾠκήθην	inhabit, live in (see ὁ οἶκος, -ου/ ὁ οἰκέτης, -ου "household slave")
φιλέω, ἐφίλησα, ἐφιλήθην	love (see ὁ φίλος, -ου/ ἡ φιλία, -ας "affection, friendship")
τηρέω, _____, _____	watch over, observe
σκευάζω, ἐσκεύασα, _____	prepare, make ready
τρέφω, ἔθρεψα, ἐθρέφθην (or ἐτράφην)	rear (a child), nourish, support (see ὁ/ἡ τροφός, -οῦ "rearer, wet nurse")

ἐρωτάω, ἠρώτησα, ἠρωτήθην   ask, question (*see* τὸ ἐρώτημα, -ατος "question")

συν-εργέω, _____, _____   work together with (*see* τὸ ἔργον, -ου)

ὀργίζω, ὤργισα, ὠργίσθην   make angry (*see* ἡ ὀργή, -ῆς "anger")

εἰκάζω, ἤκασα, ἠκάσθην   portray by a likeness, liken (*see* ἡ εἰκών, -όνος "image," *icon*)

ἥκω, (ἥξα), _____   to have come

σκώπτω, ἔσκωψα ἐσκώφθην   mock, jeer at, joke with

μειδιάω, ἐμείδησα, _____   smile

ἀν-αλίσκω (also ἀν-αλόω), ἀνήλωσα, ἀνηλώθην   expend, use up (*see* ἀλίσκομαι "be seized, be conquered," the passive idea for αἱρέω)

αὐξάνω, ηὔξησα, ηὐξήθην   increase, *augment* (*pass.* grow, increase in size)

σπείρω, ἔσπειρα, ἐσπάρην   sow seed (*see* τὸ σπέρμα, -ατος "seed")

κελεύω, ἐκέλευσα, ἐκελεύσθην   command

πλέω, ἔπλευσα, ἐπλεύσθην   sail (*see* ὁ πλοῦς, -οῦ)

πνέω, ἔπνευσα, ἐπνεύσθην   breathe (*see* ἡ πνοή, -ῆς "breath")

κρύφα   *adv.* secretly (*see* κρύπτω "hide")

ἔπειτα   *adv.* thereupon, then

ΑΣΚΗΣΙΣ

I. TRANSLATE: The Abduction of Persephone.

Πλούτων δὲ Περσεφόνης ἐρασθεὶς Διὸς συνεργοῦντος ἥρπασεν αὐτὴν κρύφα. Δημήτηρ δὲ μετὰ λαμπάδων νυκτός τε καὶ ἡμέρας κατὰ πᾶσαν τὴν γῆν ζητοῦσα περιήρχετο. μαθοῦσα δὲ παρ' Ἑρμιονέων ὅτι Πλούτων αὐτὴν ἥρπασεν, ὀργιζομένη θεοῖς κατέλιπεν οὐρανόν, εἰκασθεῖσα δὲ

5 γυναικὶ ἧκεν εἰς Ἐλευσῖνα. καὶ πρῶτον μὲν ἐπὶ τὴν ἀπ' ἐκείνης κληθεῖ- σαν Ἀγέλαστον ἐκάθισε πέτραν παρὰ τὸ Καλλίχορον φρέαρ καλούμενον, ἔπειτα πρὸς Κελεὸν ἐλθοῦσα τὸν βασιλεύοντα τότε Ἐλευσινίων, ἔνδον οὐσῶν γυναικῶν, καὶ λεγουσῶν τούτων παρ' αὐτὰς καθέζεσθαι, γραῖά τις Ἰάμβη σκώψασα τὴν θεὸν ἐποίησε μειδιᾶσαι. διὰ τοῦτο ἐν τοῖς

10 Θεσμοφορίοις τὰς γυναῖκας σκώπτειν λέγουσιν.

Ὄντος δὲ τῇ τοῦ Κελεοῦ γυναικὶ Μετανείρᾳ παιδίου, τοῦτο ἔτρεφεν ἡ Δημήτηρ παραλαβοῦσα. βουλομένη δὲ αὐτὸ ἀθάνατον ποιῆσαι, τὰς νύκτας εἰς πῦρ κατετίθει τὸ βρέφος καὶ περιῄρει τὰς θνητὰς σάρκας αὐτοῦ. καθ' ἡμέραν δὲ παραδόξως αὐξανομένου τοῦ Δημοφῶντος

15 (τοῦτο γὰρ ἦν ὄνομα τῷ παιδί) ἐπετήρησεν ἡ Πραξιθέα, καὶ καταλαβοῦ- σα εἰς πῦρ ἀνεβόησε· διόπερ τὸ μὲν βρέφος ὑπὸ τοῦ πυρὸς ἀνηλώθη, ἡ

θεὰ δὲ αὐτὴν ἐξέφηνε. Τριπτολέμῳ δὲ τῷ πρεσβυτέρῳ τῶν Μετανείρας
παίδων δίφρον κατασκευάσασα πτηνῶν δρακόντων τὸν πυρὸν ἔδωκεν, ᾧ
τὴν ὅλην οἰκουμένην δι' οὐρανοῦ αἰρόμενος κατέσπειρε.

20   Διὸς δὲ Πλούτωνι τὴν Κόρην ἀναπέμψαι κελεύσαντος, ὁ Πλούτων, ἵνα
μὴ πολὺν χρόνον παρὰ τῇ μητρὶ καταμείνῃ, ῥοιᾶς ἔδωκεν αὐτῇ φαγεῖν
κόκκον, δι' ὅπερ Περσεφόνη καθ' ἕκαστον ἐνιαυτὸν τὸ μὲν τρίτον μετὰ
Πλούτωνος ἠναγκάσθη μένειν, τὸ δὲ λοιπὸν παρὰ τοῖς θεοῖς. —Ἀπολλόδωρος

Reading Notes:

(1) ὁ Πλούτων, -ωνος, god of the underworld, so-called as the source of
wealth (see πλούσιος, -α, -ον) because, as Plato explains, ἐκ τῆς γῆς ἀνίεται
πλοῦτος/equivalent to the god ὁ Ἅιδης, -ου, a name supposedly derived from
ἀ- + ἰδεῖν

(2) ἡ Δημήτηρ, -τρος, goddess associated with grain and the earth, supposedly so named from Γη-μήτηρ or Δημο-μήτηρ. Her daughter is Persephone, whose nuptials with the lord of death formed the mythical basis
for the religion of the Eleusinian Mystery.

(2) λαμπάδων/ἡ λαμπάς, -άδος "torch," lamp (see λάμπω "shine, give light")

(2) νυκτός τε καὶ ἡμέρας partitive genitive, denoting a portion of time: "(at/
in) both night and day." The genitive in this structure may (but need not necessarily) indicate a definite part of the time during which anything takes place.
Contrast the locative dative, which fixes the time explicitly by indicating a
definite point in a given period; and the accusative, which expresses the whole
extent of time from beginning to end. See page 55.

(3) περιήρχετο/περι-έρχομαι

(3) Ἐμριονέων gen. pl. (ὁ Ἑρμιονεύς), the people of Hermione, a town on the
Argolid, where there was a chasm thought to be an entrance to the underworld

(5) Ἐλευσῖνα/ἡ Ἐλευσίς, -ῖνος, a town near Athens where the Eleusinian
Mystery was celebrated in the sanctuary of the two goddesses, Demeter and
Persephone

(6) Ἀγέλαστον/ἀγέλαστος, -ον from ἀ-+γελάω "laugh"

(6) ἐκάθισε = ἐκαθίσατο

(6) Καλλίχορον/καλλίχορος, -ον from καλός+ὁ χορός, -οῦ "dance, place for
dancing"

(6) τὸ φρέαρ, φρέατος "(dug or artificial) well, cistern:" contrast ἡ κρήνη, -ης
"(natural) well, spring"

(8) τούτων the feminine of οὗτος, αὕτη, τοῦτο (see page 24) has the stem τουτ-
only in the genitive plural.

(10) Θεσμοφορίοις/τὰ Θεσμοφόρια, -ων, a women's festival in honor of
Demeter's reunion with her daughter Persephone

(12) παραλαβοῦσα/ παρα-λαμβάνω

(13) τὰς νύκτας See note (2).

(13) κατετίθει/κατα-τίθημι

(13) τὸ βρέφος = "baby" (see τὸ παιδίον, -ου)

(13) περιῄρει/περι-αίρέω

(13) σάρκας/ἡ σάρξ, σαρκός "flesh" (see ἡ σαρκοφάγος, -ου sarcophagus, from σάρξ + φαγεῖν)

(14) παραδόξως adv. paradoxically

(15) ἐπετήρησεν/ἐπι-τηρέω

(15) καταλαβοῦσα/κατα-λαμβάνω "take, catch (by surprise)." The separable prefix κατά often has merely an intensive force.

(16) ἀνεβόησε/ἀνα-βοάω

(16) διόπερ/δι' ὅ περ "wherefore, on account of which"

(17) ἐξέφηνε/ἐκ-φαίνω

(18) δίφρον/ὁ δίφρος -ου "chariot" (see διφορέω from δίς "twice" + φορέω, see φέρω/The δίφρος ordinarily carried two.)

(18) δρακόντων/ὁ δράκων, -οντος "serpent, dragon"

(18) ᾧ instrumental dative; the antecedent is δίφρος

(19) οἰκουμένην, that is, τὴν ὅλην οἰκουμένην γῆν/ὅλος, -η, -ον "entire, whole"

(19) δι' οὐρανοῦ ablatival genitive: 'through and out of"

(19) κατέσπειρε/κατα-σπείρω

(20) Διός/ὁ Ζεύς, τοῦ Διός

(20) ἀναπέμψαι/ἀνα-πέμπω

(21) καταμείνῃ/κατα-μένω

(21) ῥοιᾶς/ἡ ῥοιά, -ᾶς "pomegranate"

(22) κόκκον/ὁ κόκκος, -ου "seed, pit"

(22) ἐνιαυτόν/ὁ ἐνιαυτός, -οῦ time period of a "year"

(22) τρίτον/τρίτος, -η, -ον "third"

II. GIVE THE LEXICAL ENTRY and then the equivalent form using the present verbal stem. (For example, ἐπράχθητε/πράττω, ἐ-πράττ-ε-σθε)

1. ἐπόθη

2. σωθῆναι

3. ἐβλήθησαν

4. νομισθέντας

5. εὑρεθείης

6. ἐτέθης

7. γραφείσῃ

8. ἐφάνθημεν

9. σταθῇς	15. ἠρωτήθημεν
10. ἐνεχθῆτε	16. θρεφθεῖσαι
11. σωθέν	17. σκωφθῶμεν
12. γραφείη	18. ἐρασθείς
13. ἐγνώσθησαν	19. νομισθεῖσι
14. λειφθέντες	20. ληφθῶσι

III. CHANGE each verb to the active (using the aorist stem).

1. ἐπέμφημεν	11. ἠρωτήθησαν
2. σωθεῖμεν	12. ὀφθείης
3. ὤφθητε	13. ἐδείχθη
4. λειφθέντες	14. ἡρέθης
5. ἐτέθη	15. σωθῶμεν
6. πραχθῆναι	16. ἐφιλήθημεν
7. ὀφθέν	17. ληφθεῖεν
8. ποθῇ	18. δοθῇ
9. ἐστάθης	19. ὤφθητε
10. ἐπείσθην	20. ἀκουσθείσαις

IV. REPHRASE each sentence, changing it from an expression of a likelihood in the past (past potential) to a likelihood in the present (present-future potential, *see* page 93).

1. Πλούτων Διὶ συνεργῶν ἂν ἠράσθη Περσεφόνης πάνυ καλῆς οὔσης.

2. Ζεὺς συνήργει ἂν Πλούτωνι τὴν Κόρην ἁρπάσαντι.

3. ᾿Αγέλαστος ἂν ἐκλήθη ἡ πέτρα ἀπὸ Δημήτρος ὀργιζομένης τοῖς θεοῖς.

4. ἀνηλώθη ἂν τὸ παιδίον κατατεθὲν εἰς πῦρ ἵνα ἀθάνατος ποιηθείη τῆς θνητῆς σαρκὸς περιαιρεθείσης.

5. Περσεφόνη ἡρπάσθη ἂν ὑπὸ Πλούτωνος ἐρασθέντος αὐτῆς.

6. ἔμαθεν ἂν Δημήτηρ τὴν Κόρην ἁρπαθεῖσαν ὑπὸ Πλούτωνος Διὶ συνεργοῦντος.

7. ἐβουλήθη ἂν Δημήτηρ πρὸς ᾿Ελευσῖνα ἐλθεῖν ἵνα τὴν Κόρην ζητοίη.

8. ἀνεβόα ἂν ἡ Πραξιθέα καταλαβοῦσα τὸν Δημοφῶντα κατατεθέντα εἰς πῦρ.

9. Τριπτολέμῳ τῷ πρεσβυτέρῳ τῶν Μετανείρας παίδων τὸν πυρὸν ἂν ἔδωκεν ἡ Μήτηρ ἵνα κατασπείροι τὴν οἰκουμένην γῆν.

10. ὑπὸ ᾿Ιάμβης σκωφθεῖσα ἐμειδία ἂν ἡ Μήτηρ.

V. REPHRASE the following groups of sentences, combining them into a single sentence by the use of participles or dependent clauses (relative, purpose, etc.).

1. Πλούτων Περσεφόνης ἠράσθη. ὁ δὲ Ζεὺς αὐτῷ συνήργει. ἐβουλήθη γὰρ αὐτὴν ἁρπάσαι ἵνα καταμείναι παρ' αὐτῷ.

2. ἔπειτα δὲ ἡ Δημήτηρ κατὰ πᾶσαν τὴν οἰκουμένην γῆν περιήρχετο. ἐζήτει γὰρ τὴν Κόρην. ἡρπάσθη δὲ αὕτη ὑπὸ Πλούτωνος. οὗτος γὰρ αὐτῆς ἠράσθη.

3. ἔμαθε δὲ Δημήτηρ ὅτι ἁρπασθείη ἡ Κόρη ὑπὸ Πλούτωνος. δι' ὅπερ ὠργίσθη τοῖς θεοῖς. τὸν δὲ οὐρανὸν κατέλιπεν.

4. ἠκάσθη δὲ γυναικὶ γεραιᾷ. ἧκε δὲ εἰς τοὺς Ἐλευσινίους. τούτων δὲ ἐβασίλευε τότε ὁ Κελεός.

5. πρῶτον δὲ ἐκαθίσατο ἐπί τινα πέτραν. τῇ δὲ πέτρᾳ ὄνομα ἦν Ἀγέλαστος. τοῦτο δὲ ἐκλήθη ὑπὸ τῆς Δημήτρος. ὠργίσθη γὰρ τοῖς θεοῖς. οὐδὲ ἤδετο τοῖς πραχθεῖσι.

6. ἔπειτα δὲ ἦλθε πρὸς τὰς Ἐλευσινίας γυναῖκας. αὗται δὲ ἦσαν ἐν τῷ οἴκῳ. ἐκεῖ (see page 78) δὲ ἐσκώφθη ὑπό τινος γραίας. ταύτῃ δὲ ὄνομα ἦν Ἰάμβη.

7. ἦν δὲ τῇ τοῦ Κελεοῦ γυναικὶ παιδίον τι. τούτῳ δὲ ὄνομα ἦν Δημοφῶν. τοῦτο δὲ τὸ παιδίον παρέλαβε Δημήτηρ. ἐβουλήθη γὰρ αὐτὸν ἀθάνατον ποιῆσαι.

8. ἐθρέφθη δὲ οὗτος ὁ Δημοφῶν ὑπὸ τῆς Δημήτρος. αὕτη γὰρ αὐτὸν κατετίθει ἑκάστην νύκτα εἰς πῦρ. ἐβουλήθη γὰρ περιαιρεῖν αὐτοῦ τὰς θνητὰς σάρκας.

9. καθ' ἡμέραν δὲ ηὐξάνετο παραδόξως ὁ Δημοφῶν. ἀλλ' ηὑρέθη ὑπὸ Πραξιθέας εἰς πῦρ κατατεθείς. αὕτη δὲ ἀνεβόησε. φοβερὰ γὰρ ἦν μὴ ἀναλωθείη ἡ σάρξ καὶ ἀποθάνοι τὸ παιδίον.

10. δι' ὅπερ ἀνηλώθη τὸ παιδίον. ἡ δὲ Δημήτηρ αὐτὴν ἐξέφηνε. ἐβουλήθη γὰρ δοῦναι τῷ πρεσβυτέρῳ παιδὶ τὸν πυρόν.

IV. NOTE THE PATTERN in each of the quotations and compose a translation of the English sentences, using the same pattern.

1. εἶδον γὰρ θεὸν καὶ ἐσώθη μου ἡ ψυχή. —Εὐσέβιος

I fell in love with truth and was called a philosopher.

We died and were abducted to heaven.

You shouted and were heard.

2. ἐρωτηθεὶς τίς ἐστι φίλος, "ἄλλος," ἔφη, "ἐγώ". —Διογένης Λαέρτιος (Ζήνων)

When asked who are wealthy, "Only," he said, "the philosophers."

Once we were seen by the others, we all shouted.

When recognized, the women were forced to leave.

3. προσθεὶς γὰρ ὁ σπείρας τε καὶ θρέψας πατήρ
   φερνὰς ἀπῴκισ᾽, ὡς ἀπαλλαχθῇ κακοῦ. —Εὐριπίδης

(ἡ φερνή, -ῆς "dowry, that which is brought, that is, φέρω, by a wife"/ἀπ-
αλλάσσω, ἀπήλλαξα, ἀπηλλάχθην "set free, release"/ἀπ-οικίζω, ἀπῴκισα
"send away from home"/ὡς = ἵνα/ on the tense of the verb, *see* page 36,
gnomic aorist)

After she has educated her, the mother who bore her and nourished her sends
her to a husband so that the daughter be likened to herself.

Type III Noun-Adjective Stems in Υ, I, and Σ

πᾶσα πολιτεία ψυχὴ πόλεώς ἐστιν. —᾽Ισοκράτης

Lesson 17
Semi-Consonant Stems

Although the letters -ι- and -υ- usually represent vowels, in certain contexts they can also represent consonantal sounds (ι = y, υ = w) and they are therefore classed as *semi-consonants*. Noun and adjective stems ending in *iota* and *upsilon* belong accordingly to the Type III declension.

Type III nouns and adjectives ending in semi-consonants show various apparent irregularities inasmuch as the final semi-consonant of the stem can shift between its consonantal and vocalic values as its immediate context changes through the addition of the declensional suffixes.

Semi-Consonantal Stems In Υ

Between vowels, -υ- has its consonantal value ("w"); but "w" is a consonant that was lost in the Greek language: in fact, early Greek once had a letter that represented "w," the *digamma* or double gamma, so called because of its shape (F); in most dialects, it was lost before the classical period. Hence, wherever -υ- would occur between vowels through the addition of the Type III declensional suffixes, it is lost.

Nouns ending in -ευ-ς show this loss of consonantal -υ- between vowels.

ὁ βασιλεύ	-ς		οἱ βασιλεῖς	
τὸν βασιλέ-	-ᾱ		τοὺς βασιλέ-	-ᾱς
τοῦ βασιλέ-	-ως		τῶν βασιλέ-	-ων
τῷ βασιλε-	-ῖ		τοῖς βασιλεῦ	-σι

Note that the nominative plural results from the contraction βασιλέ-ες → βασιλεῖς.

Note that the genitive singular has -ως (instead of -ος) as the suffix. This is because noun stems ending in -ευ-ς originally had -ηυ-ς, a form that is retained in the Homeric dialect (τοῦ βασιλῆος, τὸν βασιλῆα, τοὺς βασιλῆας). In Attic, the two adjacent vowels have "exchanged their quantity": τοῦ βασιλῆος → βασιλέως. So also in the accusative singular and plural: τοὺς βασιλῆας → βασιλέᾱς.

A similar pattern occurs in noun stems ending in -ου-ς and -αυ-ς. Note the declensions for ὁ/ἡ βοῦς "ox, cow" (*see* Latin bovis) and ἡ γραῦς (*see* ἡ γραῖα, -ᾱς).

ὁ βοῦ	-ς		ἡ γραῦ	-ς
τὸν βοῦ	-ν		τὴν γραῦ	-ν
τοῦ βο-	-ός		τῆς γρα-	-ός
τῷ βο-	-ί		τῇ γρα-	-ί
οἱ βό-	-ες		αἱ γρᾶ-	-ες
τοὺς βοῦ	-ς		τὰς γραῦ	-ς
τῶν βο-	-ῶν		τῶν γρα-	-ῶν
τοῖς βου	-σί		ταῖς γραυ	-σί

Note that in the accusative singular, the declensional suffix is retained as the consonant -ν (instead of shifting to -α, *see* page 13); hence the -υ- is not lost since it does not occur between vowels. The accusative plural similarly retains the -υ- through the contraction of the suffix ν-ς with the diphthong -αυ-.

Note that the accent pattern is regular for Type III monosyllabic nouns (*see* page 44).

In nouns ending in -υ-ς, the -υ- does not ever occur between vowels and therefore maintains its vocalic value and is retained throughout the declension. In the accusative singular and plural, however, the vocalic value causes the -ν/ -νς suffixes to be maintained (instead of shifting to -α/ -ας): ὁ ἰχθύ-ς "fish," τὸν ἰχθύ-ν, τοῦ ἰχθύ-ος, τῷ ἰχθύ-ῑ, οἱ ἰχθύ-ες, τοὺς ἰχθῦ-ς, τῶν ἰχθύ-ων, τοῖς ἰχθύ-σι.

Some noun stems ending in -υ-ς, however, alternate between -υ- and -ε(υ)- and therefore resemble βασιλεύς in certain cases of the declension. These nouns are indicated in lexica by a genitive singular in -ε-ως. *Note* the declensional paradigms for ὁ πῆχυς "forearm" and τὸ ἄστυ "town."

ὁ πῆχυ	-ς		τὸ ἄστυ	
τὸν πῆχυ	-ν		τὸ ἄστυ	
τοῦ πήχε-	-ως		τοῦ ἄστε-	-ως
τῷ πήχε-	-ι		τῷ ἄστε-	-ι
οἱ πήχεις			τὰ ἄστη	
τοὺς πήχεις			τὰ ἄστη	
τῶν πηχέ-	-ων		τῶν ἀστέ-	-ων
τοῖς πήχε-	-σι		τοῖς ἄστε-	-σι

Note that τὰ ἄστη is contracted from τὰ ἄστε(υ)-α.

Note that τοὺς πήχεις imitates the nominative plural form.

Type III adjectives with stems in -υ- also alternate with -ε(υ)- and therefore resemble ὁ πῆχυς for the masculine and τὸ ἄστυ for the neuter, except that the genitive singular does not imitate the exchange of quantity of βασιλέ-ως and the neuter plural nominative and accusative do not contract -ε(υ)-α to -η. The feminine is formed by the suffix -ι- (*see* page 64) and is declined accordingly as a Type I adjective: ἡδε(ύ)-ι-α → ἡδεῖα.

Note the paradigm for ἡδύς, ἡδεῖα, ἡδύ "sweet" (*see* ἥδομαι).

ἡδύ	-ς		ἡδεῖ	-α		ἡδύ	
ἡδύ	-ν		ἡδεῖ	-αν		ἡδύ	
ἡδέ-	-ος		ἡδεί	-ας		ἡδέ-	-ος
ἡδε-	-ῑ		ἡδεί	-ᾳ		ἡδε-	-ῑ

ἡδεῖς		ἡδεῖ	-αι	ἡδέ-	-α
ἡδεῖς		ἡδεί	-ας	ἡδέ-	-α
ἡδέ-	-ων	ἡδει	-ῶν	ἡδέ-	-ων
ἡδέ-	-σι	ἡδεί	-αις	ἡδέ-	-σι

Semi-Consonantal Stems IN _I_   Noun stems in -ι-ς alternate between -ι- and -ε(ι)-. *Note* the paradigm for ἡ πόλις "city." The genitive singular derives from a collateral form, πόλη-ος, by exchange of quantity.

ἡ πόλι	-ς	αἱ πόλεις	
τὴν πόλι	-ν	τὰς πόλεις	
τῆς πόλε-	-ως	τῶν πόλε-	-ων
τῇ πόλε-	-ι	ταῖς πόλε-	-σι

Note that the accent of the genitive plural imitates the singular.

Stems In _Σ_   Between vowels, *sigma* is unstable in Greek and usually has been lost. Hence, in noun stems ending in *sigma*, wherever -σ- would occur between vowels through the addition of the declensional suffixes, it will be lost and the resultant adjacent vowels contracted. *Note* the paradigms for ἡ τριήρης "trireme" and τὸ γένος "race, kin." The stems are τριηρεσ- and γενεσ-. The -η-ς of the nominative singular results from τριήρεσ-ς → τριήρης.

ἡ τριήρης	τὸ γένος
τὴν τριήρη	τὸ γένος
τῆς τριήρους	τοῦ γένους
τῇ τριήρε- -ι	τῷ γένε- -ι
αἱ τριήρεις	τὰ γένη
τὰς τριήρεις	τὰ γένη
τῶν τριήρων	τῶν γενῶν
ταῖς τριήρε- -σι	τοῖς γένε- -σι

Note that the declensional forms result from contraction after the loss of intervocalic *sigma*: τριήρε(σ)α → τριήρη/τριήρε(σ)-ος → τριήρους/τριήρε(σ)-ι → τριήρει/γενέ(σ)-ων → γενῶν. The accent on τριήρων is irregular.

Type III adjectives with stems in -ε(σ)- resemble nouns like ἡ τριήρης and τὸ γένος in their declension; they have one form for the masculine and feminine and another for the neuter. *Note* the paradigm for ἀληθής, ἀληθές "true" (*see* ἡ ἀλήθεια, -ας).

ἀληθής	ἀληθές
ἀληθῆ	ἀληθές
ἀληθοῦς	ἀληθοῦς

ἀληθε- -ῖ	ἀληθε- -ῖ
ἀληθεῖς	ἀληθῆ
ἀληθεῖς	ἀληθῆ
ἀληθῶν	ἀληθῶν
ἀληθέ- -σι	ἀληθέ- -σι

The noun Σωκράτης is a Type III *sigma* stem: ὁ Σωκράτης, τὸν Σωκράτη, τοῦ Σωκράτους, τῷ Σωκράτει/also τὸν Σωκράτην, by analogy to Type I.

ΟΝΟΜΑΤΑ ΚΑΙ ΡΗΜΑΤΑ

ἡ φύσις, -εως	origin, natural form (resulting from growth), nature (*see* φύω bring forth, produce/*mid.* become, grow)
τὸ γένος, -ους	race, kin, *gen*der
ὁ γονεύς, -έως	parent
ἡ ἰσχύς, -έως	bodily strength
τὸ εἶδος, -ους	form, kind (*see* ὁράω, εἶδον)
τὸ ὄνειδος, -ους	reproach, blame
τὸ μέλος, -ους	limb, musical phrase (*see* mel*ody*)
τὸ σκέλος, -ους	leg
ἡ τριήρης, -ους	trireme
ὁ πῆχυς, -εως	forearm, cubit
τὸ ἄστυ, -εως	town
ἡ πόλις, -εως	city
ὁ ἰχθύς, -ύος	fish
ὁ/ἡ βοῦς, βοός	ox, cow
ἡ γραῦς, -αός	=ἡ γραῖα, -ας
ὁ ἥλιος, -ου	sun
ἡ σελήνη, -ης	moon
ἡ μηχανή, -ῆς	*mach*ine, *mechan*ism, contrivance
ὁ κύκλος, -ου	circle, *cycle* (*see* κυκλοτερής, -ές circular, round)
ἡ χείρ, -ρός	hand (*see* ἐπιχειρέω put one's hand to, attempt)
τὸ πρόσωπον, -ου	face, countenance, mask, facade (*see* ὁράω, ὤφ-θην)

ἡδύς, ἡδεῖα, ἡδύ	sweet (see ἥδομαι)
θῆλυς, θήλεια, θῆλυ	female, feminine
ἄρρην, ἄρρεν (gen. ἄρρενος)	male, masculine
ταχύς, ταχεῖα, ταχύ	swift
ἀληθής, -ές	true (see ἡ ἀλήθεια, -ας)
ὅλος, -η, -ον	whole, entire
πορεύω, ἐπόρευσα, ἐπορεύθην	carry (mid. go, walk) (see ἡ πορεία, -ας mode of walking)
ἀπορέω, ἠπόρησα, ἠπορήθην	be without means (see ἄπορος, -ον without means, impassable, unmanageable)
ἐρείδω, ἤρεισα, ἠρείσθην	prop
ὁρμάω, ὥρμησα, ὡρμήθην	start out, hasten, set in motion (see ἡ ὁρμή, -ῆς rapid motion forward, impulse)
βουλεύω, ἐβούλευσα	take counsel, deliberate (see ἡ βουλή, -ῆς the government Council in Athens, deliberation)
ἐάω (imperf. εἴων), εἴασα, εἰάθην	permit
νοέω, ἐνόησα, ἐνοήθην	think, perceive (see ὁ νοῦς, -οῦ)
τέμνω, ἔτεμον, ἐτμήθην	cut
χρή	it is necessary
δοκέω, ἔδοξα, -εδόχθην	seem, think, seem good

Note that the suffix -σις forms feminine abstract nouns expressing verbal ideas: ἡ φύσις, -εως "growth, nature"/ἡ ποίησις, -εως "poetry, creation"/ἡ δόσις, -εως "act of giving"/ἡ λέξις, -εως (see λέγω) "style"/ἡ θέσις, -εως (see τίθημι) "placing"/ ἡ γένεσις, -εως (see γίγνομαι) "generation, manner of birth."

Note that χρή is an indeclinable noun meaning "necessity." It is used in nominal sentences (with ἐστί omitted) as the predicate for an infinitive phrase: χρή με μαθεῖν "It is necessary for me to learn" (literally, "Me to learn exists as a necessity"). (*See* δεῖ, page 79; δεῖ takes the same structure: δεῖ με μαθεῖν/δεῖ is the third person singular of the contract verb δέω "bind.") Χρή unites with verbs other than the omitted present indicative: χρή + ἦν→χρῆν "it was necessary"/χρή + εἶναι → χρῆναι "to be necessary"/χρή + ᾖ (subjunctive) → χρῇ/χρή + εἴη (optative) → χρείη.

Note that δοκέω is structured both personally (δοκῶ μοι μαθεῖν "I think it good for me to learn. I am determined to learn") and impersonally (δοκεῖ μοι τοῦτο μαθεῖν "It seems good to me to learn this. I am determined to learn this"). It was used impersonally in the official phraseology for government decrees: ἔδοξε τῇ βουλῇ) . . . "The Council decided . . ." (literally, "It seemed good to the Council . . .").

ΑΣΚΗΣΙΣ

I. TRANSLATE: The Androgyne and the Creation of Mankind.

Δεῖ δὲ πρῶτον ὑμᾶς μαθεῖν τὴν ἀνθρωπίνην φύσιν καὶ τὰ παθήματα αὐτῆς. ἡ γὰρ πάλαι ἡμῶν φύσις οὐχ αὐτὴ ἦν ἥπερ νῦν, ἀλλ' ἀλλοία. πρῶτον μὲν γὰρ τρία ἦν τὰ γένη τὰ τῶν ἀνθρώπων, οὐχ ὥσπερ νῦν δύο, ἄρρεν καὶ θῆλυ, ἀλλὰ καὶ τρίτον προσῆν κοινὸν ἀμφοτέρων τούτων, οὗ
5 νῦν ὄνομα μόνον λοιπόν. ἀνδρόγυνον γὰρ ἓν τότε μὲν ἦν καὶ εἶδος καὶ ὄνομα ἐξ ἀμφοτέρων κοινὸν τοῦ τε ἄρρενος καὶ θήλεος, νῦν δὲ οὐκ ἔστιν ἀλλ' ἢ ἐν ὀνείδει ὄνομα κείμενον. ἔπειτα ὅλον ἦν ἑκάστου τοῦ ἀνθρώπου τὸ εἶδος στρογγύλον, νῶτον καὶ πλευρὰς κύκλῳ ἔχον, χεῖρας δὲ τέτταρας εἶχε, καὶ σκέλη τὰ ἴσα ταῖς χερσίν, καὶ πρόσωπα δύ' ἐπ' αὐχένι κυκλο-
10 τερεῖ, ὅμοια πάντῃ· κεφαλὴν δ' ἀμφοτέροις τοῖς προσώποις ἐναντίοις κειμένοις μίαν, καὶ ὦτα τέτταρα, καὶ αἰδοῖα δύο, καὶ τἆλλα πάντα ὡς ἀπὸ τούτων ἄν τις εἰκάσειεν. ἐπορεύετο δὲ καὶ ὀρθὸν ὥσπερ νῦν, ὁποτέ- ρωσε βουληθείη. καὶ ὁπότε ταχὺ ὁρμήσειεν θεῖν, ὥσπερ οἱ κυβιστῶντες καὶ εἰς ὀρθὸν τὰ σκέλη περιφερόμενοι κυβιστῶσι κύκλῳ, ὀκτὼ τότε οὖσι
15 τοῖς μέλεσιν ἀπερειδόμενοι ταχὺ ἐφέροντο κύκλῳ. ἦν δὲ διὰ ταῦτα τρία τὰ γένη καὶ τοιαῦτα, ὅτι τὸ μὲν ἄρρεν ἦν τοῦ ἡλίου τὴν ἀρχὴν ἔκγονον, τὸ δὲ θῆλυ τῆς γῆς, τὸ δὲ ἀμφοτέρων μετέχον τῆς σελήνης, ὅτι καὶ ἡ σελήνη ἀμφοτέρων μετέχει· περιφερῆ δὲ δὴ ἦν αὐτὰ καὶ ἡ πορεία αὐτῶν διὰ τὸ τοῖς γονεῦσιν ὅμοια εἶναι. ἦν οὖν τὴν ἰσχὺν δεινὰ καὶ τὴν ῥώμην,
20 καὶ τὰ φρονήματα μεγάλα εἶχον, ἐπεχείρησαν δὲ τοῖς θεοῖς, καὶ ὃ λέγει Ὅμηρος περὶ Ἐφιάλτου τε καὶ Ὤτου, περὶ ἐκείνων λέγεται, τὸ εἰς τὸν οὐρανὸν ἀνάβασιν ἐπιχειρεῖν ποιεῖν, ὡς ἐπιθῶνται τοῖς θεοῖς. ὁ οὖν Ζεὺς καὶ οἱ ἄλλοι θεοὶ ἐβουλεύοντο ὅτι χρὴ αὐτοὺς ποιῆσαι, καὶ ἠπόρουν. οὔτε γὰρ ὅπως ἀποκτείναιεν εἶχον καὶ ὥσπερ τοὺς γίγαντας κεραυνώσαν-
25 τες τὸ γένος ἀφανίσαιεν—αἱ τιμαὶ γὰρ αὐτοῖς καὶ τὰ ἱερὰ τὰ παρὰ τῶν ἀνθρώπων ἠφανίζετο—οὔτε ὅπως ἐῷεν ἀσελγαίνειν. μόγις δὴ ὁ Ζεὺς ἐννοήσας λέγει ὅτι "Δοκῶ μοι," ἔφη, "ἔχειν μηχανήν, ὡς ἂν εἶέν τε ἄνθρωποι καὶ παύσαιντο τῆς ἀκολασίας ἀσθενεῖς γενόμενοι." ταῦτα εἰπὼν ἔτεμνε τοὺς ἀνθρώπους δίχα, ὥσπερ οἱ τὰ ὄα τέμνοντες καὶ
30 μέλλοντες ταριχεύειν. —Πλάτων (Ἀριστοφάνης)

Reading Notes:

(1) τὰ παθήματα/τὸ πάθημα, -ατος (=τὸ πάθος, -ους) "that which happens (or happened) to a person or is *suffered* by a person" (*see* πάσχω, ἔπαθον)

(2) ἀλλοία/ἀλλοῖος, -α, -ον "of another sort or kind" (*see* ἄλλος, -η, -ον/ ποῖος, -α, -ον/ οἷος, -α, -ον, page 78/ ὅμοιος, -α, -ον)

(3) τρία/τρεῖς (masc. -fem.), τρία (neut.)/declension: acc. τρεῖς, τρία/gen. τριῶν/dat. τρισί "three"

(3) δύο (masc. -fem. -neut.)/declension: acc. δύο/gen. δυοῖν/dat. δυοῖν "two"

(4) προσῆν/πρόσ-ειμι

(4) κοινός, -ή, -όν "common"/κοινὸν ἀμφοτέρων "common to both"/ contast: καινός, -ή, -όν

(5) ὁ ἀνδρόγυνος, -ου (from ὁ ἀνήρ + ἡ γύνη)

(7) ἀλλ' ἤ = ἀλλὸ ἤ "other than"

(7) κείμενον/κεῖμαι see page 69/ used as a passive to τίθημι; hence, ὄνομα κεῖται = ὄνομα τίθεται

(8) στρογγύλος, -η, -ον "round, spherical"

(8) τὸ νῶτον, -ου, "back" (both of men and animals)

(8) πλευράς/ἡ πλευρά, -ᾶς "rib," pl. "sides"

(8) ἔχον participle

(8) τέτταρες (masc. -fem.), τέτταρα (neut.)/declension: acc. τέτταρας, τέτταρα/gen. τεττάρων/dat. τέτταρσι "four"

(9) αὐχένι/ ὁ αὐχήν, -ένος "neck"

(10) πάντη adv. "every way, on every side" (see πᾶς, πᾶσα, πᾶν)

(10) ἐναντίοις/ἐναντίος -α, -ον "opposite" (= ἀντίος, -α, -ον/ See ἀντί preposition with gen. "over against"

(11) ὦτα/ τὸ οὖς, ὠτός "ear"

(11) αἰδοῖα/τὸ αἰδοῖον, -ου "sexual organ, pundendum" (see αἰδοῖος, -α, -ον "having a claim to reverence or awe and shame"

(11) τἆλλα = τὰ ἄλλα

(12) εἰκάσειεν = εἰκάσαι/The sigmatic aorist has alternate forms: -σαις = -σειας/-σαι = -σειε(ν)/-σαιεν = -σειαν.. These so-called Aeolic optative terminations are common in Attic.

(12–13) ὁποτέρωσε adv. "toward which of two directions" (see ὁπότερος, -α, -ον "which of two"/ See page 42 for the suffix -σε indicating destination.

(13) ὁπότε see page 78

(13) ταχύ = ταχέως/The adverbial accusative of the neuter adjective is often used as an adverb.

(13) θεῖν/θέω = τρέχω

(13) κυβιστῶντες/κυβιστάω "tumble head foremost" (especially like a professional tumbler or acrobat, ὁ κυβιστής, -οῦ)

(14) περιφερόμενοι/περι-φέρω

(14) ὀκτώ "eight" indeclinable

(14) οὖσι participle

(15) ἀπερειδόμενοι/ἀπ-ερείδω

(15) διά (with accusative) "on account of"

(16) τοιαῦτα *see* page 78

(16) ὅτι resumes the idea of διὰ ταῦτα/*see* διότι "because"

(16) τὴν ἀρχήν adverbial accusative

(16) ἔκγονον/ἔκγονος, -ον "born from, offspring" (*see* ἐκγίγνομαι)

(17) μετέχον participle

(18) περιφερῆ/περιφερής, -ές "circular, revolving" = στρογγύλος, -η, -ον (*see* ἡ περιφέρεια, -ας "circumference")

(19) τὴν ἰσχύν adverbial accusative

(19) ῥώμην/ἡ ῥώμη, -ης = ἡ ἰσχύς (*see* ῥώομαι "move with speed")

(20) φρονήματα/τὸ φρόνημα, -ατος "mind, purpose, will, pride" (*see* ἡ φρήν)

(21) ὁ Ἐφιάλτης, -ου a nightmare demon, twin brother to ὁ Ὦτος, -ου; they were gigantic sons of Poseidon and challenged the gods to battle, piling mountains upon moutains to reach up to the heavens

(21) ἀνάβασιν/ἡ ἀνάβασις, -εως (*see* ἀνα-βαίνω)

(22) ἐπιθῶνται/ἐπι-τίθημι

(24) ὅπως (*see* page 78) = ἵνα, ὡς

(24) εἶχον/ἔχω can mean "*have* power to do, be able"

(24) γίγαντας/ὁ γίγας, -αντος "*giant*" (from ἡ γῆ + γίγνομαι because the giants were earth born)

(25) κεραυνώσαντες/κεραυνόω "strike with thunderbolts" (*see* ὁ κεραυνός, -οῦ "thunderbolt")

(25) ἀφανίσαιεν/ἀ-φαν-ίζω (*see* φαίνω)

(26) ἠφανίζετο The verb is singular since the subject (αἱ τιμαί... καὶ τὰ ἱερά) is treated as a neuter plural; *see* page 62 exercise 4. /τὰ ἱερά (ἱερός, -ά, -όν) "sacred things," that is, "religious observances and sacrifices"

(26) ἀσελγαίνειν/ἀσελγαίνω "behave licentiously" (*see* ἀσελγής, -ές)

(26) μόγις *adv.* "with trouble, scarcely" (*see* ὁ μόγος, -ου = ὁ πόνος, -ου)

(27) ἐννοήσας/ἐν-νοέω

(28) ἄνθρωποι = οἱ ἄνθρωποι

(28) ἀκολασίας/ἡ ἀκολασία, -ας = ἡ ἀσέλγεια, -ας (*see* ἀ + κολάζω "chastise restrain")

(28) ἀσθενεῖς/ἀσθενής, -ές "weak" (ἀ + τὸ σθένος, -ους = ἡ ἰσχύς)

(29) δίχα *adv.* "in two" (*see* δύο, δίς)

(29) ὄα/τὸ ὄον, -ου "sorb apple or service berry," the fruit of the tree *Sorbus domestica*, which was split and pickled for use

(30) ταριχεύειν/ταριχεύω "preserve food by salting, pickling, or smoking; embalm"

II. MATCH the second phrase to the first by changing it into the same case.

1. τὴν καλὴν σελήνην
   (τὸ ἄρρεν γένος)

2. αἱ θήλειαι βόες
   (τὸ ταχὺ σκέλος)

3. τῇ ὅλῃ πόλει
   (τό ἀληθὲς εἶδος)

4. τὰς αἰσχρὰς γραῦς
   (τὸ ἡδὺ μέλος)

5. πάντες γονεῖς
   (πᾶν ὄνειδος)

6. ταῖς ἀναγκαίαις μηχαναῖς
   (ἡ ἡδεῖα φωνή)

7. τοὺς καινοὺς βασιλέας
   (ἡ μεγίστη πόλις)

8. τῷ ἀληθεῖ δεσπότῃ
   (ὁ εὐδαίμων ἀνήρ)

9. τῶν λοιπῶν τριήρων
   (τὸ εὔδαιμον ἄστυ)

10. τοῦ προτέρου ἰσχέως
    (ἡ γεραιὰ γραῦς)

11. τοὺς ταχεῖς ἵππους
    (ἡ ἀληθὴς φιλοσοφία)

12. ταῖς καιναῖς φύσεσι
    (ὁ ἡδὺς οἶνος)

13. ἰχθύσι ἀγαθοῖς
    (ἰσχὺς μεγάλη)

14. ἄρρενος παιδός
    (ἀληθὴς ἐπιστήμη)

15. ἄλλαι χεῖρες
    (καλὸν ἄστυ)

16. πολλὰς τριήρεις
    (παῖς θήλεια)

17. ὅμοια εἴδη
    (μέγα ἄστυ)

18. θερμοῦ ὕδατος
    (ἀληθὴς δόξα)

19. ἐχθροὶ βασιλεῖς
    (ἄρρην θήρ)

20. βασιλέων βροτῶν
    (ἕτερος ἰχθύς)

III. MATCH the second noun to the first by changing it into the same form.

1. πατέρες (ὁ γονεύς)

2. ποιητῶν (τὸ γένος)

3. γέροντας (ἡ γραῦς)

4. ἄνδρας (ὁ βοῦς)

5. πένης (ὁ πῆχυς)

6. βωμοῦ (ἡ βοῦς)

7. βίον (ὁ Σωκράτης)

8. ἀληθείας (τὸ ἄστυ)

9. θυγατρί (ἡ πόλις)

10. θῆρες (τὸ ἄστυ)

11. ἀνθρώπου (ἡ πόλις)

12. οἰωνούς (ὁ ἰχθύς)

13. φρενός (ἡ γραῦς)

14. λέωντι (ὁ βοῦς)

15. ἔργοις (ἡ τριήρης)

16. λόγῳ (τὸ εἶδος)

17. δεῖπνα (τὸ ὄνειδος)

18. δούλων (ὁ βασιλεύς)

19. δεσπότην (ἡ φύσις)

20. γυναικός (τὸ σκέλος)

IV. MATCH the adjective to the noun by changing it into the same form.

1. πόλεως (τερπνός)

2. παίδων (ἄρρην)

3. βοΐ (θῆλυς)

4. βασιλέας (δίκαιος)

5. γραῦς (ἄδικος)

6. μηχανῇ (ἡδύς)

7. ἄστη (μέγας)

8. ἰχθῦς (ταχύς)

9. πόλιν (πᾶς)

10. βουσί (θῆλυς)

11. ὀνείδη (ἀληθής)

12. ἄστεως (εὐδαίμων)

13. ἰσχεῖ (ἀληθής)

14. μέλους (ἡδύς)

15. γονεῦσι (ἀληθής)

16. ἰχθύων (ταχύς)

17. οἴνου (ἡδύς)

18. λόγους (ἀληθής)

19. πηχέως (μέγας)

20. σκέλος (ἄλλος)

V. REPHRASE the following sentences as indirectly quoted material introduced by ἔφη ὁ Ἀριστοφάνης . . . ; use the infinitive structure instead of ὅτι. (See pages 68, 94.)

1. ἡ πάλαι ἀνθρώπων φύσις οὐχ ἡ αὐτὴ ἦν ἥπερ νῦν.

2. πρῶτον μὲν γὰρ τρία ἦν τὰ γένη τὰ τῶν ἀνθρώπων, ἄρρεν καὶ θῆλυ καὶ τρίτον ᾧ ὄνομα ἐτίθετο ἀνδρόγυνον.

3. τὸ δὲ ἀνδρόγυνον ἀμφοτέρων μετεῖχε τῶν ἄλλων γενῶν, τοῦ τε ἄρρενος καὶ τοῦ θήλεος.

4. ὅλον δὲ ἦν πάντων τῶν ἀνθρώπων τὸ πάλαι εἶδος στρογγύλον.

5. ἐπορεύετο δὲ καὶ ὀρθὸν ὥσπερ νῦν, ὁποτέρωσε βουληθείη, καὶ ἐκυβίστων κύκλῳ ὅτε ταχὺ ὁρμήσαι δραμεῖν.

VI. REPHRASE the following sentences, changing to a past tense context and using the optative of secondary subordination.

1. δεινὰ δὲ τὰ τρία γένη τὰ τῶν ἀνθρώπων ἐστὶ τὴν ἰσχὺν ἐὰν βουληθῇ ἄδικα εἶναι.

2. βούλονται γὰρ ἀναβῆναι εἰς οὐρανὸν ἵνα ἐπιθῶνται τοῖς θεοῖς μαχόμενοι ὥσπερ Ἐφιάλτης τε καὶ Ὦτος.

3. ὁ οὖν Ζεὺς καὶ οἱ ἄλλοι θεοὶ βουλεύονται ὅ τι ἂν χρῇ αὐτοὺς ποιῆσαι.

4. ἀλλ' ἀποροῦσιν οὐδ' ἔχουσιν ὅπως ἀποκτείνωσι τοῦτο τὸ ἀνθρώπων γένος ὥσπερ τοὺς γίγαντας κεραυνώσαντες.

5. δοκεῖ δὲ τῷ Διὶ τὰ τρία γένη ἕκαστα δίχα τεμεῖν ἵνα γένωνται ἄνθρωποι ὥσπερ νῦν ἐσμεν.

VII. MATCH the second verb to the first by changing it into the same form.

1. προσῇσαν (ὁράω)

2. ἔσωζε (ἀπορέω)

3. ζῴη (εὐτυχέω)

4. ἐδόκει (ὁρμάω)

5. ἐπορεύομεν (ἐάω)

6. ἐγράφου (δίδωμι)

7. νοεῖν (ζάω)

8. ὑπεκρίνω (πορεύω)

9. ὁρῷεν (ποιέω)

10. ἐβούλου (χράομαι)

11. ἑώρα (γαμέω)
12. δηλοῖο (τιμάω)
13. ἠπόρουν (τέμνω)
14. ἀξιοῦμεν (εὐτυχέω)
15. ἔθου (ποιέω)

16. ἐδίδου (ὁρμάω)
17. εἶμεν (βαίνω)
18. βουλεύῃς (ἐάω)
19. ἐᾶν (ἵστημι)
20. δοῦναι (τέμνω)

VII. GIVE THE LEXICAL ENTRY and then the equivalent form using the present verbal stem (for example, ἐπράχθητε/ πράττω, ἐπράττεσθε).

1. ἐβουλήθημεν
2. τεθείη
3. τμηθῶσι
4. νοηθεῖεν
5. ἐγράφης
6. ἐγράφω
7. νομισθέντα
8. ἐλειφθείην
9. ἔγνωμεν
10. ἤχθητε

11. ὀφθείημεν
12. βληθέν
13. ἔβης
14. δοθῇ
15. ἧκε
16. ποθῆναι
17. ἔλαβε
18. ηὑρέθητε
19. ἁρπασθείσης
20. εἴθη

IX. NOTE THE PATTERN in each of the quotations and compose a translation of the English sentences, using the same pattern.

1. δεῖ ὑμᾶς μαθεῖν τὴν ἀνθρωπίνην φύσιν. —Πλάτων

We must listen to Socrates.

The old woman had to find the cow.

2. οὔτε ὅπως ἀποκτείναιεν εἶχον. —Πλάτων

He did not have it in his power to save Socrates.

No one could fight with nature.

3. φίλοις τ' ἀληθὴς ἦν φίλος, παροῦσί τε
   καὶ μὴ παροῦσιν. —Εὐριπίδης

For everyone he was a good teacher, both when they learned and when they didn't.

Life is always sweet for mortals, both when they are fortunate and when they are not. (εὐτυχέω/δυστυχέω)

18

Future

*κόσμον τόνδε οὔτε τις θεῶν οὔτε ἀνθρώπων ἐποίησεν, ἀλλ' ἦν ἀεὶ καὶ ἔστιν
καὶ ἔσται πῦρ. —Ἡράκλειτος*

Lesson 18
Future Tense

The future expresses a verbal action that will occur at some future time. In English, the future is expressed by the auxiliary verb "will/shall"; in Greek, the future has a separate conjugation, but this same connotation of will or volition can be noted in the Homeric dialect, where the future sometimes is used in structures that would ordinarily have required a subjunctive. For the same reason, certain forms of the future can be used to express purpose; and the future conjugation often is deponent, expressing as the middle voice a verbal idea that is active in other tenses.

**Future/
Conjugation**

The sign of the future tense is the suffix -σ^ϵ/o-. This is a thematic suffix (unlike the athematic -$\sigma\alpha$- suffix of the aorist) and the future is accordingly always conjugated thematically.

The suffix is added to the present verbal stem to form the future active and middle.

παιδεύ-σ-ο-μεν.	We shall teach.
παιδευ-σ-ό-μεθα.	We shall teach (for ourselves).

The future has a distinct form for the passive. (Only the future and the aorist passive can distinguish between middle and passive meanings other than by context.) To form the future passive, the future suffix is added to the aorist passive stem.

παιδευ-θη-σ-ό-μεθα.	We shall be taught.

The aspect of the future active and middle is progressive, like that of the present stem from which it is formed. The aspect of the future passive is punctual, like that of the aorist passive stem.

The personal suffixes for the future are primary (*see* page 28) and the future is a primary tense, that is, appropriate with subjunctives but not with the optative of secondary subordination. The future passive has middle-passive personal suffixes.

The future has a participle, an infinitive, and an optative, but it has no subjunctive since it is itself close to the volitional meaning of the subjunctive.

The future passive is completely predictable from the aorist passive stem, but the stem for the future active and middle has certain unpredictable elements and must, therefore, be learned as one of the "principle-parts" of the verb.

There are, however, general patterns that will facilitate your familiarity with the future principle part.

1. The -σ^ϵ/o- suffix may combine with the final consonant of the verbal stem.

γραφ-σ-ο-μεν → γράψομεν (*see* aorist: ἐγράψαμεν)

2. Present stems ending in a liquid (λ, μ, ν, ρ) add -$\epsilon\sigma^\epsilon$/o- to form the future active and middle; the sigma is lost between vowels and thus is conjugated like an -έω contract verb.

κριν-έσ-ο-μεν → κρινοῦμεν (*see* aorist: ἐκρίναμεν)

3. In some verbs, the future active and middle stem is actually a completely different verb that functions as the future for another verb.

οἴ-σ-ο-μεν (*see* present: φέρομεν/aorist: ἠνέγκαμεν)

4. In some verbs, the future active and middle stem is conjugated deponently with middle-passive personal suffixes.

ἀκου-σ-ό-μεϑα (*see* present: ἀκούομεν)

The chart summarizes the future conjugation.

Active	Middle (only)	Passive (only)
Indicative:		
παιδεύ-σ-ω	παιδεύ-σ-ο-μαι	παιδευ-ϑή-σ-ο-μαι
-εις	-ει	-ει
etc.	etc.	etc.
Optative:		
παιδεύ-σ-ο-ι-μι	παιδευ-σ-ο-ί-μην	παιδευ-ϑη-σ-ο-ί-μην
-ο-ι-ς	-ο-ι-ο	-ο-ι-ο
etc.	etc.	etc.
Infinitive:		
παιδεύ-σ-ειν	παιδεύ-σ-ε-σϑαι	παιδευ-ϑή-σ-ε-σϑαι
Participle:		
παιδεύ-σ-ων, -ουσα,	παιδευ-σ-ό-μενος,	παιδευ-ϑη-σ-ό-μενος,
-ον	-η, -ον	-η, -ον

Future Participle/ Purpose

The future participle (with its connotation of volition or intention) can express purpose.

καταβαίνω εἰς Πειραιᾶ προσευξόμενος τῇ ϑεῷ.

"I go down to the Piraeus in order to pray to the goddess (that is, I, intending to pray to the goddess, go...)." Contrast the structure with the subjunctive: καταβαίνω εἰς Πειραιᾶ ἵνα προσεύχωμαι τῇ ϑεῷ. (The Piraeus is the port city of Athens: ὁ Πειραιεύς, -έως/acc. τὸν Πειραιέα → Πειραιᾶ.)

κατέβην εἰς Πειραιᾶ προσευξόμενος τῇ ϑεῷ. —Πλάτων

"I went down to the Piraeus, intending to pray to the goddess." Contrast the optative: κατέβην εἰς Πειραιᾶ ἵνα προσευχοίμην τῇ ϑεῷ.

Future Optative/ Future in Secondary Subordination

The future optative may represent a future tense indirectly quoted in a past tense context. This is the only use for the future optative. This structure is not obligatory; a future indicative may be retained as an indicative in a past tense context for greater vividness of expression.

εἶπον ὅτι αὔριον Σωκράτης καταβήσεται εἰς Πειραιᾶ.

I said that tomorrow Socrates will go down to the Piraeus.

εἶπον ὅτι αὔριον Σωκράτης καταβήσοιτο εἰς Πειραιᾶ.

I said that tomorrow Socrates would go down to the Piraeus.

Principle Parts For Reference/ Some Familiar Verbs

ἀγανακτέω, ἀγανακτήσω, ἠγανάκτησα

ἀγγέλλω, ἀγγελῶ, ἤγγειλα, ἠγγέλθην

ἄγω, ἄξω, ἤγαγον, ἤχθην

ἀδικέω, ἀδικήσομαι, ἠδίκησα, ἠδικήθην

αἱρέω, αἱρήσω, εἷλον, ᾑρέθην

αἴρω, ἀρῶ, ἦρα, ἤρθην

αἰσθάνομαι, αἰσθήσομαι, ᾐσθόμην

ἀκούω, ἀκούσομαι, ἤκουσα, ἠκούσθην

ἀπο-δύω, ἀπο-δύσω, ἀπ-έδυσα (ἀπ-έδυν), ἀπ-εδύθην

ἀπο-θνῇσκω, ἀπο-θανοῦμαι, ἀπ-έθανον

ἀπο-κτείνω, ἀπο-κτενῶ, ἀπ-έκτεινα

ἀπ-όλλυμι, ἀπ-ολῶ, ἀπ-ώλεσα (ἀπ-ωλόμην)

ἁρπάζω, ἁρπάσομαι, ἥρπασα, ἡρπάσθην

ἄρχω, ἄρξω, ἦρξα, ἤρχθην

βαίνω, βήσομαι, ἔβην

βάλλω, βαλῶ, ἔβαλον, ἐβλήθην

βοάω, βοήσομαι, ἐβόησα

βοηθέω, βοηθήσω, ἐβοήθησα, ἐβοηθήθην

βούλομαι, βουλήσομαι, _____, ἐβουλήθην

γαμέω, γαμῶ (γαμήσω), ἔγημα, ἐγαμήθην

γίγνομαι, γενήσομαι/γενηθήσομαι, ἐγενόμην

γιγνώσκω, γνώσομαι, ἔγνων, ἐγνώσθην

γράφω, γράψω, ἔγραψα, ἐγράφην

δείκνυμι, δείξω, ἔδειξα, ἐδείχθην

διδάσκω, διδάξω, ἐδίδαξα, ἐδιδάχθην

δίδωμι, δώσω, ἔδωκα, ἐδόθην

διώκω, διώξομαι (διώξω), ἐδίωξα, ἐδιώχθην

δύναμαι, δυνήσομαι, ἐδυνήθην

ἐθέλω (θέλω), ἐθελήσω (θελήσω), ἠθέλησα

εἰμί, ἔσομαι ("regular" in the future except for third sing.: ἔσται)

ἐράω, ἐρασθήσομαι, ἠράσθην (passive with active meaning in future and aorist; also a deponent present: ἔραμαι)

ἔρχομαι, ἐλεύσομαι, ἦλθον

ἐρωτάω, ἐρωτήσω (ἐρήσομαι), ἠρώτησα (ἠρόμην)

ἐσθίω, ἔδομαι, ἔφαγον

εὑρίσκω, εὑρήσω, ηὗρον, ηὑρέθην

εὔχομαι, εὔξομαι, ηὐξάμην

ἔχω, ἕξω (σχήσω), ἔσχον

ζάω, ζήσω (ζήσομαι)

ἡγέομαι, ἡγήσομαι, ἡγησάμην

θαυμάζω, θαυμάσομαι, ἐθαύμασα

θύω, θύσω, ἔθυσα, ἐτύθην

ἵημι, ἥσω, ἧκα, εἵθην

ἵστημι, στήσω, ἔστησα (ἔστην), ἐστάθην

καθίζω (καθίζομαι), καθιῶ (καθιζήσομαι), ἐκάθισα (ἐκαθισάμην)

καλέω, καλῶ, ἐκάλεσα, ἐκλήθην

καλύπτω, καλύψω, ἐκάλυψα, ἐκαλύφθην

κελεύω, κελεύσω, ἐκέλευσα, ἐκελεύσθην

κομίζω, κομιῶ, ἐκόμισα, ἐκομίσθην

κρίνω, κρινῶ, ἔκρινα, ἐκρίθην

λαμβάνω, λήψομαι, ἔλαβον, ἐλήφθην

λέγω, λέξω (ἐρῶ), ἔλεξα (εἶπον), (δι-)ελέγην (ἐρρήθην)

λείπω, λείψω, ἔλιπον, ἐλείφθην

λούω (loses υ before a short vowel and contracts: λού-ο-μεν → λοῦμεν/
    λοῦτε/λοῦσι/ἔλουν), λούσομαι, ἔλουσα

μανθάνω, μαθήσομαι, ἔμαθον

μάχομαι, μαχοῦμαι, ἐμαχεσάμην

μέλλω, μελλήσω, ἐμέλησα

μένω, μενῶ, ἔμεινα

νικάω, νικήσω, ἐνίκησα, ἐνικάθην

νοέω, (δια-)νοήσομαι, ἐνόησα, ἐνοήθην

νομίζω, νομιῶ, ἐνόμισα, ἐνομίσθην

οἴχομαι, οἰχήσομαι

ὄμνυμι, ὀμοῦμαι, ὤμοσα, ὠμόθην

ὁράω, ὄψομαι, εἶδον, ὤφθην

παιδεύω, παιδεύσω, ἐπαίδευσα, ἐπαιδεύθην

παίω, παίσω (παιήσω), ἔπαισα, ἐπαίσθην

πάσχω, πείσομαι, ἔπαθον

παύω, παύσω, ἔπαυσα, ἐπαύθην

πείθω, πείσω, ἔπεισα, ἐπείσθην

πέμπω, πέμψω, ἔπεμψα, ἐπέμφθην

πίνω, πιοῦμαι, ἔπιον, (κατ-)επόθην

πίπτω, πεσοῦμαι, ἔπεσον

πλάττω, _____, ἔπλασα, ἐπλάσθην

πράττω, πράξω, ἔπραξα, ἐπράχθην

σημαίνω, σημανῶ, ἐσήμηνα, ἐσημάνθην

σῴζω, σώσω, ἔσωσα, ἐσώθην

τέμνω, τεμῶ, ἔτεμον, ἐτμήθην

τίθημι, θήσω, ἔθηκα, ἐτέθην

τίκτω, τέξομαι, ἔτεκον

τρέφω, θρέψω, ἔθρεψα, ἐτράφην

τρέχω, δραμοῦμαι, ἔδραμον

τυγχάνω, τεύξομαι, ἔτυχον

φαίνω, φανῶ, ἔφηνα, ἐφάνθην (ἐφάνην)

φέρω, οἴσω, ἤνεγκα (ἤνεγκον), ἠνέχθην

φεύγω, φεύξομαι, ἔφυγον

φημί (φάσκω), φήσω, ἔφησα

φθείρω, φθερῶ, ἔφθειρα, ἐφθάρην

φιλέω, φιλήσω, ἐφίλησα, ἐφιλήθην

φύω, φύσω, ἔφυσα (ἔφυν)

χράω, χρήσω, ἔχρησα, ἐχρήσθην

ΟΝΟΜΑΤΑ ΚΑΙ ΡΗΜΑΤΑ

ἡ ναῦς, νεώς	ship (declensional stem alternates between -αυ- and -ηυ-, with loss of intervocalic upsilon: τὴν ναῦ-ν/τῆς νε-ώς, by exchange of quantity/τῇ νη-ΐ/αἱ νῆ-ες/τὰς ναῦ-ς/ τῶν νε-ῶν/ ταῖς ναυ-σί)
ὁ νεώς, νεώ	temple (Type II declension, the so called Attic declension: derived from ὁ νηός,-οῦ by exchange of quantity: τὸν νεών/τοῦ νεώ/τῷ νεῴ/οἱ νεῴ/ τοὺς νεώς/τῶν νεών/τοῖς νεῴς)
τὸ ἄλσος, -ους	grove of trees, especially a sacred grove
τὸ δέρας (δέρος), -ατος (-ους)	(common only in nom. and acc.) = τὸ δέρμα, -ατος
ὁ ποῦς, ποδός	foot
ὁ ταῦρος, -ου	bull

τὸ μέγεθος, -ους	greatness, magnitude (*see* μέγας, μεγάλη, μέγα)
τὸ στόμα, -ατος	mouth
ὁ ὀδούς, -όντος	tooth
ἡ ἀσπίς, -ίδος	shield
τὸ δόρυ, δόρατος (δουρός)	stem, tree, beam, shaft of a spear, spear
ὁ σίδηρος, -ου	iron, anything made of iron: tool sword, knife, etc.
ὁ χαλκός, -οῦ	copper, bronze, anything made of metal (*see* χάλκεος, -α, -ον, "brazen," contracted in Attic: χαλκοῦς, -ῆ, -οῦν)
ἀλλήλους, -ας, -α	(accusative) one another/(reflexive, used only in acc., gen., and dat. plural: ἀλλήλων/ἀλλήλοις, -αις, -οις)
μέσος, -η, -ον	middle, in the middle
ἥμισυς, -εια, -υ	half
ἄγριος, -α, -ον	living in the fields (that is, ὁ ἀγρός, -οῦ), wild, savage
ἄθροος, -α, -ον	in crowds, heaps, or masses; crowded together
πλείων, -ον (gen. πλείονος)	more (*see* πολύς, πολλή, πολύ)
πλέω, πλεύσομαι (πλευσοῦμαι), ἔπλευσα, ἐπλεύσθην	sail (*see* ὁ πλόος, -οῦ/contracted in Attic: ὁ πλοῦς, πλοῦ)
ὁρμίζω, ὁρμιοῦμαι, ὥρμισα, ὡρμίσθην	bring into harbor or safe anchorage (*see* ὁ ὅρμος, -ου "chain, anchorage, the inner part of a harbor, haven, refuge")
τάσσω, τάξω, ἔταξα, ἐτάχθην (ἐτάγην)	draw up in order of battle, appoint to a task (*see* ἡ τάξις, -εως "arrangement"/ἐπι-τάσσω "enjoin, order, put upon one as a duty")
ζεύγνυμι, ζεύξω, ἔζευξα, ἐζεύχθην (ἐζύγην)	yoke (*see* τὸ ζεῦγος, -ους "yoke of beasts, carriage drawn by yoked beasts")
φυσάω, φυσήσω, ἔφυσα, ἐφυσήθην	blow
φθάνω, φθήσομαι, ἔφθασα (ἔφθην)	anticipate, be beforehand, come or act first/ (The action in which one

is beforehand is usually expressed
by the participle agreeing with the
subject: ἔφϑασε ἀποϑανών "he died
first"; but also reversed, with
φϑάνω as the participle: φϑάσας
ἀπέϑανεν.)

φοβέω, φοβήσω, ἐφόβησα, ἐφοβήϑην	frighten (*mid.* be afraid) (*see* φοβερός, -ά, -όν)
χρίω, χρίσω, ἔχρισα, ἐχρίσϑην	annoint (*see* χριστός, -ή, -όν)
ϑεάομαι, ϑεάσομαι, ἐϑεασάμην	gaze at, behold (with a sense of wonder), view as a spectator (*see* ἡ ϑέα, -ας "viewing"/τὸ ϑέατρον, -ου)
ἀνα-τέλλω, _____, ἀνέτειλα	cause to rise, rise (*see* τέλλω "accomplish"/ τὸ τέλος, -ους "consumation, ritual, completion, end")
μαστεύω, μαστεύσω, ἐμάστευσα	seek, search after

ΑΣΚΗΣΙΣ

I. TRANSLATE: Jason and Medea at Colchis.

Παραπλεύσαντες δὲ Θερμώδοντα καὶ Καύκασον ἐπὶ Φᾶσιν ποταμὸν
ἦλθον· οὗτος τῆς Κολχικῆς ἐστιν. ἐγκαθορμισθείσης δὲ τῆς νεώς, ἧκε
πρὸς Αἰήτην Ἰάσων καὶ τὰ ἐπιταγέντα ὑπὸ Πελίου λέγων παρεκάλει
δοῦναι τὸ δέρας αὐτῷ. ὁ δὲ δώσειν ὑπέσχετο, ἐὰν τοὺς χαλκόποδας
5 ταύρους μόνος καταζεύξῃ. ἦσαν δὲ ἄγριοι παρ' αὐτῷ ταῦροι δύο, μεγέθει
διαφέροντες, δῶρον Ἡφαίστου, οἳ χαλκοῦς μὲν εἶχον πόδας, πῦρ δὲ ἐκ
στομάτων ἐφύσων. τούτους αὐτῷ ζεύξαντι ἐπέτασσε σπείρειν δράκοντος
ὀδόντας. εἶχε γὰρ λαβὼν παρ' Ἀθηνᾶς τοὺς ἡμίσεις ὧν Κάδμος ἔσπειρεν
ἐν Θήβαις· ἀποροῦντος δὲ τοῦ Ἰάσονος πῶς ἂν δύναιτο τοὺς ταύρους
10 καταζεῦξαι, Μήδεια αὐτοῦ ἔρωτα ἴσχει· ἦν δὲ αὕτη θυγάτηρ Αἰήτου
καὶ Εἰδυίας τῆς Ὠκεανοῦ, φαρμακίς. φοβουμένη δὲ μὴ πρὸς τῶν
ταύρων διαφθαρῇ, κρύφα τοῦ πατρὸς συνεργήσειν αὐτῷ πρὸς τὴν
κατάζευξιν τῶν ταύρων ἐπηγγείλατο καὶ τὸ δέρας ἐγχειριεῖν ἐὰν ὀμόσῃ
αὐτὴν ἕξειν γυναῖκα καὶ εἰς Ἑλλάδα σύμπλουν ἀγάγηται. ὀμόσαντος δὲ
15 Ἰάσονος, φάρμακον δίδωσιν ᾧ καταζευγνύναι μέλλοντα τοὺς ταύρους
ἐκέλευσε χρῖσαι τήν τε ἀσπίδα καὶ τὸ δόρυ καὶ τὸ σῶμα· τούτῳ γὰρ
χρισθέντα ἔφη πρὸς μίαν ἡμέραν μητ' ἂν ὑπὸ πυρὸς ἀδικηθήσεσθαι
μήτε ὑπὸ σιδήρου. ἐδήλωσε δὲ αὐτῷ σπειρομένων τῶν ὀδόντων ἐκ γῆς
ἄνδρας μέλλειν ἀναδύεσθαι αὐτῷ μαχησομένους, οὓς ἔλεγεν ἐπειδὰν
20 ἀθρόους θεάσηται, βάλλειν εἰς μέσον λίθους ἄποθεν, ὅταν δὲ ὑπὲρ τούτου
μάχωνται πρὸς ἀλλήλους, τότε κτείνειν αὐτούς. Ἰάσων δὲ τοῦτο ἀκούσας
καὶ χρισάμενος τῷ φαρμάκῳ, παραγενόμενος εἰς τὸ τοῦ νεὼ ἄλσος
ἐμάστευε τοὺς ταύρους, καὶ σὺν πολλῷ πυρὶ ὁρμήσαντας αὐτοὺς κατέζευξε.
σπείραντος δὲ αὐτοῦ τοὺς ὀδόντας ἀνέτελλον ἐκ τῆς γῆς ἄνδρες ἔνοπλοι.
25 ὁ δὲ ὅπου πλείονας ἑώρα, βάλλων ἀφανῶς λίθους, πρὸς αὐτοὺς μαχομένους
πρὸς ἀλλήλους προσελθὼν ἀνῄρει. καὶ καταζευχθέντων τῶν ταύρων οὐκ

ἐδίδου τὸ δέρας Αἰήτης, ἐβούλετο δὲ τήν τε Ἀργὼ καταφλέξαι καὶ κτεῖναι τοὺς ἐμπλέοντας. φθάσασα δὲ Μήδεια τὸν Ἰάσονα νυκτὸς ἐπὶ τὸ δέρας ἤγαγε καὶ τὸν φυλάσσοντα δράκοντα κατακοιμίσασα τοῖς φαρμάκοις
30 μετὰ Ἰάσονος, ἔχουσα τὸ δέρας, ἐπὶ τὴν Ἀργὼ παρεγένετο.
    —Ἀπολλόδωρος

Reading Notes:

(1) Θερμώδοντα (namely ποταμόν)

(1) Καύκασον/ὁ Καύκασος, -ου a mountain between the Euxine and Caspian seas

(2) Κολχικῆς (namely γῆς)

(4) χαλκόποδας/χαλκό-πους, -ποδος

(5) δύο see page 128, note 3

(6) διαφέροντες/δια-φέρω "differ" (with instrumental dative)

(6) ὁ Ἥφαιστος, -ου a lame god, the son of Hera

(8) Ἀθηνᾶς/ἡ Ἀθήνη, -ης (also ἡ Ἀθηναία, -ας, contracted after the fifth century to Ἀθηνᾶ, -ᾶς) Athene, daughter of Zeus

(8) ὁ Κάδμος, -ου the mythical king of Thebes who founded the city by sowing the teeth of a serpent in the land; from the teeth grew the so-called Spartoi or "sown men," the autochthonous people of Thebes

(9) πῶς ἂν δύναιτο indirect quotation of the question: πῶς ἂν δυναίμην; (The particle ἄν is lost in indirect quotation only when a generalized subjunctive clause is shifted to an optative of secondary subordination in a past tense context—see page 94.)

(10) ἴσχει/ἴσχω = ἔχω

(11) τῆς Ὠκεανοῦ patronymic (see page 52, note 2)

(11) ἡ φαρμακίς, -ίδος (feminine of ὁ φαρμακεύς, -έως) "witch" (see τὸ φάρμακον, -ου)

(12) διαφθάρῃ see page 85, subjunctive clauses of fearing

(13) κατάζευξιν/ἡ κατά-ζευξις, -εως

(13) ἐχειριεῖν/ἐγ-χειρίζω, ἐγ-χειριῶ

(14) σύμπλουν/σύμ-πλοος, -ον, contracted to σύμ-πλους, -ουν (see πλέω)

(17) πρὸς μίαν ἡμέραν "(for up) to one day"

(17) ἂν ... ἀδικηθήσεσθαι The ἄν indicates that a potential, either past or present, is being quoted; the future infinitive is the result of the future implications of a present-future potential: ἀδικοῖτο ἄν "he is likely to be hurt." (Very rarely ἄν is used with a future indicative as the equivalent for an optative in this sense of present-future likelihood; hence Apollodorus has used the future infinitive. More commonly a Greek writer would have written: ἔφη ἂν ἀδικεῖσθαι (or ἂν ἀδικηθῆναι).

(20) ἄποθεν "from (far) away" (*see* page 42 for the suffix -θεν)

(20) ὑπέρ "on behalf of"

(24) ἔνοπλοι/ἔν-οπλος, -ον (*see* τὸ ὅπλον, -ου)

(25) ὅπου *see* page 78

(25) ἀφανῶς/ἀ-φανῶς (*see* φαίνω)

(26) ἀνῄρει/ἀν-αίρέω = κτείνω

(27) Ἀργώ/ἡ Ἀργώ, -όος the name of Jason's ship/ a Type III noun with a stem ending in -ο(ι); declined with loss of intervocalic iota and subsequent contraction: τὴν Ἀργό-α → Ἀργώ/τῆς Ἀργό-ος → Ἀργοῦς/τῇ Ἀργο-ῖ

(27) καταφλέξαι/κατα-φλέγω, -φλέξω, -έφλεξα "burn up"

(28) νυκτός *see* page 118, note 2

(29) φυλάσσοντα/φυλάσσω (*see* ὁ φύλαξ, -ακος)

(29) κατακοιμίσασα/κατα-κοιμίζω, -κοιμιῶ, -εκοίμισα "put to sleep"

II. IDENTIFY the basic pattern in the formation of the future principle part for each verb listed on pages 136–138.

III. CHANGE each verb to the passive; to aid you, the aorist principle part is given in parentheses.

1. δώσει (ἐδόθην)

2. ὄψομαι (ὤφθην)

3. θήσουσι (ἐτέθην)

4. φθερεῖς (ἐφθάρην)

5. γαμοῦμεν (ἐγαμήθην)

6. στήσεις (ἐστάθην)

7. φιλήσετε (ἐφιλήθην)

8. αἱρήσειν (ἡρέθην)

9. ἀδικησοίμην (ἠδικήθην)

10. ἀκούσεσθαι (ἠκούσθην)

11. ἀρεῖς (ἤρθην)

12. πέμψουσι (ἐπέμφθην)

13. τεμεῖτε (ἐτμήθην)

14. κομιοίης (ἐκομίσθην)

15. φθεροῖεν (ἐφθάρην)

16. οἴσεις (ἠνέχθην)

17. σημανεῖς (ἐσημάνθην)

18. φανεῖ (ἐφάνθην)

19. φιλήσεις (ἐφιλήθην)

20. ἤσεις (εἴθην)

IV. CHANGE each verb to the corresponding future; to aid you, the future principle part is given in parentheses.

1. ἔδραμες (δραμοῦμαι)

2. ἔπαθεν (πείσομαι)

3. ἔθεμεν (θήσω)

4. ἐνίκα (νικήσω)

5. ποιήσαιμι (ποιήσω)

6. ἔπιε (πίουμαι)

7. ᾤχου (οἰχήσομαι)

8. κρίναιεν (κρινῶ)

9. βάντες (βήσομαι)

10. ἀγάγοις (ἄξω)

11. ἤγγειλε (ἀγγελῶ)   16. εἶμεν (ἤσω)

12. ἠκούσαμεν (ἀκούσομαι)   17. εἰσί (ἔσομαι)

13. ἀγαγοῦσαν (ἄξω)   18. ὄντες (ἔσομαι)

14. εἶχες (ἕξω)   19. ἑώρα (ὄψομαι)

15. ἐδυνάμεθα (δυνήσομαι)   20. ὄμνυς (ὀμοῦμαι)

V. GIVE THE LEXICAL ENTRY and then the equivalent form using the present verbal stem, for example: (1) ἐπράχθητε/πράττω, ἐπράττεσθε; (2) πράξετε/πράττω, πράττετε.

1. ἀποθανεῖται   11. φθαρῇ

2. ηὑρέθης   12. ὄψει

3. γαμεῖς   13. δραμεῖ

4. θήσει   14. δράμοι

5. ὀφθείημεν   15. γενήσεται

6. ὀφθησόμεθα   16. ἔδωκας

7. κληθήσοιτο   17. σημανεῖ

8. φιλήσουσιν   18. πιεῖται

9. νικηθήσεσθε   19. τραφῶμεν

10. ἀπέθανεν   20. φευξόμεθα

VI. MATCH the second verb to the first by changing it into the same form.

1. σημανεῖς (πίνω)   11. δῷς (νομίζω)

2. ἔθηκας (δίδωμι)   12. ὄντα (ὁράω)

3. ἐνίκα (ποιέω)   13. ὦσι (ποιέω)

4. πείσαιμι (τρέχω)   14. μάχοιντο (χράομαι)

5. ἴδοιεν (σῴζω)   15. ἠνέγκατε (φιλέω)

6. ἐκρίνω (λαμβάνω)   16. ἔτεκον (τρέφω)

7. ἔπεσες (δίδωμι)   17. ἐλθοῦσα (ἵημι)

8. ἔθου (πράττω)   18. γράψωσι (ἐσθίω)

9. νικῶμεν (νοέω)   19. εἶεν (ἵημι)

10. ἑωρῶμεν (πλέω)   20. ἡγοῖο (εὔχομαι)

VII. MATCH the second phrase to the first by changing it into the same case.

1. αἱ ταχεῖαι νῆες   3. χαλκῆν ἀσπίδα
   (ὁ ταχὺς ταῦρος)   (χαλκοῦς πούς)

2. πολλοὺς ὀδόντας   4. βοῦς πολλούς
   (ἕκαστον μέγεθος)   (ἄλσος ἱερόν)

5. νεὼς καλούς
(γραῦς σοφή)

6. μεγάλα ἄστη
(ταχὺς ποῦς)

7. πολλὰς ναῦς
(πλεῖον ὄνειδος)

8. ἀληθεῖς λόγους
(θῆλυ γένος)

9. νεὼς πολλούς
(ὁδοὺς μέγας)

10. νεὼ ἱεροῦ
(γονεὺς ἄρρην)

VIII. REPHRASE the following sentences, changing the future participle to a purpose clause (either subjunctive or optative of secondary subordination).

1. κατέβη εἰς Πειραιᾶ προσευξαμένη τῇ θεῷ.

2. κατέβημεν εἰς τὸ ἄστυ θεασόμενοι τὴν ἑορτήν.

3. ἦλθεν Ἰάσων τοὺς ταύρους ἀποκτενῶν.

4. ἐνέβησαν εἰς τὴν ναῦν ἐμπλευσόμενοι εἰς Πειραιᾶ.

5. εἰς τὸ ἄλσος προσέρχονται ὀψόμενοι τοὺς ταύρους.

6. ἐγκαθώρμισαν τὰς ναῦς ἐκβησόμενοι εἰς ξένην γῆν.

7. φαρμάκῳ ἔχρισε Μήδεια Ἰάσονα σώσουσα.

8. Ἰάσονα πέμπει ὁ Πελίας εἰς Κολκίδα ἀποθανούμενον.

9. μετεπέμψατο Ἰάσων Αἰήτην ἀκουσόμενον τὰ ὑπὸ Πελίου ἐπιταγέντα.

10. Ἰάσονα μεταπέμπεται Μήδεια δώσουσα τὸ φάρμακον.

IX. REPHRASE the following sentences, changing the indirectly quoted statements from the infinitive structure to an optative of secondary subordination.

1. ἔφη δώσειν τὸ δέρας Ἰάσονι.

2. ἔφη Μήδεια βοηθήσειν Ἰάσονι φάρμακον διδοῦσα.

3. ἔφη Ἰάσονα ἀδικηθήσεσθαι ὑπὸ τῶν ταύρων.

4. ἔφη ἄνδρας ἐνόπλους γενήσεσθαι ἐκ τῶν ὀδόντων σπαρέντων.

5. ἔφη προσελεύσεσθαι εἰς ἄλσος ἱερόν.

6. ἔφη καταζεύξειν τοὺς ταύρους φαρμάκῳ χρισθείς.

7. τοὺς ταύρους ἔφη ἀποθανεῖσθαι ὑπὸ Ἰάσονος.

8. Μήδεια ἔφη δώσειν Ἰάσονι φάρμακον.

9. ἔφη θεάσεσθαι τοὺς ταύρους μετὰ Μηδείας.

10. Μήδεια ἔφη ἄξειν Ἰάσονα εἰς ἄλσος ἱερόν.

X. NOTE THE PATTERN in each of the quotations and compose a translation of the English sentences, using the same pattern.

1. ἐρωτηθεὶς πότερον γῆμαι ἢ μή, ἔφη, "ὃ ἂν αὐτῶν ποιήσῃς, μεταγνώσει."
—Διογένης Λαέρτιος (Σωκράτης)
(πότερον "whether?"/πότερος, -α, -ον "which of two?"/μεταγιγνώσκω "change one's mind, repent")

Whichever of the two women you see, you will love.

Whatever you write, I shall send.

Whatever you are able, you will do.

2. ἐγὼ μισῶν γυναῖκας οὐδέποτε παύσομαι. —Ἀριστοφάνης
(μισέω "hate")

We shall never stop loving women.

I shall never stop her from hating Socrates.

He will never by chance do wrong. (*See* page 74 sentence 5.)

3. δὶς ἐν τὸν αὐτὸν ποταμὸν οὐκ ἂν ἐμβαίης. —Πλάτων (Ἡράκλειτος)
(δίς "twice," *see* page 108–109, note)

You are not likely ever to stop loving women.

Socrates is likely to die unjustly.

4. ἀλλὰ γὰρ ἐν ᾍδου δίκην δώσομεν ὧν ἂν ἐνθάδε ἀδικήσωμεν, ἢ αὐτοὶ ἢ παῖδες παίδων. —Πλάτων
(ὁ ᾍδης, -ου *see* page 118, note 1/ἐν ᾍδου (namely οἴκῳ)/ἡ δίκη, -ης "justice"/δίκην δίδωμι "pay the penalty"/ἐνθάδε "here," *see* page 42 for the suffix -δε/ἢ ... ἢ "either ... or")

In Athens, you will be honored for whatever good you did while you were away.

They will exact the penalty for whatever wrong he did.

19

Comparison of Adjectives

καὶ τὸ ὅλον μεῖζον τοῦ μέρους ἐστίν. —Εὐκλείδης

Lesson 19
Adjectives/
Comparative and
Superlative
Degrees

The quality or attribute denoted by an adjective may be expressed in different degrees of intensity. In the *comparative degree*, the adjective describes an object as being more intensely qualified by the particular attribute, whereas in the *superlative degree*, the adjective describes the object as surpassing all others with regard to the attribute. The simple adjective is called the *positive degree*. In English, such degrees of comparison are expressed either by the adverbs "more" and "most" or by the use of comparative suffixes: "more wise" or "wiser" and "most wise" or "wisest."

In Greek, adverbs similarly can be used for the comparative and superlative degrees of an adjective.

μᾶλλον σοφός	more wise
μάλιστα σοφός	most wise

Greek can also express such comparison by the use of the suffixes *-τερος* for the comparative and *-τατος* for the superlative. Normally these suffixes are added directly onto the adjectival stem and the resultant form is declined like *σοφός, -ή, -όν*.

Type III *σ*-stem: *ἀληθής, -ές*
                  ἀληθέσ-τερος, -α, -ον truer
                  ἀληθέσ-τατος, -η, -ον truest

Type III *υ*-stem: *θῆλυς, -εια, -υ*
                  θηλύ-τερος, -α, -ον
                  θηλύ-τατος, -η, -ον

For adjectives like *σοφός, -ή, -όν* that belong to the declensional Types I and II, the final omicron of the adjectival stem is lengthened if the preceding syllable is short. This lengthening avoids an unpleasant succession of short syllables. (*Note* that a syllable is long if it contains a long vowel or a diphthong or if it ends in two or more consonants other than a mute followed by a liquid.)

σοφός, -ή, -όν	*καινός, -ή, -όν*
σοφώ-τερος, -α, -ον	*καινό-τερος, -α, -ον*
σοφώ-τατος, -η, -ον	*καινό-τατος, -η, -ον*

Type III adjectives ending in *-ων* add the suffixes *-έστερος -έστατος* to form the comparative and superlative degrees.

εὐδαίμων, -ον (gen. *εὐδαίμονος*)

εὐδαιμον-έστερος, -α, -ον

εὐδαιμον-έστατος, -η, -ον

Some adjectives, however, form the comparative and superlative degrees with the suffixes *-ίων* and *-ιστος*. The suffix *-ίων* has *-ιον* for the neuter; such comparative adjectives are declined like the Type III adjective *εὐδαίμων, -ον* (gen.

εὐδαίμονος). The superlative is declined like σοφός, -ή, -όν. There is no way of predicting which adjectives will form the comparative and superlative degrees in this manner; they are, however, easily recognizable in reading.

κακός, -ή, -όν	ἡδύς, -εῖα, -ύ
κακίων, -ιον	ἡδίων, -ιον
κάκιστος, -η, -ον	ἥδιστος, -η, -ον
καλός, -ή, -όν	ἐχθρός, -ά, -όν
καλλίων, -ιον	ἐχθίων, -ιον
κάλλιστος, -η, -ον	ἔχθιστος, -η, -ον
αἰσχρός, -ά, -όν	
αἰσχίων, -ιον	
αἴσχιστος, -η, -ον	

Irregular Comparisons

Some adjectives form the comparative and superlative degrees irregularly or with completely different words (English: "good," "better," "best"). Such irregular comparisons must be learned as new lexical entries.

ἀγαθός, -ή, -όν

βελτίων, -ιον	better, more virtuous	βέλτιστος, -η, -ον
ἀμείνων, -ον	better, more capable	ἄριστος, -η, -ον
κρείσσων, -ον	better, stronger	κράτιστος, -η, -ον

κακός, -ή, -όν

κακίων, -ιον	worse, more immoral	κάκιστος, -η -ον
χείρων, -ον	worse, more inferior	χείριστος, -η, -ον
ἥσσων, -ον	worse, less	ἥκιστος, -η, -ον

πολύς, πολλή, πολύ

πλείων, -ον	πλεῖστος, -η, -ον

μέγας, μεγάλη, μέγα

μείζων, -ον	μέγιστος, -η, -ον

Genitive of Comparison

The object with reference to which a comparison is made may be expressed by the conjunction ἤ "than."

σοφώτερος Σωκράτης ἢ Εὐριπίδης.   Socrates is wiser than Euripides.

The same meaning can be expressed by viewing the reference object as the point of departure away from which one moves in making the comparison, hence as an ablatival genitive.

σοφώτερος Σωκράτης Εὐριπίδου.   Socrates is wiser (if you compare him) against Euripides.

τὸ ὅλον μεῖζον τοῦ μέρους ἐστίν.
—Εὐκλείδης

The whole is greater than the part.

The reference object for the superlative is similarly an ablatival genitive.

πάντων σοφώτερος Σωκράτης.

Of all, Socrates is wisest.

Dative of Comparison

The measure or means by which one object is compared to another is viewed as an instrumental dative. This is the so-called dative of degree of difference.

πολλῷ σοφώτερος Σωκράτης Εὐριπίδου.

Socrates is much wiser than Euripides.

μιᾷ νυκτὶ πρεβύτερος Ἡρακλῆς Ἰφικλέους.

Heracles is one night older than Iphicles.

Comparison of Adverbs

Adverbs are regularly formed from adjectives. Normally, the adverb can be predicted by changing the -ν of the genitive plural of the adjective to -ς: καλός, -ή, -όν /(καλῶν) καλῶς; ταχύς, -εῖα, -ύ/(ταχέων) ταχέως; πᾶς, πᾶσα, πᾶν/ (πάντων) πάντως.

The neuter (adverbal) accusative (either singular or plural) may also be used as an adverb: πολύς, πολλή, πολύ/πολύ, πολλά; μόνος, -η, -ον/μόνον.

Similarly, the comparative degree of an adverb is identical with the comparative adjective's neuter accusative *singular* (only): σοφώτερον, ἥδιον. And the superlative degree of an adverb is identical with the superlative adjective's neuter accusative *plural* (only): σοφώτατα, ἥδιστα.

ΟΝΟΜΑΤΑ ΚΑΙ ΡΗΜΑΤΑ

τὸ κάλλος, -ους	beauty (*see* καλός, -ή, -όν)
ἡ χάρις, -ιτος (acc τὴν χάριν)	gratitude, kindness, favor, beauty, grace
ὁ ἔπαινος, -ου	praise (*see* ἐπ-αινέω praise/αἰνέω tell, speak of/ὁ αἶνος, -ου tale)
τὸ εἰκός, -ότος	likelihood, probability (*see* εἰκάζω represent by a likeness/εἰκότως likely, reasonably, probably)
ὁ δικαστής, -οῦ	juror (*see* ἡ δίκη, -ης/δίκαιος, -α, -ον/ἄδικος, -ον/δικάζω) for the suffix -της, *see* page 38, note
ἡ εἰρήνη, -ης	peace
ὁ πόλεμος, -ου	war
τὸ πάθος, -ους	experience, misfortune, passion (*see* πάσχω, ἔπαθον)
τὸ τέκνον, -ου	child (*see* τίκτω, ἔτεκον)

τὸ μέρος, -ους	part
ὠφέλιμος, -ον	useful, beneficial (*see* ὠφελέω)
πότερος, -α, -ον	which (of two)?
ἐλεύθερος, -α, -ον	free, fit for a freeman (contrast ὁ δοῦλος, -ου)
σώφρων, -ον (gen. σώφρονος)	of sound mind (*see* σῴζω/ἡ φρήν, φρενός), prudent
βελτίων, -ιον/βέλτιστος, -η, -ον	
ἀμείνων, -ον/ἄριστος, -η, -ον	
κρείσσων, -ον/κράτιστος, -η, -ον	
χείρων, -ον/χείριστος, -η, -ον	
ἥσσων, -ον/ἥκιστος, -η, -ον	
πλείων, -ον/πλεῖστος, -η, -ον	
μείζων, -ον/μέγιστος, -η, -ον	
ἀκολουθέω, ἀκολουθήσω, ἠκολούθησα	follow, go after or with (with comitative dative)
κερδαίνω, κερδανῶ, ἐκέρδανα	gain, derive profit (*see* τὸ κέρδος, -ους gain)
ἐπι-θυμέω, -θυμήσω, -εθύμησα	set one's heart upon, long for (*see* ὁ θυμός, -οῦ human organ of emotions: desire, passion, anger)
ἅπτω, ἅψω, ἧψα, ἥφθην	fasten, kindle (*mid.* touch)
κνίζω, κνίσω, ἔκνισα, ἐκνίσθην	scratch, chafe, tease, provoke
ποθέω, ποθήσω, ἐπόθησα	yearn after, long for (*see* ὁ πόθος, -ου yearning, regret)
θεραπεύω, θεραπεύσω, ἐθεράπευσα, ἐθεραπε ύθην	serve, heal, pay court to (*see* ἡ θεραπεία, -ας service, attendance, *therapy*)
θορυβέω, θορυβήσω, ἐθορύβησα	make a noise, uproar, or disturbance (*see* ὁ θόρυβος, -ου noise, uproar)
φρονέω, φρονήσω, ἐφρόνησα	have understanding, think (*see* ἡ φρήν, φρενός)
ὑπερ-φέρω, -οίσω, -ήνεγκα, -ηνέχθην	surpass
φροντίζω, φροντιῶ, ἐφρόντισα	consider, take thought (*see* ἡ φρήν, φρενός)
ἰτέον	one must go

ἐκτέον   one must have (see ἔχω, ἕξω)

ἤδη   already

Note that the suffix -τέος, -α, -ον forms verbal adjectives denoting necessity or obligation: φιλητέον "one must love"/ἐκτέον "one must have." Such verbal adjectives can be used personally (μήτηρ φιλητέα "A mother must be loved"), but more commonly they are impersonal, with the person on whom the obligation rests expressed by the dative: ἡμῖν φιλητέον "There is an obligation on us to love." These verbal adjectives can also be used as an equivalent to the impersonal δεῖ, with the agent expressed by the accusative: ταύτην φιλητέον "There is an obligation that she love."/ταύτην ἡμῖν χάριν ἐκτέον "There is an obligation that she have gratitude for us, that is, she ought to be thankful to us."

ΑΣΚΗΣΙΣ

I. TRANSLATE: The Oracle of Apollo concerning the Wisdom of Socrates.

"Χαιρεφῶντος γάρ ποτε ἐπερωτῶντος ἐν Δελφοῖς περὶ ἐμοῦ, πολλῶν παρόντων, ἀνεῖλεν ὁ Ἀπόλλων μηδένα εἶναι ἀνθρώπων ἐμοῦ μήτε ἐλευθεριώτερον μήτε δικαιότερον μήτε σωφρονέστερον."

ὡς δ᾽ αὖ ταῦτ᾽ ἀκούσαντες οἱ δικασταὶ ἔτι μᾶλλον εἰκότως ἐθορύβουν,
5 ἔφη αὖθις εἰπεῖν τὸν Σωκράτην.

"'Ἀλλὰ μείζω μέν, ὦ ἄνδρες, εἶπεν ὁ θεὸς ἐν χρησμοῖς περὶ Λυκούργου τοῦ Λακεδαιμονίοις νομοθετήσαντος ἢ περὶ ἐμοῦ. λέγεται γὰρ εἰς τὸν ναὸν εἰσερχόμενον προσειπεῖν αὐτόν· 'Φροντίζω πότερα θεόν σε εἴπω ἢ
10 ἄνθρωπον.' ἐμὲ δὲ θεῷ μὲν οὐκ εἴκασεν, ἀνθρώπων δὲ πολλῷ προέκρινεν ὑπερφέρειν." —Ξενοφῶν

Socrates and the Courtesan.

Γυναικὸς δέ ποτε οὔσης ἐν τῇ πόλει καλῆς, ᾗ ὄνομα ἦν Θεοδότη, καὶ οἵας συνεῖναι τῷ πείθοντι, μνησθέντος αὐτῆς τῶν παρόντων τινὸς καὶ εἰπόντος ὅτι κρεῖττον εἴη λόγου τὸ κάλλος τῆς γυναικός, καὶ ζωγράφους
15 φήσαντος εἰσελθεῖν πρὸς αὐτὴν ἀπεικασομένους, οἷς ἐκείνην ἐπιδεικνύειν ἑαυτῆς ὅσα καλῶς ἔχοι, "Ἰτέον ἂν εἴη θεασομένους," ἔφη ὁ Σωκράτης. "οὐ γὰρ δὴ ἀκούσασί γε τὸ λόγου κρεῖττόν ἐστι καταμαθεῖν." καὶ ὁ διηγησάμενος, "Οὐκ ἂν φθάνοιτ᾽," ἔφη, "ἀκολουθοῦντες." οὕτω μὲν δὴ πορευθέντες πρὸς τὴν Θεοδότην καὶ καταλαβόντες ζωγράφῳ τινὶ παρισ-
20 τᾶσαν, ἐθεάσαντο. παυσαμένου δὲ τοῦ ζωγράφου, "Ὦ ἄνδρες," ἔφη ὁ Σωκράτης, "πότερον ἡμᾶς δεῖ μᾶλλον Θεοδότῃ χάριν ἔχειν, ὅτι ἡμῖν τὸ κάλλος ἑαυτῆς ἐπέδειξεν, ἢ ταύτην ἡμῖν, ὅτι ἐθεασάμεθα; ἆρ᾽ εἰ μὲν ὠφελιμωτέρα ἐστὶν ἡ ἐπίδειξις, ταύτην ἡμῖν χάριν ἐκτέον, εἰ δὲ ἡμῖν ἡ θέα, ἡμᾶς ταύτῃ;" εἰπόντος δέ τινος ὅτι δίκαια λέγοι, "Οὐκοῦν,"
25 ἔφη, "αὕτη μὲν ἤδη τε παρ᾽ ἡμῶν ἔπαινον κερδαίνει καὶ ἐπειδὰν εἰς πλείους διαγγείλωμεν, πλείω ὠφελήσεται· ἡμεῖς δὲ ἤδη τε ὧν ἐθεασάμεθα ἐπιθυμοῦμεν ἅψασθαι καὶ ἀπελευσόμεθα ὑποκνιζόμενοι καὶ ἀπελθόντες ποθήσομεν. ἐκ δὲ τούτων εἰκὸς ἡμᾶς μὲν θεραπεύσειν, ταύτην δὲ θεραπεύεσθαι."
30   καὶ ἡ Θεοδότη, "Νὴ Δί᾽," ἔφη, "εἰ τοίνυν ταῦθ᾽ οὕτως ἔχει, ἐμὲ ἂν δέοι ὑμῖν τῆς θέας χάριν ἔχειν." —Ξενοφῶν

Reading Notes:

(1) ὁ Χαιρεφῶν, -όντος· φίλος τις καὶ μαθητὴς τοῦ Σωκράτους

(1) ἐπερωτῶντος/ἐπ-ερωτάω

(1) οἱ Δελφοί, -ῶν Delphi, an oracular sanctuary sacred to Apollo

(2) παρόντων/πάρ-ειμι

(2) ἀνεῖλεν/ἀν-αιρέω reply, ordain (of an oracle's answer)

(2) ἀνθρώπων partitive genitive with μηδένα

(4) ὡς = ὅτε

(6) μείζω = μείζονα (shortened μείζο(ν)α → μείζω)/see (26) πλείους, shortened from πλείο(ν)ας/(26) πλείω)

(7) νομοθετήσαντος/νομοθετέω, see ὁ νομοθέτης, -ου

(7) λέγεται (namely ὁ Ἀπόλλων)

(8) ναόν = νεών

(9) εἴπω subjunctive; a hortatory subjunctive (see page 84) as a question is the so-called deliberative subjunctive: ... σε εἴπω ... "should I call you ... ?"

(10) προέκρινεν/προ-κρίνω choose before others, select/that is, ἐμὲ (πρὸ) πάντων προέκρινεν

(12) οἵας see page 78/ καλῆς ... καὶ οἵας συνεῖναι τῷ πείθοντι part of the genitive absolute: γυναικὸς οὔσης: "beautiful ... and of such a sort as to keep company with a man who wins over her affections by gifts and favors"

(13) μνησθέντος/μιμνήσκω, -μήσω, ἔμνησα, ἐμνήσθην "remind" (mid. "remind oneself of, remember, make mention of" with the genitive)/μνησθέντος ... τινος a second genitive absolute

(13) τῶν παρόντων partitive genitive with τινος/πάρ-ειμι

(14) κρεῖττον see page 89, note 5

(14) ζωγράφους/ὁ ζωγράφος, -ου (see ἡ ζωή, -ῆς/γράφω) artist

(15) φήσαντος/φημί, ἔφησα

(15) ἀπεικασομένους/ἀπ-εικάζω

(15) ἐπιδεικνύειν = ἐπιδεικνύναι/ἐπι-δείκνυμι

(15) ἑαυτῆς ὅσα καλῶς ἔχοι (see page 78) "how much of herself was in good condition, that is, how beautiful she was"

(16) ἰτέον ἂν εἴη "it is likely that there is an obligation (for us) to go ..."

(17) ἀκούσασι (namely ἡμῖν)

(17) τὸ λόγου κρεῖττον "the (thing) greater than report, that is, that which is more than you can describe in words"

(17) ἔστι (note the accent) "it exists, it is possible"/ the whole clause: "because it is not possible for us to understand that which is greater than report if we have heard it only" (note the particle γε)

(19) πορευθέντες Deponent verbs sometimes have passive forms for the aorist.

(19–20) παριστᾶσαν/παρ-ίστημι "pose for a portrait"

(20) ὦ ἄνδρες see page 110, note 6

(23) ἡ ἐπίδειξις, -εως/see ἐπι-δείκνυμι

(24) ἡ θέα, -ας/see θεάομαι

(24) ἡμᾶς ταύτῃ (namely χάριν ἐκτέον)

(24) οὐκοῦν "therefore"/contrast οὔκουν "not therefore"/ In οὐκοῦν, the stress lies on the inferential οὖν; when used in a question, an affirmative answer is expected as a matter of course.

(27) ὑποκνιζόμενοι/ὑπο-κνίζω

(30) νὴ Δί'/νὴ Δία/νή is an affirmative adverb of swearing: "yes, by Zeus!"

(30) τοίνυν inferential particle: "therefore"

(30) ταῦθ' = ταῦτα

II. REPHRASE the following phrases, using the comparative suffixes instead of the adverbs μᾶλλον and μάλιστα.

1. γυνή τις μᾶλλον ἄδικος

2. ἄνδρας τοὺς μάλιστα σοφούς

3. ταῖς μᾶλλον ἐλευθέραις πόλεσι

4. τὰς μᾶλλον ὠφελίμους μηχανάς

5. τῷ μᾶλλον εὐδαίμονι ἄστει

6. ὁ θὴρ ὁ μᾶλλον ἄγριος

7. αἱ μάλιστα ἀληθεῖς φιλοσοφίαι

8. τῶν μᾶλλον θηλειῶν χωρῶν

9. τὸ μάλιστα ὅμοιον εἶδος

10. ταῖς μᾶλλον καιναῖς ἑορταῖς

11. τὰ μάλιστα θερμὰ ὕδατα

12. ἄνδρες οἱ μάλιστα πλούσιοι

13. ἡ μᾶλλον δήλη ἀρετή

14. τὰς τύχας τὰς μᾶλλον τερπνάς

15. ἄνδρας τοὺς μάλιστα δειλούς

16. μᾶλλον ἐμπείρους γυναῖκας

17. τὸν μᾶλλον γεραιὸν ἄνδρα

18. μάλιστα ἀξίοις βασιλεῦσι

19. χρήματα τὰ μάλιστα ἀναγκαῖα

20. γονεῦσι τοῖς μάλιστα ἀληθέσι

III. REPHRASE the following sentences, using the genitive of comparison instead of the conjunction ἤ.

1. οὔποτε εἶδον ἄνδρα τινὰ σοφώτερον ἢ Σωκράτη.

2. κρεῖσσον τὸ ἀδικεῖσθαι ἢ τὸ ἀδικεῖν.

3. γυναῖκες ἀεὶ ἀμείνονες ἢ ἄνδρες.

4. ὁ Σωκράτης δικαιότερος ἦν ἢ οἱ δικασταί.

5. οὐδὲν κάκιον ἢ τὸ κακῶς φρονεῖν.

6. μεῖζον τὸ ὅλον ἢ τὸ μέρος.

7. κρεῖσσον ἢ λόγος ἦν τὸ κάλλος Θεοδότης.

8. πλείονες ἄνδρες ἦλθον ἢ γυναῖκες.

9. σωφρονέστεροι φιλόσοφοι ἢ οἱ πολλοί.

10. ἄμεινον εἰρήνη ἢ πόλεμος.

IV. MATCH the second phrase to the first by changing it into the same case.

1. ἀμείνονες νῆες
   (κάλλιον ἄλσος)

2. πολλῷ μεγέθει
   (γεραιοτέρα γραῦς)

3. ἥδιστα ἄστη
   (θηλεῖα βοῦς)

4. κρατίστοις βασιλεῦσι
   (αἰσχίων γέρων)

5. ἀρίστου γένους
   (χεῖρον ἄστυ)

6. βελτίονας βασιλέας
   (καλλίστη τριήρης)

7. εὐδαιμονέστατοι θεοί
   (αἴσχιστος ποιητής)

8. ἥσσονι ἐχθρῷ
   (μεῖζον μέρος)

9. δικαιοτάτους δικαστάς
   (ἥκιστον πάθος)

10. σωφρονεστάτοις γένεσι
   (ἀληθὲς κάλλος)

V. GIVE THE LEXICAL ENTRY and then the equivalent form using the present verbal stem, for example: (1) ἐπράχθητε/πράττω, ἐπράττεσθε; (2) πράξετε/πράττω, πράττετε.

1. θεραπευθῇς

2. ἀφθείη

3. ἐσώθημεν

4. οἴσοις

5. ἐρεῖ

6. σχοῖμεν

7. φροντιεῖς

8. ἔλθω

9. ὑπερεχθεῖεν

10. ἐσοίμεθα

11. βουληθέντες	16. ἰδεῖν
12. ἔδου	17. πιεῖ
13. βληθέν	18. τμηθείην
14. καθεῖσο	19. φιλήσεις
15. ῥηθέντα	20. ὀφθεῖεν

VI. MATCH the second verb to the first by changing it into the same form.

1. ἐνίκα (φρονέω)	11. ἐκρίνω (λαμβάνω)
2. ζεύγνυς (φυσάω)	12. βουλοίμεθα (θεάομαι)
3. φθάνοις (φοβέω)	13. φήσας (τίκτω)
4. ἔδωκε (ἄγω)	14. θεῖναι (τέμνω)
5. βαῖεν (τίθημι)	15. μεινάσῃ (ὁράω)
6. δῷς (τρέχω)	16. πιεῖν (παύω)
7. ἐτίθεις (ὁράω)	17. ἔπαθε (ἀγγέλλω)
8. εἷμεν (δείκνυμι)	18. ὁρῷεν (φοβέω)
9. ἵει (ἔχω)	19. ἔπεμψαν (δίδωμι)
10. δοῖεν (σῴζω)	20. ἐμάχου (θεάομαι)

VII. REPHRASE the following groups of sentences, combining them into a single sentence by the use of participles or dependent clauses (relative, purpose, etc.).

1. γυνή τις ἦν ποτε ἐν τῇ πόλει. ὄνομα δὲ ταύτῃ ἦν Θεοδότη. τοιαύτη δὲ ἦν ἡ Θεοδότη συνεῖναι ἀνδράσιν.

2. ἐμνήσθη δὲ αὐτῆς τις τῶν ἐρασθέντων. ὁ δὲ Σωκράτης παρῆν.

3. εἶπε δὲ ὁ ἐραστὴς ὅτι κρεῖσσον εἴη λόγου τὸ κάλλος τῆς Θεοδότης. ἔφη δὲ εἰσελθεῖν ζωγράφους πρὸς αὐτήν. ἐβουλήθησαν γὰρ αὐτὴν ἀπεικάζεσθαι. τοῖς δὲ ζωγράφοις ἐπεδείκνυ ἡ γυνὴ τὸ κάλλος ἑαυτῆς. ὁ δὲ Σωκράτης ἐβουλήθη καὶ αὐτὸς ἰδεῖν.

4. ὁ δὲ Σωκράτης ἔφη ἰτέον εἶναι. ἐβούλετο γὰρ θεᾶσθαι.

5. οὕτω δὲ ἐπορεύθησαν πρὸς τὴν Θεοδότην. κατέλαβον δὲ αὐτὴν ἔνδον οὖσαν σὺν ζωγράφῳ τινί.

6. ἐπηρώτα δὲ Χαιρεφῶν ποτε περὶ Σωκράτους. πολλοὶ δὲ παρῆσαν. καὶ ὁ θεὸς ἀνεῖλεν ὅτι οὐδεὶς ἀνθρώπων δικαιότερος εἴη αὐτοῦ.

7. οἱ δὲ δικασταὶ ἐθορύβουν πάντες. ἤκουσαν γὰρ ὃ εἶπεν ὁ Σωκράτης.

8. ἀλλὰ μεῖζον εἶπέ ποτε ὁ Ἀπόλλων περὶ ἄλλου τινὸς ἀνθρώπων. τούτῳ δὲ ὄνομα ἦν Λυκοῦργος. οὗτος δὲ τοῖς Λακεδαιμονίοις ποτε νόμους ἔθηκεν.

9. εἰσήρχετο γὰρ ὁ Λυκοῦργος εἰς τὸν νεώ. αὐτὸν δὲ προσεῖπεν ὁ θεός. ἤκασε Λυκοῦργον θεῷ τινι.

10. ἀλλὰ τὸν Σωκράτη οὐκ ἤκασεν ὁ θεὸς θεῷ. τὸν γὰρ Σωκράτη προσεῖπεν
ὡς ἄνθρωπον πάντων τὸν σοφώτατον.

VIII. NOTE THE PATTERN in each of the quotations and compose a translation of the English sentences, using the same pattern.

1. οὐκ ἂν φθάνοιτε ἀκολουθοῦντες. —Ξενοφῶν

I would not be likely to speak first.

She is apt to come first.

2. ἤρετο γὰρ δὴ Χαιρεφῶν εἰ τις ἐμοῦ εἴη σοφώτερος. —Πλάτων

They asked if anything was better than peace.

I asked whether I was more just than Socrates.

3. πολέμου κρεῖσσον εἰρήνη βροτοῖς. —Εὐριπίδης

Reproach is more beneficial than praise for children.

Nature is always stronger than law for cities.

4. ἥδιστος γάρ τοι θάνατος
συνθνήσκειν θνήσκουσι φίλοις. —Εὐριπίδης.
(τοι particle meaning "surely, you must know")

The most beautiful love is to be in love with someone who shares the love.
(συνεράω or συμφιλέω)

5. τί γὰρ ἂν μεῖζον τοῦδ' ἔτι θνητοῖς
πάθος ἐξεύροις
ἢ τέκνα θανόντ' ἐσιδέσθαι. —Εὐριπίδης
(ἐξ-ευρίσκω/θανόντα/εἰσ-οράω)

What death more sweet than this might you discover, than to die with dying friends.

6. ἔστιν ὁ μὲν χείρων, ὁ δ' ἀμείνων ἔργον ἕκαστον.
οὐδεὶς δ' ἀνθρώπων αὐτὸς ἅπαντα σοφός. —Θέογνις

Some women are wealthier, others more poor, as regards their beauty or descent; but no one woman is best in every way.

20   Perfect

τέθνηκ' ἔγωγε πρὶν θανεῖν κακῶν ὕπο. —Εὐριπίδης

Lesson 20
Perfect Aspect

In addition to the progressive and punctual aspects, the Greek language can view a verbal action as a *state or condition* resulting from the completed (or "perfected") action.

τέθνηκα.	I am dead.
πέπωκα.	I am drunk.
ἔγημα νέος ὢν καὶ ἔτι καὶ νῦν γεγάμηκα.	I married as a young man and still now am married.

The present perfect denotes such a state as existing in present time. It resembles the archaic English "I am come" rather than the more common "I have come" because unlike the English present perfect, it does not express the past completed action but only the present resultant state. Since there is no exact equivalent for the Greek perfect in English, it often is difficult to express in translation. For example, through a contrast in aspects the Greek verbal system can communicate what in English would be a contrast in tenses.

τέθνηκ' ἔγωγε πρὶν θανεῖν κακῶν ὕπο.	I am dead from my troubles before having died. (Here, as often, the aorist by context expresses what in English would be the perfect "to have died." *Note* also that the shift in accent on the preposition *ὑπό* indicates that its object precedes it.)
ἀποθανόντες οἱ τεθνηκότες εἶδον θεόν.	After having died, the dead saw god.

The perfect aspect can be expressed in the subjunctive, optative, infinitive, and participle, as well as the indicative. Only the indicative marks the perfect with tense or time; all the other forms express only aspect.

Σωκράτη φησὶ τεθνηκέναι.	Socrates he says is dead.
Σωκράτη ἔφη τεθνηκέναι.	Socrates he said was dead.

Perfect/Conjugation

The perfect stem is not completely predictable from the present stem and is listed as a principle part of the verb. There are, however, general patterns that will facilitate your familiarity with the perfect stem.

Reduplication.

The perfect stem is characterized by *reduplication* or the doubling of the sound that stands at the beginning of the word. (You have already seen reduplication in some present stems, for example, *γί-γνομαι* as compared to the unreduplicated aorist *ἐγενόμην* and the noun *τὸ γένος.*) The perfect reduplication in most verbs repeats the initial consonant with an epsilon.

πε-παιδεύκαμεν (*παιδεύω*)

γε-γράφαμεν (*γράφω*)

An initial aspirate is reduplicated by the corresponding unaspirated consonant.

πε-φεύγαμεν (φεύγω)

τε-θύκαμεν (θύω)

If the present stem begins with a vowel, the reduplication is identical with the augment.

ᾑρήκαμεν (αἱρέω)

ἤρχαμεν (ἄρχω)

The reduplication is also identical with the augment when the present stem begins with two consonants (except a stop plus a liquid).

ἀπ-ε-κτόναμεν (ἀπο-κτείνω)

ἐ-ψαύκαμεν (ψαύω)

Some verbs, moreover, have an *irregular* reduplication.

ἑ-στήκαμεν (ἵστημι)

ἑ-ωράκαμεν (ὁράω/imperfect ἑώρων)

εἰ-λήφαμεν (λαμβάνω)

Perfect Active Suffixes
In addition to reduplication, which characterizes all perfect stems, the perfect active stem has either the suffix -κα- (*first perfect*) or the suffix -α- (*second perfect*). Both of these suffixes are conjugated athematically with the personal suffixes and there is, therefore, only an athematic conjugation for the perfect indicative.

πε-παιδεύ-κα-μεν

γε-γράφ-α-μεν

In some verbs, the final consonant of the basic stem is aspirated before the addition of the suffix.

εἰ-λήφ-α-μεν (ἔ-λαβ-ον)

ἤχ-α-μεν (ἄγω)

Sometimes, moreover, the perfect stem is actually formed from a completely different verb from the one that functions as its present stem.

ἐδη-δό-κα-μεν (ἐσθίω/future ἔδομαι)

ἐ-σχή-κα-μεν (ἔχω/aorist ἔσχον)

ἀπο-δε-δραμή-κα-μεν (ἀπο-τρέχω/future ἀπο-δραμοῦμαι)

ἐλ-ηλύθ-α-μεν (ἔρχομαι/aorist ἦλθον)

ἐν-ηνόχ-α-μεν (φέρω/aorist ἤνεγκα)

Perfect Middle-Passive
The perfect middle-passive stem has the same reduplication as the active but

it does not have the -κα- or -α- suffixes. It also is always conjugated athematic-ally.

πε-παιδεύ-μεθα

Although the perfect middle-passive stem is easily predictable from the per-fect active stem (merely by removal of the suffix), it usually is listed as a prin-ciple part since the athematic conjugation of the personal suffixes may modify the final consonant of the stem for euphonic reasons.

γε-γράμ-μεθα (Since γε-γράφ-μεθα is difficult to pronounce.)

The chart summarizes the perfect active and middle-passive conjugations.

Note that the present perfect indicative uses primary personal suffixes.

Note that for the subjunctive and optative middle-passive a periphrasis is used: the perfect middle-passive participle plus the subjunctive or optative of the verb εἰμί.

Note that the thematic vowel is substituted for the α of the suffixes in the sub-junctive, optative, participle, and infinitive and that these forms, therefore, are thematic in conjugation.

Active

Indicative			Subjunctive		Optative	
πε-παίδευ-κα		1	πε-παιδεύ-κ | ω		πε-παιδεύ-κ | ο-ι-μι	
γέ- γραφ- α			γε- γράφ -		γε- γράφ -	
πε-παίδευ-κα	ς	2		η-ς		ο-ις
γέ- γραφ- α	ς					
πε-παίδευ- κε		3		η		ο-ι
γέ- γραφ- ε						
πε-παιδεύ-κα	μεν	1		ω-μεν		ο-ι-μεν
γε- γράφ- α	μεν					
πε-παιδεύ-κα	τε	2		η-τε		ο-ι-τε
γε- γράφ- α	τε					
πε-παιδεύ-κα	σι	3		ω-σι		ο-ι-τε
γε- γράφ- α	σι					

Middle-Passive

πε-παίδευ-	μαι	1	πε-παιδευ-μένος	ὦ	πε-παιδευ-μένος	εἴην
γέ- γραμ -	μαι		γε -γραμ -μένος		γε- γραμ- μένος	
πε-παίδευ-	σαι	2		ᾖς		εἴης
γέ- γρα-	φαι					
πε-παίδευ-	ται	3		ᾖ		εἴη
γέ- γραπ -	ται					
πε-παιδεύ-	μεθα	1	-μένοι	ὦμεν	-μένοι	εἴημεν
γε- γράμ -	μεθα					

πε-παίδευ-	σθε	2		-μένοι	ἦτε	-μένοι	εἶητε
γέ- γρα- -	φθε					

πε-παίδευ-	νται	3		ὦσι	εἶησαν
(γε- γραμ-μένοι					
εἰσίν)*					

Participle Active:

masc.   fem.   neut.

πε-παιδευ-κ-ώ- -	ς	πε-παιδευ-κ-υῖ-	α	-κ-ό-ς
γε-γραφ- -ώ		γε- γραφ- - υῖ-		
-ό-τ-	α			αν	-κ-ό-ς
-ό-τ-	ος			ας	-κ-ό-τ-	ος

dat. pl.
πε-παιδευ-κ-ό- -	σι	πε-παιδευ-κ-υί-	αις	-κ-ό- -	σι
γε- γραφ- - ό- -	σι	γε- γραφ- - υί-	αις		

Participle Middle-Passive: πε-παιδευ-μέν-ος, -η, -ον
γε-γραμ -μέν-ος, -η, -ον

Infinitives:

Active: πε-παιδευ-κ-έ-ναι   Mid. -Pass.: πε-παιδεῦ-σθαι
γε-γραφ- -έ-ναι   γε-γρά - -φθαι

Note (*) that a periphrasis is used for the third person plural of the indicative middle-passive of second perfects with consonant stems because the personal suffix (-νται) cannot be added to the verbal stem without losing its distinctive character through euphonic change.

Note that in the periphrastic forms the participle will modify the subject: γυναῖκες ὦμεν πεπαιδευμέναι.

Note that the accent on the middle-passive participle and infinitive is not recessive: πεπαιδευμένος, πεπαιδεῦσθαι; so also on the active participle: πεπαιδευκώς, -κότος.

Note that the active participle does not have the -ντ- suffix as with all other verbal stems. The suffix for the perfect active is -(F)ώ/ότ-, hence: πε-παιδευ-κ-(F)ώτ-ς → πεπαιδευκώς, πε-παιδευ-κ-(F)ότ-ος → πεπαιδευκότος. The feminine derives from πε-παιδευ-κ-F(σ)-ια→πεπαιδευκυῖα.

Note that the modification of the final stem consonant in second perfects is predictable if you attempt to repeat quickly the unmodified form: γε-γράφ-μεθα→γεγράμμεθα, etc. The modified form is much easier to pronounce. Notice how these euphonic modifications occur in the following paradigms of perfect stems ending in various consonants.

(β)	(π)	(γ)
εἴλημμαι	λέλειμμαι	ἦγμαι
εἴληψαι	λέλειψαι	ἦξαι
εἴληπται	λέλειπται	ἦκται
εἰλήμμεθα	λελείμμεθα	ἤγμεθα

εἴληφθε	λέλειφθε	ἦχθε
εἰλημμένοι εἰσίν	λελειμμένοι εἰσίν	ἠγμένοι εἰσίν
(χ)	(κ)	(ϑ)
ἦργμαι	δέδειγμαι	πέπεισμαι
ἦρξαι	δέδειξαι	πέπεισαι
ἦρκται	δέδεικται	πέπεισται
ἦργμεθα	δεδείγμεθα	πεπείσμεθα
ἦρχθε	δέδειχθε	πέπεισθε
ἠργμένοι εἰσίν	δεδειγμένοι εἰσίν	πεπεισμένοι εἰσίν

**Perfect Passive/
Dative of Agent**

Since the perfect denotes a verbal action in the aspect of a state of being or condition, in the passive voice the agent for the action is normally no longer considered as its source (hence, as an ablatival genitive with a preposition of source: *see* page 50), but as the possessor of the designated verbal state of being. Such possession is expressed by the dative (*see* page 55).

τὸ βιβλίον μοι γέγραπται.

The book is (one) written by me, that is, the book written is mine. (Notice that English uses the auxiliary verb "have" to form the perfect: I have written the book/ the book has been written by me.)

**Principle Parts
For Reference/
Some Familiar
Verbs**

ἀγανακτέω, ἀγανακτήσω, ἠγανάκτησα

ἀγγέλλω, ἀγγελῶ, ἤγγειλα, ἠγγέλθην, ἤγγελκα, ἤγγελμαι

ἄγω, ἄξω, ἤγαγον, ἤχθην, ἦχα, ἦγμαι

ἀδικέω, ἀδικήσομαι, ἠδίκησα, ἠδικήθην, ἠδίκηκα, ἠδίκημαι αἱρέω,

αἱρήσω, εἷλον, ἡρέθην, ᾕρηκα, ᾕρημαι

αἴρω, ἀρῶ, ἦρα, ἤρθην, ἦρκα, ἦρμαι

αἰσθάνομαι, αἰσθήσομαι, ἠσθόμην, _____, _____, ᾔσθημαι

ἀκούω, ἀκούσομαι, ἤκουσα, ἠκούσθην, ἀκήκοα

ἁλίσκομαι, ἁλώσομαι, ἑάλων or ἥλων, ἑάλωκα or ἥλωκα

ἀν-αλίσκω, ἀν-αλώσω, ἀν-ήλωσα, ἀν-ηλώθην, ἀν-ήλωκα, ἀν-ήλωμαι

ἀνα-τέλλω, _____, ἀν-έτειλα, _____, _____, (ἐν-)τέταλμαι

ἀπο-δύω, ἀπο-δύσω, ἀπ-έδυσα (ἀπ-έδυν), ἀπ-εδύθην, ἀπο-δέδυκα, ἀπο-δέδυμαι

ἀπο-θνῄσκω, ἀπο-θανοῦμαι, ἀπ-έθανον, _____, τέθνηκα (sometimes shortened by omission of -ηκ-: τέθναμεν, etc.; so also in the participle: τεθνηκώς/τεθνεώς)

ἀπο-κτείνω, ἀπο-κτενῶ, ἀπ-έκτεινα, _____, ἀπ-έκτονα (ἀπο-θνῄσκω is generally used as the passive of ἀπο-κτείνω) ἀπ-όλλυμι, ἀπ-ολῶ, ἀπ-ώλεσα (ἀπ-ωλόμην), ἀπ-ολώλεκα (ἀπ-όλωλα intrans.)

ἅπτω, ἅψω, ἦψα, ἤφθην, _____, ἧμμαι

ἁρπάζω, ἁρπάσομαι, ἥρπασα, ἡρπάσθην, ἥρπακα, ἥρπασμαι

ἄρχω, ἄρξω, ἦρξα, ἤρχθην, _____, ἦργμαι (mid.)

βαίνω, βήσομαι, ἔβην, (παρ-)εβάθμν, βέβηκα (sometimes shortened by omission of -ηκ-: βεβᾶσι, βεβώς), (παρα-)βέβαμαι

βάλλω, βαλῶ, ἔβαλον, ἐβλήθην, βέβληκα, βέβλημαι

βοάω, βοήσομαι, ἐβόησα

βοηθέω, βοηθήσω, ἐβοήθησα, ἐβοηθήθην, βεβοήθηκα, βεβοήθημαι

βούλομαι βουλήσομαι, _____, ἐβουλήθην, _____, βεβούλημαι

γαμέω, γαμῶ (γαμήσω), ἔγημα, ἐγαμήθην, γεγάμηκα, γεγάμημαι

γίγνομαι, γενήσομαι/γενηθήσομαι, ἐγενόμην, _____, γέγονα, γεγένημαι

γιγνώσκω, γνώσομαι, ἔγνων, ἐγνώσθην, ἔγνωκα, ἔγνωσμαι

γράφω, γράψω, ἔγραψα, ἐγράφην, γέγραφα, γέγραμμαι

δείκνυμι (δεικνύω), δείξω, ἔδειξα, ἐδείχθην, δέδειχα, δέδειγμαι

δέω, δήσω, ἔδησα, ἐδέθην, δέδεκα, δέδεμαι

διδάσκω, διδάξω, ἐδίδαξα, ἐδιδάχθην, δεδίδαχα, δεδίδαγμαι

δίδωμι, δώσω, ἔδωκα, ἐδόθην, δέδωκα, δέδομαι

διώκω, διώξομαι (διώξω), ἐδίωξα, ἐδιώχθην, δεδίωχα

δύναμαι, δυνήσομαι, _____, ἐδυνήθην, _____, δεδύνημαι

ἐάω, ἐάσω, εἴασα, εἰάθην, εἴακα, εἴαμαι

ἐθέλω (θέλω), ἐθελήσω (θελήσω), ἠθέλησα, ἠθέληκα

εἰμί, ἔσομαι

ἐράω, ἐρασθήσομαι, _____ ἠράσθην (passive with active meaning in future and aorist; also a deponent present: ἔραμαι)

ἔρχομαι, ἐλεύσομαι, ἦλθον, _____, ἐλήλυθα

ἐρωτάω, ἐρωτήσω (ἐρήσομαι), ἠρώτησα (ἠρόμην), ἠρώτηκα

ἐσθίω, ἔδομαι, ἔφαγον, _____, ἐδήδοκα, (κατ-)εδήδεσμαι

εὑρίσκω, εὑρήσω, ηὗρον, ηὑρέθην, ηὗρηκα, εὕρημαι (aor., aor. pass., and perfect active also with εὑ- instead of ηὑ-)

εὔχομαι, εὔξομαι, ηὐξάμην, _____, _____, ηὖγμαι

ἔχω, ἕξω (σχήσω), ἔσχον, _____, ἔσχηκα, (παρ-)έσχημαι

ζάω (βιόω), ζήσω (ζήσομαι/βιώσομαι), ἐβίων, _____, βεβίωκα, βεβίωται (impersonal only, with dative of agent) ζεύγνυμι, ζεύξω, ἔζευξα, ἐζεύχθην (ἐζύγην), _____, ἔζευγμαι

ἡγέομαι, ἡγήσομαι, ἡγησάμην, ἡγήθην, _____, ἥγημαι

θαυμάζω, θαυμάσομαι, ἐθαύμασα, ἐθαυμάσθην, τεθαύμακα, τεθαύμασμαι

θύω, θύσω, ἔθυσα, ἐτύθην, τέθυκα, τέθυμαι

ἵημι, ἥσω, ἧκα, εἵθην, εἷκα, εἷμαι

ἵστημι, στήσω, ἔστησα (ἔστην), ἐστάθην, ἔστηκα, ἔσταμαι

καθίζω (καθίζομαι), καθιῶ (καθιζήσομαι), ἐκάθισα (ἐκαθισάμην)

καλέω, καλῶ, ἐκάλεσα, ἐκλήθην, κέκληκα, κέκλημαι

καλύπτω, καλύψω, ἐκάλυψα, ἐκαλύφθην, _____, κεκάλυμμαι

κελεύω, κελεύσω, ἐκέλευσα, ἐκελεύσθην, κεκέλευκα, κεκέλευσμαι

κερδαίνω, κερδανῶ, ἐκέρδανα, _____, (προσ-)κεκέρδηκα

κνίζω, κνίσω, ἔκνισα, ἐκνίσθην

κομίζω, κομιῶ, ἐκόμισα, ἐκομίσθην, κεκόμικα, κεκόμισμαι

κρίνω, κρινῶ, ἔκρινα, ἐκρίθην, κέκρικα, κέκριμαι

λαμβάνω, λήψομαι, ἔλαβον, ἐλήφθην, εἴληφα, εἴλημμαι

λέγω, λέξω (ἐρῶ), ἔλεξα (εἶπον), (δι-)ελέγην (ἐρρήθην) (κατ-) εἴλοχα,
  (εἴρηκα), (δι-)είλεγμαι and (ἀπο-)λέλεγμαι (εἴρημαι)

λείπω, λείψω, ἔλιπον, ἐλείφθην, λέλοιπα, λέλειμμαι

λούω, λούσομαι, ἔλουσα, _____, λέλουμαι

λύω, λύσω, ἔλυσα, ἐλύθην, λέλυκα, λέλυμαι

μανθάνω, μαθήσομαι, ἔμαθον, _____, μεμάθηκα

μάχομαι, μαχοῦμαι, ἐμαχεσάμην, _____, μεμάχημαι

μέλλω, μελλήσω, ἐμέλησα

μένω, μενῶ, ἔμεινα, _____, μεμένηκα

νικάω, νικήσω, ἐνίκησα, ἐνικάθην, νενίκηκα, νενίκαμαι

νοέω, (δια-) νοήσομαι, ἐνόησα, ἐνοήθην, νενόηκα, νενόημαι

νομίζω, νομιῶ, ἐνόμισα, ἐνομίσθην, νενόμικα, νενόμισμαι

οἴχομαι, οἰχήσομαι

ὄμνυμι, ὀμοῦμαι, ὤμοσα, ὠμόθην, ὀμώμοκα, ὀμώμομαι

ὁράω, ὄψομαι, εἶδον, ὤφθην, ἑόρακα (ἑώρακα), ἑώραμαι (ὦμμαι)

παιδεύω, παιδεύσω, ἐπαίδευσα, ἐπαιδεύθην, πεπαίδευκα, πεπαίδευμαι

παίω, παίσω (παιήσω), ἔπαισα, ἐπαίσθην, (ὑπερ-)πέπαικα

πάσχω, πείσομαι, ἔπαθον, _____, πέπονθα

παύω, παύσω, ἔπαυσα, ἐπαύϑην, πέπαυκα, πέπαυμαι

πείϑω, πείσω, ἔπεισα, ἐπείσϑην, πέπεικα (πέποιϑα), πέπεισμαι

πέμπω, πέμψω, ἔπεμψα, ἐπέμφϑην, πέπομφα, πέπεμμαι

πίνω, πιοῦμαι, ἔπιον, (κατ-)επόϑην, πέπωκα, (κατα-)πέπομαι

πίπτω, πεσοῦμαι, ἔπεσον, _____, πέπτωκα

πλάττω, _____, ἔπλασα, ἐπλάσϑην, _____, πέπλασμαι

πλέω, πλεύσομαι (πλευσοῦμαι), ἔπλευσα, _____, πέπλευκα, πέπλευσμ

πράττω, πράξω, ἔπραξα, ἐπράχϑην, πέπραχα (πέπραγα), πέπραγμαι

σημαίνω, σημανῶ, ἐσήμηνα, ἐσημάνϑην, _____, σεσήμασμαι

σῴζω, σώσω, ἔσωσα, ἐσώϑην, σέσωκα, σέσωμαι (σέσῳσμαι)

τάσσω, τάξω, ἔταξα, ἐτάχϑην, τέταχα, τέταγμαι

τέμνω, τεμῶ, ἔτεμον, ἐτμήϑην, (ἀπο-)τέτμηκα, τέτμημαι

τίϑημι, ϑήσω, ἔϑηκα, ἐτέϑην, τέϑηκα, τέϑειμαι

τίκτω, τέξομαι, ἔτεκον, ἐτέχϑην, τέτοκα

τρέφω, ϑρέψω, ἔϑρεψα, ἐτράφην, τέτροφα, τέϑραμμαι

τρέχω, δραμοῦμαι, ἔδραμον, (περι-)δεδράμηκα, (ἐπι-)δεδράμημαι

τυγχάνω, τεύξομαι, ἔτυχον, _____, τετύχηκα

φαίνω, φανῶ, ἔφηνα, ἐφάνϑην (ἐφάνην), πέφαγκα (πέφηνα), πέφασμαι

φέρω, οἴσω, ἤνεγκα (ἤνεγκον), ἠνέχϑην, ἐνήνοχα, ἐνήνεγμαι

φεύγω, φεύξομαι, ἔφυγον, _____, πέφευγα

φημί (φάσκω), φήσω, ἔφησα

φϑάνω, φϑήσομαι, ἔφϑασα (ἔφϑην)

φϑείρω, φϑερῶ, ἔφϑειρα, ἐφϑάρην, ἔφϑαρκα (δι-έφϑορα), ἔφϑαρμαι

φιλέω, φιλήσομαι, ἐφίλησα, ἐφιλήϑην, πεφίληκα, πεφίλημαι

φοβέω, φοβήσω, ἐφόβησα, ἐφοβήϑην, _____, πεφόβημαι

φύω, φύσω, ἔφυσα (ἔφυν), _____, πέφυκα

χράω, χρήσω, ἔχρησα, ἐχρήσϑην, κέχρηκα, κέχρησμαι

χρίω, χρίσω, ἔχρισα, ἐχρίσϑην, _____, κέχριμαι

ΟΝΟΜΑΤΑ ΚΑΙ ΡΗΜΑΤΑ

ἡ ἰδέα, -ας	form, semblance, outward appearance (*see* ὁράω, εἶδον)
τὸ ἔϑνος, -ους	nation, group of people

τὸ κλέος (τὰ κλέα/nom. and acc. sing. and pl. only) — fame, good repute (*see* καλέω)

ὁ χορός, -οῦ — dance, band of dancers, place for dancing

ἡ ἄνοια, -ας — folly (*see* νοέω/ ὁ νοῦς, -οῦ)

ὁ κίνδυνος, -ου — danger

ἡ ἀπειρία, -ας — inexperience (*see* ἄπειρος, -ον/ ἔμπειρος, -ον/ ἡ ἐμπειρία, -ας/ πειράω "attempt, try, make trial of")

ὁ ἀριθμός, -οῦ — number

ἡ συμφορά, -ᾶς — event, circumstance, mishap (*see* συμ-φέρω)

παλαιός, -ά, -όν — aged (τὸ παλαιόν adv, "formerly, anciently")

ἐναντίος, -α, -ον — opposite, opponent

μάχιμος, -η, -ον — warlike (*see* μάχομαι/ ἡ μάχη, -ης)

σφέτερος, -α, -ον — their own (*see* σφᾶς page 23)

ἀλλότριος, -α, -ον — belonging to another (*see* ἄλλος, -η, -ον)

ἑκών, -οῦσα, -όν — willing (contrast ἄκων, -ουσα, -ον)

ἄφωνος, -ον — voiceless, dumb (*see* ἡ φωνή, -ῆς)

ἔσχατος, -η, -ον — extreme, hindmost

ὁπλίζω, ὁπλίσομαι, ὥπλισα, ὡπλίσθην, ὥπλικα, ὥπλισμαι — equip with weapons (*see* τὸ ὅπλον, -ου/ ὁ ὁπλίτης, -ου)

ἐλπίζω, ἐλπίσω, ἤλπισα, ἠλπίσθην, ἤλπικα, ἤλπισμαι — hope, expect (*see* ἡ ἐλπίς, -ίδος "hope, expectation"/ἀν-ελπίστως adv.)

ἁμαρτάνω, ἁμαρτήσομαι, ἥμαρτον, ἡμαρτήθην, ἡμάρτηκα, ἡμάρτημαι — err, fail (*see* τὸ ἁμάρτημα, -ατος "failure")

ᾄδω, ᾄσομαι, ᾖσα, ᾔσθην, _____, ᾖσμαι — sing (*see* ἡ ᾠδή, -ῆς "song, ode")

κτάομαι, κτήσομαι, ἐκτησάμην ἐκτήθην, _____, κέκτημαι — possess

δουλόω, δουλώσω, ἐδούλωσα, ἐδουλώθην, δεδούλωκα, δεδούλωμαι — enslave (*see* ὁ δοῦλος, -ου)

δράω, δράσω, ἔδρασα, ἐδράσθην, δέδρακα, δέδραμαι — do (*see* τὸ δρᾶμα, -ατος)

μιμνῄσκω (μιμνήσκω), (ἀνα-)μνή- remind (*mid.* remember) (*see* ἡ
σω, (ἀν-)έμνησα, ἐμνήσθην,   μνήμη, -ης "remembrance, memory,
_____, μέμνημαι   memorial")

δια-φέρω, etc.   differ

πρίν   before (+ gen.)/ also adverb and
   conjunction

ΑΣΚΗΣΙΣ

I. EXAMINE each of the verbs in the list of principle parts on pages 160–163
to determine the nature of its perfect.

II. TRANSLATE: The Defeat of the Amazons at Athens.

Ἀμαζόνες γὰρ Ἄρεως μὲν τὸ παλαιὸν ἦσαν θυγατέρες, οἰκοῦσαι παρὰ
τὸν Θερμώδοντα ποταμόν, μόναι μὲν ὡπλισμέναι σιδήρῳ τῶν περὶ αὐτάς,
πρῶται δὲ τῶν πάντων ἐφ' ἵππους ἀναβᾶσαι, οἷς ἀνελπίστως δι'
ἀπειρίαν τῶν ἐναντίων ᾕρουν μὲν τοὺς φεύγοντας, ἀπέλειπον δὲ τοὺς
5 διώκοντας. ἐνομίζοντο δὲ διὰ τὴν εὐψυχίαν μᾶλλον ἄνδρες ἢ διὰ τὴν
φύσιν γυναῖκες. πλέον γὰρ ἐδόκουν τῶν ἀνδρῶν ταῖς ψυχαῖς διαφέρειν ἢ
ταῖς ἰδέαις ἐλλείπειν. ἄρχουσαι δὲ πολλῶν ἐθνῶν, καὶ ἔργῳ μὲν τοὺς
περὶ αὐτὰς καταδεδουλωμέναι, λόγῳ δὲ περὶ τῆσδε τῆς χώρας ἀκούουσαι
κλέος μέγα, πολλῆς δόξης καὶ μεγάλης ἐλπίδος χάριν παραλαβοῦσαι τὰ
10 μαχιμώτατα τῶν ἐθνῶν ἐστράτευσαν ἐπὶ τήνδε τὴν πόλιν. τυχοῦσαι δ'
ἀγαθῶν ἀνδρῶν ὁμοίας ἐκτήσαντο τὰς ψυχὰς τῇ φύσει, καὶ ἐναντίαν
τὴν δόξαν τῆς προτέρας λαβοῦσαι μᾶλλον ἐκ τῶν κινδύνων ἢ ἐκ τῶν
σωμάτων ἔδοξαν εἶναι γυναῖκες. μόναις δ' αὐταῖς οὐκ ἐξεγένετο ἐκ τῶν
ἡμαρτημένων μαθούσαις περὶ τῶν λοιπῶν ἄμεινον βουλεύσασθαι, οὐδ'
15 οἴκαδε ἀπελθούσαις ἀπαγγεῖλαι τήν τε σφετέραν αὐτῶν δυστυχίαν καὶ
τὴν τῶν ἡμετέρων προγόνων ἀρετήν. αὐτοῦ γὰρ ἀποθανοῦσαι, καὶ
δοῦσαι δίκην τῆς ἀνοίας, τῆσδε μὲν τῆς πόλεως διὰ τὴν ἀρετὴν ἀθάνατον
τὴν μνήμην ἐποίησαν, τὴν δὲ ἑαυτῶν πατρίδα διὰ τὴν ἐνθάδε συμφορὰν
ἀνώνυμον κατέστησαν. ἐκεῖναι μὲν οὖν τῆς ἀλλοτρίας ἀδίκως ἐπιθυμή-
20 σασαι τὴν ἑαυτῶν δικαίως ἀπώλεσαν. —Λυσίας

The Joys of Marriage.

Δύ' ἡμέραι γυναικός εἰσιν ἥδισται,
ὅταν γαμῇ τις κἀκφέρῃ τεθνηκυῖαν. —Ἱππῶναξ

Ask not for Whom the Bell Tolls.

Πενθεῖν δὲ μετρίως τοὺς προσήκοντας φίλους.
οὐ γὰρ τεθνᾶσιν ἀλλὰ τὴν αὐτὴν ὁδόν,
25 ἣν πᾶσιν ἐλθεῖν ἐστ' ἀναγκαίως ἔχον,
προεληλύθασιν. —Ἀντιφάνης

Manes' Epitaph.

Μάνης οὗτος ἀνὴρ ἦν ζῶν ποτέ. νῦν δὲ τεθνηκὼς
ἴσον Δαρείῳ τῷ μεγάλῳ δύναται.— Ἄνυτος

The Hollow Men.

Ὥσπερ τῶν χορῶν

30 οὐ πάντες ᾄδουσ᾽, ἀλλ᾽ ἄφωνοι δύο τινὲς
    ἢ τρεῖς παρεστήκασι πάντων ἔσχατοι
    εἰς τὸν ἀριθμόν, καὶ τοῦθ᾽ ὁμοίως πως ἔχει.
    χώραν κατέχουσι, ζῶσι δ᾽ οἷς ἐστιν βίος. —Μένανδρος

Reading Notes:

(1) Ἄρεως/ὁ Ἄρης, -εως the war god

(2) τῶν περὶ αὐτὰς partitive with μόναι: "the only women out of those around them"/ so also in (3) τῶν πάντων is partitive with πρῶται

(3) ἐφ᾽ ἵππους ἀναβᾶσαι/ ἐφ᾽ ἵππους ἀνα-βαίνω "mount (onto) horses"

(4) τῶν ἐναντίων partitive with τοὺς φεύγοντας

(4) ἀπέλειπον/ἀπο-λείπω

(5) εὐψυχίαν/ἡ εὐψυχία, -ας (εὐ + ψυχή)

(7) ἐλλείπειν/ ἐν-λείπω + gen. "fall short of, be inferior to"

(8) περὶ τῆσδε τῆς χώρας The speaker is an Athenian.

(9) χάριν adverbial accusative/πολλῆς δόξης καὶ μεγάλης ἐλπίδος χάριν "*for the sake of* (or *thanks to*) fame and (their) great expectations"/ The adverbial usage of the accusative of χάρις is common; it functions like a preposition and is usually placed after its object.

(9) παραλαβοῦσαι/παρα-λαμβάνω "take to one's side as an ally"

(12) τῆς προτέρας (namely δόξης) ablatival genitive with ἐναντίαν: "the reknown opposite from their former"

(15) οἴκαδε see page 42

(15) ἀπελθούσαις/ἀπ-έρχομαι

(15) ἀπαγγεῖλαι/ἀπ-αγγέλλω

(15) τὴν σφετέραν αὐτῶν δυστυχίαν "their *own* misfortune"/αὐτῶν is intensive agreeing with the reflexive pronoun ("of themselves") implied in the reflexive adjective σφετέραν

(16) προγόνων/ὁ πρό-γονος, -ου forefather (*see* ὁ γονεύς, -εως/γίγνομαι, ἐγενόμην)

(16) αὐτοῦ locative adverb, "in that very place, there"

(17) δοῦσαι δίκην see page 145, no. 4

(17) τῆς ἀνοίας with δίκην/ In judicial contexts, the "genitive of price" (*see* page 40) may indicate the crime.

(18) ἐνθάδε *see* page 78, "here, there"

(19) ἀνώνυμον/ἀνώνυμος, -ον (ἀ(ν) + ὄνομα)

(21) δύ᾽/δύο two

(22) κἀκφέρῃ/καὶ ἐκ-φέρῃ/ἐκ-φέρω "carry out (as a corpse for a funeral)"

(23) πενθεῖν/πενθέω mourn/The infinitive is used as a command.

(23) μετρίως "moderately, with measure"/ *see* τὸ μέτρον, -ου

(23) προσήκοντας/προσ-ήκω (ἥκω) "belong to"/ προσήκων is the opposite of ἀλλότριος

(25) ἐστ(ι) ἀναγκαίως ἔχον = ἀναγκαίως ἔχει/ἔχον is the neuter participle/ "it is necessary, that is, having it necessarily or as a necessary condition"

(26) προεληλύθασιν/προ-έρχομαι

(28) Δαρείῳ the great Persian king Darius

(29) ὥσπερ/ὥσ-περ *see* page 78

(31) τρεῖς three

(31) παρεστήκασι/παρ-ίστημι

(32) τοῦθ'/τοῦτο

(32) ὁμοίως πως ἔχει "is *more or less* (or *somehow*) similar"/ *see* the use of ἔχω with an adverb in line 25

(33) κατέχουσι/κατ-έχω

III. GIVE THE LEXICAL ENTRY and then the equivalent form using the present verbal stem. (For example, (1) ἐπράχθητε/πράττω, ἐπράττεσθε (2) πράξετε/πράττω, πράττετε (3) πεπράχατε/πράττω, πράττετε (4) πέπραχθε/ πράττω, πράττεσθε.)

1. πεφίληκας	11. ἥγησαι
2. πέπεισαι	12. ἐρασθέντος
3. νενομίκασι	13. γέγονε
4. μεμάχηται	14. βέβλησθε
5. ἐνίκησας	15. τεθνήκατε
6. κεκαλυμμέναι εἰσίν	16. ἥρπακε
7. λέλειπται	17. ἀκηκόατε
8. ἐρρήθη	18. ἠδίκηνται
9. ἠρωτήκαμεν	19. ἦρξε
10. γεγαμηκυῖαν	20. δεδώκασι

IV. CHANGE from the passive to an equivalent statement in the active, for example, (1) πέπρακταί μοι/πέπραχα (2) πεπέμμεθά σοι/πέπεμφας ἡμᾶς.

1. πέπεισαί μοι	5. νενίκανται αὐτοῖς
2. ἐσώθης ὑφ' ἡμῶν	6. εἴρηταί σοι
3. πεφίληνταί σοι	7. κεκόμισθε αὐτῷ
4. πέπλευσταί μοι	8. ἕστασαί μοι

9. ἐκλήθητε ὑφ' ὑμῶν

10. ἑώραταί μοι

11. πέπαυσθέ μοι

12. ἐμοὶ πεπαιδευμένοι εἰσίν

13. ἐφιλήθητε ὑπ' αὐτοῦ

14. τέθεισαί μοι

15. ἐνήνεκταί σοι

16. κεκελεύσμεθα ὑμῖν

17. ἐστάθημεν ὑφ' ὑμῶν

18. γέγραπταί μοι

19. πεπαιδευμένοι εἴημεν ὑμῖν

20. νενόηταί μοι

V. COMPLETE the blanks with the appropriate form of the perfect. (The principle part is given in parentheses.) For example, ἔπιες οἶνον πολὺν καὶ ἔτι καὶ νῦν πέπωκας. "You drank much wine and still even now *are drunk.*"

1. τοῦτ' ἐνόμισε καὶ ἔτι καί νῦν _____ (νενόμικα)

2. ἐγράφη ὁ νόμος ὃς ἔτι καὶ νῦν _____ (γέγραμμαι)

3. δίκη ἐδόθη ἣ ἔτι καὶ νῦν _____ (δέδομαι)

4. ἐθαυμάσαμεν ἃ ἔτι καὶ νῦν _____ (τεθαύμακα)

5. ἐδιδάχθητε ἃ ἔτι καὶ νῦν _____ (δεδίδαγμαι)

6. ἐβουλήθης ποιεῖν ἃ ἔτι καὶ νῦν _____ (βεβούλημαι)

7. ἐμάθετε ἃ ἔτι καὶ νῦν _____ (μεμάθηκα)

8. εἶδες ἃ ἔτι καὶ νῦν _____ (ἑώρακα)

9. ἐπάθετε ὃ ἔτι καὶ νῦν _____ (πέπονθα)

10. ἔτυχον ὥσπερ ἔτι καὶ νῦν _____ (τετύχηκα)

VI. REPHRASE the following sentences, changing the indirectly quoted statements from the infinitive structure to an optative of secondary subordination.

1. ἔφη τὰς Ἀμαζόνας μόνας ὡπλίσθαι σιδήρῳ τῶν περὶ αὐτάς.

2. ἔφη αὐτὰς πρώτας πάντων ἐφ' ἵππους ἀναβεβηκέναι.

3. ἔφη τὰς Ἀμαζόνας νενομίσθαι ἄνδρας μᾶλλον ἢ γυναῖκας εἶναι.

4. ἔφη τὰς γυναῖκας καταδεδουλῶσθαι τοὺς περὶ αὐτάς.

5. ἔφη αὐτὰς ἀκηκοέναι περὶ τῶν Ἀθηνῶν κλέος μέγα.

6. ἔφη αὐτὰς νενικάσθαι τοῖς Ἀθηναίοις.

7. ἔφη τὰς μαχιμωτάτας γυναῖκας ᾑρηκέναι τῶν ἐναντίων τοὺς φεύγοντας.

8. ἔφη αὐτὰς οὐκ ἀπεληλυθέναι οἴκαδε ἀποθανούσας.

9. ἔφη τὰς γυναῖκας εἰληφέναι ἐναντίαν τὴν δόξαν τῆς προτέρας νικαθείσας.

10. ἔφη αὐτὰς τὴν ἑαυτῶν πατρίδα ἀνώνυμον κατεστηκέναι.

VII. REPHRASE the following sentences, making all dependent clauses more general by the use of the subjunctive.

1. γύνη ἀεὶ ἡδίστη ὅτε τέθνηκεν.

2. εὐδαίμονες πάντες οἳ οὐ γεγαμήκασιν.

3. ὃς θεῷ πεφίληται ἀποθνῄσκει νέος.

4. ἀεὶ καλὸς πλοῦς ἐστ᾽ ὅτε πέφευγας κακά.

5. οἳ καταδεδουλωμένοι εἰσὶν στρατεύουσι μετ᾽ αὐτῶν.

VIII. MATCH the second verb to the first by changing it into the same form.

1. ἔδραμον (ὁράω)   11. ἥδεσθαι (δύναμαι)

2. ἔθηκε (δίδωμι)   12. ποιῇς (ἐρωτάω)

3. πιούσης (νομίζω)   13. ᾖσε (ἐλπίζω)

4. ἐκαλέσαμεν (ἔρχομαι)   14. ἔδει (βοάω)

5. ἐδίδου (ἵστημι)   15. ἔχον (ποιέω)

6. διδῷς (λείπω)   16. δηλοῖς (τιμάω)

7. ἐμάχου (ἐράω)   17. ἀποθανών (ἐσθίω)

8. ποιοίης (ὁράω)   18. τιθείσης (φθείρω)

9. ἐδύνασο (τίθημι)   19. ἐγένετο (εὔχομαι)

10. ἔδου (κρίνω)   20. φοβούμενοι (τίθημι)

IX. MATCH the second phrase to the first by changing it into the same form.

1. ἀλλότρια ἔθνη   6. βουσὶ καλαῖς
   (μάχιμος βασιλεύς)   (ἄστυ παλαιόν)

2. παλαιοῦ κάλλους   7. ἀληθοῦς φιλοσοφίας
   (σφετέρα χάρις)   (θῆλυς παῖς)

3. ἄφωνον βοῦν   8. χείροσι πάθεσι
   (εὐδαίμων πόλις)   (μεῖζον ἄστυ)

4. ἡδεῖαι φωναί   9. ἐλευθέρας πόλεως
   (ἄρρην γέρων)   (ἄδικος δικαστής)

5. παῖδες πεπαιδευμένοι   10. σώφρονι παιδίῳ
   (γραῦς ἑκοῦσα)   (ὅλον γένος)

X. NOTE THE PATTERN in each of the quotations and compose a translation of the English sentences, using the same pattern.

1. τί τοὺς θανόντας οὐκ ἐᾷς τεθνηκέναι; —Εὔπολις

Why don't you allow the drinkers to be drunk?

He did not want the men who married still to be married.

2. πέπεισμαι ἐγὼ ἑκὼν εἶναι μηδένα ἀδικεῖν ἀνθρώπων. —Πλάτων

She is convinced that she herself is willing to pass judgement on no woman.

They are thought (νομίζω) to be willing to teach all of them.

It is thought that all mortals are unwilling to die.

3. ἐλεύθερος πᾶς ἑνὶ δεδούλωται, νόμῳ. —Μένανδρος

Every wise man is taught by one person, himself.

All mortals are conquered by one thing, chance.

4. φαίνεται μὲν ὁ ἥλιος ποδιαῖος, πεπίστευται δ' εἶναι μείζων τῆς οἰκουμένης. —'Αριστοτέλης

(ποδιαῖος, -α, -ον "as big as a foot," *see* ὁ ποῦς, ποδός/πιστεύω "believe"/ οἰκουμένης, namely γῆς)

The philosopher appears stupid, but he is said to be wiser than Socrates.

The danger seems great, but it is considered less than death.

21

Pluperfect

καὶ σκοτία ἤδη ἐγεγόνει, καὶ οὐκ ἐληλύθει πρὸς αὐτοὺς ὁ Ἰησοῦς
—Ἰωάννης.

Lesson 21
Pluperfect/Tense
And Aspect

The Greek pluperfect (or past perfect) expresses the perfect aspect (of state or condition of being) in the past tense.

σκοτία γέγονε. Perfect: It is dark, that is, darkness has come into being.

σκοτία ἐγεγόνει. Pluperfect: It was dark, that is, darkness had come into being.

Pluperfect
Conjugation

Like all past tenses, the pluperfect shows augment and secondary personal suffixes. It is formed from the perfect stem because that stem expresses the perfect aspect. There is only an indicative mood for the pluperfect since only the indicative can express tense.

The chart summarizes the pluperfect conjugation.

Active			Middle Passive	
ἐ-πεπαιδεύκ -	η*	1	ἐ-πεπαιδεύ-	μην
ἐ-γεγράφ-			ἐ- γεγράμ -	μην
	ης*	2	ἐ-πεπαίδευ-	σο
			ἐ- γέγρα -	ψο
	ει(ν)*	3	ἐ-πεπαίδευ-	το
			ἐ- γέγραπ -	το
	ε-μεν	1	ἐ-πεπαιδεύ-	μεθα
			ἐ- γεγράμ -	μεθα
	ε-τε	2	ἐ-πεπαίδευ-	σθε
			ἐ- γέγρα -	φθε
	ε-σαν	3	ἐ-πεπαίδευ-	ντο
			ἐ- γεγραμ -	μένοι ἦσαν

Note (*) that the perfect -κα- or -α- suffixes are modified to- κε- or -ε- for the pluperfect. In the singular active, the personal suffixes are identical with the endings of the sigmatic aorist (-α, -ας, -ε), but in the Attic dialect, these endings contract with the epsilon of the perfect suffix: ἐπεπαιδεύκε-α → ἐπεπαιδεύκη/ ἐπεπαιδεύκε-ας → ἐπεπαιδεύκης/ἐπεπαιδεύκε-ε(ν) → ἐπεπαιδεύκει(ν).

Note that the pluperfect middle passive shows the same euphonic modifications as the perfect when the stem ends in a consonant (*see* page 159–160).

Note that if the perfect stem has the augment type of reduplication (*see* page 157), no additional augment is normally added to form the pluperfect: ἐλήλυθα (perfect) "I am present, having come" ἐληλύθη (pluperfect) "I was present, having come."

Future Perfect

The perfect aspect can also be expressed in the future tense. The future perfect, however, occurs very rarely in Greek and there is no need to master its conjugation.

The future perfect is formed by adding the future suffix (-σε/ο-, *see* page 134) to the stem of the perfect middle passive; it is conjugated thematically with primary middle passive personal suffixes. There is only one form for all three voices although normally the future perfect is only passive in meaning.

πε-παιδευ-σ-ό-μεθα.   We shall be in an educated condition.

The Verb ΟΙΔΑ   The verb οἶδα ("I know") is a perfect formed from the stem ἰδ- (εἶδον "I saw") Etymologically, it assumes that the state of knowing results from the experience of seeing. Its conjugation presents certain "irregularities" in the Attic dialect.

Indicative		Subjunctive	Optative	Pluperfect
οἶδα	1	εἰδ-|ῶ	εἰδε-ίη-|ν	ἤδη (ἤδειν)
οἶσθα	2	ῇς	ς	ἤδησθα (ἤδεισθα)
οἶδε	3	ῇ	-	ἤδει(ν)
ἴσμεν	1	ῶ-μεν	μεν (εἰδεῖμεν)	ᾔσμεν
ἴστε	2	ῆ-τε	τε (εἰδεῖτε)	ᾖστε
ἴσασι	3	ῶ-σι	σαν (εἰδεῖεν)	ᾖσαν (ᾔδεσαν)

Participle εἰδώς, εἰδυῖα, εἰδός/ εἰδότος, εἰδυίας, εἰδότος/ etc.

Infinitive εἰδέναι

Future (Perfect) εἴσομαι

ΟΝΟΜΑΤΑ ΚΑΙ ΡΗΜΑΤΑ

ὁ ἀνεψιός, -οῦ	(first) cousin
ὁ ἡλικιώτης, -ου	comrade (of the same age group) (*see* ἡ ἡλικία, -ας "time of life, age")
ὁ ἀδελφός, -οῦ/ἡ ἀδελφή, -ῆς	brother/sister
ὁ κηδεστής, -ῆς	relative by marriage, in-law (*see* τὸ κῆδος, -ους "care, object of care, funeral rites, connection by marriage"/κήδω "trouble, distress"; *pass.* "care for")
ἡ αἰτία, -ας	cause, responsibility, blame
τὸ πρᾶγμα, -ατος	deed, occurrence, affair, thing (*see* πράττω)
τὸ ὄμμα, -ατος	eye (= ὁ ὀφθαλμός, -οῦ) see ὁράω, ὄψομαι, εἶδον, ὤφθην, ἑόρακα, ὦμμαι)
ὁ ὄχλος, -ου	crowd
ὁ ἡγεμών, -όνος	guide, leader (*see* ἡγέομαι "lead, think")

ὁ φϑόνος, -ου	envy
ὁ οἶκτος, -ου	pity, lamentation
τὸ ἦτρον, -ου	lower abdomen, belly
ὁ ἀλεκτρυών, -όνος	cock
τὸ εἰκός, -ότος	likelihood, probability
δέσμιος, -ον	bound, captive (*see* δέω/ τὸ δεσμωτή-ριον, -ου "prison"/ ὁ δεσμώτης, -ου "prisoner"/ὁ δεσπότης, -ου "despot, master")
πρόϑυμος, -ον	willing, eager, bearing good will (*see* ἐπι-ϑυμέω/ ὁ ϑυμός, -οῦ "spirit, will")
τελευταῖος, -α, -ον	last (*see* τὸ τέλος, -ους "end, consumation"/ ἡ τελευτή, -ῆς "completion, death"/τελευτάω "finish, die")
κλείω (κλήω), κλείσω, ἔκλεισα, ἐκλείσϑην, κέκλεικα, κέκλειμαι	shut, close, bar (*see* ἡ κλείς, κλειδός "bar, bolt, key")
οἶδα	know
εἴωϑα	be accustomed (perfect of ἔϑω/ ἐϑίζω "accustom")
κλαίω (κλάω), κλαιήσω (κλαήσω, κλαύσομαι), ἔκλαυσα, _____, _____, κέκλαυμαι (κέκλαυσμαι)	weep
ὀδύρομαι, ὀδυροῦμαι, ὠδυράμην, (κατ-)ωδύρϑην	lament (*see* ὁ ὀδυρμός, -οῦ "lamenta-tion")
λυπέω, λυπήσω, ἐλύπησα	grieve (*see* ἡ λυπή, -ῆς "pain of body or mind")
ὀφείλω, ὀφειλήσω, ὠφείλησα (ὤφελον), ὠφειλήϑην, ὠφείληκα	owe
ψύχω, ψύξω, ἔψυξα, ἐψύχϑην, _____, ἔψυγμαι	cool
ἀμελέω, _____, ἠμέλησα, _____, ἠμέληκα, ἠμέλημαι	have no care for (*see* μέλω "care for")
ἀνιάω, ἀνιάσω, ἠνίασα, ἀνιήϑην, ἠνίακα, ἠνίημαι	grieve, distress
φϑέγγομαι, φϑέγξομαι, ἐφϑεγξάμην, _____, ἔφϑεγμαι	utter a sound or voice (*see* ὁ φϑόγγος, -ου "distinct sound voice")

εἶτα   *adv.* then, next

σχεδόν   *adv.* near, approximately, more or
                                       less (see ἔχω, ἔσχον)

ΑΣΚΗΣΙΣ

I. TRANSLATE: Barabbas and Christ.

Κατὰ δὲ ἑορτὴν εἰώθει ὁ ἡγεμὼν ἀπολύειν ἕνα τῷ ὄχλῳ δέσμιον ὃν
ἤθελον. εἶχον δὲ τότε δέσμιον ἐπίσημον, λεγόμενον Βαραββᾶν.
συνηγμένων οὖν αὐτῶν, εἶπεν αὐτοῖς ὁ Πιλᾶτος, "Τίνα θέλετε ἀπολύσω
ὑμῖν; Βαραββᾶν ἢ Ἰησοῦν τὸν λεγόμενον Χριστόν;" ᾔδει γὰρ ὅτι διὰ
5 φθόνον παρέδωκαν αὐτόν. —ἐκ τοῦ κατὰ Ματθαῖον εὐαγγελίου.

Andocides in Prison is Begged to Inform on his Fellow Culprits.

Ἐπειδὴ δὲ ἐδεδέμεθα πάντες ἐν τῷ αὐτῷ, καὶ νύξ τε ἦν καὶ τὸ
δεσμωτήριον συνεκέκλητο, ἧκον δὲ τῷ μὲν μήτηρ, τῷ δὲ ἀδελφή, τῷ
δὲ γυνὴ καὶ παῖδες, ἦν δὲ βοὴ καὶ οἶκτος κλαιόντων καὶ ὀδυρομένων τὰ
παρόντα κακά, λέγει πρός με Χαρμίδης, ὢν μὲν ἀνεψιός, ἡλικιώτης δὲ
10 καὶ συνεκτραφεὶς ἐν τῇ οἰκίᾳ τῇ ἡμετέρᾳ ἐκ παιδός, ὅτι "Ἀνδοκίδη, τῶν
μὲν παρόντων κακῶν ὁρᾷς τὸ μέγεθος, ἐγὼ δ' ἐν μὲν τῷ παρελθόντι
χρόνῳ οὐδὲν ἐδεόμην λέγειν οὐδέ σε λυπεῖν, νῦν δὲ ἀναγκάζομαι διὰ τὴν
παροῦσαν ἡμῖν συμφοράν. οἷς γὰρ ἐχρῶ καὶ οἷς συνῆσθα ἄνευ ἡμῶν τῶν
συγγενῶν, οὗτοι ἐπὶ ταῖς αἰτίαις δι' ἃς ἡμεῖς ἀπολλύμεθα οἱ μὲν αὐτῶν
15 τεθνᾶσιν, οἱ δὲ οἴχονται φεύγοντες, σφῶν αὐτῶν καταγνόντες ἀδικεῖν.
εἰ δ' οὖν ἤκουσάς τι τούτου τοῦ πράγματος τοῦ γενομένου, χρή σε εἰπεῖν
καὶ πρῶτον μὲν σεαυτὸν σῶσαι, εἶτα δὲ τὸν πατέρα, ὃν εἰκός ἐστί σε
μάλιστα φιλεῖν, εἶτα δὲ τὸν κηδεστήν, ὃς ἔχει σου τὴν ἀδελφὴν ἥπερ σοι
μόνη ἐστίν, ἔπειτα δὲ τοὺς ἄλλους συγγενεῖς καὶ ἀναγκαίους τοσούτους
20 ὄντας, ἔτι δὲ ἐμέ, ὃς ἐν ἅπαντι τῷ βίῳ ἡνίασα μέν σε οὐδὲν πώποτε,
προθυμότατος δὲ εἰς σὲ καὶ τὰ σὰ πράγματά εἰμι, ὅ τι ἂν δέῃ ποιεῖν.
—Ἀνδοκίδης

Socrates' Last Words.

Ἤδη οὖν σχεδόν τι αὐτοῦ ἦν τὰ περὶ τὸ ἦτρον ψυχόμενα, καὶ ἐκκαλυψά-
μενος—ἐνεκεκάλυπτο γάρ—εἶπεν (ὃ δὴ τελευταῖον ἐφθέγξατο):
25 "Ὦ Κρίτων," ἔφη, "τῷ Ἀσκληπιῷ ὀφείλομεν ἀλεκτρυόνα. ἀλλὰ ἀπόδοτε
καὶ μὴ ἀμελήσητε." "Ἀλλὰ ταῦτα," ἔφη, "ἔσται," ὁ Κρίτων. "ἀλλ' ὅρα
εἴ τι ἄλλο λέγεις."
Ταῦτα ἐρομένου αὐτοῦ, οὐδὲν ἔτι ἀπεκρίνατο, ἀλλ' ὀλίγον χρόνον
διαλιπὼν ἐκινήθη τε καὶ ὁ ἄνθρωπος ἐξεκάλυψεν αὐτόν, καὶ ὃς τὰ
30 ὄμματα ἔστησεν. ἰδὼν δὲ ὁ Κρίτων συνέλαβε τὸ στόμα καὶ τοὺς
ὀφθαλμούς. Ἥδε ἡ τελευτή, ὦ Ἐχέκρατες, τοῦ ἑταίρου ἡμῖν ἐγένετο,
ἀνδρός, ὡς ἡμεῖς φαῖμεν ἄν, τῶν τότε ὧν ἐπειράθημεν ἀρίστου καὶ
ἄλλως φρονιμωτάτου καὶ δικαιοτάτου. —Πλάτων

Reading Notes:

(1) ἀπολύειν/ ἀπο-λύω

(2) ἐπίσημον/ ἐπίσημος, -ον notable, significant (see σημαίνω)

(3) συνηγμένων/ συν-άγω

(5) παρέδωκαν = παρέδοσαν/ παρα-δίδωμι hand over to another

(6) ἐν τῷ αὐτῷ (namely τόπῳ) "in the same place"/Andocides, together with numerous other people, including many of his own relatives, was imprisoned as a result of the investigation into several notorious acts of impiety that were committed in the year 415 B.C.. Andocides turned state's evidence to gain indemnity and obtain his own and his relatives' release. He claimed that although he knew of the proposed act he had actually opposed his friends' plans and took no active part in them himself; he also attempted to excuse his betrayal of his comrades by claiming that his information won his father's release and occasioned no additional harm to his comrades because they actually by that time had either gone into exile or had been already put to death. The scandalous events that were involved were of two kinds: the mutilation of a great number of religious effigies throughout Athens and the profane performance of the Eleusinian Mystery in private homes.

(7) συνεκέκλητο/συγ-κλείω

(7) ἧκον/ἧκω "come, have come"/ contrast ἵημι, ἧσω, ἧκα

(7–8) τῷ μέν... τῷ δέ... τῷ δέ... see page 19

(8) βοή/ ἡ βοή, -ῆς (see βοάω)

(9) παρόντα/πάρ-ειμι

(10) συνεκτραφείς/συν-εκ-τρέφω

(10) οἰκίᾳ/ ἡ οἰκία, -ας = ὁ οἶκος, -ου

(10) 'Ανδοκίδη the form of Andocides' name used for calling him

(11) παρελθόντι/παρ-έρχομαι go by (the side), pass

(12) ἐδεόμην uncontracted, see page 104

(13) παροῦσαν/πάρ-ειμι

(13) οἷς... ἐχρῶ/χράομαι + dat. (those people) with whom you associated

(13) συνῆσθα/σύν-ειμι

(14) συγγενῶν/συγ-γενής, -ές

(14–15) οἱ μὲν αὐτῶν... οἱ δέ... see page 19

(15) σφῶν (gen. of σφᾶς see page 23) =ἑαυτῶν/see σφέτερος, -α, -ον

(15) καταγνόντες/κατα-γιγνώσκω lay as a charge against someone (gen.) for a crime (inf.)

(19) ἀναγκαίους that is, connected by necessary or natural ties, related by blood

(19) τοσούτους see page 78

(20) πώποτε/πω (up to this time, yet) + ποτε

(23) Socrates in prison has just drunk the lethal dose of hemlock and the executioner (ὁ ἄνϑρωπος) has explained that its effects will be felt as a progressive chill moving upwards on his body.

(23–24) ἐκκαλυψάμενος/ἐκ-καλύπτω see ἐγ-καλύπτω

(25) ὦ Κρίτων see note 10

(25) ὁ Ἀσκληπιός, -οῦ the son of Apollo who was patron of the healing art; his temple sancturaries were like hospital asylums or spas where the sick recuperated; after experiencing a cure, the patient offered the god a gift *ex voto* in thanksgiving. Socrates' remark about his debt of a cock to Asclepius is an ironic comment on the sickness of living from which his approaching death is about to cure him.

(25) ἀπόδοτε καὶ μὴ ἀμελήσητε commands: pay it and don't neglect (this debt)!/*see* ὅρα see!

(28) ἐρομένου/*see* λέγω

(29) διαλιπών/δια-λείπω

(29) ἐκινήϑη/κινέω, κινήσομαι, ἐκίνησα, ἐκινήϑην, _____, κεκίνημαι move, disturb, stir

(29) ὅς (that is, Socrates) *see* page 110, note 24

(30) συνέλαβε/συλ-λαμβάνω

(31) ὦ Ἐχέκρατες *see* note 10/The description of Socrates' death is being narrated to Echecrates by Phaedo.

(31) ἑταίρου/ὁ ἑταῖρος, -ου = φίλος, comrade, companion

(32) τῶν τότε of the people then/ partitive gen. with the superlative, *see* page 148.

(32) ἐπειράϑημεν/πειράω, πειράσω, ἐπείρασα, ἐπειράϑην, πεπείρακα, experience, make trial of + gen., hence the relative ὧν

(33) ἄλλως adv. otherwise (*see* ἄλλος, -η, -ον/ ἀλλά)

(33) φρονιμωτάτου/φρόνιμος, -ον (*see* ἡ φρήν, φρενός/σώφρων, -ον, gen. -ονος)

II. CHANGE from perfect to pluperfect.

1. τεϑνήκασι	7. ἐλήλυϑε
2. ἠδίκηται	8. δέδεσαι
3. γέγονε	9. γέγραψαι
4. δεδιδάγμεϑα	10. ἐκκεκάλυπται
5. τεϑαυμάκατε	11. εἰώϑαμεν
6. γεγάμηνται	12. ἑστήκασι*

*Usually augments to εἱ–.

13. νενόμισθε

14. νενίκαμαι

15. πεποίηνται

16. ἐδήδοκας

17. πέπεισθε

18. πεπραγμένοι εἰσίν

19. πέφευγε

20. πέπλασμαι

III. GIVE THE LEXICAL ENTRY and then the equivalent form using the present verbal stem.

1. ἐγέγραφθε

2. ἀποθανεῖ

3. ἠκούσθημεν

4. εἴληψο

5. τεθνηκότες

6. ἐδέδοτο

7. γεγραφυίαις

8. εἶτο

9. λυθέντα

10. λελειμμένας

11. εἴκη

12. ἐκεκλήκεσαν

13. εἴστηκε

14. ἔστη

15. ἴδοιεν

16. μενεῖς

17. παιδευθείη

18. ἑορακέναι

19. τεθνήκοις

20. λελοίπωμεν

IV. CHANGE from the passive to an equivalent statement in the active (*see* page 160). The required principle part is given in parentheses when necessary.

1. εὕρηταί μοι (ηὕρηκα)

2. ἐγέγραπτο ἡμῖν (γέγραφα)

3. ἐδεδίδαξο ὑμῖν (δεδίδαχα)

4. ἐγνώσθημεν ὑπ’ αὐτῶν

5. βληθήσεται ὑφ’ ὑμῶν

6. λελειμμέναι ἦσάν σοι (λέλοιπα)

7. εἰλήμμεθα ὑμῖν (εἴληφα)

8. ᾕρητό σοι (ᾕρηκα)

9. ἤρχοντο ὑπ’ αὐτῶν

10. τεθαυμασμένη μοι εἴη (τεθαύμακα)

V. REPHRASE the following groups of sentences, combining them into a single sentence by the use of participles or dependent clauses (relative, purpose, etc.).

1. ἐδέδεντο πάντες ἐν τῷ δεσμωτηρίῳ. ἐγεγόνει δὲ ἤδη νύξ. τὸ δὲ δεσμωτήριον συνεκέκλητο.

2. ἧκον δὲ τοῖς δεσμώταις πᾶσι οἱ συγγενεῖς. ἔκλαιον δὲ πάντες ὠδύροντό τε.

3. εἶπε δὲ Χαρμίδης πρὸς Ἀνδοκίδην. ὁ δὲ Χαρμίδης ἦν ἀνεψιὸς αὐτοῦ καὶ ἡλικιώτης.

4. ἔφη δὲ αὐτὸς οὔποτε δεῖσθαι λέγειν οὐδὲν οὐδὲ λυπεῖν Ἀνδοκίδην, νῦν δὲ

ἔφη ἀναγκάζεσθαι εἰπεῖν διὰ τὴν παροῦσαν αὐτοῖς συ μφοράν. ἐβεβούλητο γὰρ ἑαυτόν τε καὶ τοὺς συγγενεῖς σῶσαι.

5. ἔφη δὲ χρῆναι Ἀνδοκίδην λέγειν περὶ τοῦ πράγματος εἴ τι εἰδείη. οὕτως γὰρ ἂν σῶσαι ἑαυτόν τε καὶ τοὺς συγγενεῖς τόν τε πατέρα. τοῦτον δὲ εἰκὸς Ἀνδοκίδην μάλιστα φιλεῖν.

VI. REPHRASE each sentence, changing it from an expression of a likelihood in the past (past potential) to a likelihood in the present (present future potential, *see* page 93).

1. εἰώθει δ' ἂν ὁ ἡγεμὼν ἀπολύειν τῶν δεσμωτῶν ἕνα τῷ ὄχλῳ.

2. ᾔδει γὰρ ἂν ὅτι διὰ φθόνον παραδοίη τὸν Χριστόν.

3. ἔψυκτο δ' ἂν Σωκράτους τὰ περὶ τὸ ἦτρον.

4. ἐξεκεκάλυπτο δ' ἂν ὁ Σωκράτης ἀποθνήσκων.

5. ἐληλύθει δὲ ὁ Χριστὸς ἄν.

VII. REPHRASE each sentence, changing to a past tense context and using the optative of secondary subordination.

1. πάντες δὲ λέγουσιν ὅτι ὁ Χριστὸς ἐλήλυθε.

2. ὅταν νὺξ γεγόνῃ, πάντες οἱ δεσμῶται ἐν τῷ δεσμωτηρίῳ δέδενται.

3. λέγουσιν ὅτι ὁ Χριστὸς παραδέδοται τῷ ὄχλῳ διὰ φθόνον.

4. ἴσμεν τὸν Χριστὸν ὅτι παραδέδοται τῷ ὄχλῳ.

5. ὅταν τεθνήκῃ θεός, ὀδυρόμεθα ἀεί.

VIII. MATCH the second phrase to the first by changing it into the same form.

1. πρόθυμοι ἡγεμόνες (ἑκὸν ἔθνος)

2. ἀληθῆ εἰκότα (ὠφέλιμον μέρος)

3. βελτίοσι βασιλεῦσι (νεὼς καλός)

4. νῆες ταχεῖαι (πόλις ἐλευθέρα)

5. σώφρονος δικαστοῦ (θῆλυ γένος)

6. ἀμείνονα γραῦν (σφέτερος γονεύς)

7. πλείστου μεγέθους (μέγιστος πούς)

8. νεὼς μαχίμης (νεὼς ἄριστος)

9. ἰχθῦς ἄρρενας (βοῦς ἄγριος)

10. γραὸς θηλείας (ἔθνος πεφευγός)

IX. NOTE THE PATTERN in each of the quotations and compose a translation of the English sentences, using the same pattern.

1. οὐδὲ τῶν πραγμάτων προορᾶτε οὐδὲν πρὶν ἂν ἢ γεγενημένον ἢ γιγνόμενόν τι πύθησθε. —Δημοσθένης (προ-οράω/ πυνθάνομαι, πεύσομαι, ἐπυθόμην, _____, _____, πέπυσμαι "learn, inquire")

Nor does anyone know a man before he sees him drunk or drinking.

We do not know of mortals the blessed ones before we see them dead or dying.

He chose (αἱρέομαι) no man before he knew him either having done wrong or doing wrong. (Use the optative of secondary subordination.)

2. διαφέρουσιν οἱ πεπαιδευμένοι τῶν ἀπαιδεύτων ὅσῳ οἱ ζῶντες τῶν
τεθνεώτων. —'Αριστοτέλης (ἀπαίδευτος, -ον, see παιδεύω/ὅσῳ see pages
78 and 148/τεθνεώτων = τεθνηκότων see page 160)

The enslaved (δουλόω/δεδούλωμαι) differ from the free by as much as the lover
from the beloved (φιλέω/πεφίλημαι).

3. ἐπακήκο' ὑμῶν... ἅπαντας οὓς εἰρήκατ' ἐξ ἀρχῆς λόγους. —Μένανδρος
(ἐπακήκο' = ἐπ-ακήκοα/εἰρήκατ' = εἰρήκατε)

We know all his books that he's written since a child.

We had seen of their enemies as many as they'd conquered.

22

Conditional Clauses

εἰ ἵπποι χεῖρας εἶχον, ἵπποις ὁμοίας καὶ ἂν θεῶν ἰδέας ἔγραφον.
—Ξενοφάνης

Lesson 22
Conditional
Clauses

A conditional clause is one introduced by εἰ ("if") or in some other way stating a supposition or hypothesis (for example, a relative clause with the force or implication of a hypothesis).

You have already learned that such hypotheses are regularly negated by μή (*see* page 68) and that they can be made general in meaning, like any dependent clause, by the addition of the particle ἄν and the shift of the verb to a subjunctive (*see* page 85); in past tense contexts, such generalized clauses may shift to the optative of secondary subordination, omitting the particle ἄν (*see* page 94).

In certain contexts, however, the combination of a conditional clause with an independent statement produces particular patterns of meaning that you have not yet studied.

Contrary-to-Fact
Conditions

As you know, a past tense of the indicative with the particle ἄν states a likelihood in the past, a so-called "past potential" (*see* page 93–94). When a past tense hypothesis is added to such a past potential, the combination of the two clauses implies that the potential was never realized and that the hypothesis is a supposition of something that in fact is not true.

εἰ ἵπποι χεῖρας εἶχον, θεῶν ἰδέας ἂν ἔγραφον.

If horses had hands, they were likely to be drawing pictures of gods. (The *implication* is that horses do not actually have hands; otherwise I would not have stated their drawing merely as a likelihood instead of an actuality: the statement of their drawing as a past likelihood implies that the potential, as can now be judged by my own placement in present time, was never realized in actuality. Contrast: εἰ ἵπποι χεῖρας εἶχον, θεῶν ἰδέας ἔγραφον. If horses had hands —which perhaps they did—they were actually drawing pictures of gods.)

All past tense indicatives in any combination function alike in this structure for contrary-to-fact suppositions; the difference between imperfect, aorist, and pluperfect is one only of verbal aspect.

εἰ ἦσαν ἄνδρες ἀγαθοί, οὐκ ἂν ποτε ταῦτα ἔπασχον. —Πλάτων

If they were good men, they would never have suffered these things.

εἰ ἀπεκρίνω, ἂν ἐμεμαθήκη. —Πλάτων

If you had answered, I would have understood.

Future Less Vivid
Conditions

As you know, an optative with the particle ἄν expresses a present likelihood, the so-called present-future potential (*see* page 93). A conditional clause added to such a present potential tends to be attracted also into the optative as an optative of secondary subordination.

εἰ μὴ γαμοίη ἄνθρωπος, οὐκ ἂν ἔχοι κακά. —Μένανδρος	If a man not marry, he is likely not to have troubles. (Or: If a man should not marry, he would not have troubles.) (Unlike the contrary-to-fact condition, nothing is implied about the irreality of the supposition; since the likelihood exists in present time, we cannot know whether it will be fulfilled until some future time which is obviously beyond our knowledge.)

Since such clauses were named in terms of their English equivalents, they were called *future less vivid* (that is "should–would") to contrast them with the so-called more vivid form ("shall–will").

εἰ μὴ γαμεῖ ἄνθρωπος, οὐχ ἕξει κακά.	If a man shall not marry, he will not have troubles.

Since this terminology has nothing to do with the Greek structures, it is better to pay no attention to it and to consider the future less vivid as a present potential with an optative hypothesis in secondary subordination and the so-called more vivid as simply a future hypothesis.

Note that the negative for past and present potentials is always οὐ (*see* page 95), whereas the negative for all hypotheses is always μή.

The Verb *EIMI*

The verb εἶμι (contrast the enclitic εἰμί "to be") means "to go" and is irregular in its conjugation. Normally it functions as a *future* for ἔρχομαι (whose future ἐλεύσομαι is rare in Attic prose), although sometimes the indicative may have present tense meaning. In prose εἶμι is ordinarily used as the subjunctive, optative, infinitive, participle, imperfect, and future for ἔρχομαι.

The chart summarizes the conjugation of εἶμι.

Indicative		Subjunctive	Optative	Imperfect
εἶμι	1	ἴ-|ω	ἴ-οι-|μι (ἰοίην)	ᾖα (ᾔειν)
εἶ	2	ῃς	ς	ᾔεις (ᾔεισθα)
εἶσι	3	ῃ	—	ᾔει (ᾔειν)
ἴ-|μεν	1	ω-μεν	μεν	ᾖ-|μεν
ἴ-|τε	2	η-τε	τε	ᾖ-|τε
ἴ-|ασι	3	ω-σι	εν	ᾖ-|σαν (ᾖσαν)

Infinitive: ἰέναι
Participle: ἰών, ἰοῦσα, ἰόν/ἰόντος, ἰούσης, ἰόντος/etc.

Result Clauses/ *ΩΣΤΕ*

The adverb ὥστε introduces an expression of the result ensuing from some other statement. There are two structures used with ὥστε.

If the result is one that the other statement *tends* to produce, ὥστε is followed by an infinitive.

πᾶν ποιοῦσιν ὥστε δίκην μὴ διδόναι. —Πλάτων

They do everything so as not to pay the penalty. (Contrast this *intention* or *expected result* with a subjunctive clause of purpose, *see* page 84.)

If the result is one that actually is produced, ὥστε is followed by an indicative.

πᾶν ποιοῦσιν ὥστε δίκην οὐ διδόασιν.

They do everything so that, actually, they do not pay the penalty.

ONOMATA KAI PHMATA

ἡ ἡλικία, -ας	time of life, age (*see* ὁ ἡλικιώτης, -ου)
ἡ δίκη, -ης	right, justice, lawsuit, trial/δίκην διδόναι pay the penalty (*see* δίκαιος, -α, -ον/ἄδικος, -ον/ὁ δικαστής, -οῦ)
ἡ μάχη, -ης	battle (*see* μάχομαι/μάχιμος, -η, -ον)
ὁ κατήγορος, -ου	accusor (*see* κατ-ηγορέω speak against, accuse/ἡ ἀγορά, -ᾶς assembly, marketplace, *see* ἄγω/ἀγορεύω speak in the assembly)
ἡ ἀπορία, -ας	lack of means (*see* πορεύω carry/ἀπορέω be without means/ἄπορος, -ον)
ἡ πονηρία, -ας	wickedness, baseness (*see* ὁ πόνος, -ου work, labor, pain/ὁ πένης, -ητος poor man/πονηρός, -ά, -όν bad)
ὁ πρεσβύτης, -ου	= ὁ γέρων, -οντος elder, old man (*see* πρεσβύτερος, -α, -ον)
ἡ ἱκετεία, -ας	supplication, suppliant approach (*see* ἱκνέομαι come)
ἡ τόλμα, -ης	courage, overboldness, recklessness (*see* τολμάω dare, have the courage or hardihood)
ἡ αἰσχύνη, -ης	shame, dishonor (*see* αἰσχρός, -ά, -όν/αἰσχύνω make ugly, be ashamed/ἡ ἀν-αισχυντία, -ας shamelessness)
ἡ μοχθηρία, -ας	wickedness, depravity (*see* ὁ μόχθος, -ου hardship, distress/μοχθηρός, -ά, -όν/μοχθέω be weary)
ὀλίγος, -η, -ον	little, few

χαλεπός, -ή, -όν	difficult, hard
βραδύς -εῖα, -ύ	slow, dull, sluggish
ὀξύς, -εῖα, -ύ	sharp, keen, quick, sour
θάττων, -ον	comparative of ταχύς, -εῖα, -ύ swift
λοιδορέω, λοιδορήσομαι, ἐλοιδόρησα, ἐλοιδορήθην, λελοιδόρηκα, λελοιδόρημαι	abuse, revile
ὀνειδίζω, ὀνειδιῶ, ὠνείδισα, ὠνειδίσθην, ὠνείδικα	reproach (see τὸ ὄνειδος, -ους)
οἴομαι, οἰήσομαι, _____, ᾠήθην (present and imperfect are often athematic: οἶμαι, ᾤμην: these forms are probably perfect and pluperfect of οἴομαι)	think
θρηνέω, θρηνήσω, ἐθρήνησα, _____, _____, τεθρήνημαι	lament (see θρῆνος, -ου dirge)
μέλει, μελήσει, ἐμέλησε, _____, μεμέληκε	it is a concern (see ἀ-μελέω/μετα-μέλει it causes repentance)
τρέπω, τρέψω, ἔτρεψα (ἐτραπόμην), τέτροφα, τέτραμμαι	turn, mid. flee
θέω, θεύσομαι, other forms supplied by τρέχω/ἔδραμον	run
ἐθίζω, ἐθιῶ, εἴθισα, εἰθίσθην, εἴθικα, εἴθισμαι	accustom (see εἴωθα/τὸ ἔθνος, -ους)
ψηφίζω, ψηφιῶ, ἐψήφισα, ἐψηφίσθην, ἐψήφικα, ἐψήφισμαι	cast one's vote (with a pebble) (see ἡ ψῆφος, -ου pebble)
ἀπο-λογέομαι, _____, ἀπελογησάμην, ἀπελογήθην, _____, ἀπολέλογμαι	speak in one's own defense
μηχανάομαι, μηχανήσομαι, ἐμηχανησάμην, _____, _____, μεμηχάνημαι	make by art, devise (see ἡ μηχανή, -ῆς contrivance, machine)
ἕνεκα	on account of (+ gen.)/see χάριν + gen.
ἐγγύς	adv. near (+ gen.)
ἴσως	adv. perhaps, equally, probably (see ἴσος, -η, -ον)
πρόσω (πόρρω)	adv. forward (of time, far into + gen.)
ἅτε	inasmuch as (+ participle)

ΑΣΚΗΣΙΣ

I. TRANSLATE: Socrates Addresses the Jurors Who Have Just Voted for his Death.

οὐ πολλοῦ γ᾿ ἕνεκα χρόνου, ὦ ἄνδρες ᾿Αθηναῖοι, ὄνομα ἕξετε καὶ αἰτίαν
ὑπὸ τῶν βουλομένων τὴν πόλιν λοιδορεῖν ὡς Σωκράτη ἀπεκτόνατε, ἄνδρα
σοφόν—φήσουσι γὰρ δὴ σοφὸν εἶναι, εἰ καὶ μή εἰμι, οἱ βουλόμενοι ὑμῖν
ὀνειδίζειν—εἰ γοῦν περιεμείνατε ὀλίγον χρόνον, ἀπὸ τοῦ αὐτομάτου ἂν
5 ὑμῖν τοῦτο ἐγένετο· ὁρᾶτε γὰρ δὴ τὴν ἡλικίαν ὅτι πόρρω ἤδη ἐστὶ τοῦ
βίου θανάτου δὲ ἐγγύς. λέγω δὲ τοῦτο οὐ πρὸς πάντας ὑμᾶς, ἀλλὰ πρὸς
τοὺς ἐμοῦ καταψηφισαμένους θάνατον. λέγω δὲ καὶ τόδε πρὸς τοὺς αὐτοὺς
τούτους. ἴσως με οἴεσθε, ὦ ἄνδρες ᾿Αθηναῖοι, ἀπορίᾳ λόγων ἑαλωκέναι
τοιούτων οἷς ἂν ὑμᾶς ἔπεισα, εἰ ᾤμην δεῖν ἅπαντα ποιεῖν καὶ λέγειν ὥστε
10 ἀποφυγεῖν τὴν δίκην. πολλοῦ γε δεῖ. ἀλλ᾿ ἀπορίᾳ μὲν ἑάλωκα, οὐ μέντοι
λόγων, ἀλλὰ τόλμης καὶ ἀναισχυντίας καὶ τοῦ μὴ ἐθέλειν λέγειν πρὸς
ὑμᾶς τοιαῦτα οἷ᾿ ἂν ὑμῖν μὲν ἥδιστα ἦν ἀκούειν—θρηνοῦντός τέ μου καὶ
ὀδυρομένου καὶ ἄλλα ποιοῦντος καὶ λέγοντος πολλὰ καὶ ἀνάξια ἐμοῦ, ὡς
ἐγώ φημι, οἷα δὴ καὶ εἴθισθε ὑμεῖς τῶν ἄλλων ἀκούειν. ἀλλ᾿ οὔτε τότε
15 ᾤήθην δεῖν ἕνεκα τοῦ κινδύνου πρᾶξαι οὐδὲν ἀνελεύθερον, οὔτε νῦν μοι
μεταμέλει οὕτως ἀπολογησαμένῳ, ἀλλὰ πολὺ μᾶλλον αἱροῦμαι ὧδε
ἀπολογησάμενος τεθνάναι ἢ ἐκείνως ζῆν. οὔτε γὰρ ἐν δίκῃ οὔτ᾿ ἐν πολέμῳ
οὔτ᾿ ἐμὲ οὔτ᾿ ἄλλον οὐδένα δεῖ τοῦτο μηχανᾶσθαι, ὅπως ἀποφεύξεται
πᾶν ποιῶν θάνατον. καὶ γὰρ ἐν ταῖς μάχαις πολλάκις δῆλον γίγνεται ὅτι
20 τό γε ἀποθανεῖν ἄν τις ἐκφύγοι καὶ ὅπλα ἀφεὶς καὶ ἐφ᾿ ἱκετείαν τραπόμε-
νος τῶν διωκόντων. καὶ ἄλλαι μηχαναὶ πολλαί εἰσιν ἐν ἑκάστοις τοῖς
κινδύνοις ὥστε διαφεύγειν θάνατον, ἐάν τις τολμᾷ πᾶν ποιεῖν καὶ λέγειν.
ἀλλὰ μὴ οὐ τοῦτ᾿ ᾖ χαλεπόν, ὦ ἄνδρες, θάνατον ἐκφυγεῖν, ἀλλὰ πολὺ
χαλεπώτερον πονηρίαν· θᾶττον γὰρ θανάτου θεῖ. καὶ νῦν ἐγὼ μὲν ἅτε
25 βραδὺς ὢν καὶ πρεσβύτης ὑπὸ τοῦ βραδυτέρου ἑάλων, οἱ δ᾿ ἐμοὶ κατήγοροι
ἅτε δεινοὶ καὶ ὀξεῖς ὄντες ὑπὸ τοῦ θάττονος, τῆς κακίας. καὶ νῦν ἐγὼ
μὲν ἄπειμι ὑφ᾿ ὑμῶν θανάτου δίκην ὀφλών, οὗτοι δ᾿ ὑπὸ τῆς ἀληθείας
ὠφληκότες μοχθηρίαν καὶ ἀδικίαν. καὶ ἐγώ τε τῷ τιμήματι ἐμμένω καὶ
οὗτοι. ταῦτα μέν που ἴσως οὕτως καὶ ἔδει σχεῖν, καὶ οἶμαι αὐτὰ μετρίως
30 ἔχειν.—Πλάτων

Reading Notes:

(1) ὦ ἄνδρες ᾿Αθηναῖοι the form for direct address or naming, the so-called vocative; so also in lines 8 and 23

(3) εἰ καί even if, although

(4) περιεμείνατε/περι-μένω wait

(4) αὐτομάτου/αὐτόματος, -η, -ον acting by itself or of its own will, *automatic*/ τὸ αὐτόματον, -ου accident

(7) καταψηφισαμένους/κατα-ψηφίζομαι vote (a penalty, acc.) *against* (some-one, gen.)

(7–8) τοὺς αὐτοὺς τούτους these same (people)

(8) ἑαλωκέναι/ἁλίσκομαι, which functions as the passive for αἱρέω

(9) τοιούτων *see* page 78

(10) δεῖ/δέω, δεήσω, ἐδέησα, ἐδεήθην, δεδέηκα, δεδέημαι need, lack (contrast: δέω, δήσω, ἔδησα, ἐδέθην, δέδεκα, δέδεμαι bind)/πολλοῦ δεῖ far from it (literally: "it lacks of much," the genitive being an ablatival idea expressing quantity) Do not confuse this δεῖ with the impersonal usage of the other δεῖ, δήσω (*see* page 127).

(12) θρηνοῦντός τέ μου Note that this is a genitive absolute but that by pure grammar it could be nominative since μου refers to the same person as the subject of ἑάλωκα.

(13) ἀνάξια/ἀν-άξιος, -ον

(15) ἀνελεύθερον/ἀν-ελεύθερος, -ον *not* free, servile, not befitting a free man

(16) αἱροῦμαι choose (*middle* of αἱρέω take)

(16) ὧδε *see* page 78

(17) τεθνάναι = τεθνηκέναι *see* page 160

(18) ὅπως ἀποφεύξεται Sometimes, although rarely, a future indicative occurs instead of a subjunctive in a purpose clause (*see* page 134).

(23) μὴ οὐ τοῦτ' ᾖ χαλεπόν The negative μὴ with a subjunctive introduces a so-called doubtful assertion; μή οὐ with the subjunctive a doubtful negation. This structure is really only μὴ/μὴ οὐ in clauses of fearing (*see* page 85) with the idea of fearing not expressed but merely to be inferred from the context: (φοβοῦμαι) μὴ οὐ τοῦτ' ᾖ χαλεπόν (I fear or suspect) this may not be difficult.

(24) θεῖ (namely ἡ πονηρία)

(25) ἑάλων/ἁλίσκομαι

(27) ὀφλών/ὀφλ-ισκ-άνω (*see* ὀφείλω), ὀφλήσω, ὤφλησα (ὦφλον), _____, ὤφληκα, ὤφλημαι owe, be guilty, incur a penalty or fine/ δίκην ὀφλεῖν lose a lawsuit/ ὑφ' ὑμῶν θανάτου δίκην ὀφλών by you(r doing, that is, ablatival gen. of agent) having lost a lawsuit (with the assessed penalty) of death (that is, gen. of value, *see* page 40)

(27–28) ὑπὸ τῆς ἀληθείας ὠφληκότες μοχθηρίαν by truth('s agency) guilty of baseness

(28) τιμήματι/τὸ τίμημα, -ατος estimate of damages, penalty (*see* ἡ τιμή, -ῆς/ τιμάω)

(28) ἐμ-μένω abide, remain in

II. REPHRASE each sentence, making all conditions contrary-to-fact.

1. εἰ ἵπποι χεῖρας ἔχουσι, θεῶν ἰδέας ἵπποις ὁμοίας γράφουσιν.

2. εἰ περιμένετε ὀλίγον χρόνον, Σωκράτης ἀπὸ τοῦ αὐτομάτου ἀποθανεῖται.

3. εἰ ἅπαντα ἐποίουν, τοὺς δικαστὰς ἔπεισα.

4. εἰ θρηνοίη Σωκράτης ἀπολογούμενος, ἡδὺ ἂν εἴη τοῖς δικασταῖς.

5. εἰ ᾤήθη Σωκράτης πᾶν ποιεῖν ἕνεκα τοῦ κινδύνου, οὐκ ὦφλε θανάτου δίκην.

6. ἐὰν μὴ πᾶν ποιῇ τις ὥστε ἀποφυγεῖν, μεταμελήσει αὐτῷ ἀπολογησαμένῳ.

7. εἰ μὴ ὅπλα ἀφίῃς ἐν ταῖς μάχαις, οὐκ ἐκφεύξει τὸ ἀποθανεῖν.

8. ἐάν τις μὴ οἶται δεῖν πάντα ποιεῖν καὶ λέγειν ὥστε ἀποφυγεῖν τὴν δίκην, δίκαιός ἐστι καὶ ἄξιος τιμῆς.

9. οἳ βούλοιντο τὴν πόλιν ὀνειδίζειν, φαῖεν ἂν ὡς Σωκράτη ἀπεκτόνατε.

10. ὅταν βουλώμεθα τοὺς Ἀθηναίους λοιδορεῖν, Σωκράτη φαμὲν ἄνδρα σοφὸν ἀποθανεῖν ὑπ' αὐτῶν.

III. REPHRASE each sentence, changing from contrary-to-fact to present potential (future-less-vivid).

1. εἰ ἐβουλήθην Ἀθηναῖόν τινα λοιδορεῖν, ἔφην ἂν αὐτὸν Σωκράτη ἀπεκτονέναι.

2. εἰ μὴ Σωκράτους κατεψηφίσαντο, οὐκ ἂν ἀπέθανε.

3. εἰ ᾤσθε Σωκράτη ἀπορίᾳ λόγων ἑαλωκέναι, ἠδικεῖσθε ἄν.

4. εἰ ἐθρήνει Σωκράτης ἀπολογούμενος, ἐξέφυγεν ἂν τὸ ἀποθανεῖν.

5. εἰ ἔδει με ἀπολογεῖσθαι θρηνοῦντά τε καὶ ὀδυρόμενον, εἱλόμην ἂν μᾶλλον τεθνάναι ἢ ζῆν.

IV. REPHRASE each sentence, changing from the particular to a generalized dependent clause in a present tense context (the so-called present general condition).

1. εἰ Ἀθηναῖοί ἐστε, ὀνειδισθήσεσθε ἀεὶ ἅτε Σωκράτη ἀπεκτονότες.

2. εἰ οἶσθά τινα ἀδικοῦντα, δεῖ καταψηφίσασθαι αὐτοῦ θάνατον.

3. εἰ μεταμέλει μοι ἀπολογησαμένῳ, αἱροῦμαι μᾶλλον ἀποθανεῖν ἢ ζῆν ἀδίκως.

4. εἴ τις νικηθεὶς ἐν μάχῃ ἐφ' ἱκετείαν τρέπεται, ἐκφεύξεται τὸ ἀποθανεῖν.

5. εἰ τολμᾷ τις πᾶν ποιεῖν, οὐ δώσει δίκην.

V. REPHRASE each sentence, changing from the particular to a generalized dependent clause in a past tense context with the optative of secondary subordination (the so-called past general condition).

1. εἰ ἐλοιδόρεις Σωκράτη, οὐκ ἐμεμαθήκης.

2. εἰ μὴ ἠκηκόεσάν τινος ἀεὶ θρηνοῦντός τε καὶ ὀδυρομένου, κατεψηφίσαντο αὐτοῦ οἱ δικασταὶ θάνατον.

3. εἴ τις ἀφῆκέ ποτε τὰ ὅπλα νικαθεὶς ἐν μάχῃ, ἐσώθη.

4. εἰ μὴ ἐτόλμων πᾶν ποιεῖν ὥστε σωθῆναι, ἐνικάθησαν.

5. εἰ Σωκράτης ἐτεθνήκει καταψηφισθείς, ἠδίκουν πάντες οἱ Ἀθηναῖοι.

VI. REPHRASE each sentence, changing the result clause from a statement of the intended or expected result to a statement of the actual result.

1. τολμῶσιν οἱ πονηροὶ πᾶν ποιεῖν ὥστε σωθῆναι.

2. κατεψηφίσαντο Σωκράτους θάνατον ὥστε τεθνάναι λοιδορηθέντα.

3. μηχαναὶ πολλαί εἰσιν ἐν ἑκάστοις τοῖς κινδύνοις ὥστε διαφυγεῖν θάνατον.

4. οἱ Σωκράτει κατήγοροι ἅτε δεινοὶ καὶ ὀξεῖς ὄντες βραδέως ἔδραμον ὥστε ὑπὸ τοῦ θάττονος ἑαλωκέναι, τῆς κακίας.

5. τὰ ὅπλα ἀφεῖσαν ἐν μάχαις ὥστε μὴ ἑαλωκέναι ὑπὸ τῶν ἐχθρῶν φυγόντας.

VII. GIVE THE LEXICAL ENTRY and then the equivalent form using the present verbal stem.

1. ἑαλώκεσαν

2. ἀκηκόωμεν

3. ἀποθανεῖ

4. ἀδικηθήσονται

5. ἑλοίμην

6. ἁρπασθῆναι

7. δεδιδαγμένη εἴη

8. ἠράσθη

9. ἐτεθαυμάκει

10. γεγάμηνται

11. ἐδεδώκεμεν

12. ἔδωκα

13. λελείμμεθα

14. ὀφθεῖμεν

15. εἰρήκῃς

16. νομεῖς

17. ἐκεκάλυφο

18. σωθήσεσθαι

19. ἔπιε

20. ἐτεθήκεμεν

VIII. MATCH the second phrase to the first by changing it into the same form.

1. βραδεῖς πρεσβῦται (ἑκὼν κηδεστής)

2. ἄριστον βασιλέα (ἄφωνος γραῦς)

3. σώφρονι γραΐ (φωνὴ ὀξεῖα)

4. εἰκότος μείζονος (πῆχυς βραχύς)

5. κάλλη ὠφέλιμα (μέρος ὀξύ)

6. νεῶν ταχειῶν (ἄστυ ἀληθές)

7. γρᾶες βραδεῖαι (ναῦς θάττον)

8. μεγάλου εἰκότος (ἧσσον μέρος)

9. νεῷς πλείοσι (γονεὺς βραδύς)

10. μέρους ὀλιγωτέρου (πόλις σφετέρα)

XI. NOTE THE PATTERN in each of the quotations and compose a translation of the English sentences, using the same pattern.

1. εἰ μὴ γαμοίη ἄνθρωπος, οὐκ ἂν ἔχοι κακά. —Μένανδρος

If Socrates not do wrong, he is not likely to pay the penalty.

Should Socrates die, those wanting to revile the city would say that you killed him.

If you go to Athens, you are likely to be in a state of wonder (θαυμάζω/ τεθαύμακα) that Socrates died at their hands (ὑπ' αὐτῶν).

2. εἰ ἀπεκρίνω, ἄν ἐμεμαθήκη. —Πλάτων

If you had not drunk wine, you would not have been drunk.

If they had gone to the city, they would have known Socrates (to be/being) a wise man.

Had he thrown away his shield, he would not have died but would be living now.

3. ἢν ἐγγὺς ἔλθῃ θάνατος, οὐδεὶς βούλεται θνῄσκειν. —Εὐριπίδης

If a child drinks wine, he is drunk.

Whenever you teach, I always understand (μανθάνω/ μεμάθηκα).

If ever he is put to death by the jurors, this city will be reviled.

4. θαυμάζοιμ' ἄν εἰ οἶσθα. —Πλάτων

He is likely to lament if you (do) die. (Contrast: He is likely to lament if you should die.)

They are likely to be captive (ἁλίσκομαι/ἑάλωκα) if you do flee.

5. εἰ μὴ καθέξεις γλῶσσαν, ἔσται σοι κακά. —Εὐριπίδης (καθέξω, κατ-έχω hold *down* (under control))

Unless you do everything to be saved, you will pay the penalty.

If they will not cast away their weapons, they will not escape.

6. εἰ μή πατὴρ ἦσθ', εἶπον ἄν σ' οὐκ εὖ φρονεῖν. —Σοφοκλῆς

If you had not said anything, I would never have known you didn't understand.

Were he not dead, I'd consider him happy (εὐδαίμων or εὐτυχής).

23

Vocative and Imperative

Πάτερ ἡμῶν ὁ ἐν τοῖς οὐρανοῖς, ἀγιασθήτω τὸ ὄνομά σου. —Ματθαῖος

Lesson 23
Vocative case

The Greek noun has a special case to signify the person or thing directly addressed or called to; this case is named the "vocative."

παῖ.	(Hey, you!) boy!
γύναι.	(Hey) woman!
πάτερ.	(Oh) father!

**Vocative/
Declension**

In the plural of all three types of nouns, the vocative is identical in form with the nominative plural.

In the singular, the vocative is the *noun stem alone with no declensional suffix.* Type I nouns ending in the suffix -*της* (*see* page 38) show the stem in -*α*, whereas other Type I nouns show the stem in -*η*. Type II masculine and feminine nouns have -*ε* in place of the final -*o*; Type II neuter nouns are identical with the nominative in the vocative case. Some Type III nouns lose the final consonant of the noun stem for euphonic reasons in forming the vocative case.

The chart presents examples of the vocative case for the three noun declensional types.

I

ψυχή (τὴν ψυχή-ν)
ποιητά (τὸν ποιητή-ν)

II

ἄνθρωπε (τὸν ἄνθρωπο-ν)
παιδίον (τὸ παιδίον)

III

παῖ (τὸν παῖ/δ-α)
γύναι (τὴν γυναῖ/κ-α)
πάτερ (τὸν πατέρ-α)
Σώκρατες (τὸν Σωκράτε(σ)-α → Σωκράτη)
βασιλεῦ (τὸν βασιλέ(υ)-α → βασιλέα)
πόλι (τὴν πόλι-ν)
πῆχυ (τὸν πῆχυ-ν)
σῶμα (τὰ σώμα/τ-α)

Note that the vocative sometimes has a recessive accent, for example *ἄδελφε (τὸν ἀδελφό-ν)/Σώκρατες (τὸν Σωκράτη)/Ἄπολλον (τὸν Ἀπόλλον-α)/δέσποτα (τὸν δεσπότη-ν).*

Ordinarily, the exclamatory *ὦ* precedes the vocative. Without *ὦ* the vocative is less polite, expressing astonishment, joy, contempt, a threat, or the like.

There is no distinctive vocative form for demonstratives, relatives, articles, or participles. The nominative case may be in apposition to the vocative or function as its predicate.

ὦ ἄνδρες οἱ παρόντες	You gentlemen here present!
φίλος ὦ Μενέλαε	O Menelaos, my dear! (Contrast: ὦ φίλε Μενέλαε O my dear Menelaos!)

The nominative of the demonstrative οὗτος regularly is used as a vocative.

οὗτος, τί πάσχεις;	Hey you there, what's wrong with you?

Imperative Mood

The imperative mood of the verb gives direct and subjective expression to a command or a prohibition (negative command: μή).

παῖ, ἔσθιε.	(Hey you) child, eat! (Contrast the indicative statement of the same command: κελεύω τὸν παῖδα ἐσθίειν I command the child to eat.)

The imperative mood has no tense (although commands obviously imply future time) but, like all the Greek moods except for the indicative, it expresses only verbal aspect; the imperative, therefore, can be formed from the present, aorist, or perfect verbal stems and it can distinguish active, middle-passive, and passive voices.

A command may be addressed to the second person (as in the example above) or to the third person.

ὁ παῖς ἐσθιέτω.	Let the child eat.
ἁγιασθήτω τὸ ὄνομά σου.	Sanctified be your name.

A command addressed to the first person in Greek is expressed by the *hortatory* subjunctive (see page 84): ἐσθίωμεν "Let's eat!" This same subjunctive (*in the aorist aspect only*) is also commonly used instead of the aorist imperative to express *prohibitions addressed to the second and third persons.*

μὴ γράψῃς.	Don't write!

Imperative/ Conjugation

The imperative is indicated by distinctive personal suffixes for the second and third persons; these suffixes are added to the verbal stem either thematically or athematically.

Active	Middle-Passive	Passive
-θι	-σο	-θι
-ς } 2 -τε	-αι } 2 -σθε	(-τι) } 2 -τε
-ον		
-τω 3 -ντων (-τωσαν)	-σθω 3 -σθων (-σθωσαν)	-τω 3 -ντων (-τωσαν)

The chart summarizes the imperative conjugation.

Thematic

	Present			Aorist	
παίδευ-	ε____	2	λίπ-	ε____	
	έ-τω	3		έ-τω	
	ε-τε	2		ε-τε	

παιδευ-	ό-ντων	3	λίπ-	ό-ντων	
	(έ-τωσαν)			(έ-τωσαν)	
	ου*	2		ου*	
	έ-σθω	3		έ-σθω	
	ε-σθε	2		ε-σθε	
	έ-σθων	3		έ-θων	
	(έ-σθωσαν)			(έ-σθωσαν)	

Athematic

ἵστα-	ε ___ **	2	θέ-	-ς	παιδευ-σ-	ου
τίθε-	-τω	3	δό-	-τω	-σά	-τω
δίδο-	-τε	2	ἔ-	-τε		-τε
ἵε-	-ντων	3		-ντων		-ντων
δείκνυ-	(-ντωσαν)			(-ντωσαν)		(-ντωσαν)
	-σο	2		-σο**		-σαι
	-σθω	3		-σθω	-σά	-σθω
	-σθε	2		-σθε		-σθε
	-σθων	3		-σθων		-σθων
	(-σθωσαν)			(-σθωσαν)		(-σθωσαν)

So also for βῆ-/γνῶ-/
δῦ-/στῆ-, except 2 sg. act.
has -θι (βῆ-θι, etc.)
and 3 pl. act. has short
stem vowel (βά-ντων, etc.).

Note (*) that παιδεύου is contracted for παιδεύ-ε-σο.

Note (**) that the uncontracted form is given for these forms on the chart.
The actual form is always contracted: ἵστη/τίθει/δίδου/ἵει/δείκνῡ; so also
θέ-σο → θοῦ/δέ-σο → δοῦ/ἔ-σο → οὗ.

The aorist passive is always athematic in its conjugation of the imperative.

παιδεύ-θη-	τι	2	(The personal suffix -τι is a
	τω	3	euphonic development of -θι to
	τε	2	avoid an aspirated consonant in two
	ντων (ντωσαν)	3	adjacent syllables.)

The imperative of εἰμί is used with the perfect participle to form a periphrasis
for the perfect imperative.

πεπαιδευκὼς (-υῖα, -ὸς)	ἴσ-	θι	2
	ἔσ-	τω	3
πεπαιδευκότες (-υῖαι, -ότα)	ἔσ-	τε	2
	ὄ -	ντων	3

| πεπαιδευμένος (-η, -ον) | ἴσ- | θι | 2 |
| | | etc. | |

The simple forms of the perfect imperative are rare.

πεπαίδευκ-	ε ____	2
	έ-τω	3
	ε-τε	2
		3
πεπαίδευ-	-σο	2
	-σϑω	3
	-σϑε	2
	-σϑων	3

Note that the infinitive also can function as a command addressed to the second person (see page 166, note 23); it is more common in poetry than in prose and has a more solemn or formal connotation.

Note also the imperative forms for the irregular verbs οἶδα and εἶμι: (οἶδα) ἴσ-ϑι/ἴσ-τω/ἴσ-τε/ἴσ-των and (εἶμι) ἴ-ϑι/ἴ-τω/ἴ-τε/ἰ-ό-ντων.

Note that thematic contract verbs will show the regular patterns of contraction (see page 104) in the imperative forms.

ΟΝΟΜΑΤΑ ΚΑΙ ΡΗΜΑΤΑ

ἡ διαβολή, -ῆς	slander, false accusation (see δια-βάλλω slander, reproach)
ὁ/ἡ μάρτυς, -υρος	witness (see μαρτυρέω bear witness, testify)
ὁ ἑταῖρος, -ου/ἡ ἑταίρα, -ας	comrade, companion/companion, courtesan
τὸ πλῆϑος, -ους	great number, multitude, the commons (see πλείων, -ον/πλεῖστος, -η, -ον/πίμπλημι fill/πληϑύνω multiply)
ὁ πολίτης, -ου	citizen (see ἡ πόλις, -εως/ἡ πολιτεία, -ας/πολιτικός, -ή, -όν political, relating to citizens)
ἡ ϑέμις, -ιδος (acc. ϑέμιν)	justice, the goddess Themis, that which is laid down or established (see τίϑημι)
μικρός (σμικρός), -ά, -όν	small
σφοδρός, -ά, -όν	vehement, excessive (see σφόδρα adv. exceedingly)
ἀξιόχρεως, -εων ("Attic declension" adjective *see* ὁ νεώς, τοῦ νεώ temple,	noteworthy (see ἄξιος, -α, -ον/ἀξιόω/τὸ χρέως, χρείους that which

page 138, by exchange of quantity from, -ηος, -ηον)

one *needs* must pay, obligation, debt)

περισσός (περιττός), -ή, -όν

beyond the regular number or size, extraordinary, strange (*see* περί + ἴσος)

μαντεύομαι (μαντεύω), μαντεύσομαι, ἐμαντευσάμην, (ἐμαντεύθην), _____, μεμάντευμαι

prophesy, consult an oracle (*see* ὁ μάντις, -εως diviner, prophet/ μαντικός, -ή, -όν *mantic*, prophetic/ τὸ μαντεῖον, -ου seat of an oracle, see ὁ χρησμός, -οῦ/μαίνομαι be mad, intoxicated)

τελευτάω, τελευτήσω, ἐτελεύτησα, ἐτελευτήθην, τετελεύτηκα

bring to pass, finish, die (*see* τὸ τέλος, -ους consummation, ritual, completion, end/ τέλλω accomplish/ ἀνα-τέλλω cause to rise/τελευταῖος, -α, -ον last/ ἡ τελευτή, -ῆς completion, termination/ τὸ τελεστήριον, -ου place for initiation)

σκέπτομαι (σκοπέω), σκέψομαι, ἐσκεψάμην, (ἐσκέφθην), _____, ἔσκεμμαι

view, look about carefully, consider, examine (*see* δια-σκοπέω look at in different ways, examine well)

μέλλω, μελλήσω, ἐμέλησα

intend, be about to (contrast: μέλω care for/ ἀ-μελέω have no care for/ μέλει it is a concern)

ἐν-θυμέομαι, ἐνθυμήσομαι, _____, ἐνεθυμήθην, _____, ἐντεθύμημαι

lay to heart, ponder, be angry (*see* πρόθυμος, -ον, willing, bearing good will/ἐπι-θυμέω desire)

αἰνίσσομαι (αἰνίττομαι), αἰνίξομαι, ᾐνιξάμην, ᾐνίχθην, _____, ᾔνιγμαι

speak in riddles (*see* τὸ αἴνιγμα, -ατος dark saying, riddle, *enigma*/ ὁ αἶνος, -ου tale/αἰνέω tell, praise)

ἐλέγχω, ἐλέγξω, ἤλεγξα, ἠλέγχθην, _____, ἐλήλεγμαι

cross-examine, refute (*see* ὁ ἔλεγχος, -ου argument of disproof or refutation/τὸ ἔλεγχος, -ους reproach)

ἀπ-εχθάνομαι, ἀπεχθήσομαι, ἀπηχθόμην

incur hatred (*see* ἡ ἀπέχθεια, -ας hated/ἡ ἔχθρα, -ας hatred/ἐχθρός, -ά, -όν hated, hostile)

λογίζομαι, λογιοῦμαι, ἐλογισάμην, ἐλογίσθην, _____, λελόγισμαι

count, reckon, calculate

ἔοικα (perfect of εἴκω resemble)

seem, resemble

πειράω, πειράσω, ἐπείρασα, ἐπειράσθην, πεπείρακα, πεπείραμαι

attempt, make trial of (*see* ἡ πεῖρα, -ας attempt)

αὐτοσχεδιάζω

speak or act offhand, extemporize, act or speak or think unadvisedly

	(*see* αὐτοσχεδόν *adv.* near at hand/ αὐτοσχέδιος, -α, -ον in close fight, improvised)
παίζω, παίσομαι, ἔπαισα, _____, πέπαικα, πέπαισμαι	play, jest (*see* ὁ παῖς, παιδός)
κινδυνεύω, κινδυνεύσω, ἐκινδύνευσα, ἐκινδυνεύθην, κεκινδύνευκα	make a venture, hazard, run the risk of (doing or being) (*see* ὁ κίνδυνος, -ου danger)
ἐπίσταμαι, ἐπιστήσομαι, _____, ἠπιστήθην	understand
ψεύδω, ψεύσω, ἔψευσα, ἐψεύσθην, _____, ἔψευσμαι	deceive, (*mid.* lie) (*see* ψευδής, -ές false)
θορυβέω, θορυβήσω, ἐθορύβησα, _____, _____, τεθορύβημαι	make a noise or disturbance (*see* ὁ θόρυβος, -ου noise, confused noise of a crowd, tumult)
ἄρτι	*adv.* just now, presently
ἐντεῦθεν	*adv.* hence, thereupon

ΑΣΚΗΣΙΣ

I. TRANSLATE: Socrates Explains his Mission in Life.

Ὑπολάβοι ἂν οὖν τις ὑμῶν ἴσως· "᾽Αλλ᾽, ὦ Σώκρατες, τὸ σὸν τί ἐστι
πρᾶγμα; πόθεν αἱ διαβολαί σοι αὗται γεγόνασιν; οὐ γὰρ δήπου σοῦ γε
οὐδὲν τῶν ἄλλων περιττότερον πραγματευομένου ἔπειτα τοσαύτη φήμη
τε καὶ λόγος γέγονεν, εἰ μή τι ἔπραττες ἀλλοῖον ἢ οἱ πολλοί. λέγε οὖν
5 ἡμῖν τί ἐστιν, ἵνα μὴ ἡμεῖς περὶ σοῦ αὐτοσχεδιάζωμεν." ταυτί μοι δοκεῖ
δίκαια λέγειν ὁ λέγων, κἀγὼ ὑμῖν πειράσομαι ἀποδεῖξαι τί ποτ᾽ ἐστιν
τοῦτο ὃ ἐμοὶ πεποίηκεν τό τε ὄνομα καὶ τὴν διαβολήν. ἀκούετε δή. καὶ
ἴσως μὲν δόξω τισὶν ὑμῶν παίζειν· εὖ μέντοι ἴστε, πᾶσαν ὑμῖν τὴν
ἀλήθειαν ἐρῶ. ἐγὼ γάρ, ὦ ἄνδρες ᾽Αθηναῖοι, δι᾽ οὐδὲν ἀλλ᾽ ἢ διὰ σοφίαν
10 τινὰ τοῦτο τὸ ὄνομα ἔσχηκα. ποίαν δὴ σοφίαν ταύτην; ἥπερ ἐστὶν ἴσως
ἀνθρωπίνη σοφία· τῷ ὄντι γὰρ κινδυνεύω ταύτην εἶναι σοφός. οὗτοι δὲ
τάχ᾽ ἄν, οὓς ἄρτι ἔλεγον, μείζω τινὰ ἢ κατ᾽ ἄνθρωπον σοφίαν σοφοί
εἶεν, ἢ οὐκ ἔχω τί λέγω· οὐ γὰρ δὴ ἔγωγε αὐτὴν ἐπίσταμαι, ἀλλ᾽ ὅστις
φησὶ ψεύδεταί τε καὶ ἐπὶ διαβολῇ τῇ ἐμῇ λέγει. καί μοι, ὦ ἄνδρες
15 ᾽Αθηναῖοι, μὴ θορυβήσητε, μηδ᾽ ἐὰν δόξω τι ὑμῖν μέγα λέγειν. οὐ γὰρ
ἐμὸν ἐρῶ τὸν λόγον ὃν ἂν λέγω, ἀλλ᾽ εἰς ἀξιόχρεων ὑμῖν τὸν λέγοντα
ἀνοίσω. τῆς γὰρ ἐμῆς, εἰ δή τίς ἐστιν σοφία καὶ οἵα, μάρτυρα ὑμῖν παρέξο-
μαι τὸν θεὸν τὸν ἐν Δελφοῖς. Χαιρεφῶντα γὰρ ἴστε που. οὗτος ἐμός τε
ἑταῖρος ἦν ἐκ νέου καὶ ὑμῶν τῷ πλήθει ἑταῖρός τε καὶ συνέφυγε τὴν φυγὴν
20 ταύτην καὶ μεθ᾽ ὑμῶν κατῆλθε καὶ ἴστε δὴ οἷος ἦν Χαιρεφῶν, ὡς σφοδρὸς
ἐφ᾽ ὅ τι ὁρμήσειεν. καὶ δή ποτε καὶ εἰς Δελφοὺς ἐλθὼν ἐτόλμησε τοῦτο
μαντεύσασθαι—καί, ὅπερ λέγω, μὴ θορυβεῖτε, ὦ ἄνδρες—ἤρετο γὰρ δὴ
εἴ τις ἐμοῦ εἴη σοφώτερος. ἀνεῖλεν οὖν ἡ Πυθία μηδένα σοφώτερον εἶναι.
καὶ τούτων πέρι ὁ ἀδελφὸς ὑμῖν αὐτοῦ οὑτοσὶ μαρτυρήσει, ἐπειδὴ ἐκεῖνος
25 τετελεύτηκεν.

Σκέψασθε δὴ ὧν ἕνεκα ταῦτα λέγω· μέλλω γὰρ ὑμᾶς διδάξειν ὅθεν μοι
ἡ διαβολὴ γέγονεν. Ταῦτα γὰρ ἐγὼ ἀκούσας ἐνεθυμούμην οὑτωσί· "Τί
ποτε λέγει ὁ θεός, καὶ τί ποτε αἰνίττεται; ἐγὼ γὰρ δὴ οὔτε μέγα οὔτε
σμικρὸν σύνοιδα ἐμαυτῷ σοφὸς ὤν· οὐ γὰρ δήπου ψεύδεταί γε· οὐ γὰρ
30 θέμις αὐτῷ." καὶ πολὺν μὲν χρόνον ἠπόρουν τί ποτε λέγει· ἔπειτα μόγις
πάνυ ἐπὶ ζήτησιν αὐτοῦ τοιαύτην τινὰ ἐτραπόμην. ἦλθον ἐπί τινα τῶν
δοκούντων σοφῶν εἶναι, ὡς ἐνταῦθα εἴπερ που ἐλέγξων τὸ μαντεῖον καὶ
ἀποφανῶν τῷ χρησμῷ ὅτι "Οὑτοσὶ ἐμοῦ σοφώτερός ἐστι, σὺ δ' ἐμὲ
ἔφησθα." διασκοπῶν οὖν τοῦτον—ὀνόματι γὰρ οὐδὲν δέομαι λέγειν, ἦν
35 δέ τις τῶν πολιτικῶν πρὸς ὃν ἐγὼ σκοπῶν τοιοῦτόν τι ἔπαθον, ὦ ἄνδρες
Ἀθηναῖοι, καὶ διαλεγόμενος αὐτῷ—ἔδοξέ μοι οὗτος ὁ ἀνὴρ δοκεῖν μὲν
σοφὸς ἄλλοις τε πολλοῖς ἀνθρώποις καὶ μάλιστα ἑαυτῷ, εἶναι δ' οὔ.
κἄπειτα ἐπειρώμην αὐτῷ δεικνύναι ὅτι οἴοιτο μὲν εἶναι σοφός, εἴη δ' οὔ.
ἐντεῦθεν οὖν τούτῳ τε ἀπηχθόμην καὶ πολλοῖς τῶν παρόντων· πρὸς
40 ἐμαυτὸν δ' οὖν ἀπιὼν ἐλογιζόμην ὅτι τούτου μὲν τοῦ ἀνθρώπου
ἐγὼ σοφώτερός εἰμι· κινδυνεύει μὲν γὰρ ἡμῶν οὐδέτερος οὐδὲν καλὸν
κἀγαθὸν εἰδέναι. ἐντεῦθεν ἐπ' ἄλλον ᾖα τῶν ἐκείνου δοκούντων
σοφωτέρων εἶναι καί μοι ταὐτὰ ταῦτα ἔδοξε, καὶ ἐνταῦθα κἀκείνῳ καὶ
ἄλλοις πολλοῖς ἀπηχθόμην. —Πλάτων

Reading Notes:

(1) ὑπολάβοι/ὑπο-λαμβάνω take up (what is said), take up (a notion)

(1) σὸν τί ἐστι πρᾶγμα Socrates has just denied that he has ever been a
teacher for pay. He now imagines that his interlocutor is apt to turn on him
and ask what then his business is.

(2) πόθεν see page 78

(3) δήπου (δή + που see page 78) certainly perhaps

(3) πραγματευομένου/πραγματεύομαι (see τὸ πρᾶγμα, -ατος) be engaged
in business

(3) τοσαύτη see page 78

(4) ἀλλοῖος, -α, -ον of another sort (see ποῖος, etc., page 78)

(5) ταυτί an intensified demonstrative = ταῦτα/ so also (24) οὑτοσί and (27)
οὑτωσί

(6) κἀγώ/καὶ ἐγώ

(6) ἀποδεῖξαι/ἀπο-δείκνυμι

(7) ὄνομα, that is, the epithet of σοφός

(11) τῷ ὄντι instrumental dative of the neuter participle of εἰμί: by the thing
that is, in other words, in reality

(11) ταύτην (namely ἀνθρωπίνην σοφίαν) adverbial accusative with σοφός

(12) τάχ'/τάχα adv. perhaps (see ταχύς, -εῖα, -ύ swift)

(12) μείζω see page 151, note 6

(12) κατ' ἄνθρωπον *in accordance with* man, that is, human

(17) ἀνοίσω/ἀνα-φέρω refer

(17) οἷα *see page* 78

(17) παρέξομαι/παρ-έχω furnish, hand over, produce (a person) on demand

(19) ὑμῶν τῷ πλήθει ἑταῖρός τε καὶ συνέφυγε τὴν φυγὴν ταύτην/An ἑταῖρος can be both a personal friend (as in ἐμός τε ἑταῖρος ἦν ἐκ νέου) and a political associate (as in ὑμῶν τῷ πλήθει ἑταῖρος). These two aspects of Chaerephon are joined by the coordinating conjunctions ἐμός τε... καὶ. Three aspects of Chaerephon's political activities are further joined in coordination by the next sequence of conjunctions: ἑταῖρός τε καὶ... καὶ. Chaerephon was one of the "democrats" who went into exile *along with* the others (συν-έφυγε τὴν φυγὴν) during the oligarchic *coup d'état*, that recently (hence ταύτην) had been overthrown. Upon the restoration of the democracy, Chaerephon returned from exile (κατ-ῆλθε literally, "came down," that is, from the mountains back to the city) along with the others. Thus Socrates can assume that his jurors are all "democrats."

(20–21) ὡς σφοδρὸς ἐφ' ὅτι ὁρμήσειεν how vehement (he was) towards whatever he would start out upon/ for the form of ὁρμήσειεν, *see page* 129, note 12

(21) καὶ δή... καὶ This conjunctional phrase always introduces a particular example illustrative of the preceding statement: "and in particular."

(23) ἀνεῖλεν/ἀν-αιρέω *see page* 151, note 2

(24) τούτων πέρι When the accent on a preposition is recessive (πέρι instead of περί), its object precedes.

(28–29) οὔτε μέγα οὔτε σμικρόν adverbial accusative with σοφός

(29) σύνοιδα/σύν-οιδα know something about a person as a potential witness for or against him (dative)

(30) μόγις adv. with toil and pain, scarcely, hardly (*see* ὁ μόγος, -ου toil)/ πάνυ very (*see* πᾶς, πᾶσα, πᾶν)

(31) ζήτησιν/ἡ ζήτησις, -εως (*see* ζητέω/ for the -σις suffix, *see page* 127 note)

(31) ἦλθον ἐπί τινα Note the lack of a conjunction (δέ, etc.); this lack is called *asyndeton* and it usually means that the sentence is an explanation (that is, asyndeton equals γάρ).

(34) ἔφησθα = ἔφης

(34) διασκοπῶν/δια-σκοπέω

(38) κἄπειτα/καὶ ἔπειτα

(39) παρόντων/πάρ-ειμι

(41) οὐδέτερος/οὐδὲ ἕτερος neither

(43) ταὐτά/τὰ αὐτά

(43) ἐνταῦθα here, there (*see* ἐντεῦθεν)

II. MATCH the second verb to the first by changing it into the same form.

1. ἄγγειλον (ἀκούω)
2. ἀπόθανε (ἵστημι)
3. δός (ἵημι)
4. βουλήθητι (ἐράω)
5. γνῶθι (τίθημι)
6. δίδασκε (τίθημι)
7. τίμα (ποιέω)
8. θοῦ (φιλέω)
9. δίδου (λέγω)
10. εἰπέ* (τρέχω)

11. γεγραμμένον ἔστω (εὑρίσκω)
12. βῆθι (ἔρχομαι)
13. σωθήντωσαν (πέμπω)
14. ἰδέ (πίνω)
15. σημήνατε (ὁράω)
16. φόβησον (λέγω)
17. τμηθήτω (νικάω)
18. θέντων (φιλέω)
19. ἕς (λαμβάνω)
20. ἀποκτείνατε (ἄγω)

Note (*) that the accent on the aorist imperative of five verbs is irregular: εἰπέ, ἐλθέ, εὑρέ, ἰδέ, λαβέ/εἴπετε, ἔλθετε, εὕρετε, ἴδετε, λάβετε. Compounds, however, have the normal recessive accent: ἄπελθε, κάτειπε, etc.

III. CHANGE from the present imperative to the aorist imperative.

1. ὅρα
2. βούλου
3. κρινέσθων
4. λειπέτω
5. ἔα
6. ἔρχου
7. ἡγοῦ
8. λέγε
9. κομιζέσθω
10. μανθανέτωσαν

11. βαῖνε
12. τίθει
13. δίδου
14. τίθεσο
15. καλείσθων
16. ὁρᾶτε
17. ἵει
18. ἐρχέσθων
19. φίλει
20. λάμβανε

IV. CHANGE from the third person imperative to the second person imperative.

1. λαβέτω
2. δότω
3. κρινάτω
4. ἐρασθήτω
5. γενέσθων
6. βουλέσθωσαν
7. ἔτω

8. ἔστω
9. γνώτω
10. ἴτω
11. ὄντων
12. δέσθω
13. ἰδέτω
14. διωξάτω

15. βουληθήτω	18. ἡγησάσθω
16. ἰόντων	19. τιθέτω
17. βήτω	20. διδόσθω

V. GIVE THE LEXICAL ENTRY and then the corresponding form using the present verbal stem.

1. ἔτε	11. ἀπελέλοξο
2. εἶτε	12. θές
3. ἐπιστηθείης	13. ἴδετε
4. ἀκηκόατε	14. ἐτετόκεσαν
5. ἔλωμεν	15. λιπέτωσαν
6. ἦρξαι	16. ἔβης
7. ἀδικηθεῖεν	17. γνοίη
8. σχές*	18. εἴληψαι
9. νικαθήσει	19. ἄγγειλαι
10. ὤφθη	20. δοῦναι

Note (*) that this is the second person imperative of the aorist of ἔχω/ἔσχον. *See* θές, δός, ἔς.

VI. REPHRASE each sentence as a direct command (vocative and second person imperative).

1. Σωκράτη κελεύω εἰπεῖν πόθεν αἱ διαβολαὶ γεγόνασιν αὐτῷ.

2. κελεύομεν τοὺς ἄνδρας δικαστὰς οὐ θορυβῆσαι ἀλλ' ἀκούειν.

3. κελεύω τὸν δικαστὴν σκέψασθαι ὧν ἕνεκα λέγω ὃ ἔπραξε Χαιρεφῶν εἰς Δελφοὺς ἐλθών.

4. κελεύει ὁ Μένανδρος τὸν ἄνθρωπον οὔποτε γῆμαι οὐδὲ γήμασθαι τὴν γυναῖκα.

5. κελεύω Σωκράτη εἰδέναι ὅτι πάντων σοφώτατός ἐστιν.

6. τὸν παῖδα κελεύω οὐκ ἀπεχθέσθαι πᾶσι τῶν παρόντων.

7. τὸν ποιητὴν κελεύομεν ἀπιέναι νικαθέντα.

8. Χαιρεφῶντα κελεύω μαρτύρησαι εἰπόντα ὃ εἶπεν ὁ θεός.

9. τὴν πόλιν κελεύει λογίζεσθαι ὅτι οὐδεὶς βροτῶν σοφώτερός ἐστι Σωκράτους.

10. τὸν θεὸν κελεύω οὐκ αἰνίττεσθαι ἀεὶ οὐδὲ ψεύδεσθαί ποτε ἀλλ' εἰπεῖν μοι σαφῶς τἀληθῆ.*

Note (*) that in classical Greek the vocative of θεός is never used; instead, the god is addressed as a nominative apposition to the vocative (*see* page 189):

ὦ θεός "Oh you, my god." In later Greek, the vocative, however, does occur (θεέ).

VII. REPHRASE each sentence in the above exercise as a direct command to the third person (nominative and third person imperative). The vocative would indicate that the speaker is addressing the person commanded, whereas the third person imperative would indicate that the speaker is addressing someone other than the person commanded.

VIII. NOTE THE PATTERN in each of the quotations and compose a translation of the English sentences, using the same pattern.

1. μὴ κρίνετε ἵνα μὴ κριθῆτε. —Ματθαῖος

Don't reproach so that you not be reproached.

Don't do wrong so that you not be done wrong.

2. ἀποκρίνου, ὦ ἀγαθέ· καὶ γὰρ ὁ νόμος κελεύει ἀποκρίνεσθαι. —Πλάτων

Marry, Woman! For even god wants you to marry.

Speak, Socrates. For all here present also want to hear.

3. τοῦτο ἴτω ὅπῃ τῷ θεῷ φίλον. —Πλάτων (ὅπῃ in what way, in whichever direction = ὅπου, see page 78)

Let the penalty be as much as seems enough to the jurors.

Let Socrates say what seems best to him.

4. εὖ γὰρ ἴστε· ἐὰν με ἀποκτείνητε, οὐκ ἐμὲ μείζω βλάψετε ἢ ὑμᾶς αὐτούς. —Πλάτων (βλάπτω harm)

Consider this well: if the jurors don't understand, they will not wrong Socrates so much as themselves.

Advice for Further Study

Vocabulary

The Greek language is extraordinarily rich in words, with a literature that spans over a millenium in the ancient period and continues on through late antiquity into the Byzantine period before showing pronounced characteristics of the modern Demotic. The modern language, moreover, is not so much a new and separate language as a natural dialectal derivative of the ancient tongue. It is only fair to say that even after years of reading Greek you will still come upon words that are unfamiliar and will necessitate the use of a lexicon. You will find, however, that your vocabulary will grow rapidly if you follow a few simple procedures in your reading.

Always attempt to guess the meaning of unfamiliar words from the context and by recognition of the basic component roots. Never look up a word in the lexicon as soon as you come upon it in your reading, but instead read whole sentences or even whole paragraphs to establish the context—you must at least know, for example, whether the word is a verb or a noun before looking it up since the system of verbal prefixes makes simple alphabetizing in a lexicon impossible. When you do look up a word, notice the roots out of which it is composed and look at other words that surround it in the lexicon in order to get some feeling for its "family." It is probably not a good practice to write the word's meaning above the Greek word in the text since you will tend to disregard the Greek word and notice only its gloss. If you feel that you must make some notation in your text, place the gloss at least in the margin. Always devote some of your study time to reading the Greek passage out loud. You will not learn any Greek words that you cannot pronounce, and by reading aloud you will begin to get a firmer feeling for the cadences of the language. This is very important. *Read aloud.* If you are an energetic person, it will also be helpful to make flash cards of new words, drill yourself, and eventually compose basic vocabularies of words involved in particular subjects, as, for example, the parts of the body or words relative to shipping, eating, banqueting, etc.

Grammar Review

You will quickly lose an active command of grammar unless you set yourself specific review tasks. This book has been designed to facilitate its use as a review text as well as a beginning method. Once every week or two you should review a chapter and do the exercises again, especially those that practice forms. If you are involved in formal learning, it is hoped that your course will apportion some part of its activity to drill and review and to practice in composition like the NOTE THE PATTERN exercises. Eventually, you will find it useful to become familiar with a good reference grammar. There are two that are available in English. Unfortunately, neither is entirely satisfactory since they both approach Greek grammar not in terms of its organic structures but in terms of the various segments of English that might more or less be converted into Greek. Thus, the sense of the language's coherent structural system is largely lost and instead the student finds what seems like a senseless multiplicity of forms and grammatical patterns, with related items often separated from each other since their relationship depends upon Greek rather than English. Nevertheless, you will find a reference grammar useful in learning dialectal forms and in becoming aware of some of the rarer stylistic variants.

The following are the standard reference grammars in English: Herbert Smyth, *Greek Grammar* (Cambridge: Harvard University Press, 1920, often reprinted and revised); William Goodwin, *A Greek Grammar* (London: Macmillan Co., 1879, often reprinted).

Readings

Opinions differ greatly about which Greek authors are best suited for the elementary student. The following list of suggestions attempts to reflect the order of ascending difficulty, but your particular interests or reasons for reading Greek may well make it preferable for you to read something more "difficult" that you love instead of something more elementary but for you perhaps somewhat boring.

Greek New Testament: written in the standard Greek of the Hellenistic period, the so-called *koine* or "common" tongue, and exhibiting a few trends that will develop into the modern language, but basically a quite easy text essentially in the language that you have learned.

Lucian's *True History*: the account of a fantastic sea voyage to fabulous places, including a flight to the moon, written in the second century A.D. by a person whose native tongue may have been Aramaic but who writes a good standard Attic; the first few paragraphs, however, present the author's purpose in composing this piece of fiction and are considerably more "difficult" than the remainder of the work; the elementary student should begin at paragraph five.

Apollodorus' *Bibliotheke* (*Library*): an encyclopedia of Greek mythical narratives, composed around the first century A.D.

Lucian's *The Ass*: the story of a man's unfortunate metamorphosis into an ass and his subsequent adventures; perhaps falsely attributed to Lucian.

Xenophon's *Anabasis*: the account of an adventure of mercenary Greek soldiers who find themselves having to retreat overland to the Black Sea when the Persian prince whom they had come to support in an attempted revolution is killed in the first engagement; the *Anabasis* is interesting, but only if read rather rapidly, which unfortunately is often not the case when it is used as an elementary reading. Many consider this work the standard introductory text, but other works of Xenophon are perhaps better suited for that purpose, for example, his *Memorabilia of Socrates*, an account of his impressions of the great teacher.

Lysias' *Orations*: in particular, the first oration, which is for a trial of murder committed by a jealous husband against his wife's alleged adulterer; or the twelfth oration, a trial directed against a politian who used a period of political unrest to harass Lysias' family and to steal their property. Lysias was a fifth century speech writer; it was at his father's house that the conversations reported in Plato's *Republic* are supposed to have taken place.

Plato's *Apology of Socrates*: the speech purported to have been made by Socrates at his trial for impiety in 399 B.C. but actually an imaginative reconstruction of the event by Plato. Other works of Plato are also possible, in particular his *Phaedo, Phaedrus, Euthyphro, Crito,* or *Symposium*.

Herodotus' *History of the Persian Wars*: the historical and mythological background to the hostile relations of Greece and the growing Persian Empire.

Herodotus writes in the Ionic dialect, a major dialect of which Attic is a variant; the novelty of the dialect will cause some difficulty at first, as will Herodotus' digressive and parenthetical style of narration, but apart from that, his prose is quite "easy." School texts that present selected passages from Herodotus rewritten in the Attic dialect are available. You should probably read some Herodotus before attempting anything in other dialects.

Homer's *Odyssey* or *Iliad*: the epic dialect is initially quite confusing for a beginning student, but the simplicity of epic style, with its repeated formulaic phrases and scenes, makes Homer quite accessible to the dedicated beginner. Homer is often read at the second-year level; and students sometimes are taught the epic dialect as the base dialect instead of Attic.

Euripides' tragedies: the *Alcestis* and the *Medea* are often read at the second-year level, but all of the tragedies are of about the same "difficulty."

Demosthenes' *Oration against Neaera* (59): the trial of a man who has been living illegitimately with a woman who used to be a courtesan and whose daughter from those earlier times has been introduced into high Athenian society and has become involved in a religious scandal; perhaps falsely attributed to Demosthenes, the great fourth century B.C. lawyer and politician.

Andocides' *On the Mysteries*: a trial for impiety in 399 B.C., directed against the author because of his role earlier in the scandalous mutilation of religious effigies and the alleged profanation of the Eleusinian Mystery in 415 B.C.

Texts   The following are the most available texts of Greek authors.

Oxford Classical Texts (Oxford Press): texts of some of the more standard Greek authors.

Loeb Classical Library (Harvard University Press): an extensive collection of texts with English translations on the facing pages.

Association Guillaume Budé (Société d'éditions "Les Belles lettres" Paris): an extensive collection of texts with French translations on the facing pages.

Bibliotheca Teubneriana (Teubner, Leipzig): the most complete collection of Greek authors.

In addition, there are often school texts of particular works with notes on language and background.

Dual

δυοῖν γὰρ θάτερόν ἐστι τὸ τεθνάναι. —Πλάτων

Appendix 1:
Degrees of
Plurality

In addition to the singular and plural number for nouns, adjectives, and verbs, Greek has a special degree of plurality that indicates no more or less than two, the so-called dual. It is never obligatory to use the dual for a plurality of two unless the twoness is specifically to be emphasized. The dual died out as a living form in the Attic dialect by about 300 B.C. and had disappeared earlier from other dialects; it is common in the language of the Homeric epics.

δυοῖν θάτερόν ἐστι τὸ τεθνάναι.   The other of the two (possibilities for what happens when you die) is to be dead. (*θάτερον = τὸ ἕτερον*)

Dual/Declension

There are only two declensional forms for the dual: one for the nominative, accusative, and vocative and another for the genitive and dative.

The chart summarizes the declensional suffixes for the dual of nouns and adjectives.

Types I and II		Type III
N. A. V.	_____	-ε
G. D.	-ιν	-οιν

Examples

I	II	III
τὼ ποιητά	*τὼ ἀνθρώπω*	*τὼ παῖδ-ε*
τοῖν ποιητα-ῖν	*τοῖν ἀνθρώπο-ιν*	*τοῖν παιδ-οῖν*
τὼ ψυχά	*τὼ ὁδώ*	*τὼ γυναῖκ-ε*
τοῖν ψυχα-ῖν	*τοῖν ὁδο-ῖν*	*τοῖν γυναικ-οῖν*
	τὼ παιδίω	*τὼ σώματ-ε*
	τοῖν παιδίο-ιν	*τοῖν σωμάτ-οιν*

Attic declension (p. 138)

τὼ νεώ
τοῖν νεῴν

EY-Stem (p. 123)

τὼ βασιλῆ (βασιλεύ-ε)
τοῖν βασιλέ-οιν

Contract (p. 88)

τὼ νώ
τοῖν νο-ῖν

OY-Stem (p. 123)

τὼ βό-ε
τοῖν βο-οῖν

AY-Stem (p. 123)

τὼ γρᾶ-ε
τοῖν γρα-οῖν

ἡ ναῦς (p. 138)

τὼ νῆ-ε
τοῖν νε-οῖν

Y-Stem (p. 124)

τὼ ἄστει (ἄστε-ε)

τοῖν ἀστέ-οιν

τὼ ἰχθύ-ε

τοῖν ἰχθύ-οιν

Adjectives (p. 124)

ἡδέ-ε

ἡδέ-οιν

I-Stem (p. 125)

τὼ πόλει

τοῖν πολέ-οιν

Σ-Stem (p. 125)

τὼ γένει (γένε-ε)

τοῖν γενοῖν (γενέ-οιν)

Adjectives (p. 125)

ἀληθεῖ

ἀληθοῖν

The numeral "two" obviously is declined as a dual: δύο/δυοῖν.

Dual/Personal Conjugational Suffixes

The chart summarizes the personal suffixes of the dual number. The first person dual is supplied by the first person plural (except for a few instances in poetry, where the first person dual suffix occurs: -μεθον).

	Primary	Secondary	Imperative
Active			
2	-τον	-τον	-τον
3	-τον	-την	-των
Middle-Passive			
2	-σθον	-σθον	-σθον
3	-σθον	-σθην	-σθων

Examples

Thematic	Athematic
Present	
2/3 παιδεύ-ε-τον/-σθον	2/3 τίθε-τον/-σθον
2/3 ποιεῖ-τον/-σθον	2/3 ἵστα-τον/-σθον
2/3 ὁρᾶ-τον/-σθον	2/3 δίδο-τον/-σθον
2/3 δηλοῦ-τον/-σθον	2/3 ἵε-τον/-σθον
Imperfect	
2 ἐ-παιδεύ-ε-τον/-σθον	2 ἐ-τίθε-τον/-σθον

3   ἐ-παιδευ-έ-την/-σθην   3   ἐ-τιθέ-την/-σθην

2   ἐ-ποιεῖ-τον/-σθον   2   ἵστα-τον/-σθον

3   ἐ-ποιεί-την/-σθην   3   ἱστά-την/-σθην

2   ἑωρᾶ-τον/-σθον   2   ἐ-δίδο-τον/-σθον

2   ἐθρά-την/-σθην   3   ἐ-διδό-την/-σθην

2   ἐ-δηλοῦ-τον/-σθον   2   ἵε-τον/-σθον

3   ἐ-δηλού-την/-σθην   3   ἱέ-την/-σθην

Future

2/3   παιδεύ-σ-ε-τον/-σθον   2/3   παιδευ-θή-σ-ε-σθον (Fut. Pass.)

Aorist

2   ἐ-λίπ-ε-τον/-σθον   2   ἔ-θε-τον/-σθον

3   ἐ-λιπ-έ-την/-σθην   3   ἐ-θέ-την/-σθην

                                       2   ἐ-παιδεύ-σα-τον/-σθον

                                       3   ἐ-παιδευ-σά-την/-σθην

Subjunctive

2/3   παιδεύ-η-τον/-σθον

Optative

2   παιδεύ-ο-ι-τον/-σθον   2   τιθε-ῖ-τον/-σθον

3   παιδευ-ο-ί-την/-σθην   3   τιθε-ί-την/-σθην

Aorist Passive

                                       2   ἐ-παιδεύ-θη-τον

                                       3   ἐ-παιδευ-θή-την

Perfect

                                       2/3   πε-παιδεύ-κα-τον/
                                                   πε-παίδευ-σθον

Pluperfect

                                       2   ἐ-πε-παιδεύ-κε-τον/
                                                   -παίδευ-σθον

                                       3   ἐ-πε-παιδευ-κέ-την/
                                                    -παιδεύ-σθην

etc.

2 Numbers

εἷς, δύο, τρεῖς. ὁ δὲ δὴ τέταρτος ἡμῖν, ὦ φίλε Τίμαιε, ποῦ; —Πλάτων

Appendix 2

1.	α′ εἷς, μία, ἕν	πρῶτος, -η, -ον	ἅπαξ
2.	β′ δύο	δεύτερος	δίς
3.	γ′ τρεῖς, τρία	τρίτος	τρίς
4.	δ′ τέσσαρες, τέσσαρα	τέταρτος	τετράκις
5.	ε′ πέντε	πέμπτος	πεντάκις
6.	ϛ′ ἕξ	ἕκτος	ἑξάκις
7.	ζ′ ἑπτά	ἕβδομος	ἑπτάκις
8.	η′ ὀκτώ	ὄγδοος	ὀκτάκις
9.	θ′ ἐννέα	ἔνατος	ἐνάκις
10.	ι′ δέκα	δέκατος	δεκάκις
11.	ια′ ἕνδεκα	ἑνδέκατος	ἑνδεκάκις
12.	ιβ′ δώδεκα	δωδέκατος	δωδεκάκις
13.	ιγ′ τρεῖς καὶ δέκα	τρίτος καὶ δέκατος	τρεισκαιδεκάκις
14.	ιδ′ τέσσαρες καὶ δέκα	τέταρτος καὶ δέκατος	τεσσαρεσκαιδεκάκις
15.	ιε′ πεντεκαίδεκα	πέμπτος καὶ δέκατος	πεντεκαιδεκάκις
16.	ιϛ′ ἑκκαίδεκα	ἕκτος καὶ δέκατος	ἑκκαιδεκάκις
17.	ιζ′ ἑπτακαίδεκα	ἕβδομος καὶ δέκατος	ἑπτακαιδεκάις
18.	ιη′ ὀκτωκαίδεκα	ὄγδοος καὶ δέκατος	ὀκτωκαιδεκάκις
19.	ιθ′ ἐννεακαίδεκα	ἔνατος καὶ δέκατος	ἐννεακαιδεκάκις
20.	κ′ εἴκοσι(ν)	εἰκοστός	εἰκοσάκις
21.	κα′ εἷς καὶ εἴκοσι	πρῶτος καὶ εἰκοστός	εἰκοσάκις ἅπαξ
30.	λ′ τριάκοντα	τριακοστός	τριακοντάκις
40.	μ′ τεσσαράκοντα	τεσσαρακοστός	τεσσαρακοντάκις
50.	ν′ πεντήκοντα	πεντηκοστός	πεντηκοντάκις
60.	ξ′ ἑξήκοντα	ἑξηκοστός	ἑξηκοντάκις
70.	ο′ ἑβδομήκοντα	ἑβδομηκοστός	ἑβδομηκοντάκις
80.	π′ ὀγδοήκοντα	ὀγδοηκοστός	ὀγδοηκοντάκις
90.	ϟ′ ἐνενήκοντα	ἐνενηκοστός	ἐνενηκοντάκις
100.	ρ′ ἑκατόν	ἑκατοστός	ἑκατοντάκις
200.	σ′ διακόσιοι, -αι, -α	διακοσιοστός	διακοσιάκις
300.	τ′ τριακόσιοι	τριακοσιοστός	τριακοσιάκις

Note that the cardinal numbers from one to four are declined: N. A. τρεῖς, τρία/G. τριῶν/D. τρισί(ν); N. A. τέσσαρες, τέσσαρα/G. τεσσάρων/D. τέσσαρσι(ν). So also τρεῖς (τρία) καὶ δέκα/τριῶν καὶ δέκα/τρισὶ καὶ δέκα; etc.

Note that the letters of the alphabet are used as numeral digits, with the inclusion of a few letters (like koppa ϙ) that had disappeared from the ordinary alphabet.

Appendix 3

You have learned the Attic dialect as your basic tongue in ancient Greek. This is the dialect of Greek that survives in the writings of the major authors of the city of Athens from the fifth and fourth centuries B.C. The Attic dialect also was the model for the *koine* or "common tongue," the Greek that was spoken and written throughout the ancient world during the international period that came into being with the rise of the city of Alexandria as a center of culture and that lasted until the sixth century A.D., when the ancient world came to an end. The living language slowly diverged from this *koine* dialect and evolved into the dialect of modern spoken and, for the most part, literary Greek, the so-called demotic or popular tongue, whereas the *koine* continued to serve as the model for the repeated attempts to restore the ancient Attic to its role as the official tongue, first during the Byzantine period, when the center of Greek culture was the city of Constantinople, and in modern times, when conservative governments have tended to favor the adoption of the artificial, academic, and legalistic *katharevousa*, the so called purifying tongue.

In the different cities and regions of ancient Greece, numerous dialects were spoken, bearing general affinities to the ancestral tribal affinities of each city, but displaying particular local divergences. Neighboring cities often spoke quite different dialects; examples survive in inscriptional remains. A few of these dialects became somewhat standardized as literary dialects and were associated with particular genres of literature that evolved in the various tribal groups. This identification of genre with dialect was so strong that even Attic writers used the characteristics of such alien literary dialects when they wrote in that particular genre.

The standard reference work for both the local and literary dialects of ancient Greek is Carl Buck's *The Greek Dialects* (University of Chicago, 1955, revised from the edition of 1928).

This appendix is intended merely as the barest introduction to the salient features of the literary dialects. You will find that the best way to become familiar with a new dialect is simply to begin reading it, letting the strange new forms remind you of the Attic that is your basic tongue.

Ionic Greek

Ionic was the dialect of the Ionian peoples, who were akin to the inhabitants of Attica and the neighboring regions along the shores of the Saronic and Corinthian gulfs and who migrated to the Aegean islands and the adjacent regions of Asia Minor. The chief examples of Ionic are the poetry of Archilochus, the history of Herodotus, and the medical writings of the Hippocratic school. In addition, the epic dialect of Homer and Hesiod is largely Ionic.

Characteristics

1. Successive adjacent vowels are often not contracted as in Attic (that is, Attic contract verbs, pluperfect singular endings, declensional endings, verb endings of the second person middle-passive with lost *sigma*, etc.).

2. Forms of the article beginning with *tau* are used as the ordinary relative pronoun.

3. The particle ἄν occurs as κέ (or κέν).

4. The chart summarizes typical sound changes from the Attic.

Attic	Ionic	example
$\bar{\alpha}$	η	χώρᾱ/χώρη
ε	$\varepsilon\iota$	ξένος/ξεῖνος
o	ov	μόνος/μοῦνος
$\varepsilon\iota$	$\eta\ddot{\iota}$	βασίλειος/βασιλήϊος

5. The chart summarizes typical vowel changes in the uncontracted -αω verbs, which are normally contracted in Attic.

	example: Attic/Ionic
$-\alpha\omega \rightarrow -\varepsilon\omega$	ὁράω: ὁρῶ/ὁρέω
$-\alpha o \rightarrow -\varepsilon o-$	ὁράοντες: ὁρῶντες/ὁρέοντες
$-\alpha ov \rightarrow -\varepsilon ov-$	ὁράουσι: ὁρῶσι/ὁρέουσι

6. The -έω contract verbs in Attic contract -εο-, -εου- to -ευ- in Ionic: ποιέομεν: ποιοῦμεν/ποιεῦμεν; ποιέουσι: ποιοῦσι/ποιεῦσι

7. The chart summarizes typical differences in declensional endings.

Attic		Ionic	example: Attic/Ionic
Type I			
gen. sing..	-ου	-εω	Ἀτρείδου/Ἀτρείδεω
acc. sing.	-ην	-εα	δεσπότην/δεσπότεα
gen. pl.	-ων	-εων	χωρῶν/χωρέων
dat. pl.	-αις	-ησι	χώραις/χώρησι
Type II			
dat. pl.	-οις	-οισι	ἵπποις/ἵπποισι
Adjectives			
Υ-Stem	-εια	-εα	γλυκεῖα/γλυκέα

8. The adjective πολύς, πολλή, πολύ is completely regular in Ionic: πολλός, πολλή, πολλόν.

9. Ionic has -αται and -ατο for the verbal personal suffixes -νται, -ντο in the perfect and pluperfect: and -ατο for -ντο in the optative.

10. The iterative suffix -σκ- is often added to the imperfect and to thematic aorists: ἔχ-ε-σκ-ο-ν, λάβ-ε-σκ-ο-ν. *Note* that the augment can be omitted on past tenses and is always omitted on the forms with this suffix.

11. The optative has different endings from Attic: -ειας for -οις, -ειε for -οι, and -ειαν for -οιεν.

12. The chart summarizes the personal pronouns that differ from the Attic forms.

	Attic/Ionic	Attic/Ionic	Attic/Ionic
gen. sing.	ἐμοῦ/ἐμέο, ἐμεῦ, μευ	σοῦ/σέο, σεῦ	αὐτοῦ/εὖ
acc. sing.	_____	_____	αὐτόν/μίν
dat. sing.	_____	σοί/σοί, τοί	αὐτῷ/οἷ
gen. pl.	_____	_____	αὐτοί/σφεῖς
acc. pl.	ἡμᾶς/ἡμέας	ὑμᾶς/ὑμέας	αὐτούς/σφέας, σφέ
dat. pl.	_____	_____	αὐτοῖς/σφίσι, σφί(ν)

Example   The opening sentence of the history of Herodotus will serve as an illustration.

Ionic

'Ηροδότου 'Αλικαρνησσέος
ἱστορίης ἀπόδεξις ἥδε, ὡς
μήτε τὰ γενόμενα ἐξ ἀνθρώπων τῷ χρόνῳ ἐξίτηλα γένηται, μήτε ἔργα μεγάλα τε καὶ
θωμαστά, τὰ μὲν Ἕλλησι, τὰ
δὲ βαρβάροισι ἀποδεχθέντα,
ἀκλεᾶ γένηται, τά τε ἄλλα
καὶ δι' ἣν αἰτίην ἐπολέμησαν
ἀλλήλοισι.

Attic

'Ηροδότου 'Αλικαρνησσέως
ἱστορίας ἀπόδειξις ἥδε, ὡς
μήτε τὰ γενόμενα ἐξ ἀνθρώπων τῷ χρόνῳ ἐξίτηλα γένηται, μήτε ἔργα μεγάλα τε καὶ
θαυμαστά, τὰ μὲν Ἕλλησι, τὰ
δὲ βαρβάροις ἀποδεχθέντα,
ἀκλεᾶ γένηται, τά τε ἄλλα
καὶ δι' ἣν αἰτίαν ἐπολέμησαν
ἀλλήλοις.

Translation: Of Herodotus the Halicarnassian's inquiry the results are the following: with this purpose, so that neither the things that came into being out of human agency become transitory through time's instrumentality, nor the actions, both great and marvellous—some displayed for Greeks, others for non-Greeks—become without fame: and amongst other things, in particular for what reason they went to war against each other.

Homeric Dialect   The dialect of the epic poems was not spoken by any particular peoples but was an art or poetic language, preserving forms from various locales where these traditional poems had evolved over the ages. It is largely a variety of Old Ionic, with some additional characteristics of the Aeolic dialect, the language of the people of northern Greece who had migrated to Asia Minor. The dialect of Hesiod is essentially the same as that of the Homeric epics, but with additional characteristics of the Boeotian and Dorian peoples with whom Hesiod lived. In addition to Homer and Hesiod, the epic dialect was used by elegaic and iambic poets such as the Athenian Solon, the Spartan Tyrtaeus, and the Megarian Theognis; in the Hellenistic period, the Homeric dialect was copied by "new epic" writers like Apollonius of Rhodes.

Characteristics (in addition to those listed above as Ionic):

1. The chart summarizes typical differences in declensional endings.

Attic	Homeric	Example: Attic/Homeric
Type I		
nom. sing. -ης	-ᾱ	ἱππότης/ἱππότᾱ
gen. sing. -ου	-αο	'Ατρεΐδου/'Ατρεΐδαο

gen. sing.	-ου	-ω	Βορέου/Βορέω
gen. pl.	-ῶν	-άων	κλισιῶν/κλισιάων
dat. pl.	-αις	-ης	σχίζαις/σχίζης

Type II

gen. sing.	-ου	-οιο (-οο)	θεοῦ/θεοῖο

Type III

dat. pl.	-σι	-εσσι, -εσι, -σσι	ποσί/πόδεσσι

EY–Stem lengthen ε to η: βασιλεῖ/βασιλῆι

I–Stem maintain ι in all the cases: πόλεως/πόλιος

2. The ending -φι(ν) serves for the genitive and dative singular and for the dative plural: ἐξ εὐνῆς/ἐξ εὐνῆφι; βίᾳ/βίηφι

3. Thematic aorists, active and middle, are often reduplicated like ἄγω/ἤγαγον, which is the only such reduplicated form in Attic: πείθω/πέπιθον. Note also that verbs do not always form their principle parts in the same way as in Attic; thus, instead of a sigmatic aorist, πείθω has here a thematic aorist.

4. Variant verbal personal suffixes may occur. Thus, the suffixes that normally are associated with the athematic conjugation in Attic may occur in thematic conjugation in Homeric Greek: ἐθέλ-ω-μι, ἐθέλ-η-σι. Similarly, the personal suffix for the third person plural -σαν is often interchangeable with -ν: ἐ-φοβήθη-σαν/φόβηθε-ν; ἔ-βη-σαν/ βά-ν; ἵε-σαν/ἵε-ν. For the first person plural -μεσθα is interchangeable with -μεθα. For the infinitive, -μεναι and -μεν can occur instead of -ειν. And in thematic aorists, instead of -εῖν, the uncontracted -έειν can occur.

5. The sign of the subjunctive in Attic is the lengthened variable vowel, but in Homeric Greek the subjunctive can occur with a short variable vowel and thus be identical with the indicative: ἴωμεν/ἴομεν.

6. "Expanded" contract verbs occur in Homeric Greek. This "expansion" consists of the insertion of an additional vowel before the vowel that results from contraction; the inserted vowel is identical with the contracted vowel, but may be either long or short: ὁρά-ει → ὁρᾷ/ὁράᾳ; ὁρά-ω → ὁρῶ/ὁρόω.

7. The chart summarizes the personal pronouns that differ from the Attic (and Ionic, *see* page 210) forms.

	Attic/Homeric	Attic/Homeric	Attic/Homeric
nom. sing.	ἐγώ/ἐγών		
acc. sing.	————	————	αὐτόν/ἕ, ἑέ
gen. sing.	ἐμοῦ/ἐμεῖο, ἐμέθεν	σοῦ/σεῖο, σέθεν	αὐτοῦ/ἕο
dat. sing.	————	σοί/τεΐν	αὐτῷ/ἑοῖ

nom. pl.	ἡμεῖς/ἄμμες	ὑμεῖς/ὕμμες	_____
acc. pl.	ἡμᾶς/ἄμμε	ὑμᾶς/ὕμμε	_____
gen. pl.	ἡμῶν/ἡμείων	ὑμῶν/ὑμείων	αὐτῶν, σφῶν/σφείων
dat. pl.	ἡμῖν/ἄμμι	ὑμῖν/ὕμμι	_____

Example

The opening verses of Homer's *Odyssey* will serve as an illustration.

Homeric	Attic
Ἄνδρα μοι ἔννεπε, Μοῦσα	Ἄνδρα μοι ἔννεπε, Μοῦσα,
πολύτροπον, ὃς μάλα πολλὰ	πολύτροπον, ὃς μάλα πολλὰ
πλάγχθη, ἐπεὶ Τροίης	ἐπλάγχθη, ἐπεὶ Τροίας
ἱερὸν πτολίεθρον ἔπερσε·	ἱερὸν πτολίεθρον ἔπερσε·
πολλῶν δ' ἀνθρώπων ἴδεν	πολλῶν δ' ἀνθρώπων εἶδεν
ἄστεα καὶ νόον ἔγνω,	ἄστη καὶ νοῦν ἔγνω,
πολλὰ δ' ὅ γ' ἐν πόντῳ	πολλὰ δ' αὐτός γ' ἐν πόντῳ
πάθεν ἄλγεα ὃν κατὰ θυμόν,	ἔπαθεν ἄλγη ὃν κατὰ θυμόν,
ἀρνύμενος ἥν τε ψυχὴν	ἀρνύμενος ἥν τε ψυχὴν
καὶ νόστον ἑταίρων.	καὶ νόστον ἑταίρων.

Translation: Muse, tell me about the man of twisted ways, who very much wandered after he destroyed Troy's sacred citadel: and many men's cities did he see and he knew their minds; and much suffering did he experience on the sea in his passionate heart as he tried to win his own life's breath and the homecoming of his companions.

Doric Greek

The Doric dialect was the language of the Dorian Greeks, who came originally from the Northwest and settled in the Peloponnesus, eventually sending out colonists to Crete, southern Asia Minor, and to southern Italy and Sicily. Choral poetry, such as the odes of the Theban Pindar, was the genre associated with this dialect; and even Athenian tragedians use some Doric forms in the choral parts of their dramas. In the Hellenistic period, pastoral poetry, like the idylls of Theocritus, was also composed in the Doric dialect.

Characteristics

1. Attic η occurs as ᾱ in Doric: λήθη/λάθᾱ.

2. The chart summarizes typical differences in declensional endings.

Attic		Doric	example: Attic/Doric
Type I			
gen. sing.	-ου	-αο	Ἀτρείδου/Ἀτρείδαο
gen. pl.	-ῶν	-ᾶν	ἱπποτῶν/ἱπποτᾶν
Type II			
gen. sing.	-ου	-ω	θεοῦ/θεῶ
acc. pl.	-ους	-ως, -ος	νόμους, τοὺς λύκους/ νόμως, τὼς λύκος

3. The chart summarizes the personal pronouns that differ from the Attic forms.

	Attic/Doric	Attic/Doric	Attic/Doric
nom. sing.	ἐγώ/ἐγών	σύ/τύ	————
acc. sing.	————	σέ/τέ, τύ	————
gen. sing.	ἐμοῦ/ἐμέος, ἐμοῦς, ἐμεῦς	σοῦ/τέος, τεοῦ, τεοῦς, τεῦς	————
dat. sing.	ἐμοί/ἐμίν	σοί/τοί, τίν	αὐτῷ/ἵν
nom. pl.	ἡμεῖς/ἁμές	ὑμεῖς/ὑμές	————
acc. pl.	ἡμᾶς/ἁμέ	ὑμᾶς/ὑμέ	αὐτούς, σφέ/ψέ
gen. pl.	ἡμῶν/ἁμέων	————	————
dat. pl.	ἡμῖν/ἁμίν	————	————

4. Several of the verbal personal suffixes differ from the Attic: -τι instead of -σι: δίδωσι/δίδωτι; -μες instead of -μεν: παιδεύομεν/ παιδεύομες; -μαν instead of -μην: ἐπορευόμην/ἐπορευόμαν; -μεσθα instead of -μεθα: πορευόμεθα/πορευόμεσθα. Also, the infinitive ends in -εν instead of -ειν: ἀείδειν/ἀείδεν.

Example

The opening verses of Pindar's *First Pythian Ode* will serve as an illustration.

Doric	Attic
Χρυσέα φόρμιγξ, Ἀπόλλωνος	Χρυσῆ φόρμιγξ, Ἀπόλλωνος
καὶ ἰοπλοκάμων σύνδικον	καὶ ἰοπλοκάμων σύνδικον
Μοισᾶν κτέανον. τᾶς ἀκούει	Μουσῶν κτέανον. ἧς ἀκούει
μὲν βάσις ἀγλαΐας ἀρχά,	μὲν βάσις ἀγλαΐας ἀρχή,
πείθονται δ' ἀοιδοὶ σάμασιν	πείθονται δ' ἀοιδοὶ σήμασιν
ἁγησιχόρων ὁπόταν προοιμίων	ἡγησιχόρων ὁπόταν προοιμίων
ἀμβολὰς τεύχῃς ἐλελιζομένα.	ἀμβολὰς τεύχῃς ἐλελιζομένη.

Translation: Golden lyre, Apollo's and the violet tressed Muses' jointly claimed possession: (you) to whom harkens the dance step, the festivity's beginning; and poets obey your rhythmic signs whenever you, as you are strummed, fashion the beats for the prelude that leads in the choral dancers.

Aeolic Greek

The Aeolic dialect was the language of the peoples of Thessaly and Boeotia, who migrated to the island of Lesbos and the northern regions of Asia Minor. It was associated with the genre of lyric poetry and survives in literary form in very few works, primarily the fragmentary poems of Sappho and Alcaeus. Of the standarized literary dialects, it appears most difficult and strange to the student of Attic, perhaps because of the scantiness of the extant literature composed in it.

Characteristics

1. Aeolic shows many of the variant forms already listed for the other dialects. In addition, Attic contract verbs are athematically conjugated: φιλῶ/

φίλημμι. Liquid and nasal consonants are often doubled: κρίνω/κρίννω; φθείρω/φθέρρω. The infinitive ending -ειν occurs as -ην: κρίνειν/κρίννην.

2. The chart summarizes typical differences in declensional endings.

	Attic	Aeolic	example: Attic/Aeolic
Type I			
acc. pl.	-ας	-αις	ἄρχας/ἄρχαις
Type II			
gen. sing.	-ου	-ω	θεοῦ/θεῶ
acc. pl.	-ους	-οις	ἀλλήλους/ἀλλάλοις
dat. pl.	-οις	-οισι	γενεθλίοις/γενεθλίοισι

Example:

A few verses from a poem by Sappho will serve as an illustration.

Aeolic (Lesbian)
Τεθνάκην δ' ἀδόλως θέλω·
ἄ με ψισδομένα κατελίμπανε,
πόλλα καὶ τόδ' ἔειπέ μοι·
"ὤιμ' ὡς δεῖνα πεπόνθαμεν,
Ψάπφ', ἦ μάν σ' ἀέκοισ'
ἀπυλιμπάνω."

Attic
Τεθνηκέναι δ' ἀδόλως θέλω·
ἡ δέ με ψιζομένη κατέλειπε,
πολλὰ καὶ τόδ' εἶπέ μοι·
"οἴ μ' ὡς δεῖνα πεπόνθαμεν,
Σάπφ', ἦ μήν σ' ἄκουσ'
ἀπολείπω."

Translation: I want absolutely to be dead! And she weeping was leaving me and often did she say this to me: "Alas, what a terrible thing this is that we are suffering, Sappho. I swear, against my will I am leaving you."

Modern Demotic Greek

The linguistic changes that have resulted in the modern spoken language of Greece are extensive enough to require that one learn modern Greek as a new language, especially since an active ability is the obvious goal; but the continuity with the ancient language is remarkable, although often regrettably disregarded by the Classicist. Ideally, the student of ancient Greek should continue the study by learning the modern language at some point, probably after a year or so of reading in the ancient literature. The experience of learning modern Greek will in effect resurrect the ancient language from the silence of so many ages past and place it in the context of the living language as one of the more extreme dialects diverging from the ancient Attic. The Greek language has, in fact, been extraordinarily conservative, changing so little in two millenia that it is still recognizable as the same language.

Characteristics

1. Modern Greek has lost the optative mood and the infinitive, the latter being replaced by an expanded usage of the subjunctive (introduced by νά, which is derived from the ancient ἵνα). The dative case, furthermore, has also been lost, except for a few formal phrases, and the loss has been compensated for by an expanded dependence upon prepositions to clarify syntactic relations.

2. The future is indicated by the particle θά, and the perfect tenses have be-

come analytic, using the auxiliary verb ἔχω. The language, however, retains the distinction between progressive and aorist aspects, the middle- passive voice, the participles, although not in so extensive usage, and the contract verbs, although with different resultant contractions. For the most part, the thematic mode of conjugation is used; and some of the personal suffixes for the verb are changed, although still recognizable: -μεν/-με; -ουσι/-ουν; -μεθα/-μαστε; -σθε/-στε; -το/-ταν; -ντο/-νταν.

3. As is to be expected, new words have been added from various other languages in the course of time; and many ancient words have developed new meanings or have surfaced with meanings that were not their dominant meaning in antiquity. Often, the initial syllable of an ancient word has been lost as it evolves into the modern language. Nouns often have been reformed from the oblique cases into a new nominative form: τὸν ἄνδρα/ό ἄνδρας.

Example

A few verses from a poem by Kavafis will serve as an illustration. The Atticized version would probably not have been comprehensible to a reader in antiquity since no attempt has been made to Atticize the syntactic structures.

Modern Demotic	Attic
"Τί περιμένουμε στὴν ἀγορᾷ συναθροισμένοι;"	"Τί περιμένομεν ἐν τῇ ἀρορᾷ συνηθροισμένοι;"
"Εἶναι οἱ βάρβαροι νὰ φθάσουν σήμερα."	"Ἔστιν (ὅτι περιμένομεν) οἱ βάρβαροι ἵνα φθάσωσι σήμερον."
"Γιατὶ μέσα στὴ Σύγκλητο μιὰ τέτοια ἀπραξία; τί κάθονται οἱ συγκλητικοὶ καὶ δὲν νομοθετοῦνε;"	"Διὰ τί μέσα ἐν τῇ Συγκλήτῳ τοιαύτη τις ἀπραξία; τί κάθηνται οἱ συγκλητικοὶ καὶ οὐδὲν νομοθετοῦσιν;"
"Γιατὶ οἱ βάρβαροι θά φθάσουν σήμερα· τί νόμους πιὰ νὰ κάμουν οἱ συγκλητικοί; οἱ βάρβαροι, σὰν ἔρθουν, θὰ νομοθετήσουν."	"Δι' ὅτι οἱ βάρβαροι φθάσουσι σήμερον· τί νόμους πλέον (θέλουσιν) ἵνα κάμνωσιν οἱ συγκλητικοί; οἱ βάρβαροι, ὅταν ἔλθωσι, νομοθετήσουσιν."

Translation: "Why do we wait assembled in the market place?"
"It is that we are waiting for the barbarians to come today."
"Why in the midst of the Senate is there such a lack of activity?
Why do the senators sit and pass no laws?"
"Because the barbarians are going to arrive today: why do the senators want to pass more laws? The barbarians, whenever they come, will pass the laws."

Glossary

Included in this glossary are all words introduced in the lesson vocabularies and in the notes to the reading selections. The principle parts of verbs are not listed. For the principle parts of the more common verbs, refer to pages 160–163 or to the list that follows this glossary.

A

ἀγαθός, -ή, -όν	good, noble
ἄγαν	*adv.* very much, too much
ἄγγελος, -ου, ὁ	messenger
ἀγγέλλω	announce
ἀγέλαστος, -ον	humorless, grave
ἁγιάζω	make sacred
ἀγορά, -ᾶς, ἡ	assembly, marketplace
ἀγορεύω	speak in the assembly
ἄγριος, -α, -ον	living in the fields, wild, savage
ἀγρός, -οῦ, ὁ	field, country
ἄγχω	strangle
ἄγω	lead
ἀδελφός, -οῦ, ὁ/ἀδελφή, -ῆς, ἡ	brother/sister
ἀδικέω	be unjust, do wrong, be guilty
ἄδικος, -ον	unjust
ᾄδω	sing
ἀεί	*adv.* always
ἀηδῶς	*adv.* without pleasure
ἀθανασία, -ας, ἡ	immortality
ἀθάνατος, -ον	immortal
᾿Αθήναζε	*adv.* toward Athens
᾿Αθήνηθεν	*adv.* from Athens
ἆθλος, -ου, ὁ	contest
ἄθροος, -α, -ον	in crowds, heaps, or masses; crowded together
αἰδοῖον, -ου, τό	sexual organ
αἰδοῖος, -α, -ον	having a claim to reverence or awe or shame
αἰνέω	tell, speak of, praise
αἴνιγμα, -ατος, τό	dark saying, riddle, enigma

αἰνίσσομαι	speak in riddles
αἰνίττομαι	v. αἰνίσσομαι
αἶνος, -ου, ὁ	tale
αἱρέω	take (mid. choose)
αἴρω	raise
αἰσθάνομαι	perceive, see, hear
αἰσχρός, -ή, -όν	ugly, shameful
αἰσχύνη, -ης, ἡ	shame, dishonor
αἰσχύνω	make ugly, be ashamed
αἰτία, -ας, ἡ	cause, responsibility, blame
ἀκολασία, -ας, ἡ	licentiousness
ἀκολουθέω	follow, go after or with (+ comitative dat.)
ἀκούω	hear, listen to
ἄκων, -ουσα, -ον	unwilling
ἀλεκτρυών, -όνος, ὁ	cock
ἀλήθεια, -ας, ἡ	truth
ἀληθής, -ές	true
ἀλίσκομαι	be seized or conquered
ἀλλά	but
ἀλλήλους, -ας, -α	(acc.) of one another
ἀλλοῖος, -α, -ον	of another sort or kind
ἄλλος, -η, -ον	other
ἀλλότριος, -α, -ον	belonging to another
ἄλλως	otherwise
ἄλσος, -ους, τό	grove of trees, especially a sacred grove
ἁμαρτάνω	err, fail
ἁμάρτημα, -ατος, τό	failure, mistake
ἀμελέω	have no care for, be unconcerned
ἀμφότερος, -α, -ον	both
ἄν	= ἐάν/also the particle
ἀνά	adv. up toward
ἀνάβασις, -εως, ἡ	journey upward or inland

ἀνα-βαίνω	mount
ἀνα-βοάω	raise a shout
ἀναγκάζω	force, compel
ἀναγκαῖος, -α, -ον	necessary
ἀναγκαίως	*adv.* necessarily
ἀνάγκη, -ης, ἡ	necessity
ἀν-αιρέω	kill; reply, ordain (of an oracle's answer); *v.* αἱρέω
ἀναισχυντία -ας, ἡ	shamelessness
ἀνα-λαμβάνω	take up
ἀν-αλίσκω	expend, use up
ἀν-αλόω	expend, use up
ἀν-άξιος, -ον	unworthy
ἀνα-πέμπω	send up
ἀνα-τέλλω	cause to rise, rise
ἀνα-φέρω	refer
ἀνδρόγυνος, -ου, ὁ	androgyne
ἀνελεύθερος, -ον	not free, servile, not befitting a free man
ἀν-ελίσσω	unroll, read a book roll
ἄνευ	without (+ gen.)
ἀνεψιός, -οῦ, ὁ	(first) cousin
ἀνήρ, ἀνδρός, ὁ	man
ἀνθρώπινος, -η, -ον	human
ἄνθρωπος, -ου,	man, human, mankind
ἀνιάω	grieve, distress
ἄνοια, -ας, ἡ	folly
ἀντί	instead of, over against (+ gen.)
ἀντίος, -α, -ον	opposite
ἄνω	*adv.* upward
ἀνώνυμος, -ον	nameless
ἄξιος, -α, -ον	worthy
ἀξιόχρεως, -εων	worthy, noteworthy
ἀξιόω	esteem worthy, place a value upon

ἀπ-αγγέλλω	announce, report
ἀπαίδευτος, -ον	uneducated
ἀπαλλαγή, -ῆς, ἡ	deliverance
ἀπ-αλλάσσω	release, deliver, set free
ἅπαξ	*adv.* once
ἀπ-εικάζω	take a likeness of, paint a portrait
ἀπειρία, -ας, ἡ	inexperience
ἀπ-ερείδω	prop away or up
ἀπ-ερύκω	keep off or away
ἀπ-έρχομαι	go away
ἀπ-εχθάνομαι	incur hatred
ἀπέχθεια, -ας, ἡ	hatred
ἀπό	away from (+ ablatival gen.)
ἀπο-δείκνυμι	reveal
ἀπο-δίδωμι	pay back
ἄποθεν	*adv.* from far away
ἀπο-θνήσκω	die
ἀπ-οικίζω	send away from home
ἀπο-κρίνομαι	answer, reply
ἀπο-κτείνω	kill
ἀπο-λείπω	leave behind
ἀπ-όλλυμι	destroy (*mid.* perish, die)
ἀπο-λογέομαι	speak in one's own defense
ἀπο-λύω	release, untie
ἀπορέω	be without means
ἀπορία, -ας, ἡ	lack of means
ἄπορος, -ον	without means, impassable, un-manageable
ἅπτω	fasten, kindle (*mid.* touch)
ἆρα	particle that introduces questions
ἄρα	therefore
ἀρά, -ᾶς, ἡ	curse
ἀρετή, -ῆς, ἡ	excellence

ἀριθμός, -οῦ, ὁ	number
ἄριστος, -η, -ον	superl. of ἀγαθός
ἄρμα, -ατος, τό	chariot
ἁρπάζω	snatch away, seize
ἄρρην, ἄρρεν (ἄρρενος)	male, masculine
ἄρτι	*adv.* just now, presently
ἄρτος, -ου, ὁ	bread
ἀρχή, -ῆς, ἡ	beginning, rulership
ἀσελγαίνω	behave licentiously
ἀσελγής, -ές	licentious
ἀσθενής, -ές	weak
ἄσκησις, -εως, ἡ	exercise
ἄσοφος, -ον	stupid
ἀσπίς, -ίδος, ἡ	shield
ἄστυ, -εως, τό	town
ἄτε	inasmuch as (+ participle)
αὖθις	*adv.* again
αὐξάνω	increase, augment (*pass.* grow, increase in size)
αὐτίκα	*adv.* immediately
αὐτόματον, -ου, τό	accident
αὐτόματος, -η, -ον	acting by itself or of its own will
αὐτός, -ή, -ό	*see* page 23
αὐτοσχεδιάζω	speak or act offhand, extemporize
αὐτοσχέδιος, -α, -ον	in close fight, improvised
αὐτοσχεδόν	*adv.* near at hand
αὐτοῦ	*adv.* in that very place, there
αὐχέω	boast
αὐχήν, -ένος, ὁ	neck
ἀφανίζω	make disappear
ἀφανῶς	*adv.* invisibly, unseen
ἄφωνος, -ον	voiceless, dumb

B

βαίνω	walk
βάλλω	throw
βασίλειος, -ον	royal, kingly
βασιλεύς, -έως, ὁ	king
βασιλεύω	rule as king
βέλτιστος, -η, -ον	superl. of ἀγαθός
βελτίων, -ιον	comp. of ἀγαθός
βίος, -ου, ὁ	life
βιοτεύω	live
βιόω	live, pass one's life
βλάπτω	harm
βοάω	shout
βοή, -ῆς, ἡ	shout
βορά, -ᾶς, ἡ	food
βουλεύω	take counsel, deliberate
βουλή, -ῆς, ἡ	the government Council in Athens, deliberation
βούλομαι	want
βοῦς, βοός, ὁ/ἡ	ox/cow
βραδύς, -εῖα, -ύ	slow, dull, sluggish
βρέφος, -ους, τό	baby
βροτός, -ή, -όν	mortal
βωμός, -οῦ, ὁ	altar

Γ

γαμέω	marry
γάμος, -ου, ὁ	marriage, wedding
γάρ	for, because
γε	indeed
γένεσις, -εως, ἡ	generation, manner of birth
γενναῖος, -α, -ον	noble
γενναίως	*adv.* nobly
γεννάω	beget, bear

γένος, -ους, τό	race, kin, gender
γεραιός, -ά, -όν *geraios*	old
γέρων, -οντος, ὁ	old man
γεύω	give a taste of (*mid.* taste)
γῆ, -ῆς, ἡ	earth
γηράσκω	grow old
γίγας, -αντος, ὁ	giant
γίγνομαι	be, come to be, become, be born
γιγνώσκω	know, recognize
γλῶσσα, -ης, ἡ	tongue, language
γνώμη, -ης, ἡ	thought, mind
γονεύς, -έως, ὁ	parent
γραῖα, -ας, ἡ	old woman
γράμμα, -ατος, τό	letter, lines of a drawing (*pl.* epistle, letter)
γραφή, -ῆς, ἡ	indictment
γράφω	write (*mid.* indict)
γραῦς, -αός, ἡ	old woman
γυνή, γυναικός, ἡ	woman

Δ

δαιμόνιον, -ου, τό	a divine power, deity
δαίμων, -ονος, ὁ	a divine power, deity
δέ	but, and
δεῖ	it is necessary
δείκνυμι	show
δειλός, -ή, -όν	cowardly
δεινός, -ή, -όν	terrible, clever
δεῖπνον, -ου, τό	dinner
δέρας (δέρος), -ατος (-ους), τό	skin of an animal
δέρμα, -ατος, τό	skin of an animal, hide
δέρω	flay, skin
δέσμιος, -ον	bound, captive
δεσμωτήριον, -ου, τό	prison

δεσμώτης, -ου, ὁ	prisoner
δεσπότης, -ου, ὁ	despot, master, lord, husband
δεύτερος, -α, -ον	second
δέω	need, lack
δέω	bind, tie
δή	indeed
δῆλος, -η, -ον	manifest, visible
δηλόω	make manifest, show
δῆμος, -ου, ὁ	populace
δημόσιος, -α, -ον	belonging to the populace
δήπου	certainly- -I suppose
διά	through and out of (+ ablatival gen.), throughout, on account of (+ acc.)
δια-βάλλω	slander, reproach
διαβολή, -ῆς, ἡ	slander, false accusation
δι-αγγέλλω	announce
διάκονος, -ου, ὁ	servant
δια-λέγομαι	converse, have a dialogue
δια-λείπω	leave an interval
δι-αν-ίστημι	rise, stand up
δια-σκοπέω	investigate
δια-φέρω	differ (+ instrumental dat. and ablatival gen.)
διδάσκαλος, -ου, ὁ	teacher
διδάσκω	teach
δίδωμι	give
δι-έρχομαι	go through
διόπερ	wherefore, on which account
διότι	because
δικάζω	judge
δίκαιος, -α, -ον	just, right
δικαστής, -οῦ, ὁ	juror
δίκη, -ης, ἡ	right, justice, lawsuit, trial (δίκην

	διδόναι pay the penalty)
δίς	twice
διφορέω	bear, carry double
δίφρος, -ου, ὁ	chariot
δίχα	*adv.* in two
διώκω	pursue
δοκέω	seem, think, seem good
δόξα, -ης, ἡ	opinion, public opinion
δόρυ, δόρατος (δουρός), τό	stem, tree, beam, shaft of a spear, spear
δόσις, -εως, ἡ	act of giving
δοῦλος, -ου, ὁ	slave, servant
δουλόω	enslave
δράκων, -οντος, ὁ	serpent
δρᾶμα, -ατος, τό	action
δραχμή, -ῆς, ἡ	drachma (a unit of currency worth six obols and equal to about three times a day's wage of a common worker)
δράω	do
δύναμαι	be able
δύο	two
δυσείδεια, -ας, ἡ	ugliness
δυστυχέω	be unfortunate
δύω	go down, enter, cause to enter
δώδεκα	twelve
δῶρον, -ου, τό	gift

E

ἐάν	= εἰ ἄν
ἑαυτόν, -ήν, -ό	himself/herself/itself
ἐάω	permit
ἔβην	v. βαίνω
ἐγγύς	*adv.* near/ prep. + gen.
ἐγ-καλύπτω	cover up

ἔγνων	v. γιγνώσκω
ἐγ-χειρίζω	give, put in the hand
ἐγώ	I
ἔδραμον	v. τρέχω
ἔδωκα	v. δίδωμι
ἔθανον	v. θνήσκω
ἐθέλω	want
ἔθηκα	v. τίθημι
ἐθίζω	accustom
ἔθνος, -ους, τό	nation, group of people
ἔθω	accustom
εἶδον	v. ὁράω
εἶδος, -ους, τό	form, kind
εἰκάζω	portray by a likeness, liken
εἰκός, -ότος, τό	likelihood, probability
εἰκότως	adv. likely, reasonably, probably
εἰκών, -όνος, ἡ	image
εἷλον	v. αἱρέω
εἰμί	be
εἶμι	go
εἶπον	v. λέγω
εἰρήνη, -ης, ἡ	peace
εἰς	toward, into (+ acc.)
εἷς, μία, ἕν	one
εἰσ-έρχομαι	go into
εἰσ-οράω	look upon
εἰσ-φέρω	carry in, bring in
εἶτα	adv. then, next
εἶχον	v. ἔχω
εἴωθα	be accustomed
εἴων	v. ἐάω
ἐκ	out of (+ ablatival gen.)
ἑκαστάκις	adv. each time

ἕκαστος, -η, -ον	each
ἑκάτερος, -α, -ον	each of two
ἔκγονος, -ον	born from, offspring
ἐκ-δίδωμι	give away, divorce
ἐκεῖ	*adv.* there
ἐκεῖθεν	*adv.* from that place, thence
ἐκεῖνος, -η, -ον	that
ἐκ-καλύπτω	take the cover off, uncover
ἐκ-λέγομαι	select
ἐκτέον	one must have
ἐκ-τίθημι	expose (a child to die)
ἐκ-φαίνω	reveal
ἐκ-φέρω	carry out (as a corpse for a funeral)
ἑκών, -οῦσα, -όν	willing
ἔλεγχος, -ου, ὁ	argument of refutation, reproach
ἐλέγχω	cross-examine, refute
ἑλίσσω	roll
Ἑλλάς, -άδος, ἡ	Greece
ἐλ-λείπω	fall short of, be inferior to
Ἕλλην, -ηνος, ὁ	Greek (person)
ἐλεύθερος, -α, -ον	free, fit for a free man
ἐλπίς, -ίδος, ἡ	hope
ἐμαυτόν, -ήν	myself
ἐμ-βαίνω	walk in
ἐμ-βάλλω	throw in
ἐμ-βιόω	live in
ἔμαθον	*v.* μανθάνω
ἐμέ	*v.* ἐγώ
ἐμ-μένω	abide, remain in
ἐμοί	*v.* ἐγώ
ἐμός, -ή, -όν	my
ἐμοῦ	*v.* ἐγώ
ἐμπειρέω	experience

ἐμπειρία,-ας, ἡ	experience
ἔμπειρος, -ον	experienced
ἐν	in, on (+ locative dat.)
ἐναντίος, -α, -ον	opposite, opponent
ἐν-απο-θνήσκω	die in
ἐνθάδε	*adv.* here, there
ἐνθένδε	*adv.* thence, from that place
ἐν-θυμέομαι	lay to heart, ponder, be angry
ἔν-ειμι	be in
ἔνεκα	on account of (+ gen.)
ἐνιαυτός, -οῦ, ὁ	time period of a year
ἐννέα	nine
ἐν-νοέω	consider
ἔνοπλος, -ον	in armor
ἐνταῦθα	*adv.* here, there
ἐντεῦθεν	*adv.* hence, thereupon
ἐν-τίθημι	place in
ἐξ-ευρίσκω	discover
ἔοικα	seem, resemble
ἑορτή, -ῆς, ἡ	festival
ἐπ-αινέω	praise
ἔπαθον	*v.* πάσχω
ἔπαινος, -ου, ὁ	praise
ἐπ-ακούω	listen to, overhear
ἔπειτα	*adv.* thereupon, then
ἐπίδειξις, -εως, ἡ	revelation
ἐπ-ερωτάω	ask
ἔπεσον	*v.* πίπτω
ἐπί	on (+ gen.), onto (+ acc.), on (+ dat.)
ἐπι-βοάω	shout
ἐπι-βουλή, -ῆς, ἡ	plot formed against someone
ἐπι-θυμέω	set one's heart upon, long for, desire

ἐπίθυμος, -ον	desirous
ἐπι-καλύπτω	cover up
ἐπι-νέμομαι	encroach upon, spread over
ἐπίσημος, -ον	notable, significant
ἐπίσταμαι	understand, know
ἐπιστήμη, -ης, ἡ	knowledge
ἐπι-στρἀτεύω	make war upon
ἐπι-τάσσω	enjoin , order, put upon one as a duty
ἐπιτήδειος, -α, -ον	suitable, useful, necessary
ἐπι-τηρέω	watch upon
ἐπι-τίθημι	place upon (*mid.* attack)
ἐπι-χειρέω	put one's hand to, attempt
ἔπος, -ους, τό	word, verse
ἔραμαι	love
ἐραστής, -οῦ, ὁ	lover
ἐράω	love
ἔργον, -ου, τό	work, deed
ἔρδω	do
ἐρίζω	contend, strive
ἐρείδω	prop
ἔρομαι	ask
ἔρχομαι	go, come
ἔρως, -ωτος, ὁ	love
ἐρωτάω	ask, question
ἐρώτημα, -ατος, τό	question
ἐς	= εἰς
ἐσθίω	eat
ἐσθλός, -ή, -όν	good
ἔστην	*v.* ἴστημι
ἔσχατος, -η, -ον	extreme, hindmost
ἔσχον	*v.* ἔχω
ἑταίρα, -ας, ἡ	companion, courtesan

ἑταῖρος, -ου, ὁ	comrade, companion
ἔτεκον	v. τίκτω
ἔτεμον	v. τέμνω
ἕτερος, -α, -ον	other, different
ἔτι	adv. still
ἑτοῖμος, -η, -ον	at hand, ready
ἔτυχον	v. τυγχάνω
εὖ	adv. well
εὐδαίμων, -ον/ (-ονος)	blessed with a good spirit, fortunate
εὐθύς/εὐθέως	adv. straight
εὐθύς, -εῖα, -ύ	straight
εὐνή, -ῆς, ἡ	bed
εὑρίσκω	find
εὐτυχέω	be fortunate
εὔχομαι	pray
εὐφυχία, -ας, ἡ	nobility of spirit
ἔφαγον	v. ἐσθίω
ἔχθρα, -ας, ἡ	hatred
ἐχθρός, -ά, -όν	hated, hateful, hostile, inimical
ἔχω	have, (+ adv.) be
ἑώρων	v. ὁράω
Z	
ζάω	live, be alive
ζεύγνυμι	yoke
ζεῦγος, -ους, τό	yoke of beasts, carriage drawn by yoked beasts
Ζεύς, Διός, ὁ	Zeus
ζητέω	seek, search for
ζωγράφος, -ου, ὁ	artist
ζωή, -ῆς, ἡ	life
ζῷον, -ου, τό	living creature, animal
H	
ἤ	than

ἤ	or/(ἤ... ἤ... either... or...)
ἤγαγον	v. ἄγω
ἡγεμών, -όνος, ὁ	guide, leader
ἡγέομαι	lead, think
ἡδέως	*adv.* with pleasure, pleasurably
ἤδη	*adv.* already
ἤδομαι	enjoy, take pleasure in (+ dat.)
ἡδύς, -εῖα, -ύ	sweet
ἧκα	v. ἵημι
ἤκιστος, -η, -ον	superl. of κακός
ἥκω	come, have come
ἡλικία, -ας, ἡ	time of life, age
ἡλικιώτης, -ου, ὁ	comrade (of the same age group)
ἥλιος, -ου, ὁ	sun
ἡμᾶς	v. ἐγώ
ἡμεῖς	v. ἐγώ
ἡμέρα, -ας, ἡ	day
ἡμῖν	v. ἐγώ
ἥμισυς, -εια, -υ	half
ἡμῶν	v. ἐγώ
ἤνεγκα	v. φέρω
ἤνεγκον	v. φέρω
ἡνία, -ας, ἡ	reins
ἦρα	v. αἴρω
ἥσσων, -ον	compar. of κακός
ἦτρον, -ου, τό	lower abdomen, belly

Θ

θάλασσα, -ης, ἡ	sea
θαλάσσιος, -α, -ον	sea-like, from the sea
θάνατος, -ου, ὁ *thanatos*	death
θάττων	compar. of ταχύς
θαῦμα, -ατος, τό	marvel

θαυμάζω	wonder at
θέα, -ας, ἡ	viewing
θεάομαι	gaze at, behold (with a sense of wonder), view as a spectator
θέατρον, -ου, τό	theater
θεῖος, -α, -ον	divine
θέλγω	enchant, beguile
θέμις, -ιδος, ἡ	justice, the goddess Themis, that which is laid down or established
θεός, -οῦ, ὁ/ἡ	god/goddess
θεραπεία, -ας, ἡ	service, attendance
θεραπεύω	serve, heal, pay court to
θερμός, -ή, -όν	hot
θέσις, -εως, ἡ	placing
θέω	run
θῆλυς, θήλεια, θῆλυ	female, feminine
θήρ, -ρός, ὁ	beast, animal
θησαυρός, -οῦ, ὁ	treasury
θνήσκω	die
θνητός, -ή, -όν	mortal
θορυβέω	make a noise, uproar or disturbance
θόρυβος, -ου, ὁ	noise, confused noise of a crowd, tumult
θρηνέω	lament
θρῆνος, -ου, ὁ	dirge
θυγάτηρ, -τρός, ἡ	daughter
θυμός, -οῦ, ὁ	human organ of emotions: desire, passion, anger
θύω	sacrifice

I

ἰατρός, -οῦ, ὁ	doctor
ἰδέα, -ας, ἡ	form, semblance, outward appearance
ἱέρεια, -ας, ἡ	priestess

ἱερός, -ή, -όν	sacred
ἱερός, -οῦ, ὁ	priest
ἵημι	send, let go
ἱκετεία, -ας, ἡ	supplication, suppliant approach
ἱκνέομαι	come, arrive
ἱμάτιον, -ου, τό	article of outer clothing, worn over the *chiton* or tunic
ἵππος, -ου, ὁ	horse
ἰσθμός, -οῦ, ὁ	isthmus
ἴσος, -η, -ον	equal, like
ἰσχύς, -έως, ἡ	bodily strength
ἴσχω	*v.* ἔχω
ἴσως	*adv.* perhaps, equally, probably
ἰτέον	one must go
ἰχθύς, -ύος, ὁ	fish

K

καθέζομαι	sit down
καθίζομαι	sit down
καί	and
καινός, -ή, -όν	new, novel
καίω	burn
κακός, -ή, -όν	bad
κακῶς	*adv.* badly
καλέω	call
καλλίχορος, -ον	with beautiful dancing
κάλλος, -ους, τό	beauty
καλός, -ή, -όν	beautiful, handsome
καλύπτω	cover
καλῶς	*adv.* well
καρπός, -οῦ, ὁ	fruit, harvest
κατά	down from, against (+ ablatival gen.), down toward, in accordance with (+ acc.)

κατα-βάλλω	throw down
κατα-γιγνώσκω	lay as a charge against someone (gen.) for a crime (infinitive)
κατάδηλος, -ον	very manifest, very visible
κατάζευξις, -εως, ἡ	yoking
κατα-κλύζω	flood, wash away
κατα-κοιμίζω	put to sleep
κατα-λαμβάνω	take, catch (by surprise), seize
κατα-λείπω	leave behind
κατα-μένω	stay
κατα-σπείρω	sow, cast seed down
κατα-τίθημι	place down
κατα-φλέγω	burn up
κατ-έχω	hold down (under control), occupy
κατ-ηγορέω	speak against, accuse
κατήγορος, -ου, ὁ	accusor
κατ-οπτρίζομαι	look into a mirror
κάτοπτρον, -ου, τό	mirror
κάτω	*adv.* downward
κεῖμαι	lie, repose
κελεύω	command
κεράννυμι	mix
κεραυνός, -οῦ, ὁ	thunderbolt
κεραυνόω	strike with thunderbolts
κερδαίνω	gain, derive profit
κέρδος, -ους, τό	gain, profit
κεφαλή, -ῆς, ἡ	head
κηδεστής, -ῆς, ὁ	relative by marriage, in-law
κῆδος, -ους, τό	care, object of care, funeral rites
κήδω	trouble, distress (*pass.* care for)
κινδυνεύω	make a venture, hazard, run the risk of (doing or being)
κίνδυνος, -ου, ὁ	danger
κινέω	move, disturb, stir

κλαίω	weep
κλάω	weep
κλείς, κλειδός, ἡ	bar, bolt, key
κλείω	shut, close, bar
κλέος, τό/τά κλέα	(nom. and acc. only) fame, good repute
κνίζω	scratch, chafe, tease, provoke
κοινῇ	*adv.* together, by a common way
κοινός, -ή, -όν	common, together
κοινῶς	*adv.* together
κόκκος, -ου, ὁ	seed, pit
κολάζω	chastise, restrain
κομίζω	convey, escort
κόρη, -ης, ἡ	girl, maiden
κόσμος, -ου, ὁ	universe, ornament
κρατιστεύω	be mightiest
κράτιστος, -η, -ον	superl. of ἀγαθός
κρατήρ, -ῆρος, ὁ	mixing bowl for wine and water
κράτος, -ους, τό	might, power
κρείσσων, -ον	compar. of ἀγαθός
κρήνη, -ης, ἡ	(natural) well, spring
κρίνω	judge, decide (a contest or dispute)
κριτής, -οῦ, ὁ	judge
κρύπτω	hide
κρύφα	*adv.* secretly
κτάομαι	possess
κτείνω	kill
κυβιστάω	tumble head foremost
κυβιστής, -οῦ, ὁ	acrobat
κύκλος, -ου, ὁ	circle, cycle
κυκλοτερής, -ές	circular, round
κύων, κυνός, ὁ/ἡ	dog
κατα-ψηφίζομαι	vote (a penalty, acc.) against (someone, gen.)

κώνειον, -ου, τό	juice of the herb hemlock

Λ

λαβή, -ῆς, ἡ	handle
λαμβάνω	take, grasp
λαμπάς, -άδος, ἡ	torch
λάμπω	shine, give light
λάρναξ, -ακος, ἡ	box, chest
λέγω	say, speak
λείπω	leave, depart
λέξις, -εως, ἡ	style (in speech)
λέων, -οντος, ὁ leon	lion
λήγω	cease from
λίθος, -ου, ὁ	stone, rock
λογίζομαι	count, reckon, calculate
λοιδορέω	abuse, revile
λοιπός, -ή, -όν	remaining over, left
λούω	wash
λύκος, -ου, ὁ	wolf
λυπέω	grieve
λυπή, -ῆς, ἡ	pain of body or mind
λύω	untie, release

M

μάθησις, -εως, ἡ	learning
μαθητής, -οῦ, ὁ	student
μαίνομαι	be mad, be intoxicated
μᾶλλον	*adv.* more
μάθημα, -ατος, τό	lesson
μανθάνω	learn
μαντεῖον, -ου, τό	seat of an oracle
μαντεύομαι	prophesy, consult an oracle
μαντικός, -ή, -όν	mantic, prophetic
μάντις, -εως, ὁ	diviner, prophet

μαρτυρέω	bear witness, testify
μάρτυς, -υρος, ὁ/ἡ	witness
μαστεύω	seek, search after
μάχη, -ης, ἡ	battle
μάχιμος, -η, -ον	warlike, fit for battle
μάχομαι	fight
με	v. ἐγώ
μέγας, μεγάλη, μέγα	big
μέγεθος, -ους, τό	greatness, magnitude
μέγιστος, -η, -ον	superl. of μέγας
μειδιάω	smile
μείζων, -ον	compar. of μέγας
μείς, μηνός, ὁ	month
μέλει	it is a concern
μέλλω	intend, be about to
μέλος, -ους, τό	limb, musical phrase
μέλω	care for
μέν	indeed
μέν. . . δέ	see. page 18
μένω	stay, remain
μέρος, -ους, τό	part
μέσος, -η, -ον	middle, in the middle
μετά	with, amidst (+ partitive gen.), into the midst, after (+ acc.)
μετα-γιγνώσκω	change one's mind, repent
μετα-μέλει	it causes repentance
μετ-έχω	share
μετρίως	adv. moderately, with measure
μέτρον, -ου, τό	measure
μέχρι	as far as (+ ablatival gen.)
μή	not
μηδέ	nor
μηδείς, μηδεμία, μηδέν	no one/nothing

μηκέτι	*adv.* not yet
μήν	certainly
μήνη, -ης, ἡ	moon
μηνίω	have wrath against (+ comitative dat.)
μήτηρ, μητρός, ἡ	mother
μηχανάομαι	make by art, devise
μηχανή, -ῆς, ἡ	machine, mechanism, contrivance
μικρός, -ά, -όν	small
μιμνήσκω	remind (*mid.* remind oneself of, remember, make mention of, + gen.)
μισέω	hate
μνήμη, -ης, ἡ	remembrance, memory, memorial
μνηστεία, -ας, ἡ	courtship
μνηστεύω	seek in marriage, court
μνηστής, -ῆρος, ὁ	suitor
μόγις	*adv.* with toil and pain, scarcely, hardly
μόγος, -ου, ὁ	pain, trouble
μοί	*v.* ἐγώ
μόνος, -η, -ον	alone, only
μου	*v.* ἐγώ
μοχθέω	be weary
μοχθηρία, -ας, ἡ	wickedness, depravity
μοχθηρός, -ά, -όν	suffering or causing hardship
μόχθος, -ου, ὁ	hardship, distress

N

ναῦς, νεώς, ἡ	ship
νεανίας, -ου, ὁ	young man
νέμομαι	graze like cattle
νέος, -α -ον	new, young
νεώς, νεώ, ὁ	temple
νή	affirmative adverb of swearing

νήπιος, -α, -ον	childish, stupid
νίκη, -ης, ἡ	victory
νοέω	think, perceive
νομίζω	think, consider
νομοθετέω	be a lawgiver
νομοθέτης, -ου, ὁ	lawgiver
νόμος, -ου, ὁ	law
νοῦς, -οῦ, ὁ	mind, intellect
νύμφη, -ης, ἡ	bride
νυμφίος, -ου, ὁ	bridegroom
νῦν	adv. now
νύξ, νυκτός, ἡ	night
νῶτον, -ου, τό	back

Ξ

ξένος, -η, -ον	foreign, host, guest
ξύμπας, ξύμπασα, ξύμπαν	absolutely all/everything

Ο

ὅδε, ἥδε, τόδε	this (see page 24)
ὁδός, -οῦ, ἡ	road, way
ὀδούς, -όντος, ὁ	tooth
ὀδυρμός, -οῦ, ὁ	lamentation
ὀδύρομαι	lament
ὅθεν	adv. whence, from which place
οἶδα	know
οἴκαδε	adv. toward home
οἰκέτης, -ου, ὁ	household slave
οἰκέω	inhabit, live in
οἰκία, -ας, ἡ	house
οἶκος, ου, ὁ	house
οἶκτος, -ου, ὁ	pity, lamentation
οἶμαι	v. οἴομαι
οἶνος, -ου, ὁ	wine

οἴομαι	think
οἷος, -α, -ον	which kind (of)
οἴσω	v. φέρω
οἴχομαι	be gone
οἰωνός, -οῦ, ὁ	bird (usually a large bird of prey), omen (drawn from the appearance of such a bird)
ὀκταμηνιαῖος, -α, -ον	eight months old
ὀκτώ	eight
ὄλεθρος, -ου, ὁ	death, destruction
ὀλιγάκις	*adv.* few times
ὀλίγος, -η, -ον	little, few
ὅλος, -η, -ον	entire, whole
ὄμβρος, -ου, ὁ	rain
ὄμμα, -ατος, τό	eye
ὅμοιος, -α, -ον	similar, like
ὁμοίως	*adv.* similarly
ὄναρ, τό	(nom. and acc. only) dream
ὀνειδίζω	reproach
ὄνειδος, -ους, τό	reproach, blame
ὄνειρος, -ου, ὁ	dream
ὄνομα, -ατος, τό	name
ὀνομάζω	name
ὀξύς, -εῖα, -ύ	sharp, keen, quick, sour
ὄον, -ου, τό	sorb-apple
ὄπῃ	*adv.* in what way, in whichever direction
ὁπλίζω	equip with weapons
ὁπλίτης, -ου, ὁ	armored soldier
ὅπλον, -ου, τό	weapon, armor, tool
οἰκεῖος, -α, -ον	one's own, belonging to one's family
ὁπόθεν	*adv.* whence, from which place
ὁποῖος, -α, -ον	which kind (of)
ὁπόσος, -η, -ον	as much as

ὁπότε	*adv.* when, at which time
ὁπότερος, -α, -ον	which of two
ὁποτέρωσε	*adv.* toward which of two directions
ὅπου	*adv.* where, in which place
ὅπως	=ἵνα, ὡς/as, by which way
ὁράω	see
ὀργή, -ῆς, ἡ	anger
ὀργίζω	make angry
ὀρθός, -ή, -όν	upright
ὅρκος, -ου, ὁ	oath
ὁρμάω	start out, hasten, set in motion
ὁρμή, -ῆς, ἡ	rapid motion forward, impulse
ὁρμίζω	bring into harbor or safe anchorage
ὅρμος, -ου, ὁ	chain, anchorage, the inner part of a harbor, haven, refuge
ὄρνις, ὄρνιθος, ὁ/ἡ	bird, (bird of) omen
ὅς, ἥ	he/she
ὁσάκις	*adv.* as many times as
ὅσος, -η, -ον	as much as
ὅστις, ἥτις, ὅτι	whoever/whatever
ὅταν	=ὅτε ἄν
ὅτε	*adv.* when, at which time
ὅτι	(conjunction) that
οὐ (οὐκ, οὐχ)	*adv.* not
οὗ	*adv.* where, in which place
οὐδέ	and not, nor
οὐδείς, οὐδεμία, οὐδέν	no one/nothing
οὐκοῦή	therefore
οὔκουν	not therefore
οὖν	therefore
οὐρανός, -οῦ, ὁ	sky, heaven
οὖς, ὠτός, τό	ear
οὐκέτι	not yet

οὗτος, αὕτη, τοῦτο	this (*see* page 24)
οὕτω	*adv.* thus
οὕτως	*adv.* thus
οὐχί	no
ὀφείλω	owe
ὀφθαλμός, -οῦ, ὁ	eye
ὀφλισκάνω	owe, be guilty, incur a penalty or fine
(ὀφλεῖν δίκην)	lose a lawsuit
ὄχλος, -ου, ὁ	crowd

Π

πάθημα, -ατος, τό	suffering, passive occurrence
πάθος, -ους, τό	experience, misfortune, passion, suffering
παιδεία, -ας, ἡ	education, training
παίδειος, -ον	childish
παιδεύω	teach
πάλαι	*adv.* long ago
παιδίον, -ου, τό	child
παίζω	play, jest
παίω	hit
παλαιός, -ά, -όν	aged
(τό παλαιόν)	*adv.* formerly, anciently
πάλιν	*adv.* back, backwards, again
πάντῃ	*adv.* every way, on every side
πάνυ	*adv.* altogether, very
παρά	away from the side of (+ ablatival gen.), beside (+ locative dat.), toward the side of (+ acc.)
παρα-γίγνομαι	be beside (+ dat.), arrive at (+ acc.)
παρα-δίδωμι	hand over to another
παραδόξως	*adv.* paradoxically
πάρ-ειμι	be present
παρά-κειμαι	lie beside

παρα-λαμβάνω		take to one's side as an ally
παρ-έρχομαι		go by (the side of), pass
παρ-έχω		furnish, hand over, produce (a person) on demand
πάρθενος, -ου, ἡ		virgin, maiden
παρ-ίστημι		stand by, pose for a portrait
πᾶς, πᾶσα, πᾶν		all, every
πάσχω		experience, suffer
πατήρ, πατρός, ὁ	_pater_	father
πατρίς, -ίδος, ἡ		(father) land, country
πάτταλος, -ου, ὁ		peg
παύω		stop
πείθω		persuade
πεῖρα, -ας, ἡ		attempt
πειράω		attempt, experience, make trial of (+ gen).
πέλεκυς, -εως, ὁ		axe
πέμπω		send
πένης, -ητος, ὁ		poor man, pauper
πενθέω		mourn
πενία, -ας, ἡ		poverty
περί		around, concerning (+ gen., dat., acc.)
περι-αιρέω		take off from around
περι-έρχομαι		go around
περι-μένω		wait
περισσός, -ή, -όν		beyond the regular number or size, extraordinary, strange
περιττός, -ή, -όν		_v._ περισσός
περιφέρεια, -ας, ἡ		circumference
περιφερής, -ές		circular, revolving
περι-φέρω		carry around
πέτρα, -ας, ἡ		rock
πῆχυς, -εως, ὁ		forearm, cubit

πίμπλημι	fill
πίνω	drink
πίπτω	fall
πιστεύω	believe, trust
πλάττω	form, mould
πλεῖστος, -η, -ον	superl. of πολύς
πλείων, -ον/(-ονος)	compar. of πολύς
πλευρά, -ᾶς, ἡ	rib (*pl.* sides)
πλέω	sail
πλῆθος, -ους, τό	great number, multitude, the commons
πληθύνω	multiply
πλημυρά, -ᾶς, ἡ	flood tide
πληρόω	fill
πλησμονή, -ῆς, ἡ	fullness
πλοῦς, -οῦ, ὁ	sailing, voyage
πλούσιος, -α, -ον	wealthy
πλοῦτος, -ου, ὁ	wealth
πνέω	breathe
πνοή, -ῆς, ἡ	breath
ποδιαῖος, -α, -ον	as big as a foot
πόθεν	*adv.* whence?, from which place?
ποθεν	*adv.* from some place
ποιέω	do, make
ποίημα, -ατος, τό	poem
ποίησις, -εως, ἡ	poetry, creation
ποιητής, -οῦ, ὁ	creator, poet
ποῖος, -α, -ον	what kind (of)?
ποιος, -α, -ον	some kind (of)
ποθέω	yearn after, long for
πόθος, -ου, ὁ	yearning, regret
πόλεμος, -ου, ὁ	war
πόλις, -εως, ἡ	city

πολιτεία, -ας, ἡ	constitution
πολιτικός, -ή, όν	political, relating to citizens
πολίτης, -ου, ὁ	citizen
πολλάκις	*adv.* many times
πολύς, πολλή, πολύ	much, many
πονηρία, -ας, ἡ	wickedness, baseness
πονηρός, -ή, -όν	bad, evil
πονέω	work
πόνος, -ου, ὁ	work, pain
πορεία, -ας, ἡ	mode of walking
πορεύω	carry (*mid.* go, walk)
πόρρω	*v.* πρόσω
πόσος, -η, -ον	how much?
ποσος, -η, -ον	some amount (of)
ποταμός, -οῦ, ὁ	river
πότε	*adv.* when?
ποτε	*adv.* at some time
πότερον	*adv.* whether
πότερος, -α, -ον	which (of two)?
ποῦ	*adv.* where?
που	*adv.* somewhere
πούς, ποδός, ὁ	foot
πρᾶγμα, -ατος, τό	deed, occurrence, affair, thing
πραγματεύομαι	be engaged in business
πράττω	do
πρέπω	be conspicuous, resemble/πρέπει it is fitting
πρεσβύτερος, -α, -ον	older
πρεσβύτης, -ου, ὁ	old man, elder
πρό	before (+ ablatival gen.)
προ-βαίνω	walk forward
πρόβατον, -ου, τό	cattle
πρόγονος, -ου, ὁ	forefather

προ-έρχομαι	go before, go forward
προσ-έχω	put a boat in toward land
πρόθυμος, -ον	willing, eager, bearing goodwill
προ-κρίνω	choose before others, select
προ-οράω	foresee
πρός	toward, to (+ acc.)
προσ-δέω	tie to
πρόσ-ειμι	be in addition
προσ-έρχομαι	go toward
προσ-ήκω	belong to
προσ-πατταλεύω	fasten, peg, bolt, impale
πρόσω	forward/far into (+ ablatival gen.)
πρόσωπον, -ου, τό	face, countenance, mask, facade
πρότερος, -α, -ον	previous, earlier
προ-τίθημι	place forth
πρῶτος, -η, -ον	first
πτηνός, -ή, -όν	winged, flying
πυνθάνομαι	learn, inquire
πῦρ, -ρός, τό	fire
πυρός, -οῦ, ὁ	wheat
πώποτε	*adv.* up to this time, yet, ever
πῶς	how?
πως	somehow

Ρ

ῥῆμα, -ατος, τό	that which is said, verb, phrase
ῥοιά, -ᾶς, ἡ	pomegranate
ῥώμη, -ης, ἡ	strength
ῥώομαι	move with speed

Σ

σαρκοφάγος, -ου, ἡ	sarcophagus
σάρξ, σαρκός, ἡ	flesh
σέ/σε	*v.* σύ

σεαυτόν, -ήν	yourself
σελήνη, -ης, ἡ	moon
σῆμα, -ατος, τό	sing, grave monument
σημαίνω	show by sing, signal
σθένος, -ους, τό	strength
σίδηρος, -ου, ὁ	iron, anything made of iron: tool, sword, knife, etc.
σκέλος, -ους, τό	leg
σκευάζω	prepare, make ready
σκιά, -ᾶς, ἡ	shadow
σκοπέω	contemplate, consider, examine
σκώπτω	mock, jeer at, joke with
σμικρός, -ά, -όν	μικρός
σοί/σοι	v. σύ
σοῦ/σου	v. σύ
σοφός, -ή, -όν	wise
σός, -ή, -όν	your
σπείρω	sow seed
σπέρμα, -ατος, τό	seed
σπεύδω	strive after, hasten, be eager
σπουδή, -ῆς, ἡ	haste
σπουδῇ	*adv.* hastily
στόμα, -ατος, τό	mouth
στρατός, -οῦ, ὁ	army
στρογγύλος, -η, -ον	round, spherical
σύ	you
συγγενής, -ές	related
συγ-κλείω	lock in, enclose, lock together
συλ-λαμβάνω	take together, close, help, take hold of with
σύμπλους, -ουν	sailing with
συμ-φέρω	happen, profit
συμφορά, -ᾶς, ἡ	event, circumstance, mishap

σύν	with (+ comitative dat.)
συν-άγω	lead together
σύν-ειμι	be together with
συν-ευνάζω	put to bed with (*pass.* sleep with)
συν-εκ-τρέφω	raise up together
συνεχές	*adv.* continually
συνεχῶς	*adv.* continually
συν-ίστημι	stand with, form a league with (+ comitative dat.)
σύν-οιδα	know something about a person as a potential witness for or against him (dat.)
συνουσία, -ας, ἡ	sexual intercourse
σφᾶς	them
σφέτερος, -α, -ον	their own
σφόδρα	*adv.* exceedingly
σφοδρός, -ά, -όν	vehement, excessive
σχεδόν	*adv,* near, approximately, more or less
σῴζω/σώζω	save
σῶμα, -ατος, τό	body
σώφρων, -ον/(-ονος)	of sound mind, prudent

T

τάξις, -εως, ἡ	arrangement
ταριχεύω	preserve food by salting, pickling, or smoking; embalm
τάσσω	draw up in order of battle, appoint to a task, arrange
ταῦρος, -ου, ὁ	bull
τάχα	*adv.* perhaps
ταχύς, -εῖα, -ύ	swift
τε	and
τεκμαίρομαι	judge from signs and omens
τέκμαρ, τό	(indeclinable) boundary sign

τέκνον, -ου, τό	child
τελεστήριον, -ου, τό	place for initiation
τελευταῖος, -α, -ον	last
τελευτάω	bring to pass, finish, die
τελευτή, -ῆς, ἡ	completion, death
τέλλω	accomplish
τέλος, -ους, τό	consummation, ritual completion, end
τέμνω	cut
τερπνός, -ή, -όν	delightful, pleasurable
τετράκις	*adv.* four times
τέτταρες, τέτταρα	four
τεύχω	produce (by work of art), make
τηρέω	watch over, observe
τίθημι	place
τίκτω	give birth, beget
τιμάω	honor/in legal language: estimate the amount of punishment for a condemned person (+ gen. of price)
τιμή, -ῆς, ἡ	esteem, honor, price
τίμημα, -ατος, τό	estimate of damages, penalty
τίς, τί	who?/what?
τις, τι	someone or other/something or other
τοι	surely—you must know
τοίνυν	therefore, accordingly
τοιόσδε, τοιάδε, τοιόνδε	such a kind (of)
τοιοῦτος, τοιαύτη, τοιοῦτο	such a kind (of)
τόλμα, -ης, ἡ	courage, overboldness, reo̱klessness
τολμάω	dare, have the courage or hardihood
τόπος, -ου, ὁ	place, region
τόσος, -η, -ον	so much
τοσόσδε, τοσήδε, τοσόνδε	so much
τοσοῦτος, τοσαύτη, τοσοῦτο	so much

τότε	*adv.* then, at that time
τρεῖς, τρία	three
τρέπω	turn (*mid.* flee)
τρέφω	rear (a child), nourish, support
τρέχω	run
τριήρης, -ους, ἡ	trireme
τριπλασιάζω	triple
τρίς	*adv.* thrice
τρίτος, -η, -ον	third
τρόπος, -ου, ὁ	manner, way of life
τροφός, -οῦ, ὁ/ἡ	rearer/wet-nurse
τυγχάνω	happen by chance
τύχη, -ης, ἡ	chance, luck

Υ

ὑμᾶς	*v.* σύ
ὑμεῖς	*v.* σύ
ὑμῖν	*v.* σύ
ὑμῶν	*v.* σύ
ὑπέρ	on behalf of (+ gen.)
ὑπ-εξ-έρχομαι	withdraw, go out under cover
ὑπερ-φέρω	surpass
ὑπ-έχομαι	promise
ὕπνος, -ου, ὁ	sleep
ὑπο-κνίζω	aggravate, frustrate
ὑπο-κρίνομαι	answer, reply
ὑπο-λαμβάνω	take up (what is said), take up (a notion)
ὑπο-τίθημι	enjoin, instruct, place under concern
ὑφ-ίστημι	withstand, undertake
ὑψόθεν	*adv.* from on high

Φ

φαίνω	show, (*mid.* appear)

φαρμακεύς, -έως, ὁ	wizard
φαρμακίς, -ίδος, ἡ	witch
φάρμακον, -ου, τό	drug
φάσκων	v. φημί
φερνή, -ῆς, ἡ	dowry
φέρω	carry, bring
φεύγω	flee, go into exile from
φήμη, -ης, ἡ	utterance prompted by the gods, prophetic saying, any voice or words, common report
φημί	say
φθάνω	anticipate, be beforehand, come or act first
φθέγγομαι	utter a sound or voice
φθείρω	destroy, corrupt
φθόγγος, -ου, ὁ	any clear sound, voice, utterance
φθόνος, -ου, ὁ	envy
φιλέω	love
φιλητέον	one must love
φιλία, -ας, ἡ	affection, friendship
φίλος, -ου, ὁ	friend
φιλοσοφία, -ας, ἡ	philosophy
φιλόσοφος, -ου, ὁ	philosopher
φιλόφρων, -ον/(-ονος)	friendly
φοβερός, -ά, -όν	fearful, afraid
φοβέω	frighten (*mid.* be afraid)
φόβος, -ου, ὁ	fear
φορέω	bear repeatedly
φρέαρ, φρέατος, τό	well, cistern
φρήν, φρενός, ἡ	midriff (as seat of life, intellect), heart (as seat of passions)
φρονέω	have understanding, think
φρόνημα, -ατος, τό	mind, purpose, will, pride
φρόνιμος, -ον	sensible, intelligent

φροντίζω	consider, take thought
φύλαξ, -ακος, ὁ	guard
φυλάσσω	keep, guard
φυλάττω	v. φυλάσσω
φυσάω	blow
φύσις, -εως, ἡ	origin, natural form (resulting from growth), nature
φύω	bring forth, produce, (*mid.* become, grow)
φωνή, -ῆς, ἡ	sound, tone, voice, any articulate sound
φῶς, -ωτός, τό	light

X

χαρίζω	show kindness to
χάρις, -ιτος, ἡ	gratitude, kindness, favor, beauty, grace
χαλεπός, -ή, -όν	difficult, hard
χάλκεος, -α, -ον	brazen
χαλκόπους, -ποδος	brazen-footed
χαλκός, -οῦ, ὁ	copper, bronze, anything made of metal
χείρ, -ρός, ἡ	hand
χείριστος, -η, -ον	superl. of κακός
χείρων, -ον	compar. of κακός
χιτών, -ῶνος, ὁ	chiton, tunic, article of clothing worn next to the skin
χορός, -οῦ, ὁ	dance, band of dancers, place for dancing
χράομαι	have in use as something or someone necessary (+ dat.)
χράω	proclaim an oracle, (*mid.* consult an oracle)
χρέως, χρείους, τό	that which ones needs must pay, debt
χρή	it is necessary (+ infinitive phrase)

χρῆμα, -ατος, τό	thing, a thing that one uses, (*pl.* money)
χρηστός, -ή, -όν	good
χρησμός, -οῦ, ὁ	oracular response, oracle
χριστός, -ή, -όν	annointed
χρίω	annoint
χρόνος, -ου, ὁ	time
χώρα, -ας, ἡ	country
χωρίς	without (+ ablatival gen.)
Ψ	
ψαύω	touch
ψεύδω	deceive, (*mid.* lie)
ψηφίζω	cast one's vote
ψῆφος, -ου, ἡ	pebble
ψυχή, -ῆς, ἡ	soul
ψύχω	cool
Ω	
ὦ	O!
ὧδε	*adv.* thus
ᾠδή, -ῆς, ἡ	song, ode
ὠνητός, -ή, -όν	for sale, to be bought
ὡς	= ὅτε/as, by which way
ὥσπερ	just as
ὠφελέω	benefit
ὠφέλιμος, -ον	useful, beneficial

Verbs:
List of
Unpredictable
Principal
Parts

A

ἄγω, ἄξω, ἤγαγον,
ἤχθην, ἦχα, ἦγμαι
αἱρέω, αἱρήσω, εἶλον,
ἡρέθην, ᾕρηκα,
ᾕρημαι
αἴρω, ἀρῶ, ἦρα,
ἤρθην, ἦρκα, ἦρμαι
ἀκούω, ἀκούσομαι,
ἤκουσα, ἠκούσθην,
ἀκήκοα
ἁλίσκομαι, ἁλώσομαι,
ἥλων, ἥλωκα
ἀπελαύνω, ἀπελῶ,
ἀπήλασα,
ἀπηλάθην,
ἀπελήλακα,
ἀπελήλαμαι
ἀποδύω, ἀποδύσω,
ἀπέδυν, ἀπεδύθην,
ἀποδέδυκα,
ἀποδέδυμαι
ἀποθνῄσκω,
ἀποθανοῦμαι,
ἀπέθανον, τέθνηκα
(The prefix ἀπο- is
not used in the per-
fect of this verb.)
ἀποκτείνω, ἀποκτενῶ,
ἀπέκτεινα, ——,
ἀπέκτονα
ἀπόλλυμαι, ἀπολῶ,
ἀπώλεσα or
ἀπωλόμην,
ἀπολώλεκα or
ἀπόλωλα (The sec-
ond aorist ἀπωλόμην
and the second per-
fect ἀπόλωλα are
intransitive, that is,
"perish" rather than
"destroy.")
ἁρπάζω, ἁρπάσομαι
ἥρπασα, ἡρπάσθην,
ἥρπακα, ἥρπασμαι
ἄρχω, ἄρξω, ἦρξα,
ἤρχθην, ἦρχα,
ἦργμαι

ἀφικνέομαι, ἀφίξομαι,
ἀφικόμην, ἀφῖγμαι

B

βαίνω, βήσομαι,
ἔβην, βέβηκα
βάλλω, βαλῶ, ἔβαλον,
ἐβλήθην, βέβληκα,
βέβλημαι
βλάπτω, βλάψω,
ἔβλαψα, ἐβλάφθην
or ἐβλάβην,
βέβλαφα,
βέβλαμμαι
βούλομαι, βουλήσομαι,
ἐβουλήθην,
βεβούλημαι

Γ

γαμέω, γαμῶ, ἔγημα,
γεγάμηκα
γίγνομαι, γενήσομαι,
ἐγενόμην, γέγονα,
γεγένημαι
γιγνώσκω, γνώσομαι,
ἔγνων, ἐγνώσθην,
ἔγνωκα, ἔγνωσμαι
γράφω, γράψω,
ἔγραψα, ἐγράφην,
γέγραφα,
γέγραμμαι

Δ

δείκνυμι, δείξω,
ἔδειξα, ἐδείχθην,
δέδειχα, δέδειγμαι
δίδωμι, δώσω, ἔδωκα,
ἐδόθην, δέδωκα,
δέδομαι

E

ἔρχομαι, ἐλεύσομαι,
ἦλθον, ἐλήλυθα
ἐσθίω, ἔδομαι,
ἔφαγον, ——,
ἐδήδοκα
εὑρίσκω, εὑρήσω,
εὗρον, εὑρέθην,

εὕρηκα, εὕρημαι
(The augment is
either εὑ or ηὑ-.)
ἔχω, ἕξω, ἔσχον, ——,
ἔσχηκα

I

ἵημι, ἥσω, ἧκα, εἵθην,
εἷκα, εἷμαι
ἵστημι, στήσω, ἔστησα
or ἔστην, ἐστάθην,
ἕστηκα, ἕσταμαι
(The second aorist
and perfect are in-
transitive; "stand"
rather than "set.")

K

καλέω, καλῶ, ἐκάλεσα,
ἐκλήθην, κέκληκα,
κέκλημαι

Λ

λαμβάνω, λήψομαι,
ἔλαβον, ἐλήφθην,
εἴληφα, εἴλημμαι
λέγω, λέξω or ἐρῶ, ἔλε-
ξα or εἶπον, ἐλέχ-
θην, εἴρηκα, λέλεγμαι
λείπω, λείψω, ἔλιπον,
ἐλείφθην, λέλοιπα,
λέλειμμαι

M

μανθάνω, μαθήσομαι,
ἔμαθον, μεμάθηκα
μάχομαι, μαχοῦμαι,
ἐμαχεσάμην,
μεμάχημαι
μέλει, μελήσει, ——,
ἐμέλησε, μεμέληκε
μένω, μενῶ, ἔμεινα, ——,
μεμένηκα

N

νομίζω, νομῶ,
ἐνόμισα,
ἐνομίσθην, νενόμικα,
νενόμισμαι

$O - \Phi$

O

ὁράω, ὄψομαι, εἶδον,
ὤφθην, ἑώρακα,
ἑώραμαι

Π

πάσχω, πείσομαι,
ἔπαθον, πέπονθα
πείθω, πείσω, ἔπεισα,
ἐπείσθην, πέπεικα
or πέποιθα,
πέπεισμαι (The
second perfect is
intransitive: "trust"
with a dative com-
plement rather than
"persuade"; the
middle means "be-
lieve, obey.")
πέμπω, πέμψω,
ἔπεμψα, ἐπέμφθην,
πέπομφα, πέπεμμαι
πίνω, πιοῦμαι, ἔπιον,
ἐπόθην, πέπωκα,
(κατα)πέπομαι
πίπτω, πεσοῦμαι,
ἔπεσον, πέπτωκα
πλέω, πλεύσομαι,
ἔπλευσα, ἐπλεύσθην,
πέπλευκα,
πέπλευσμαι
πράττω, πράξω,
ἔπραξα, ἐπράχθην,
πέπραχα or
πέπραγα, πέπραγμαι
πυνθάνομαι,
πεύσομαι, ἐπυθόμην,
πέπυσμαι

Σ

στρέφω, στρέψω,
ἔστρεφα, ἐστρέφθην
or ἐστράθην, ——,
ἔστραμμαι

Τ

τίθημι, θήσω, ἔθηκα,
ἐτέθην, τέθηκα,
τέθειμαι
τίκτω, τέξομαι,
ἔτεκον, τέτοκα
τρέπω, τρέψω, ἔτρεψα,
ἐτρέφθην or ἐτράπην,
τέτροφα, τέτραμμαι
τρέφω, θρέψω,
ἔθρεψα, ἐθρέφθην
or ἐτράφην, τέτροφα,
τέθραμμαι
τρέχω, δραμοῦμαι,
ἔδραμον,
(ἀπο)δεδράμηκα
τυγχάνω, τεύξομαι,
ἔτυχον, τετύχηκα

Φ

φαίνω, φανῶ, ἔφηνα,
ἐφάνθην or ἐφάνην,
πέφαγκα or
πέφηνα, πέφασμαι
φέρω, οἴσω, ἤνεγκα
or ἤνεγκον,
ἠνέχθην, ἐνήνοχα,
ἐνήνεγμαι
φεύγω, φεύξομαι,
ἔφυγον, πέφευγα

Index

δοῦλος — slave

ἄνθρωπος — mankind